RED LIVES, VOL. 1

Before you start to read this book, take this moment to think about making a donation to punctum books, an independent non-profit press,

@ https://punctumbooks.com/support/

If you're reading the e-book, you can click on the image below to go directly to our donations site. Any amount, no matter the size, is appreciated and will help us to keep our ship of fools afloat. Contributions from dedicated readers will also help us to keep our commons open and to cultivate new work that can't find a welcoming port elsewhere. Our adventure is not possible without your support.

Vive la Open Access.

Fig. 1. Detail from Hieronymus Bosch, *Ship of Fools* (1490–1500)

Published in 2026 by punctum books, Earth, Milky Way.
https://punctumbooks.com

ISBN-13: 978-1-68571-290-7 (print)
ISBN-13: 978-1-68571-291-4 (PDF)
ISBN-13: 978-1-68571-297-6 (EPUB)

DOI: 10.53288/0455.1.00

LCCN: 2025948139
Library of Congress Cataloging Data is available from the Library of Congress

Editing: SAJ
Book design: Hatim Eujayl
Cover design: Vincent W.J. van Gerven Oei
Indexing: Sherri Barnes

HIC SVNT MONSTRA

Red Lives

Our Years in the US Communist Party (1950–2000)

Volume I

Coming of Age in the Communist and Labor Movements

Edited by Jay Schaffner, Paul Friedman, Cindy Hawes, Geoffrey Jacques, Timothy Johnson, Carol Pittman, Donna Ristorucci, Daniel Rosenberg, and Jackie Saindon.
Foreword by Robin D.G. Kelley.

p.

Contents

Foreword 17
Robin D.G. Kelley

Introduction 23
Daniel Rosenberg

PART I
ON THE POST–WORLD WAR II COMMUNIST MOVEMENT IN THE UNITED STATES

Communist Labor and Political Reporter 41
Geoffrey Jacques

Flashback to My Long-Ago Communist Youth 109
Leon Wofsy

My Experience in Freedom Summer 115
Marian Gordon

PART II
GROWING UP COMMUNIST DURING THE COLD WAR

Born Red: Pages from a Socialist's Life 131
Jay Schaffner

From China to the United States 175
Peter Hodes

My Parents Were Communists 187
Naomi Chesman Smith

We Were *Movement* Organizations—People's Organizations, Not Puppets of Anyone 191
Joseph Harris

PART III
THE WORLD OF WORK AND THE PARTY OF THE WORKING CLASS

The Work We Do to Broaden Workers' Thinking Is Important 219
Dave Cohen

CPUSA Trade-Union Club in Health Care, 1970s–1992 261
Marilyn Albert

From Red-Diaper Baby to Union Leadership 265
Paul Friedman

Another World Is Possible 281
Frank Emspak

We Had a Big Victory, One That Many Thought We Couldn't Win 311
Sharon Stewart

Party Time 319
Rafael Pizarro

Building the Left in the Labor Movement 327
James Williams

Taking Organizing Seriously 339
Judy Atkins

A Series of Exposures and Experiences … Some of the Best Years of My Political Life 349
Chris Townsend

Select Annotated Bibliography 367

Books That Influenced Our Authors 373

Index 379

About the Editors 401

Acknowledgments

This project would not have been possible without the support and encouragement from our publisher, punctum books. punctum has been there for us with suggestions, encouragement, and friendly pushes and nudges — special appreciation and thanks to the entire team at punctum, but especially, Co-Directors Eileen A. Fradenburg Joy and Vincent W.J. van Gerven Oei, and Associate Director for Editorial Development SAJ. Deep appreciation to Sherri L. Barnes at Moonlight Indexing for the incredible job of indexing she did. Thanks also to Vincent W.J. van Gerven Oei for the cover design.

I would like to thank my coeditors, without whom this collection would not have been possible. We have worked together for a number of years — for some, it has now been nearly nine years. Thanks and tremendous love and gratitude to Paul Friedman, Cindy Hawes, Geoffrey Jacques, Timothy Johnson, Carol Pittman, Donna Ristorucci, Daniel Rosenberg, and Jackie Saindon. You have corrected my gaffes, edited my emails and papers, and made this collection the work that it is.

I want to also acknowledge and thank others, who were part of of our editorial committee at different times, some of whom have continued to offer suggestions and advice over the years: Mike Zagarell, John Eklund, Matthew Hallinan, Laura Montana, Mike Stein, Laura Zagarell, Barry Cohen, David Cohen, April Knutson, and Allen Silverstone.

Special thanks are in order to those who readily searched their personal or professional archives for photos, especially Ted Reich and Howard Harawitz, but also Maxine Orris, Jack Radey, Jim Williams, Mike Honey, Matt Weinstein, Mike Glick, and Pat Fry.

For me, this project was sparked by a 2013 invitation by my high school friend Josh Miller, now a professor of political science at Lafayette College in Easton, Pennsylvania, to speak to his class on why I was a socialist, why I joined the Communist Party, and why I have remained a socialist. That year and the following one, I worked together with longtime friends and comrades as we put together a unique gathering, celebrating the fiftieth anniversary of the founding of the W.E.B. Du Bois Clubs of America. Those friends were Robert (Bob) Heisler, Carmen Ristorucci, Conn (Ringo) Hallinan, and Jackie Saindon. Over many months I exchanged ideas with them, which led, at the reunion, to a panel discussion, "A Look Back, A Look Forward," with panelists Matthew Hallinan, JJ Johnson, Jackie Saindon, Naomi Chesman Smith, Jarvis Tyner, and Mike Zagarell, moderated by Mike Myerson. Out of the preparations for this event grew the ad hoc committee that has nurtured this project.

The idea that arose was to solicit the thoughts, memories, and reflections of comrades from the Communist Party USA, current and former. We felt that this history—our history—was not being told, was missing. The committee that came into being, and then the editorial committee that assembled this book, has endeavored over the past eight years to redress this lack.

I have exchanged ideas and shared drafts with many people and would like to express my thanks and gratitude for their time, thoughts, and help: all the members of the editorial committee, as well as Mike Zagarell, Barry Cohen, Van Gosse, Max Elbaum, Carl Bloice, Phyllis Willett, Sam Webb, Gene Tournour, Ethan Young, Len Polletta, and Pat Fry. Regrettably, Carl, Phyllis, Gene, Pat, and Allen have passed and will not have seen this finished work. If I have left anyone out, I apologize and ask your forgiveness and understanding. This effort would not have been possible without the love, support, editorial input, and endurance of my wife, Judith Eisenscher Schaffner.

Jay Schaffner
August 1, 2025

Foreword

Robin D.G. Kelley

In the mid-1980s, when I began research for my doctoral dissertation on the history of the CPUSA in Alabama, there was a general consensus — among the Left at least — that the Party was moribund. It had lived out its best days in the 1930s and '40s and now was merely a shadow of its former self. For those of us rooted in what Geoffrey Jacques describes in his contribution to this volume as the New Communist Movement, the CPUSA was the shadow we boxed incessantly, perhaps obsessively. To my comrades they were Stalinists, revisionists, reformists, reactionaries, *ad infinitum.* On the other hand, "progressives" and many unaffiliated radicals waxed nostalgic for the 1930s and '40s, when the Communist Party's power and popularity was unrivaled on the Left. American Communism experienced a renaissance during the early Reagan years, with the release of *Reds* in 1982, Warren Beatty's three-hour blockbuster about John Reed, Louise Bryant, and the Russian Revolution, and Jim Klein and Julia Reichert's academy award-winning documentary, *Seeing Red: Stories of American Communists,* released the following year. I cannot stress enough the impact these films had on me and my generation of budding Marxists. The renascent romance with the Reds of yesteryear is precisely what set me on the path to Marx, Lenin, Mao, and eventually to graduate school, where "New Left" historians had spawned a renaissance in studies of

American Communism. They focused on the Popular Front and contributed to a declension narrative of the death of the Old Left circa 1956, and the birth of the "new" — which is to say, their generation. There were exceptions, like Gerald Horne who arguably has written more than anyone on the CPUSA but never wrote its epitaph.

It was only when I began to interview current and former Communists, both for my book and through my work with the Abraham Lincoln Brigade Archives, that the heroic figures and reactionary shadows I had conjured up faded away, revealing multi-dimensional, complex human beings — people I grew to admire and care about. During that formative period between the mid-1980s and the early-1990s, I got to know dozens of folks who had passed through the Party's orbit, including Esther Cooper Jackson, James Jackson, Dorothy Burnham, Hosea Hudson, Clyde and Anne Johnson, Charlene Mitchell, Lloyd Brown, Dorothy Healey, Annette Rubenstein, Christopher Columbus Alston, Marge Frantz, Laurent Frantz, Rob Hall, Gil Green, Junius Scales, Herbert Aptheker, Ishmael Flory, Saul Wellman, Steve Nelson, Joe Brandt, Warren Sussman, Sylvia Thompson, Don Wheeldon, Anne Braden, not to mention later generations of Party people, notably Angela Davis, Maurice Jackson, Bettina Aptheker, Gerald Horne, Anthony Monteiro, Jarvis Tyner, Scott Douglass, Geoffrey Jacques — too many to name. When I met them, they were not sitting around reminiscing about their glorious past. Most were still active, fighting the Reagan-Bush regimes, demonstrating against the US invasions of Lebanon and Grenada, challenging South African apartheid, protesting police brutality, building a Left caucus in their trade unions, fighting for fair housing, and just trying to eke out a living on paltry wages after decades of personal sacrifice. In other words, neither the Party nor its ideals had died after 1956 — a point I made thirty-four years ago by tracing the direct line between

Alabama's Communists and the Civil Rights Movement, especially in Lowndes County and Birmingham.[1]

And yet, we are still beset with the idea that Nikita Khrushchev's revelations of Stalin's crimes and/or the Soviet invasion of Hungary, both in 1956, triggered a mass exodus from the Party, leading to its rapid demise. Quite recently Tony Pecinovsky, in a rejoinder to Michael Goldfield's essay on the history of the CPUSA in *Jacobin,* went to great pains to remind readers that the Party lived on well past 1956, did some good things along the way, and still exists. His brief but densely packed capsule history mentions, among other things, the W.E.B. Du Bois Clubs, its role in the Berkeley Free Speech Movement and the anti-war movement, the formation of the National Alliance Against Racist and Political Repression (NAARPR) and the National Anti-Imperialist Movement in Solidarity with African Liberation (NAIMSAL), as well as the CPUSA's presence in local electoral politics from the late 1960s through the 1980s.[2] For the people of "El Norte" living in the belly of the beast, the CP-organized Venceremos Brigade was the way to get to Cuba. And going to Cuba in the 1970s and '80s was like going to Palestine today — it was a badge of honor, a political education, and evidence of one's revolutionary bona fides. Even the uninitiated had heard of Angela Davis, the most famous Communist in the United States, and the world, at that time. Indeed, she was in the headlines before California Governor Ronald Reagan targeted her, before making the FBI's most wanted list, before her imprisonment and the international campaign to set her free. Through Davis's initial work with the Black Panthers, the Student Non-Violent Coordinating Committee (SNCC), and as a formative leader in the Che Lumumba Club, along with founders Franklin and Kendra Alexander and Deacon Alexander, she had earned a reputation

1 See Robin D.G. Kelley, *Hammer and Hoe: Alabama Communists During the Great Depression* (University of North Carolina Press, 1990), 227–32.

2 Tony Pecinovsky, "100 years of CPUSA: A Critical Reply to 'Jacobin,'" *Communist Party USA,* May 8, 2020, https://www.cpusa.org/article/100-years-of-cpusa-a-critical-reply-to-jacobin/.

as one of California's most popular and beloved revolutionary intellectuals.

Red Lives proves the Party had a rich and varied history after 1956, well beyond the "Free Angela" campaign. Yet, even when we acknowledge this history, it is treated as an aberration or an enigma that requires explanation. Hence the common question: Why would anyone remain in the Communist Party after 1956? The question is wrongheaded and these powerful, honest personal narratives explain why. The truth is, repression did not kill the Party, nor did it stop with the end of McCarthyism. The Subversive Activities Control Board continued its activities into the 1970s, and the FBI's Counter-Intelligence Program (COINTELPRO) targeted the CPUSA alongside Black nationalist and other militant organizations. Indeed, the running joke-turned-urban-legend was that FBI informants made up about one-third of the Party's membership. The point, of course, is that state repression failed. More importantly, liberal anticommunist reforms did not change the conditions that made life unbearable for the masses of working people on whose behalf the Party fought. To the contrary, Cold War liberals built the military-industrial complex, squandered surpluses that could have ended poverty on a global war against Third World revolutions, escalated the prospect of nuclear annihilation, weakened democracy, and strengthened corporate power. The reforms that did benefit the masses — limited antidiscrimination laws regarding race and sex, voter protection, a rise in wages, the expansion of the welfare state, etc. — were the result of *movements* often involving or led by Communists and ex-Communists. By the 1970s and early '80s, even these gains were being reversed.

And yet, despite liberalism's assault on socialist movements, here and abroad, socialism was winning. From our vantage point in 2024, it may seem hard to believe that the global political winds were shifting toward Marxism-Leninism or some version of democratic socialism. Many of these revolutions proved to be short-lived, or at later points made disastrous turns. But from the late 1960s through the 1980s, just consider all of the countries and national liberation movements moving toward a "socialist path": Chile, Mozambique, Angola, Guinea Bissau and Cape Verde Islands, People's Republic of the Congo, Vietnam, Jamaica, Grenada, Nicaragua, St. Lucia, Dominica, St. Vincent, Tanzania, South Africa, and Zimbabwe, to name a few. No one knew the political machinations occurring within the Soviet Politburo, the various movements it may or may not have betrayed in order to shore up its own strategic interests. But looking from the outside one could have easily concluded that revolution gripped the world and the USSR was the beacon lighting the way. Few predicted the imminent collapse of the Soviet Union. To be a Communist, in other words, did not appear to be a losing proposition.

Furthermore, CP members were not robots taking marching orders from Moscow. Dorothy Healey's memoir, one of the few books documenting the Party's history during the 1960s and '70s, made this point over three decades ago. She portrays the local Party apparatus in Los Angeles as fairly independent of national leadership—so much so that California earned a reputation as the "Yugoslavia" of the CPUSA. She reminds us, for example, that the Southern California district's creation of the Che Lumumba Club, an all-Black unit which Healey helped bring into existence in 1967, did not have the approval or blessings of the National Committee.[3] *Red Lives* both confirms Healey's experience of working independently, sometimes in defiance of national and Soviet leadership, and reveals instances in which Party leaders stifled local initiatives. What you will not find in these pages is "disillusionment"—the noun most commonly used by anti-communists to explain why people leave the Party. To be disillusioned is to discover that communism was essentially a lie, the false god that failed. But disagreement or recognizing the Party is no longer an effective vehicle for change is not disillusionment. No one represented in this book blindly followed orders or thought of socialism as a mind trick. Rather, they claimed the Party as their own, argued for policy changes, applied their skills

3 Dorothy Healey and Maurice Isserman, *Dorothy Healey Remembers: A Life in the American Communist Party* (Oxford University Press, 1990).

and insights to the work, changed their minds, engaged in criticism and self-criticism, and chose to stay or leave for a variety of political and personal reasons. And failure, more often than not, produced more epiphanies than heartbreak, as expressed in Dave Cohen's remark: "As Marxists, we learn from history, and recent history has shown us that a hierarchical approach to socialism—'The Party is the leader and the rest should follow orders'—failed miserably in the Soviet Union and Eastern Europe. Now is the time for new approaches." The collapse of the Soviet Union in 1989 provided just such an opportunity for "new approaches." The split that occurred at the 1991 Party convention birthed the Committees of Correspondence for Democracy and Socialism, which attracted more than half of the CP membership as well as activists from other organizations, notably Democratic Socialists of America.

Finally, *Red Lives* does much more than fill in the last half century of CPUSA history through a personal lens. It reminds us why people become Communists or join movements dedicated to replacing capitalism with a socialist commonwealth. I read these stories, full of humor and pathos and lessons and dreams, and I think about that song of global proletarian solidarity and revolution, whose lyrics Eugène Pottier penned in 1871 during his involvement in the Paris Commune, and whose melody the Belgian socialist Pierre Chrétien De Geyter composed many years later. It is that song that still brings tears to my eyes when sung with passion; that song that extols the power of a united, international working class to create a world without oppression and exploitation; that song that never lets us forget: "a better world's in birth!"

December 17, 2025

Introduction

Daniel Rosenberg[1]

What has the Communist movement meant to the United States? What have Communists done to enlarge democracy, while promoting socialism as the way to redress oppression and exploitation? When asked if he was a member of the Communist Party by the House Un-American Activities Committee (HUAC) during the mid-1950s, singer-activist-actor Paul Robeson answered:

> What do you mean by the Communist Party? Do you mean ... a party of people who have sacrificed for our people and for all Americans and workers, that they can live in dignity? Do you mean that party?[2]

Red Lives: Our Years in the US Communist Party (1950–2000) is about *that* Party. A long-prevailing practice among historians has been to portray the Party as dead and buried after 1956. *Red Lives* offers a strikingly different view. It presents evidence of hundreds of union, civil rights, anti-repression, and antiwar

1 Originally written September 2022; revised May 2023.

2 Quoted in Eric Bentley, ed., *Thirty Years of Treason: Excerpts from Hearings before the House Committee on Un-American Activities, 1938–1968* (Viking, 1971), 773.

engagements to which Party members brought their class and racial unity perspectives. Instead of providing a settled history of the Communist Party USA (CPUSA), *Red Lives* offers a lens on events through which readers may gain understanding. By way of collecting direct experiences, it surveys the continuation of the Communist Party after its alleged demise in the 1950s and the work of thousands of members during the ensuing decades.

Volume 1 surveys the Communist experience across two realms: growing up in a Communist and leftist milieu and involvement in the labor movement. The three volumes of *Red Lives: Our Years in the US Communist Party (1950–2000)* comprise the first collection of analyses and reminiscences by Communist Party members and activists covering the 1950s through the 1990s. Constituting a legacy of struggle through the decades, their stories need telling especially in light of today's protest movements and renewed interest in socialism.

Geoffrey Jacques and the late Leon Wofsy assess the questions and challenges facing Communists as they emerged from McCarthyism. Anticommunism painted a decidedly false picture of the group's activities and aims. It obscured that the Party was the first movement in the country to assert the centrality of African American equality to the progress of all social movements, and it covered up Party-led street protests against economic deprivation and exploitation during the Great Depression—defying eviction notices, blocking forced removal of tenants and farmers unable to pay mortgages or rent. McCarthyism hid the Party's role in building enormous movements (in which many contributors to this volume participated) in support of African Americans, Latinos, and European immigrants imprisoned on false charges, like Sacco and Vanzetti in the 1920s (murder), the Scottsboro Nine (rape) in the '30s, and Angela Davis (conspiracy to kidnap and murder) in the '70s. Anticommunism painted Communists as foreign agents and misfits, as treacherous and distinctly abnormal; hence Party members suffered from "an absence of individual grace and humor," going about their picnics and dances with "anxious solemnity." Or the

Party was a magnet for outcasts. Worse, said sociologist Gabriel A. Almond, Party members were "neurotically hostile people."[3]

The contributors to *Red Lives* joined the Communist movement in defiance of not only such caricature but also more concrete hazards. There were still risks in choosing to join the Communist Party in the '60s and '70s: Some states banned the organization into the '70s. The University of California fired Angela Davis from her teaching position for being a Communist as late as 1969.

This collection's common themes are many: that working people form the basic force of all progressive struggles; that an alternative to capitalism — socialism — is fundamentally necessary; that collectivity and alliances are crucial to achieving common aims; and that Black–white and multiracial unity are the catalyst to progressive action. Shared by all is the belief that mass activity and mass movements are key, that socially progressive goals cannot be met by acting solo.

Among those adhering to the revived Party, this first volume's contributors bring their family histories, upbringings, and youthful encounters to bear. These range from Communist to anticommunist, from atheist to devotedly religious. Jay Schaffner speaks of dual influences: "My political view of the world is a product of two generations: my own, the political generation of the 1960s, and that of my immigrant parents, who were radicalized in the 1920s, '30s, and '40s." Peter Hodes's father was summarily dismissed from his job as professor in Tulane University: "My father was unable to find another job in his profession, because there was a (secret) blacklist of fired Communists and those accused by Joe McCarthy's witch-hunters of being Communists." Schaffner's parents hid their Marxist books in closets during the McCarthy era.

Common to the period leading to that covered by *Red Lives* were the informers and informants — naming names, ruining lives, making up stories, concocting falsehoods, destroy-

3 Gabriel Almond, *The Appeals of Communism* (Princeton University Press, 1954), 268.

ing careers and reputations — as depicted, for example, in the account of Peter Hodes. Loyalty oaths became obligatory for work in government and in various industries. Added to this was the purposeful infiltration of the Party by the Federal Bureau of Investigation (FBI), so much so that agents and informants constituted a sizable proportion of the membership in some locales. Ruination by dint of FBI exposure of one's private opinions, books, and petition signings produced isolation, stress, and anxiety, making Party membership or clinging to principles harder. Naomi Chesman Smith's evocation of a child's fear in this atmosphere is haunting. Even given our present temporal distance, then, a number of our contributors choose to refer to friends or comrades indirectly or generically ("steelworker comrade") or by first name only ("John"), to avoid "outing" them.

But of course there were also more positive examples and lessons. Joseph Harris recounts how his upbringing taught him not only to question conventional wisdom and official doctrine but also to take action. For the CPUSA, with its history of involvement in the earliest sit-ins and boycotts targeting segregation, dating to the 1930s, was part of 1950s battles against Jim Crow and persisted in the struggles for civil rights and equality into the '60s and later. In 1964, Harris volunteered in Mississippi during Freedom Summer, registering voters in face of the Ku Klux Klan. Contributor Marian Gordon was with him there: "People from all around the country responded by volunteering to put their bodies on the line. And Communists were among them."

Inasmuch as the Communist Party was a working class–based group, a good number of contributors describe their lives as workers, union members, and labor leaders. Union experience informs David Cohen's contribution, and it taught him much: "As an elected officer of a union local, you had to maintain support from the membership and not use your elected position to advocate for something that had no support among the workers." From the same industry, Frank Emspak recalls a history of family labor and union culture: "Growing up, there was simply no separation between the 'family' and the union, the United Electrical Workers." Jim Williams labored in the same field, later became a millwright at United States Steel, and recalls, "There was a certain cachet or prestige in the Party that was attributed to steelworkers."

Barely out of his teens, Jay Schaffner put in time in a machine shop, alongside African American and Polish workers. At only seventeen, future United Electrical Workers leader Chris Townsend immersed himself in transit-union organizing in Tampa, through which he met Communists for the first time: "I did anything that needed to be done. I signed up too many members to count. I always came to the meetings with fistfuls of signed cards and all of them with the five-dollar initiation fee. I passed out literature at four and five a.m. at the gates." Geoffrey Jacques, the son of Chrysler-Ford workers, grew up in a Detroit milieu that "was such a hotbed of radicalism that simply navigating one's way through the myriad political and cultural options available was as much a learning experience as it was fun." The late Sharon Stewart, journalist and Newspaper Guild member, benefited from union, National Association for the Advancement of Colored People (NAACP), National Urban League, and Communist Party support in beating an attempt by Denver's *Rocky Mountain News* to fire her: "My personal struggle against racism and sexism at the *News* ended in victory because I wasn't alone."

An entire book could be composed solely from the remembrances of *Red Lives* workers in the field of health care. Their dedication and depth of experience are obvious. Marilyn Albert relates how she "became a hospital nurse and remained one for thirty-three years"; and Paul Friedman tells us that he "learned how to read electrograms, run a blood circulation machine for animal experiments, and monitor the electrogram machine in the open-heart operating room at the hospital.... [He] was in the operating room at least twice a week during open-heart surgeries." But beyond their professionalism, their commitment to collective action is also apparent. Rafael Pizzaro reminisces, "I was a blue-diaper baby, a son of a Local 1199 member."[4]

Red Lives: Our Years in the US Communist Party (1950–2000) aims to take its place beside the published reminiscences of labor, civil rights, peace, and LGBTQ+ veterans. Multivolume collected Black Panther Party and Student Nonviolent Coordinating Committee memoirs occupy well-earned space on the shelves of today's young activists — for instance, Sharon Monteith's *SNCC's Stories: The African American Freedom Movement in the Civil Rights South*. Parallel reflections of organized protest and action appear in Harvey Schwartz's assemblage of testimony from the International Longshoremen's and Warehousemen's Union, *Solidarity Stories: An Oral History of the ILWU*, and Shirley Hune and Gail M. Nomura's *Our Voices, Our Histories: Asian American and Pacific Islander Women*.

A Word on History

Naturally, the experiential testimony related here belongs to a longer history. Founded in 1919, the US Communist movement had emerged from socialist, working-class, and radical movements that supported labor organizing and promoted international solidarity. Radicals who steadfastly opposed World War I (1914–1918) and US entry into this commercially driven conflict over the redivision of colonies and markets by stronger powers were among the pioneers of the Communist Party. They had seen the war as profit-motivated and a clash between imperialists, in contrast with other leftists, who backed the involvements of their governments to demonstrate their loyalty to the "fatherland" and so escape persecution. The original US Communists thus resisted the nationalism that legitimized the war. They soon ran afoul of legislation banning organized opposition to the war and government and hence were compelled to function in illegality or semi-legality for much of the early 1920s.

4 1199SEIU United Health Care Workers East.

Though debilitated by internal division and factional disputes over leadership and direction in its early years, the CPUSA emerged in the 1930s as a generally more united and popularly oriented group. From then and into the '40s, members were crucial to the expansion of labor organizing and the formation of unions in the steel, automobile, electrical, rubber, food, clothing, tobacco, health-care, longshoring, and social-service industries, among others. The Party's reach extended into political, labor-based, cultural, multiracial, and multinational movements in all sections of the country. Several members were elected and reelected to public office during the 1940s.

US Communists would eventually adopt a stance toward World War II (1939–1945) different from their opposition to World War I. Like Communists around the world, however, they did not truly back the Allied effort until Germany attacked the Soviet Union in 1941. Thereafter they supported the strongest US involvement, including by maximizing war production and discouraging strikes, which they feared would hamper the full economic mobilization essential to Hitler's defeat.

In response, the notion rose in the CPUSA that the national unity accruing to and required by the war might continue in peacetime, across class lines. In the early '40s, Party leaders Earl Browder and others developed a view that the organization might better facilitate less hostile relationships between corporations and the working public by transforming itself into a non-Party pressure group. The notion sanctioned support for US corporate investments abroad, which might insure healthy levels of US production and employment. It anticipated that the US–Soviet alliance that had defeated fascism on the battlefield would persist.

The concept bore fruit with the dissolution of the Party into the Communist Political Association in 1944. The new group lasted but a year before reestablishing itself as the CPUSA, with Soviet encouragement. Belying the belief in postwar continuity, the wartime alliance of the Soviet Union and capitalist states deteriorated into the Cold War quickly after 1945, amid invocations of the "American Century." US Communists, who had so commonly been viewed and accepted as necessary allies in social struggles, came under fire as Soviet pawns, and with this followed the anticommunist laws and trials of the late '40s and beyond.

In the 1950s and '60s, HUAC conducted scores of investigations into Communist "infiltration" of civil rights, peace, labor, and other movements — hence the interrogation of Paul Robeson. HUAC subcommittees caravanned to Cleveland, Chicago, San Francisco, Los Angeles, Newark, Louisville, Denver, and other places for onsite inquisitions of local activism.

Emerging in the mid-1950s in a greatly weakened condition from the worst of McCarthyism, the Communist Party attempted to resume its activity but found itself immediately affected by events in countries whose socialist societies it supported and admired. Like Communists in other countries, US leaders and members identified with the Soviet Union, hailing the positives (social protections and aid to anticolonial and peace movements) while backing, excusing, or denying the negatives (severe repression of opponents). The dichotomy of fighting for a democratic and more egalitarian United States while justifying or ignoring antidemocratic measures in the Soviet Union posed challenges for the CPUSA at all times, inasmuch as Party members were so often in the forefront of pivotal progressive movements. Many US Communists were deeply affected by later revelations of persecutions and executions during the time when Joseph Stalin headed the Soviet Union (1922–1953). Hungarian protests against such policies in late 1956 turned violent and drew the intervention of Soviet soldiers, likewise disheartening many US Communists. In the ensuing months, the CPUSA lost most of its members. Thus, write two historians, "American Communism as an organized movement had reached the end of the road."[5] But the present volume shows otherwise.

A word on the process of gathering this collection would be in order. An editorial committee, spearheaded and facilitated by

---

5 Irving Howe and Lewis Coser, *The American Communist Party: A Critical History* (Praeger, 1957), 498.

Jay Schaffner, was formed to elicit written contributions; members were Timothy V. Johnson, Carol Pittman, Cindy Hawes, Donna Ristorucci, Daniel Rosenberg, Geoffrey Jacques, Jackie Saindon, the late Alan Silverstone, John Eklund, Paul Friedman, April Knutson, David Cohen, Matthew Hallinan, and Mike Stein. The editors themselves represent a range of experience in the Communist Party. The essays were written over a period of eight years, from spring 2015 to winter 2022, and therefore reflect the developing politics of the country, especially in how the public has come to view, understand, and even embrace socialism and socialist ideas

Seeking the broadest representation of engagement, the editors invited five hundred people to send written reflections on their experiences as members of the Communist Party or such allied organizations as the W.E.B. Du Bois Clubs of America and the Young Workers Liberation League. Sixty responded, and of their essays more than half are included in *Red Lives.* All submitted papers are deposited at one of the leading left-radical-labor collections in the United States, the Tamiment Library and Robert F. Wagner Labor Archives at New York University's Bobst Library. Here they may be read and viewed by all interested readers and researchers.

Reasons for nonparticipation included busy work schedules, health issues, and changes in lives, families, and jobs. Many who were approached found it difficult to put their feelings into words on a page. Some hesitated to reflect on public or personal history or broach memories of negative experiences. Several have pursued other interests or priorities. There were those who left the organization but wanted to avoid publicly criticizing or attacking the Party. But few viewed their past activities with bitterness. Nevertheless, the writers published in our collection testify to contradictory experiences and conclusions.

The present collection reflects the general absence of Party work in fighting for LGBTQ+ rights and equality, as some essayists note. While the Party and Communists in different parts of the country had earlier accepted gay and lesbian members, it later moved to drop them, expelling them during the McCarthy period, especially, for fear that they would testify against the Party to avoid being outed. Afterward, Party officials viewed the LGBTQ+ cause and other mass movements as non-working-class endeavors that rejected the primacy of the class struggle between capitalists and workers and the centrality of fighting racism to the struggle for progress.[6] There was a distinction, however, between official policy and the more flexible, often accepting, views of members. Some Party districts, like Northern California, welcomed gay and lesbian members, and Party clubs around the country occasionally staked out independent ground of their own.

The reflections of the authors here are thought-provoking and forthright. Some have remained in the Party or have rejoined it. Several authors deal with a single moment or movement. Others assess the entire period of their memberships, evaluating the strengths and weaknesses of the Party over time. Some analyze the organization's structure, as either facilitating or impeding its growth. A few offer perspectives on questions about the Party's theory and strategy, matters the Party took for granted about workers, industry, technology, unity, coalition, and militancy. Several perceive the difficulties in the relationship between the Party and the Soviet Union. But others affirm the benefits of solidarity, within and outside the United States, in which the Party played no small role. Promoting the common interests of working people everywhere appears as a consistent value and practice.

During a time of growing mass movements for civil rights, labor rights, peace, international solidarity, children and young people's, women's, and gay rights, these activists were both engaged and involved, coming to the conclusion that capitalism just wasn't working. They sought out socialism, and as a vehicle for both their activities and their beliefs, joined the Communist Party USA, or a youth organization that worked closely

6 Bettina Aptheker documents the Party's relationship with LGBTQ+ struggles in *Communists in Closets: Queering the History, 1930s–1990s* (Routledge, 2023).

or was affiliated with it—the W.E.B. Du Bois Clubs, the Young Workers Liberation League, Advance, Labor Youth League, or the Young Communist League. Many are still active today and hold true to their socialist beliefs. What do their stories say to today's generations that are also concluding that capitalism just doesn't work? The words of W.E.B. Du Bois upon joining the Communist Party in 1961 resonate now as they did then: "Capitalism cannot reform itself; it is doomed to self-destruction. No universal selfishness can bring social good to all."

As part of our process, the editors have endeavored to ensure that our vocabulary conformed to current usage. As this book went to press, however, we discovered that one archaism that escaped us was the term *the Ukraine.* As used in this volume, this term refers to that part of the former czarist empire from which parents and grandparents of contributors to this volume emigrated to the United States. When they came to this country, the term was in common use. After the February 1917 Russian Revolution and the Bolshevik Revolution later that year, the term *the Ukraine* continued in use, and was used as such during the years of the Soviet Union's existence. However, with Ukrainian independence in 1991, and especially with the Russian invasion of Ukraine on February 24, 2022, the term *the Ukraine* has widely come to be considered pejorative. Our writers originally used this archaic formulation in writing about their immigrant ancestors from a land that was previously part of the old czarist empire. In the second and third volumes of this series, we will not use this term and will use *Ukraine,* instead.

Fig. 1. Demonstration by Advance Youth Organization members and supporters against the Subversive Activities Control Board (SACB), outside the old Federal Building in Lower Manhattan, September 12, 1963. The SACB was holding hearings around the country, seeking to identify "Communist-front" organizations. Once so branded, an organization would be required run this banner on its leaflets and mail envelopes and make this announcement at all its meetings: "Advance Youth Organization, declared by the Attorney General of the United States to be a Communist-front organization, which seeks to overthrow the government of the United States by force and violence" — a helluva way to entice new members to join your organization during the midst of the McCarthy period. (Photo by Ted Reich)

Fig. 2. Demonstration against the war in Vietnam, San Francisco Bay, 1964. Here, Archie Brown, rank-and-file International Longshore and Warehouse Union (ILWU) Local 10 member, lifelong public Communist and Party leader, courageous and militant trade unionist, and antifascist, is speaking to the marchers. Archie fought in Spain against the Franco dictatorship with the Abraham Lincoln Brigade, later served as an officer of ILWU, was targeted under the McCarthyite Landrum–Griffin Act, and had the case reversed by the Supreme Court. The Communist Party, and leaders like Archie Brown, were an integral part of the anti–Vietnam War peace movement in the Bay Area and other cities across the country. (Photo courtesy of Jack Radey)

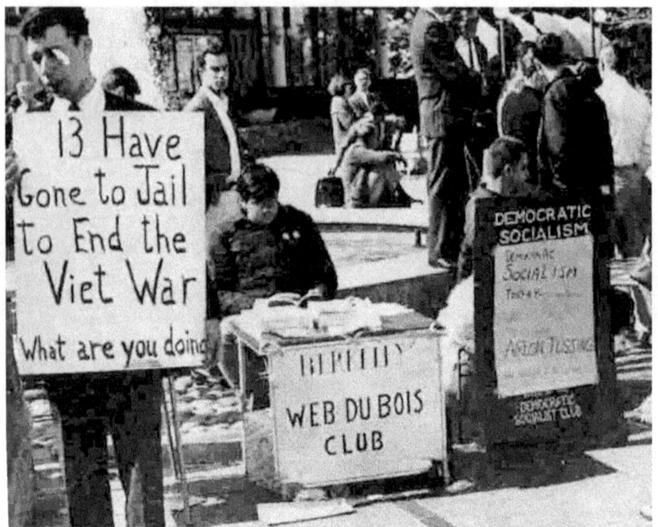

Fig. 3. The W.E.B. Du Bois Club, which the FBI called "Communist-inspired," sets up an information and recruitment table at the University of California, Berkeley, spring 1965. (Photo from the *Daily Californian*)

Fig. 4. W.E.B. Du Bois Clubs members at a demonstration against the war in Vietnam, New York City, December 1964. (Photo by Ted Reich)

PART I

ON THE POST–WORLD WAR II COMMUNIST MOVEMENT IN THE UNITED STATES

1

Communist Labor and Political Reporter

Geoffrey Jacques[1]

While it's not quite accurate to say that my first acquaintance with the Communist Party USA (CPUSA) came from an election advertisement on a bus traveling down a Detroit street, my memory of that encounter, in September or October 1974, with a poster bearing the Party's name, still registers as some kind of turning point. The ad featured the Party's top leaders in the state, the African American and white team of Thomas Dennis Jr., the Black district organizer of the Michigan CP; William "Billy" Allan, the local reporter for the *Daily World* newspaper; and Peggy Goldman Frankie, organizational secretary for the state Party. They were running for governor, lieutenant governor, and member of the state board of education, respectively, in the upcoming election. Seeing that advertisement was, for me, both curious and electrifying. It seemed like the answer to a question that I wasn't aware that I had been asking, one of those answers in front of you the whole time you remain consciously unacquainted with the question nagging at your insides. Maybe the best way of putting this is to say that a light suddenly went on, but the truth is more akin to the answer a literature professor

1 Written October 2020.

once gave me when I asked him if he understood James Joyce's *Finnegan's Wake,* the book we had been reading in class. "I've been reading this book for forty years," he said, "and the fog is just beginning to lift."

My serious interest in the Communist Party began that summer. Richard Nixon resigned the day before I turned twenty-one—the best ever birthday present. I had been born into a working-class family of Black migrants from Kansas and Missouri; my father, Austin, had come with my mother, Ida, to Detroit in 1937 for work in the auto industry, landing a job at the massive Ford Rouge plant in Dearborn, where he would work, except for a stint in the navy during World War II, until his death in 1972. My mother worked for the Chrysler plant in suburban Detroit that built tanks. She had been a "Rosie the Riveter" in a Dearborn plant during the war, helping build munitions for the fight against fascism, but at the Chrysler plant she put her business-school courses to use as a clerical worker. (In those days, "business school" meant, for women, secretarial school.) The United Auto Workers (UAW) had been a presence in my life since childhood, even though my father wasn't a union activist. We had a small collection of books in my home, mainly classics—*Wuthering Heights* and the like—but we also had a pictorial history of the UAW, which showed the famous 1930s battle in which Henry Ford's gangsters beat Walter Reuther bloody, among other incidents from the Reuther caucus's version of UAW history. Labor militancy was a part of my elementary education. Other aspects of social consciousness were part of the overall atmosphere in which I grew up. During my ten-year Roman Catholic education, anticommunism was as much a part of my education as was the spiritual and ethical side. We had tutorials and saw films about Dr. Tom Dooley, the white missionary in Vietnam who was an early US casualty in that conflict. And, of course, the Cold War was part of everyday life. On the first Saturday of every month, Detroit, the "Arsenal of Democracy," was treated to a citywide air-raid alarm that went off at noon. The Friday of the Cuban Missile Crisis, our teacher, of the Sisters of Charity order, told our class, "I might never see you again," but assured us that she would pray for our souls. I was in fourth grade. The next year, three months after my tenth birthday, I stayed home while my mother went to church (I must have been ill) and saw the live broadcast of Jack Ruby killing Lee Harvey Oswald. Meanwhile, each day the Civil Rights Movement and the Vietnam War were part of our household's daily television-news diet, as they were for everybody of my generation.

My political consciousness had been growing throughout my teen years, during which demonstrations against police brutality and the war in Vietnam were as much a part of youthful frolics as were the rock and jazz concerts and outdoor festivals I attended. My teenage years were an exciting mix of cultural and political involvement, as I was privileged enough to hang out with old beatniks, hippies, yippies, Black nationalists, and Black revolutionaries. While still in high school, I had started writing jazz, rock, blues, and rhythm-and-blues record reviews for *CREEM* magazine, the Midwest's most important rock-music periodical. The first poems I ever published, in 1972, appeared in the San Francisco–based *Journal of Black Poetry,* and a couple of months before I graduated from high school, my first nationally published essay came out in *Black World* magazine, a review of a book on jazz that brimmed with all the impetuousness of an intellectually precocious youth.

It still astonishes me that none of this seemed all that unusual at the time. The Detroit I grew up in was such a hotbed of radicalism that simply navigating one's way through the myriad political and cultural options was as much a learning experience as it was fun. And while I liked school and did well there, my formal education seemed little more than preparatory exercises for the real education that was available in the city's storefront meeting halls, concert stages, churches, theaters, offices, cafés, restaurants, boutiques, picket lines, rallies, and demonstrations in the streets. The uprising of 1967 was still fresh in everyone's minds, and the real hollowing out of the city's industrial base was just beginning to accelerate toward devastating the city. That process would take close to a quarter century. Meanwhile, one saw Black political power emerging in a multiracial city and radical politics assume a level of public presence that I've since come to understand was rare in the United States during those times.

Much of the activity centered on the neighborhoods that stretched north of downtown toward Wayne State University, and indeed it was downtown, while standing outside the main branch of the city's library that I saw the Communist campaign notice. That bus ad was not my first encounter with the CPUSA. I had participated in the campaign to free Angela Davis as a rally-goer and sympathizer and had attended the massive Detroit rally to celebrate her victory. But for the most part my contact was indirect. You could say that I share with many other radicals of my generation the distinction of having received an education in radicalism and Marxism from the Communists without having had a single substantive conversation with a real, live, self-acknowledged Party member.

One of the most important of the Detroit educational sites for radicals was Global Books, the CPUSA's bookstore, on Second Avenue, nestled in the just belowground floor of an old apartment building a few blocks from the university. It was a reservoir of knowledge about labor history, African American history and politics, and African culture, history, and politics, and it carried all the theoretical classics of the working-class political movement. You could find books by Kwame Nkrumah, Frantz Fanon, and W.E.B. Du Bois, as well as Marx and Lenin, Herbert Aptheker, Victor Perlo, and even Black US Communists like Claude M. Lightfoot, whose booklet *Black America and the World Revolution* (1970), has held an honored place in my library since I bought it there while still in high school nearly half a century ago. Yet, even as I cherished the knowledge it offered, my memory has Global Books as a musty and initially intimidating place. While there would sometimes be a clerk close to my age sitting behind the counter, most of the staff seemed old and dour. The store would later move to a lighter, airier, more distant site in a northern neighborhood of the city, but during the late 1960s and early 1970s, it seemed at one with the bohemian aura that had settled over the district just south of the university. The store was a block or so away from the offices of the *Fifth Estate,* one of the great underground newspapers of the counterculture era (it still publishes as an anarchist periodical), and just a few blocks from the record stores, restaurants, cafés, and bars of the Cass Corridor, as the Detroit neighborhood now known as Midtown was then called.

It would be too much to say that Global Books was at that point a central node of my political consciousness. Political conversations were more freewheeling at Vaughan's Bookstore, in the heart of the Black community. This is where I would meet some of the people who would become my political colleagues, friends, and comrades — those with whom I would read my first Marxist books and engage in my earliest mature political activities.

During high school, I was mostly involved in literary activities, while also nurturing what became an obsessive interest in music, first in rock and roll (my association with *CREEM,* the rock and counterculture magazine, as a writer and record reviewer, dates from my last two years of high school), but very soon in jazz. Indeed, my interest in jazz has been a major factor in my life, and proved a worthy seasoning to a political life. By the time I got to college, I had been in a number of demonstrations against both the war in Vietnam and police brutality at home. The Black consciousness of the day had affected me as I transitioned from childhood to adolescence, spurred by the rebellion that had engulfed Detroit just three weeks before my fourteenth birthday. A year later, while watching the 1968 Democratic Convention police riot in Chicago, I distinctly remember thinking that real change must now come to the United States, since we had witnessed the police bloody white people in public. While this may now seem wishful, it was the kind of thinking that spurred me to attend, while in high school, the weekly forums hosted by the local Pan African society, and to combine my growing and almost consuming interest in modern literature and jazz and other modern music with a nascent self-education in politics.

My first year in college was spent at the University of Michigan, in Ann Arbor, where I arrived the year after Black student activism rocked the campus. While the highlight of my year was a poetry class taught by Robert Hayden, it also was at Ann Arbor that I got my first taste of the intellectual study of Cold War discourse, in a class on politics in which we read a big book by Zbigniew Brzezinski, *The Soviet Bloc* (1960; rev. ed., 1967). The encounter between Black students and the school's administration had resulted in some curriculum changes and the establishment of a Black student center, but it was hard for me to relate to the students, most of whom were from the affluent classes. In contrast to the backgrounds out of which many of my affluent Black friends in Detroit came, neither the counterculture, the bohemian-beatniks, nor the protest movements of the era seem to have influenced the parents of these kids, whether Black or white. The activists of the previous years had by this time either graduated or were busy preparing to graduate, and they were largely inaccessible to a newbie like me. So I made few friends on campus and was already contemplating how unhappy I was when my father died on the last day of my freshman year. The summer of 1972 was one of grief. My father died on April 29, after being hit by a car while crossing the street. The driver was never found. The prospect of going back to the University of Michigan was definitely unappealing, so I enrolled in Wayne State University to be closer to my mother.

It seems that I met the campus revolutionaries the day I arrived at Wayne State, and I soon found myself as a staff writer and editor at the *South End,* the school paper. There, I wrote mostly reviews of jazz recordings and concerts. I had tried my hand at writing about politics for the *Michigan Daily* during my year in Ann Arbor but quickly realized that my knowledge of the subject required much more study. At the *South End,* I mostly stuck to cultural subjects.

The editorial team of the *South End,* headed by Gene Cunningham, consisted of young people associated with the League of Revolutionary Black Workers, as well as other young Black and white radicals. We were the second of the paper's student editorial teams that adhered to the League and its politics, after that led by John Watson a couple of years earlier. It was my association with this group that got me reading Marxist works seriously. Several of us were in a study group led by Ernie Mkalimoto, who, as Ernie Allen, became a well-known professor of Black Studies at the University of Massachusetts Amherst. He was one of the leaders of the League, which was then in the throes of an internal and terminal crisis. Our group included the late Arthur Bowman Jr. (my oldest friend, who died of coronavirus as I was writing this essay), Leslie Roberts (who died some years ago), Reggie Carter, Janice Hanible (my first college girlfriend), Christopher Booker, Naomi Dickerson, Thomas Walker, and a number of other young activists. We read "On Practice," "On Contradiction," "On the Correct Handling of Contradictions among the People," and "Where Do Correct Ideas Come From?" all collected in a Beijing-published pamphlet, *Four Essays on Philosophy* (1966), by Mao Zedong (or, as the old colonial spelling had it, Mao Tse-tung). Hanible and Roberts led the group to feminist political literature. We read *Women's Estate* (1971), by Juliet Mitchell, and *The Dialectic of Sex* (1970), by Shulamith Firestone. We spent the longest time on *Pedagogy of the Oppressed* (1970), by Paulo Friere, which, among other things, ruined us even further for standard institutional education. The collection of articles and essays by Lenin published as *National Liberation, Socialism, and Imperialism* (1968) helped us construct a revolutionary ethos out of our cultural and political nationalism. Talking about Lenin's ideas helped us better contextualize our understanding of the history of Black nationalism, especially as we embarked on a study of Marcus Garvey and Garveyism, with books like *Black Power and the Garvey Movement* (1970), by Theodore Vincent. My path to the Communist Party was forged in part through my studies with this group of friends, most of whom have remained friends to this day.

Wayne State University during the 1960s and early 1970s was a hotbed of political activity. As an urban campus, it prided itself on political engagement, yet during the 1950s it had adopted an anticommunist hiring policy, and even though I knew nothing of this when I entered the school in the fall of 1972, the reverberations of that policy would impact my entire relationship with Wayne State, a relationship that would last over a decade, until I moved to New York City in 1983 as a staff member of the *Daily World,* the CPUSA newspaper. Meanwhile, my year at the *South End* was an immersion in the world of the late 1960s and early 1970s revolutionary Left. We were out front in reporting on the people's struggle against racist police, as that struggle took shape in focusing on a year-old so-called anticrime unit called STRESS (Stop the Robberies, Enjoy Safe Streets), a police decoy operation that had killed eleven civilians, all of them Black, within its first year. We had taken up all the causes of the left-wing movement, from anti–Vietnam War work to solidarity with the Palestinian people, a then-new cause that would be the source of considerable trouble between the *South End* editorial staff and the university administration.

All this work had a concrete and positive outcome, in that it contributed to the election of Coleman A. Young as the first African American mayor of Detroit in 1973, a watershed moment locally as well as nationally. Young's election was like an earthquake. One could feel it, as if the ground was moving under one's feet. This was the very first election in which I participated as an adult, and it gave me my first lessons in the politics of power and governance. Like most young people that were involved in the social movements of the time, my understanding of and experience in radical politics was mostly limited to protest movements.

The presidential elections of the day, like the one that brought Nixon to power, seemed somewhat remote to us. I had little understanding of organized labor's role in politics, and even less of an understanding of how the Black Power impulse that was a significant part of everyday discourse related to voting and elections. The counterculture circles in which I moved had even less to do with politics. In Detroit, many hippies hewed closely to anarchist impulses, as a matter either of protest or of attempting to build a new society within the womb of the old. Groups like the Black Panther–inspired White Panther Party, started by poet and rock-and-roll impresario John Sinclair (who the police had famously jailed on a marijuana charge), attempted an alliance between the counterculture and the Black freedom movement, but their efforts, as loud as they were, remained somewhat marginal.

One of the White Panther Party's aims was to mount a "total assault on the culture by any means necessary, including rock 'n' roll, dope and fucking in the streets." As scandalous as such appeals to hedonism sounded to both the "silent majority" in Nixon-land and many of our own elders, in some ways, such appeals seemed almost redundant. After all, the rhythm-and-blues hit "Dancing in the Street" (1964) by Martha and the Vandellas (released on the Motown recording company's "Hitsville USA" label), was already a staple of Black urban culture, and the fashions and mores of the day (not to mention the infamous privacy problems plaguing teenagers) had made varying degrees of "public" sex almost a modern courtship rite. To all this the counterculture brought the outdoor music festival, which, in the case of Michigan at least, was often more of a rock-blues-jazz festival than was typical. And these, too, were considered political events as much as cultural ones. It was characteristic of the times, then, that mass events involving thousands of people—music festivals, political meetings, rallies, conventions, demonstrations—were all part of everyday life. In the Detroit of 1973, we would add a political campaign to this sociocultural mélange.

In addition to the outdoor music festival, the emergence of the rock-and-roll ballroom in the middle to late 1960s also helped create a new kind of social space for teenagers. In Detroit, this role was filled by the Grande Ballroom, a performance space and dance hall that featured local and national rock 'n' roll bands, and, on occasion, blues and jazz groups as well. It was here that I saw B.B. King and Sun Ra for the first time, where Iggy Pop, who was then the lead singer of the Psychedelic Stooges, performed what has got to be the loudest concert I've ever attended. The legal maximum audience for the hall may have been as many as five thousand, maybe smaller, but Iggy, dancing and gyrating in front of what seemed like ten-foot tall speakers, singing "I Just Wanna Be Your Dog," seemed to turn the ambient air itself into pure sound.

When most people use *counterculture* to refer to the youth culture of the late 1960s, they are usually referring to that culture that grew up around the various schools of rock and folk-rock music that emerged during the era. That counterculture is usually figured by historians of culture as a white youth phenomenon. This was not my experience. While there certainly was a segment of the counterculture that was mainly white, there was also a youth counterculture that was mainly Black. And between these two poles was the broader counterculture, which was primarily a mixed-race phenomenon. The African American counterculture of the 1960s and 1970s was, to a significant degree, an African-influenced cultural nationalist expression. While it shared with the rest of the counterculture the ethos of experimentalism in lifestyle, dress, and social attitudes, its political orientation was toward building Black social, cultural, and economic institutions. In Detroit, this orientation both dovetailed with and was distinguished from the rest of the counterculture. Yet during the warmer months, the city seemed filled with counterculture festivals and events of all sorts. And while the Black festivals tended to feature more political speeches and the white ones fewer, politics within the counterculture as a whole was never far offstage. This is one factor that seemed to distinguish Detroit's counterculture.

Politics seemed deeply integrated with cultural or spiritual concerns. Earlier I mentioned the *Fifth Estate,* the city's alternative newspaper. It came out two or three times a month and was a vital source of political information for most of us youth. It was here that I read Julius Lester, who had been a leader of the Student Nonviolent Coordinating Committee (SNCC) and whose columns, originally published in the New York newspaper *The Guardian,* were republished in the *Fifth Estate.* Another columnist was Frank Joyce, a white activist and writer who had been active with antiracist groups in the city, such as People against Racism, since the early 1960s. Joyce would go on to play distinguished roles in the city's New Left leadership and in the labor movement. The paper also published accounts of local demonstrations. But most important, and perhaps consequential, in my memory, the *Fifth Estate* took a strong position in favor of the local Black radical movement. It offered a running account of the upsurge taking place in the auto plants, much of it fueled by the League of Revolutionary Black Workers and their affiliates. It also championed opposition to police brutality, often linking the attacks by the police on Black teenagers with the attacks against hippies (who it proudly called "freeks"), often going out of its way to describe police attacks in detail, something that one never saw in the big commercial media.

Maybe it was because of the *Fifth Estate* that I participated in one of my earliest demonstrations, a response from the call of the defense team to be part of the crowd that attended the trial that grew out of a police assault on a Detroit church in 1969. The New Bethel Shoot-Out, as it came to be colloquially known, started one spring evening, when police attacked New Bethel Baptist Church, where a meeting of the Republic of New Africa was being held. Reverend C.L. Franklin, the father of Aretha Franklin and one of the best-known African American preachers in the country, was the pastor of the 4,500-member church, a central institution in the Black community. Hundreds of people were in attendance, and witnesses say the police assaulted the meeting after confronting some of the guards assigned to protect it. When police opened fire on the meeting, the guards fired back. As a result, one police officer was killed, another wounded, four civilians were wounded, and over one hundred were carted off to jail.

In one of the first acts of radical action on the part of a government official to hit my consciousness, an African American lawyer who was an elected judge of the Recorders Court, in a midnight hearing at police headquarters, ordered the immediate release of those subjected to mass, indiscriminate arrest by the police that night. (Contemporaneous newspaper accounts differ over whether the judge released all or only some of the prisoners, the rest allegedly having been let go by the city's prosecutor.) By that action the judge catapulted his name to the front pages, dominating the news for weeks. The judge's recognition of the arrestees' Constitutional rights, and his restoration of those rights, brought loud, public anger and vitriol from the white police and their far-right-wing friends. Calls for the judge's firing rang out from white officialdom everywhere. Of course, the judge was threatened, but he was also the subject of massive police demonstrations outside his courtroom. I hadn't heard of the judge until this moment, and had no idea that he was a famous radical of the elder generation.

The judge, George W. Crockett, had served on the defense team of the first Smith Act Communist defendants back in the late 1940s, and he had spent four months in jail on contempt charges for his trouble. He had been a New Dealer and then a UAW lawyer in the days before Reuther's elevation as UAW president. During the 1950s, he continued his defense of Smith Act defendants, including the Michigan Six, a group that included Tommy Dennis and Billy Allan, as well as Saul Wellman and others. He was a partner in one of the first racially integrated big-city law firms in the country. Before he was elected to the judicial bench, then, Crockett was a well-known progressive. The *Detroit Free Press* reminded readers of some of this history in the days after the New Bethel Shoot-Out, but such reminders, although framed in a way that aimed to alienate readers, did nothing to diminish Crockett's stature in the Black community. In 1980, some years after the shoot-out and its aftermath, Detroiters sent Crockett to Congress, where he served five terms. During his first term, I was privileged to interview him for a radio program I produced on Detroit's public radio station.

The subject was Paul Robeson in Detroit, and particularly his aid to the UAW's Ford Motor Company organizing campaign of the early 1940s. Rep. Crockett recalled how, during the early years of the Cold War, although Robeson was banned from most of the country's venues, Detroit, and in particular the Rev. Charles A. Hill, the progressive pastor of Hartford Avenue Baptist Church, welcomed him. I had already had the chance to learn about Crockett in my reporting on a tribute dinner in his honor in 1979, attended by over one thousand people. The political and legal leadership of Detroit, led by Coleman A. Young and Erma Henderson, turned out to lay accolades on then judge Crockett before a racially integrated audience that was as much a movement crowd as it was a society one — a major social event in Detroit that season. Events like the New Bethel Shoot-Out and Crockett's role in it helped reinforce the fact that for young activists in the late 1960s and early 1970s, there already was an older generation of radicals in our midst who we could learn from, and it just so happened that in the Black community, many of these elders seemed to come from or had been active in the Communist Party and its milieu.

The election campaign of 1973 that made Coleman Young mayor of Detroit was a people's movement that ushered in a people's government. One of the factors in his biography that cropped up during the campaign was Young's defiant 1952 testimony in front of the House Un-American Activities Committee hearings that terrorized the community when the committee came to town. Somehow, recordings of that testimony surfaced in the media, and we young radicals caught a thrill from hearing him, even though I'm now sure the instigators of this "revelation" meant to hurt him with it. It was stirring to see that our new mayor had enemies in the far-right wing, that he had vanquished them rhetorically during our childhood years, and was now, as the first local political hero of our generation, vanquishing them politically as well. Young opened up city government to constituencies that had been locked out. This had the effect of broadening the liberal coalition that dominated Democratic Party politics, especially as that broadening included African American and white members of labor and other organizations that weren't part of the established liberal apparatus, and to the extent that it included young people and activists in its tent. It was a milieu that, in effect, mainstreamed Left ideas and personalities that had been part of older Left movements, including those that bore the stamp of Communist Party activism.

Through all this, our Marxist study group remained active on Wayne State University's campus and in the larger community. After our year at the *South End,* we worked through the Association of Black Students on campus. One of my roles was as the host of the Association's radio program, *ABS Speaks,* but I was also writing for local periodicals, including the *Ann Arbor Sun,* a weekly newspaper that John Sinclair was heavily involved with, and *Tribe* magazine, which was initiated by Wendell Harrison, a leading local jazz musician, and the Tribe collective of which he was a part. Meanwhile, as we approached the end of our college years, our study group began to suffer an identity crisis. It seemed that, in the heady days of the mid-1970s, we were engaged in the same kind of wide-ranging inquiry that impacted many of our contemporaries.

These were also the years of the emergence of the New Communist Movement, a collection of radical groups whose membership was drawn largely from student, antiwar, and Black Power activists, many of whom were just entering the workforce. For many of us, our student Marxism grew, as we gained experience in the world of work, into a working-class consciousness. Yet many New Communist Movement groups were, to one degree or another, influenced by Maoism as well as by anti-Sovietism, both of which were deeply influential for young activists, including those of color like ourselves. We had come to Marxism through reading a mix of older US Communist texts and the canonical works of Marx, Lenin, Trotsky, Mao—and, for some, even Stalin—along with our Malcolm X, Robert F. Williams, and Franz Fanon; and in all this reading and the debates that went with it, the question of the precise moment when the USSR (or the Communist Party USA) ceased being revolutionary was an animating one.

Detroit had one of the largest, most working class–based, and most interracial groups in the entire New Communist Movement; this was an organization that grew from members and leaders of the League of Revolutionary Black Workers and affiliated groups and that eventually named itself the Communist Labor Party (CLP). The Maoist-oriented group took its lead from the general line pursued by the Communist Party of China, although the CLP's sectarianism did not rise to the level of many other Maoist groups. The CLP's domestic ideal seemed to be the Communist Party USA of the 1920s. Nevertheless, they were a sectarian bunch, whose enemies all seemed to be on the Left: the liberals, the "revisionists" of the CPUSA, the elected officials of the unions. I remember being in a meeting once in which a leader of the Motor City Labor League, a majority white organization that was one of the groups that came to constitute the CLP, described CPers as "liberals."

In a word, we had inherited a kind of "left" anticommunism, a heritage that seemed to find support in the fact that the real, existing Communist Party seemed to us visible and invisible at the same time. For example, everybody read Herbert Aptheker's work. Books from the International Publishers imprint were in the libraries of every activist and left-wing intellectual I knew. We all admired Angela Davis. But most of the real, live Communists we knew were kind of mysterious figures. Few local Communists would openly admit their Party membership. Although everyone in my circle knew something about McCarthyism, having grown up in it, few of us knew any of the details. Our sense of the de facto and de jure legal status of the Communist Party was partially obscured by the fact that, legally speaking, one had almost no problem espousing Marxist or Marxist-Leninist ideas in public, as long as you took care to distinguish your version of Marxism-Leninism from the Communist Party USA's version. So that even in a town that, in the mid-1970s, was as left-wing as Detroit, where the president of the city council, Erma Henderson, had been the Detroit leader of the Labor Youth League some twenty years earlier; where the new mayor would send a limousine to the Detroit airport to greet his old friend and roommate, James E. Jackson, who was at that moment the Educational Director of the CPUSA, just so Mayor Young could brag to his old friend Jim about his ascension to power in the fifth largest city in the country; and where the Communist candidates for statewide office would have their campaign posters mounted as advertisements on the city busses — even there, one had to search to find one's way to the real, flesh-and-blood, existing Communist Party. In this regard, you could say I lucked out. The Communists found me, and I found them, at just about the same time.

The New Communist Movement's interest in the legacy of the Communist movement in the United States was in many ways peculiar and idiosyncratic. During the mid-1970s, there were thousands of young people who had studied some of the Marxist classics, as our study group had, and had gained an interest in the older radical movement even as we were making a radical movement of our own. Yet our interest in the Communist movement was focused primarily on its past, a past that we sometimes treated as if the Party was a museum piece and we its conservators and preservationists. Our interest in the contemporary Communist Party that lived among us was completely overshadowed by our preoccupation with the Party's past. And for us, the further back that past was, the better.

One benefit of this perspective was that we eagerly sought to acquaint ourselves with the history of our parents' generation. Our parents had grown up in the middle years of the twentieth century, the years of Depression, war, and early Cold War; some had even participated in the Popular Front movement. Most of our parents, however, were reluctant to share much information about their own youthful radicalism with their children. This may be hard for some to understand, but it must be remembered that the 1970s were still Cold War years, and even though the most draconian anticommunist laws had been repealed or nullified by the courts, association with the Communist Party was not without its complications. In addition, the epidemic of midnight Smith Act raids on friends, neighbors, and prominent persons that the government conducted in the early Korean War years, the Detroit HUAC hearings of 1952, the firings and blacklisting in industry, the legal requirement of public or individual contractual disavowal of any radical associations whatsoever, past or present, in order to get a job — all these were part of our parents' lives. My mother, a government worker, and her sister Lessie, a nurse, feared that my own radical associations would land me in jail, or worse. They rarely shared these fears with me (I only learned of the depth of their concern years later, from a cousin), and they never sought to hinder my involvement in the movement. But looking back, it is clear that fear of government-instigated domestic terror of the 1950s returning was never far from their minds. The success of the Free Angela Davis movement was still very recent, and while our study group's interest in the Communist movement grew in the afterglow of that victory, the very circumstances of the case were a reminder that we had not yet transcended the anticommunist era. The reticence some of our parents showed in this regard extended to a range of public figures in Detroit, especially, but not only, those coming from the African American community. Although Coleman Young's 1940s and 1950s radicalism was well known—he'd been a national leader of the country's left wing during the years of the Korean War—few outside of those with long memories knew, for example, of the prominent role that Erma Henderson, the city's new city council president (in those years it was called the Common Council), had played in the local left wing movement just twenty years earlier.

What problematized all this even further was what we might call the Reuther paradox. Walter Reuther was the longtime liberal social democrat who became UAW president in 1946 by winning a contest between Left and social democratic union factions. We understood him to be both descended from the radical tradition and a foe of radicals. Generally speaking, Reuther was a hero, but many in the Black community were well aware of his limitations, especially when it came to the barriers that kept Black workers out of the skilled trades. It should not be so surprising, then, that the African American community leadership in Detroit in the early 1970s included both pro- and anti-Reuther factions, as well as people who were friendly to both groups. The group that was elected with Young to city leadership included many people who, like the mayor, had cut their political teeth as part of the anti-Reuther left wing. These complications were part of the overall political atmosphere. In some ways, these circumstances could lead to real political complexities, in particular for those young activists who saw the radicalism of Reuther as conservative, and especially in light of the stories we were hearing from some of our elders.

Such stories of our city and our country's radical past came to us both from our elders and from contemporaries who passed them down as a kind of oral history. This is how I first learned about the Depression-era activities of the CPUSA and first heard some of the spurious reasons that were given regarding how and why that earlier movement "failed" to achieve its objectives. The source of this history was Dave Blake, a dear friend from my *South End* days. Somewhere along the line, Dave had joined the Socialist Workers Party, the country's leading exponent of the Trotskyist Fourth International and a group that was especially active on college campuses during those years. Dave's account of this history, then, came from a standpoint of critical admiration, as did similar accounts I would hear from others, including some who had been important Communist Party leaders just a few years earlier but had now taken up with groups mainly composed of activists much younger than themselves.

All this dovetailed with transformations that involved our study group. At this point, the group had been meeting regularly for about two years. We continued to meet, even after most of us had either graduated from college or dropped out. By this time, we were searching for some activity to involve ourselves with as a collective, and at just this moment, revolution broke out in Portugal against the fascist regime of long-serving dictator António de Oliveira Salazar and Marcelo Caetano, his authoritarian successor. The regime had governed the country for half a century. When it was overthrown in the Carnation Revolution of April 1974, the event accelerated the liberation movements in Portugal's African colonies, especially Angola and Mozambique, whose peoples were waging increasingly successful wars against the old colonial power. Among youthful Black radicals of the time, these developments offered an opportunity to involve ourselves in a matter of international solidarity that coincided with our Black nationalist sentiments.

While some of the older activists among us had been involved in solidarity work around Cuba, in addition to having participated in anti–Vietnam War activities, much of our relationship with African anti-imperialist movements centered around reading Fanon and the work of some of the major revolutionaries and statesmen, like Kwame Nkrumah of Ghana and Amilcar Cabral of Guinea-Bissau. During my own high school years, I attended the weekly lectures of the local chapter of the Pan African Congress, which combined talks on African history with reports, often given by exiles from South Africa and elsewhere, about the state of the anticolonial struggle. After revolution broke out in Portugal, we had the spectacle of Gerald Ford begging Congress for funds for intervention in Angola, along with Henry Kissinger all but threatening the Portuguese people with war if they voted against his wishes. In the wake of these events, we found ourselves with a hot-button issue that directly related to our sympathies with Africans fighting colonialism. It could be said that the antiapartheid movement of the 1980s in this country had its origins in these mid-1970s struggles. The issues came to a head in the mid-1970s, in the planning and staging of the annual African Liberation Day marches and festivals. These events, which started in the spring of 1972, deftly combined political and cultural expression and ranged from day-long music-oriented events to marches in the streets. By 1974 and 1975, they'd come to pivot around a debate over which of the movements in Angola were deserving of our support, a debate that polarized around Cold War divisions, with the People's Movement for the Liberation of Angola (MPLA) finding its support with us pro-Marxist radicals, while the National Front for the Liberation of Angola (FNLA) found its support largely among Maoists and anticommunist Black nationalists. Both groups paraded together in a single demonstration through one of the city's West Side Black neighborhoods on African Liberation Day, debating with each other before settling down to the party that inevitably followed, where food, drink, and good music and companionship put debate to rest, at least temporarily. Our group also worked to establish connections with others across the country. Tom Walker and I went to Chicago in the spring of 1976 to participate in a national conference in solidarity with Angola, myself representing our group under the name of the "Anti-Imperialist Action Committee," while Walker was one of a couple of delegates from the "Detroit Marxist-Leninist Organization," a federation of study groups that included, for a time, our own. It was at this conference that I may have first encountered Communists like Ishmael Flory, who led the Illinois Party organization, and other activists who I would come to work with in the antiapartheid movement in New York City a decade later.

In the midst of this activity, our study group was itself getting attention from other organizations, including some that had famous former Communists among their members. Among the older radicals we paid attention to was Raya Dunayevskaya, one-time secretary to Leon Trotsky and a collaborator with C.L.R. James in the "Johnson-Forrest Tendency" of the 1940s–1950s Trotskyist movement. Her monthly lectures at the downtown Detroit YMCA under the title "Marxist Humanism," which I attended regularly over the course of 1974–1975, would often draw scores of people to the little lecture room. She would bring G.W.F. Hegel's ideas to life in connection with the radical protest movements of the day. Her talks were often dazzling, with their Hegelian anti-vanguardism and their call for "revolution from below." Ultimately, however, her ideas struck me as wastefully anti-institutionalist just at a moment when it appeared that mass movements were challenging and beginning to reshape institutions. Her ideas seemed oddly utopian at a time when emergent social movements were concerning themselves with the work of institution building and reshaping. Dunayevskaya was an able and brilliant justifier of the ethos of protest. Her newspaper, *News and Letters* (which was also the name of the organization she led), seemed to herald protest movements as such as the embryo of the new society. Yet for all its insight, this approach was not as helpful as it might have been when it came to thinking through what to do once protest movements started knocking down institutional barriers. In a word, her brilliance shed little light on how a radical should be engaged in the political sphere.

It was in this connection that Saul Wellman, who had been one of the Michigan Six defendants but who had left the Party sometime after the courts threw the case out, came to one of our meetings, most of which were held in the house owned by Arthur Bowman's parents in Highland Park, a smaller, separate city nestled completely within Detroit's borders. (Arthur's parents were involved in Left politics in the 1950s, most notably as leaders of the UAW Local 600 Credit Union during the union's Congress of Industrial Organizations [CIO] days. Arthur Bowman Sr. was the credit union's lawyer, and his wife Thelma was on the executive board. She would become one of the city's earliest Black yoga teachers.) Gene Cunningham and I were Bowman's roommates that year. Wellman brought a special guest along with him: Dorothy Healey, who had been a well-known leader of the California Communist Party. Healey had recently resigned from the Party and was now attached, as it seemed was Wellman, to the New American Movement, a socialist group that attorney Arthur Kinoy, among others, had recently founded. Wellman and Healey were most interested in pursuing their arguments with the Communists, and, along the way, trying to persuade us that the Party was a hopelessly outdated enterprise. We listened dutifully, asked questions, and certainly learned a few things. Whatever most of us thought about Wellman and Healey's criticisms of the Party, none of us was all that attracted to their organizational model. Whatever else we thought or knew about the Communists, we also knew that the Party included some Black people among its members and leaders, while it seemed that Wellman and Healey had traded in that kind of organization for one that appeared to be all white and seemed destined to remain so. Whatever else we as a group were searching for, it did not include becoming African American tokens in an otherwise all white left-wing organization.

At the same time, we were all honored when James Boggs and Grace Lee Boggs came to visit our study group. You could not be an African American revolutionary in Detroit in the late 1960s and early 1970s without having pored over, in detail, James Boggs's work. His books *The American Revolution: Pages from a Negro Worker's Notebook* (1963) and *Racism and the Class Struggle* (1970) were treated by us with the same reverence that the movement as a whole treated books by Fanon or *The Autobiography of Malcolm X.* Boggs's works shaped our thinking in all kinds of ways, big and small. Our understanding of the possibilities of Black political power was profoundly shaped by his theories. The essay he and Grace coauthored, "The City is the Black Man's Land" (which appears in *Racism and the Class Struggle*), counted as a manifesto among us. (Indeed, as it turns out, Boggs may have been the first to coin the phrase "Black Power"; at least, he played a significant role in the May 1, 1965, Detroit conference that founded the National Organization for Black Power.) His observations about the growing role of technology in the manufacturing sector, which in those days went by the name "automation," represented advanced thinking almost to the point of prophecy. The fact that his books were published by Monthly Review Press, the leading independent left-wing press in the country, was an added bonus. (Monthly Review published no other Black American Marxist writers save Oliver C. Cox, who taught at Wayne State University and whose books we also read and whose lectures and classes some of us attended, but whose work seemed obscure to many of us.) Yet, for all that, meeting Boggs in person was something of a letdown. Boggs was moving away from his Marxist roots and was himself searching for another way forward. Like many in the non-Communist Left in those days, he was losing his confidence in the potential of the working class as an agent of social change. By this time, much of his focus was on condemning the conservatism of organized labor's leadership, in a way that seemed more hopeless than hopeful. This was an attitude he seemed to share with Healey and Wellman, among others. Not to stretch the figure too far, but it seemed that just as we were waking up to the potential of the working class and organized labor as catalysts of social change, these elders were going to sleep on that potential.

It was also during this period that I met Christopher C. Alston, who would become, for all intents and purposes, my first mentor in the Communist movement. Chris was about sixty years old and a handsome man, with rich dark skin and a streak of grey in his hair. He had an authoritative aura, but he was wonderfully devoid of the condescension that many of our elders would visit upon young radicals. Some of our elders seemed manifestly unhappy with their lives; Chris was one of the happiest men of his generation that I'd ever met. He wasn't in the Party, having left it some years previously. I'm not sure I ever knew when he stopped being an actual Party member, but he continued to be on warm terms with local Party members and leaders. (Over the years, I was to find this to be generally the case for many in Michigan who had separated themselves relatively recently; many seem to have left during or right after the Party's late-1950s post–Stalin revelations crisis.) Chris had been an activist in the Young Communist League during the earliest years of the Great Depression and was still proud of a photograph of himself from the *Daily Worker* in 1932, standing at the funeral of the martyrs of the Ford Hunger March, in front of a huge banner-picture of Lenin that served as background to the coffins of the young workers that were slain that day. (I'll have more to say about the Ford Hunger March later.) Chris had spent his life in the working-class movement, was one of the founding militants of the United Auto Workers union, and, at the time that we met, was an administrator of a city-owned public housing project. We met at a Common Council meeting that was called in answer to the Ford administration's threats to intervene in Angola. Our study group (we were now calling ourselves the Black and Red Collective) had made some leaflets to distribute at the meeting, where we fully expected the council to issue a public statement in opposition to Ford's threatened intervention. But our amateurishly produced leaflets paled in style and beauty compared to those Chris and his friends produced. Those that testified before the council from Chris's group that day included Art McPhaul, another old radical that we'd never seen before. These were clearly Black radicals of the older generation that had the same sympathies as us, but until that moment, we had no knowledge whatsoever of their existence.

After the Common Council meeting ended, my friends and I rushed over to this small group of elders, which included Art McPhaul, Frank Sykes, Chris's wife Marti, and a few others. While McPhaul and Sykes seemed somewhat reticent, Chris was eager to talk with us. (McPhaul, it turns out, was a veteran of the Civil Rights Congress, but may no longer have been, when we met him, enrolled in the Party, while Sykes, an autoworker and another veteran of the 1932 Ford Hunger March, was still an active member.) In essence, Chris took us under his wing. He would talk with us about radical history and his history in the Party, at least up to a point. More important to us, however, was that here was a living link to the storied Black and radical labor past. Chris seemed to have known all the legendary figures of the movement, and while he was fine with talking about the distant past, the closer we got to our-contemporary times, the vaguer he seemed to become about his precise relationship to the Party, even as he made clear that his membership was a thing of the past. His friendliness toward the Party, however, was beyond dispute. (One older Black Party member would later describe Chris and some of his friends as "cheating the Party out of dues," a charge that Chris, as I remember, greeted with amusement.) The fact that Chris was an active and respected leader of the Black community only enhanced his stature in our eyes.

It was during this time, and under this array of influences, that my personal interest in the CPUSA began to grow. I started to attend forums and events sponsored by the *Daily World*, the Party's news organ, and began to read the paper regularly. I also joined in discussions, both formal and informal, with the few Party members and people close to the Party who were closer to my age. There weren't many, but after a few meetings and parties, I eventually counted myself a member of the Young Workers Liberation League (YWLL). I wish I could say how it was I became a League member, but I suspect that people like Wendell Addington Jr. and Denise Line had something to do with it. Denise was a striking and beautiful African American woman who was a few years older than me and worked, if memory serves, in one of the city's auto plants. I was somewhat in awe of her. Having spent the previous few years of my life in a radical milieu whose activities mainly consisted of intellectual pursuits that were almost devoid of practical application, it was in some ways jarring to find myself suddenly in an atmosphere where the relationship between theory and practice was far more balanced. The Communists I met all had rich and fascinating bookcases in their homes that included not only Marxist-Leninist literature, but novels and other literature from writers I'd never heard of; yet, with some notable exceptions, the Communists I met rarely wore their intellectualism on their sleeves. The ideas in the books on their shelves seemed more like tools to inform activism, rather than abstract concepts rolled out for debate. For people like Denise, the ideas of Marxism seemed to be just that: tools, rather than inert notions. What most impressed me in my earliest encounters with this group was that the ideas of Marxism seemed to live just as robustly within Communist culture as it did in books. Nobody invited me to a study group. Instead, I was invited to lectures, to read pamphlets and the *Daily World* on my own, and to participate in activities in which the people I met were involved.

Although my memory on this is somewhat imprecise, it seems that I was in the YWLL for about a year before joining, sometime in 1976, the Communist Party. What I remember about the YWLL and the CPUSA is that they were a round of meetings, parties, and demonstrations. I was also impressed by the range of brilliant people I met in that milieu. (At this point in my account, it seems that discretion is the better part of wisdom when talking about some of these people, so forgive me if I refrain from always offering full names here, especially of those that are, as of this writing, still alive.) But among the YWLLers that most impressed me was Linda, a daughter of an affluent left-wing African American family that lived in one of the city's poshest neighborhoods. She was a leader of one of the League's student chapters at a big university in the state and would later distinguish herself in political circles in Detroit and Washington; she, too, would wear her Marxism more as a set of internally held values than as a fixed ideology. She was also fun to be around. I've never known exactly how Susan, a shy yet energetic white woman with bright red hair, came to her politics. She was, as I remember, an artist who worked in one of the local advertising firms. She created witty and effective leaflets for our various attempts to organize unemployed youth.

The Detroit leader of the YWLL when I joined was Wendell Addington Jr., the son of a prominent leftist family. His father had been a local activist and developer in the nonprofit, cooperative, and affordable housing movement; he was a respected figure in the city's left-wing milieu, an anti–Vietnam War activist, and a leader of the local Free Angela Davis committee. Wendell Jr. was an affable, friendly fellow, with a great sense of humor. Like the rest of the Communists I met, he seemed unbitten by the bug of sectarianism. Yet he was a serious and dedicated activist. We worked to organize unemployed youth in the midst of the worst post–World War II recession up to that time. Our efforts included public demonstrations, support for city-council resolutions, and lobbying trips to local and state lawmakers. We would assemble coalitions that included young leaders and members of the local National Association for the Advancement of Colored People (NAACP) and people involved in the newly emerging, post–Great Society nonprofit community organizations. These latter groups constituted the beginnings of the professionally run NGO-style social-service organizations that have, over the last few decades, supplanted what was once a network of volunteer-run, membership-based community organizations and movements. The earnest and dedicated leaders of these groups were not yet hampered by the legal restrictions that would later stifle their ability to act politically. So, we were able to take a bus up to Lansing, the state capital, and lobby legislators in favor of an impending state bill that mirrored the Humphrey-Hawkins legislation on full employment that the YWLL and other progressive groups supported.

What made that particular trip so memorable for me was an aspect of it that was revelatory and deeply moving. We went from office to office in the Capitol, unimpeded, hoping to talk with (mostly Democratic) legislators about our concerns. When we would introduce ourselves as the "Detroit Youth Jobs Coalition" and offer a leaflet that had the names of more than one local leader of organized labor signed as endorsers, state representative after state representative would attempt to impress the obviously impressionable teens and young adults (I was about twenty-two) standing before them by taking out their wallets and showing us their union cards! Nothing in my half-dozen or so years of reading Communist literature and participating in rallies and demonstrations had quite prepared me for this spectacle. Here were workers — union members — in the state legislature, writing and passing laws! It was one of those myth-defying, if not myth-destroying, moments. It also helped me understand what made the Communists different from other left-wing groups.

While most left-wing organizations and personalities painted all officialdom with the same derogatory brush, the Communists distinguished among them, primarily, it turns out, because they understood the people's movement and the class struggle to be complex. In large part, these card-carrying trade unionists that were also state legislators were working-class people who had taken advantage of working-class victories in order to enter politics and try to do some good. This helped me understand that calling the Democratic Party a "bourgeois" party, even as bankers and industrialists held outsize power within the party's decision-making apparatus, could be an oversimplification. It awakened me to the understanding that some form of working-class politics was also part of the Democratic Party's identity. Aside from this, while all of the Democratic Party lawmakers we met, including those that still carried their union cards in their wallets, would publicly describe themselves as "liberals," one thing that soon became apparent to me was that this designation could also be, within the prevailing political context of the time, porous. I was soon to find, on more than one occasion, a "liberal" that knew far more Marxist theory than one had any right to expect. It would be years before I fully understood the history behind all this, but meanwhile, this episode at the state Capitol was a glimpse of an insight that would only grow within me over time: the understanding that in a democracy, politics is, by nature and above all, complicated.

This was an insight that would serve me well during my next phase of involvement with the Party and its milieu. But there were other lessons to learn, as well. Election Day 1976 was perhaps only the second time I'd voted in a presidential election. (I was barely eligible to vote in the 1972 election and don't remember if I'd cast a vote in that contest.) I was all set to register as an independent, in part because I had resolved to vote for Gus Hall and Jarvis Tyner, the Communist candidates in the general election. But the nice woman at the registration table informed me that if I registered as an independent, I would be ineligible to vote in the Democratic primary, which, in Detroit, was where the real political competition was. I registered as a Democrat on the spot and have remained a registered Democrat from that day to this. Yet I still voted for Hall and Tyner in the general election. Standing in line at the polling station at Berea Lutheran Church on Tireman Avenue in Detroit (where voters lined up by precinct), I was feeling a little self-conscious about my choice. Gerald Ford was not the most odious of Republicans, especially compared to Nixon, but he was a callous warmonger who liked to keep Henry Kissinger around. Jimmy Carter was well-enough liked by the local Democratic leadership, but his being a white Southerner did not make him especially trustworthy. A protest vote seemed like a good way out of this trap, as well as a way to help build a movement. Besides, I was impressed that the Party seemed to take elections seriously as both a protest and an organizing vehicle. This was expressed forthrightly by Gus Hall in a pamphlet he'd published a few years earlier, "A Lame Duck in Turbulent Waters: The Next Four Years of Nixon" (1972), in which he discussed the Party's rationale for running independent candidates while also remaining active in broader political circles, including in the Democratic Party, and while I came to more fully understand the concept of the "three-legged stool" (in which the Party sought to field its own candidates, help foment broader independent political movements, and work within the liberal wing of the Democratic Party), I was most impressed by Hall's insistence that the time had come for Communists to take the prospect of getting themselves elected to office seriously. At the same time, I was not unaware of the idealism of voting for the Communist candidates, especially living in a town where the Democratic Party was, for all intents and purposes, the mass leader of the progressive movement. But I was heartened by the conversation being held by two African American men who were in the precinct line next to mine. Both were dressed in the casual everyday clothes commonly worn by men of my father's generation who worked in the city's factories. Both looked to be in their early fifties, with gray just beginning to show at the temples. "Are you voting for Carter?" one of them asked the other. When his companion admitted that he was indeed voting for the Democrat, the first man said, somewhat laconically, "Well, I'm going to vote for that Communist Gus Hall fellow." I can't recall whether he said anything else to justify his choice, but I'd heard everything I needed to hear. The utility of the Party's independent work in electoral politics began to dawn on me, though I can't say I fully understood that yet. Indeed, the full extent of the nuanced approach that the Party took to electoral politics and political officeholders was not at all clear to me. I was still learning. But the lessons in this topic that I learned that year were enduring. All this stood me in good stead as I got ready for the big learning curve that lay ahead.

Sometime during that year I joined the Communist Party. Even after having been active in the YWLL and attending all sorts of Party events, it seemed that I still had to almost bang the door down to gain entry. Later I would come to understand this problem as a holdover from the McCarthy era. But at the time, it seemed really puzzling to me. Yet when I finally joined, I was welcomed with open arms. However much I may have been expecting great, new experiences and insight to come from signing a Party card, all that joining the Party added to my life at first was another annoying meeting to attend.

I was already pretty busy. During the previous year, I had been asked to take over a jazz radio program on WDET-FM, the local National Public Radio affiliate. Kenn Cox, the previous host, who championed me as his replacement, was one of Detroit's most prominent jazz musicians. This was a purely volunteer arrangement, although I do remember receiving some compensation a few years later. But until at least the late 1970s, public radio usually meant all-volunteer radio. This arrangement gave the on-air personalities a great deal of freedom. But while some hosts of the music shows aired on the station used the microphone as a political platform, I mostly resisted that temptation. For the most part, I limited my political commentary to information that would illuminate aspects of jazz history. One reason had to be that such compartmentalization meant that I could use the radio show, and the privilege I had to play the entire range of jazz music on the air, as a way of relaxing from the increasingly busy political world I was entering. For those three hours a week I had no responsibility but to enjoy playing music for an audience, and I took full advantage of that opportunity. The radio show was scheduled at different times over the years: Sometimes it broadcast on Monday evenings and sometimes on Saturday mornings. But the three-hour show was a highlight of my life during those years, and I spent my twenties as, among other things, one of the major Detroit jazz radio hosts.

My first couple of years in the Party were, nevertheless, full of activism as well as meetings. I've already mentioned some of the activities related to the work of the YWLL, and I soon found myself named chair of the local YWLL, a position I couldn't have held for long. A benefit of this was that I got to go to the national meetings held in New York City, but to tell the truth, I remember far too little about those. James Steele was the charismatic and brilliant national chair of the YWLL whose depth of political insight was impressive. That he was a big jazz fan also warmed me to him. The fact that he was older than me by about a decade perhaps limited our personal relationship, but that mattered little to me. That an African American leader of his capability was at the helm of this youth organization I'd joined and was also a national CPUSA leader was impressive. It's hard to convey what it was like for a Black kid from the Midwest to find himself in the midst of such a diverse and outstanding group of thinkers and activists. The qualities I'd come to admire in the YWLL group in Detroit were magnified by the people I was meeting in New York, people who hailed from across the country and who were, to my mind, already seasoned revolutionaries, even though few of us were older than our early thirties.

My education continued in the summer of 1977, during the two weeks spent in a northern Minnesota recreational camp of a Communist Party school. The school had many teachers, but the one that stood out to me was Party education director Jim Jackson, although I don't remember if I had yet become aware of his legend, his personage, his melodious voice, or his broad and deep intellect. In the camp, we mostly read Marxist classics and would discuss them, seminar style, with whatever teachers were made available to us. The school was named after W.E.B. Du Bois and William Z. Foster, and although I've long thought of this experience as some kind of advanced training in Marxism-Leninism, it was probably little more than an "advanced" introduction to the subject. Aside from overall good impressions, I remember little else about the experience, except that I began an affair with one of my fellow students, another Detroiter, that turned into a two-year relationship that ended, for me, with a broken heart. Perhaps it was the energy of a new relationship that enhanced this two-week adventure in the remote woods of the upper Midwest and accounts for why it stands out in my sensibility but hardly at all in my memory.

The school was located in the Mesabi Iron Range, which was Party general secretary Gus Hall's home turf. He visited and either gave a speech or led a seminar, I can't remember which, but this was perhaps my first time meeting him. By then, I'd read a bit of Gus's work, and something about his history, and was eager to meet him. Aside from "A Lame Duck in Turbulent Waters," which taught me quite a bit, essays like "Racism: The Nation's Most Dangerous Pollutant" (1971) and his book *The*

Energy Rip-Off (1973) had a real impact on my thinking. However, as much as I was impressed by his writing, and while I can't say exactly what I expected from him as a person, what I came away with was the sense that here was a man of some mystery and paradox. Gus always impressed me as a private, remote person, someone it would have been hard to get to know well. This wasn't simply about the forty-year age difference between us. I'd developed warm and comfortable relationships with others of his generation, such as Chris Alston, who was only three years younger, and Jack White, who I will talk about later. But Hall was one of those figures you rarely meet outside of certain branches of the performing arts—a person who was not only a celebrity but also involved enough with the notion of their celebrity that they always seemed to be performing a role. The singular nod to informality one had with Hall was that in CPUSA culture almost all leaders were addressed by their first names. This was far less common then in work and professional circles than it is now. Titles, when used at all in the Party, were reserved for formal settings and occasions. So, everybody called him Gus. And everybody called Party chairman Henry Winston "Winnie," a diminutive that, to my ears, took some getting used to. It sounded at first almost too casual. But my response was probably derived from my African American pride orientation and milieu, in which white people that called Black people by nicknames or diminutives were generally to be regarded with suspicion. It was only after witnessing the universal love and respect Winnie had in the Party that the jarring sound of the nickname went away. At any rate, the somewhat distant character of Gus was, in fact, not at all common among Communist Party leaders that I met during these years, and at first I didn't really catch it in his demeanor. While it's possible that he was never more relaxed in my presence than when he visited us at the Party school, nothing of my memory of him at that time counters the impression I gathered from my numerous encounters with him over the years.

I had a number of day jobs during this time, including driving a cab in Detroit, an adventure that deserves an essay all its own. One of the cab companies I drove for served, on the night shift at least, as a transportation service for sex workers visiting clients either at their homes or in the local hotels that catered to that business. Drivers at that time ran in two twelve-hour shifts, dividing their fares and their share at the end of each shift. Few taxi drivers in Detroit owned their own medallion (the city-issued license to own a cab), and so they worked on a percentage arrangement with the company or, in some cases, the medallion-owning driver who leased the cab while he slept. It was the very model of what's now called "gig" work and was related to what had been called "piece" work. My cab-driving career ended, after a couple of years, on the day I was robbed at gunpoint at high noon across the street from one of Detroit's major high schools. The night man was mad at me for "allowing" the thieves to take his eight-track tape player.

Another job seemed like an almost dystopian reversion to childhood: coloring maps for political campaigns and candidates of the Republican Party, among others. This was a job in the sampling department of a major opinion-survey concern. I colored in regions on sampling maps. While at the job, I learned some rudimentary things about opinion polling and sampling, but mostly it was grunt work performed in a two- or three-person sampling department, where we sat coloring maps at the direction of the department manager. We never knew the clients whose campaigns we were working on, but we did know that many of them were GOP politicians. This was, of course, an ironic and deeply humorous circumstance.

One of my coworkers was a man in his late forties or early fifties, an Italian-American who had left-wing politics but seemed to have been involved in movement activities in an earlier life. We had engaging political conversations, but I soon noticed that he met my exuberance in talking about politics with a set of carefully policed boundaries that excluded most topics that touched on socialism. This was surprising, because he clearly policed that boundary not because he didn't believe in socialism; indeed, he clearly was pro-socialist and admired the socialist countries. What was evident was that his motive was some kind of fear that I barely understood. His attitude was both puzzling and surprising, and even more so after I ran into him one day at the public library sitting at a table with the previous week's issues of the *Daily World* stacked up, ready for him to read. By this time, he'd probably figured out my Communist associations, if I hadn't openly shared them myself (like I said, I was exuberant about these), and although he greeted me heartily, he also warned me not to tell anyone about what he was reading. This incident was just one reminder — there would be others — that especially for people just a few years older than myself, the ghost of the McCarthyite terror was still hovering, just as it also reminded me that the memory of a strong Left movement in which the Communist Party played a big role was still fresh, for both good and ill, for many local people. But it also reminded me, once again, that for all the talk about Marxism and the reading of Marxist-Leninist classics that I'd done before getting involved with the Party, it wasn't just the ideas in books that had made a difference. The legal circumstances that had impacted the CPUSA and the movement around it twenty years earlier still reverberated, however hard the Party was working once again, after a long absence, to regain something of its public face and presence.

Nowhere was the incongruity in which anticommunism coexisted with warm memories of the Communist Party more apparent than in the way the more liberal of Detroit's two daily newspapers treated the impending retirement of Billy Allan, who would leave Detroit after nearly four decades as the city's *Daily Worker* and *Daily World* correspondent. As I've mentioned earlier, in the mid-1950s Allan had been one of the Michigan Six, the local Smith Act defendants, along with Tommy Dennis, Helen Winter, Saul Wellman, Phil Schatz, and Nat Ganley. (This group had been in the second or third wave of the more than one hundred Communists that had been arrested under the law. The Michigan group spent a few months in jail before being released on appeal. The charges were later thrown out by the Supreme Court.) By the time Billy retired, he was known as the dean of labor journalists in Detroit.

Billy Allan was an immigrant who still spoke with the rich accent of his native Scotland. He had not only been a witness to and reporter of the great events that built the CIO in Michigan, but he was a participant in those events. He had reported on and participated in the great Flint UAW General Motors (GM) sit-down strike of 1937, as well as in every other CIO organizing campaign of those years. He was a short, wiry man, with a head full of shockingly white hair. He was the labor reporter's labor reporter and a wickedly funny man. He knew everybody that was anybody in the political and labor worlds of Detroit in those days, and it seemed that he knew where all the political skeletons were buried. Billy and I got along, in part because he knew I was a writer, and so that was something we shared. I was also an enthusiastic learner, and he was a great teacher.

To that point, it had been rare for me to see a story in the daily papers about the Communist Party, though I was later to learn that the Party had been a semiregular news topic during the 1950s and earlier. But during my childhood, adolescence, and young adulthood, a near-total news blackout had contributed to rendering the Party almost invisible to the public consciousness. One reason the campaign bus advertisement I referred to at the beginning of this essay was so startling was that even though I had some knowledge that local Communists existed, they remained almost universally underground. So, it was a surprise, and not only to me, to find Allan lionized in the *Detroit Free Press* when it came time for him to retire. Here he was, introduced as a kindly old man who was good with children and liked to bake bread and cookies, but also an atheist and a Communist! The story that appeared as a two-page spread in the Sunday magazine section of the *Detroit Free Press* in early 1977 was both a kind of shock and a matter of pride. It wasn't every day that a Communist got a headline calling him "Detroit's Beloved Revolutionary," and even if the article focused on Allan the individual, with not a single word quoted from any other Party member except Billy's wife Stephanie and their children, that was fine, too.

Almost exactly a year to the day after that *Detroit Free Press* article on Billy Allan appeared, the first article in the *Daily World* was published under my byline as the paper's Detroit correspondent. I was a twenty-four-year-old college dropout who was eking out something of a living working low-wage jobs supplemented by occasional freelance writing checks from one or another periodical. (One consequence of all this activity was that I didn't finish college. It would be another two decades before I returned to school to finish my undergraduate degree before going on to earn my doctorate in English and American literature, in 2005.) Although I'd majored in journalism in college and considered myself a writer, the only employment I'd had in that profession was on college newspapers. Important college newspapers, to be sure. (The role played by our team on the Gene Cunningham–edited *South End* in the movement that helped bring Coleman A. Young to office was generally recognized.) But they were college newspapers, nevertheless. And here I was about to step into the shoes of the dean of Detroit labor journalists. Perhaps it was only the hubris of youth that made me even think I would do anything but embarrass both the Party and myself. Yet I was infected enough with the bug to do just the sort of writing the *Daily World* would require that I leaped at the chance. Sometime during this period I had read *Labor Radical,* Len De Caux's account of his tenure as editor of the *CIO News* during that labor federation's left-wing heyday. It became an inspirational text. And while I cannot say whether I read the book before or after I started working at the *Daily World,* it remains the case that this book served both to influence my approach to the task ahead and to prod me to the career that I would pursue for the next two decades.

Presumably, my journalism experience and the fact that I was already being published in local periodicals were factors that went into my being asked to replace Billy at the paper. I wasn't the only possible candidate. There was at least one other professional journalist, with much more experience, in the local Party, but he wasn't publicly known as a Communist, and my guess is that he might not have wanted to trade his career as a working journalist with a greater reputation and—let's hope—income than what was available with the notoriously low-paying life of a Party staffer. The only virtue in the fact that Party staffers earned minimum wage was that in the 1970s it was still possible, if barely, to live on such salaries. Although this was already changing in the late 1970s, the cost of living in Detroit, with its famously low rents for relatively high-quality working-class housing, was not skyrocketing like it was in other cities. And in any case, these were not considerations when I first started at the *Daily World,* because I was living with the girlfriend I had met at the Party school, and she made a comfortable living as a teacher.

Two events frame the first sixteen months of my life as a *Daily World* reporter. The first was the occasion of my first story for the paper, and the second was the Twenty-Second Convention of the Communist Party USA, which took place in Detroit. In between, I was fortunate to spend ten days in Cuba, at the Eleventh World Festival of Youth and Students, and learn a great deal about how both the labor movement and retail politics work in this country.

My education in the history and ways of the labor movement took a big leap forward when I covered a national trade union conference on the shorter workweek, attended by rank and filers and officers from two hundred locals of twenty-five national unions, some eight hundred attendees in all.

"25 Unions Say, 'Cut Workweek,'" was the front-page story in the April 13, 1978, issue of the *Daily World,* over my byline. This was my first story for the paper, and it was the headline story, published on the front page of its tabloid format. It remains a matter of personal pride. The conference was heavily weighted in favor of industrial unions, with leaders of the autoworkers, including UAW president Douglas Fraser, and officers of electrical, steel, furniture workers, meat cutters, and other such unions attending and speaking. This may have been when I first met Fred Gaboury, the glamorous, larger-than-life former Pacific Northwest logger who was one of the leaders of the Party's trade union work. What was glamorous was that he carried his lumberjack culture around as if it were a badge of honor, which it was, and with a great deal of charm. He was a physically imposing figure who looked far better in the role of Pacific Northwest lumber worker and working-class militant than anybody a Hollywood casting agent could produce. Gaboury was a writer and organizer of considerable skill and one of the leaders of the National Center of Trade Union Action and Democracy (TUAD), a Party-sponsored group that held conferences, conducted rank and file networking, and published a newsletter, *Labor Today,* which had started in Detroit in 1962 and which was successor to a long line of left-wing labor newsletters, including *Labor Herald, Labor Unity,* and *The March of Labor;* alongside Trotskyist and other left-wing labor newsletters, including *Union Democracy in Action,* out of Brooklyn, and the very successful Detroit-based *Labor Notes,* which continues to publish. Fred was a gregarious, gruff, larger-than-life figure. He was a very smart man who exuded a kind of gentle toughness. He did not suffer fools lightly and was fond of uttering short and precise statements whose truth came from his deep well of knowledge. Fred was a reflexive working-class internationalist. Talking with him confirmed my growing skepticism about the xenophobic antitrade sentiment that was beginning to grip the industrial working class and its unions. "We're essentially free traders," Gaboury said, in what I presumed to be the Party's take, when I asked him what he thought about the North America Free Trade Agreement (NAFTA) and the racist anti-NAFTA discourse that was rising throughout the industrial states. This struck me as a reasonable pro–working class response, as it took for granted that such trade pacts, which, by expanding the reach of industry, would necessarily expand the numbers of the industrial working class and effectively tie members of that class to each other across borders, just as it did the companies that employed them. It was almost a Luddite position to oppose this process, and it would have been more productive to find ways of bringing the new workers created by these trade agreements and those displaced by the shifting organization of industry into a productive relationship with each other. While it was important to point out the flaws of these agreements, very soon a xenophobic narrative began to supplant, in the broader public discussion, any working class–based assessments of them. Sad to say, a strong residue of the ideology that sees international trade as a job-killing enterprise survives in the trade-union movement, and this is one of the gateways through which right-wing ideology continues to invade the working class. Besides, if one looks closely at what has happened in industry over the last half-century, it becomes apparent that whatever worker displacement came from trade agreements pales compared to the much longer-term problem of displacement through automation. In fact, at the end of the second decade of the twenty-first century, auto-industry employment in the United States was just a few thousand jobs fewer than it was during the industry's late-1970s heyday. Automation was the problem that the shorter workweek conference aimed to address.

Everybody could see the robots coming. As I've already noted, James Boggs wrote about them as early as 1963, and my later perusal of CPUSA literature from the period found that the Party publicly discussed "automation" (the favored term of the period) as far back as the early to mid-1960s. Even the UAW, in its literature, had discussed robots off and on. Not only that, but new forms of the organization of work were also on the horizon, driven especially by management consultants such as W. Edwards Deming, whose advocacy of what came to be known as "just-in-time" production soon took hold. This idea, which started as a way of forestalling overproduction crises, changed the way work was organized throughout the economy. Deming's ideas foreshadowed many aspects of the life of precarity that many, if not most, workers now experience. By championing the shorter workweek (trade-union leaders at the 1978 conference I covered wanted a cut from forty to thirty hours, with no cut in pay), advocates sought to turn the impending technological revolution to the advantage, rather than to the disadvantage, of workers. It was a noble effort, but events would soon overtake the high hopes and idealism of conferences like this one.

These were the waning years of the Carter administration, and therefore the waning years of a certain kind liberal dominance in our politics. The twenty-five union shorter workweek conference took place near the end of the long postwar heyday of organized labor's influence in the country. Although the liberal-labor alliance of the previous three decades still held, there were cracks in its edifice. There was a great deal of labor dissatisfaction with the Carter administration, and that dissatisfaction was chronicled by myself and others, including Tim Wheeler, the *Daily World*'s Washington correspondent. This sentiment would build during Carter's administration and would help shape the presidential election to come.

Meanwhile, my everyday reporting ranged from chronicling strikes by postal, hospital, and sanitation workers to stories tracking the increasing tide of layoffs that were early warning signs that the auto-industry profit boom of the late 1970s was built on sand. I covered solidarity meetings with the beleaguered people of Chile, who were suffering under the Pinochet dictatorship, and anti–South African apartheid solidarity meetings. When the general secretary of the South African Council of Trade Unions, John Gaetsewe, visited Detroit in June 1978, I reported that he was hosted at a public meeting by, among others, Buddy Battle of the UAW. The reason I mention this detail is that Battle, an African American trade unionist who was a leading member of the Walter Reuther–founded Administration Caucus leadership group in the UAW, was also a main leader of the Trade Union Leadership Council (TULC), which was the most important local multiunion, Black-led trade unionists association after the demise of the Left-led National Negro Labor Council (NNLC) of the 1950s. Coleman Young was a NNLC founder and served as its executive director. Both groups are now generally recognized as precursors to the Coalition of Black Trade Unionists. Older comrades had told me that Battle had been a leading figure in the purge of Communists from union offices some twenty-five years earlier, and the rhetoric of anticommunism had always been a weapon in the hands of those that sought to delegitimize the South African liberation movement. But cracks like these in the Cold War edifice were becoming more and more common during these years.

My attendance at the 11th World Festival of Youth and Students, which took place in Havana in the summer of 1978, was another singular event in my life during this period. The festival had become an international institution of the world radical movement. The 1978 festival was the eleventh. World Youth Festivals had begun right after World War II. They were sponsored by the World Federation of Democratic Youth, a Soviet Union–supported nongovernmental organization that brought together Communist youth groups and similar organizations, as well as student and other youth groups. People from the United States had attended each of the previous festivals, and delegates had routinely garnered the attention of the FBI as well as often hostile reactions from the commercial press. Nevertheless, these festivals drew a host of activists and others during their, at that point, thirty years of activity.

There were some 400 of us in the US delegation to the Eleventh World Youth Festival. We were just one of the more than 18,000 people in 145 delegations from countries, colonies, and territories across the planet that attended the ten-day event. Although the number may not seem that large (I've been at conventions with more people), the festival seemed to take over the whole island during its duration. James Steele was, at least in my memory, the leader of the US delegation. (This might be a memory lapse, and perhaps the diverse delegation was also led by a diverse body, but I'm going on recall here.) The breadth of our delegation was impressive, ranging as it did from trade unionists to academics to people that worked for a variety of local governments. It seemed like it represented a large swath of the activist community of the middle and late 1970s, and, as such, gave a picture of how our country's politics were evolving at that time. A lot of the political staffers (people that worked for elected officials as well as in city government) were African American. This was a really new development, as government up to that point had been almost exclusively an all-white affair. The political-staffer delegates from cities like Detroit, Philadelphia, and Los Angeles brought with them a new type of experience. They were activists, but they were also activists in government, which, when you're talking about young people that came up in the movements of the 1960s and early 1970s, conveys an understanding of the relationship between government and activism that saw the two realms as conflicting, but not always antagonistic.

What we saw of Cuba was also enlightening. Of course, the country welcomed the attendees with open arms, and everybody was on their best behavior, but, at least on my part, the fact that as many of our encounters with Cubans were as likely to be casual as they were official helped cement the idea that the popular support for the revolution was genuine. We attended what seemed to be a huge block party that those of us from the US delegation attended, and I recall a conversation with one resident who talked, to my astonishment, about the shows currently on view on Miami television. On another level, I found myself a beneficiary of Cuba's health-care system. I'd long suffered from a cough, somehow related to continuing hay-fever allergies that had plagued me since childhood. I brought that cough with me to Cuba, and it got to the point where someone insisted that I get treated. I remember seeing a nurse (there was probably a medical team on hand to attend to the needs of festival goers), who gave me a dose of medicine with a tongue depressor. My cough cleared up. While I don't want this little adventure to go into the annals of the discourse on the miracles of Cuban medicine (there are far better stories about that aspect of revolutionary Cuba's contribution to the world's welfare than mine), I must say that my only regret is that I never learned the name of the medicine they gave me. Partly this had to do with my own overenthusiastic and perhaps incautious exuberance, such that I took things at face value. But the regret comes from the fact that the cough would return periodically, and all there was for it were the usual over-the-counter remedies and a little patience.

Our encounters with Cuban people and society during the festival were otherwise the product of guided tours, all of which were interesting and instructive. At the same time, the fact that revolutionaries and activists from all over the world attended the festival also left a deep impression. I met, at one of the seemingly interminable outdoor meetings, a trio of soldiers from revolutionary Laos, in their dress uniforms, looking as cool in the heat as I was wishing to be cool. Revolutionaries from South Africa and Angola also left an imprint on my consciousness, as it was still rare to meet such people in the United States, aside from a few refugees and an occasional official who came to town to give speeches.

While I wish I could say I remembered seeing Fidel Castro during the festival, all I can say is that I stood in a crowd of what someone told us was one million people, hearing Fidel's voice, but standing between a quarter- and a half-mile away from the speaker's platform. And as I didn't, and still don't, speak Spanish or understand it well (beyond a phrase or two), what remains in my memory is the crush of the crowd and a voice coming over the loudspeakers. In a word, I was both in and not quite in a rally at which Castro spoke.

A week or two after I got back to Detroit, I was visited by two men who identified themselves as FBI agents. I was not surprised to see them. I stood on the inside of the screen door while they stood outside, on the porch. I politely answered their general questions. From early youth I'd experienced this fishing-style of questioning. At least they didn't tell me I looked just like the guy that had just robbed a bank, as the G-men's almost-twin Detroit police detectives told me when I was twelve years old and standing at the bus stop. In about five minutes, after determining that I wasn't interested in talking to them, the FBI men left. This was my first and only encounter with self-identified members of the political police. I was shaken, but not stirred.

One of the best headlines that ever appeared above a story over my byline was "Ford Spokesmen Hail Death Car." This was a September 15, 1978, article on a grand jury indictment charging the Ford Motor Company with homicide and recklessness, due to fifty-nine deaths linked to one of its cars, the notorious Ford Pinto, whose design flaws were held responsible. Most of the big headlines in the *Daily World* in those days were the work of Seymour Joseph, the managing editor. Joseph was an old-fashioned newspaper man, who loved the quirks and obscurities of the English language enough to let any wayward writer know when they were about to step off the path of the righteous and into the realm of abuse. "That's not English," Seymour would say when you thought your latest malapropism was the work of journalistic genius. It was a mild, but effective, corrective.

What made Seymour particularly valuable was that he was a fast rewriter, was great with catchy headlines, and treated all the copy that came across his desk, whether from professional or novice, as equally subject to his sharp pen. Of course, it's doubtful if he even got to see official Party pronouncements or Gus's speeches when they came downstairs from the Party's offices on the seventh floor of its New York City headquarters. And if that is the case, then it's too bad. All good writers need good editors, and in Seymour we *Daily World* staffers had one of the best. Having had Joseph as an editor of my copy was good preparation for my second stint under a great editor: half a decade as associate editor under editor Dan North at *1199 News,* the monthly magazine of New York City's hospital workers union. (Dan North's father, Joseph North, was an editor of the *Daily Worker,* and his uncle, Alex North, was one of the top Hollywood composers. Dan played a big role in my life, politically, personally, and professionally. Nevertheless, that tale is outside the scope of this essay). Both stints were great training, but Joseph's tutelage really helped me grow as a writer, such that I was well prepared when I went to work at 1199 in 1990. Still, I didn't really know how lucky I was to have that early experience of Seymour editing my copy until I began to write longer articles for all sorts of fancy newspapers and magazines, and eventually to write books, only to discover that for most writers, a good editor is hard to find.

The rest of 1978 through 1979 saw a growing dissatisfaction with the Carter administration, alongside a growing threat from the right. Conservatives put three tax proposals on the Michigan ballot that fall. These included a freeze on state spending, a John Birch Society–sponsored proposition to cut property taxes by 50 percent, and a school-voucher plan. Statewide, the Birch Society–supported Proposition 13, also known as the Tisch amendment, went down to defeat, as did the voucher plan, while voters split on the freeze proposal. Victory in Detroit over all three tax proposals was credited in my reporting to a broad effort, led by the American Federation of State, County and Municipal Employees (AFSCME) and city council president Erma Henderson. Henderson had her own mass organization, Women's Conference of Concerns, that lobbied for progressive legislation, supported Henderson's efforts in that direction, and served overall as a hub for a diverse array of Detroit community and other organizations to discuss public policy issues that were relevant to the community. Women's Conference of Concerns was led and managed by Black women and was a true mass organization. It functioned mainly as a mobilizer and networker of the diverse set of primarily women's organizations, along with churches and other community groups. Its biggest annual event was a special riverboat party, held on a steam vessel that traveled from the docks at the foot of downtown Detroit to Bob-Lo, an amusement park on an island in the middle of the Detroit River, on the Canadian side of the border a few miles south of the city. The AFSCME–Women's Conference of Concerns alliance in that election "led to a widespread grassroots campaign which, while not nearly as well-financed as its opponents, was able to play a decisive role in routing the 'tax revolt,'" I wrote in a postelection article. Whatever some may now think of the way the right wing was able to achieve power in the 1980 election and change the shape of our politics after that point, assessments of right-wing ascendancy have to take into account the fact that people's organizations fought back vigorously, and the victories in those struggles should be credited alongside the losses. Otherwise, one can lose perspective, which can be a debilitating thing in politics.

The rising dissatisfaction with the Carter administration from within the liberal-progressive camp could be seen as early as the run-up to the 1978 elections. In October of that year, I reported on a meeting of representatives of more than one hundred organizations, including the leaders of twenty national unions, that met in Detroit at a UAW-initiated conference demanding that President Carter do more to resist the right-wing push. Rep. Ronald Dellums (D-CA) characterized the meeting as comprised of groups that "have spoken up against racism, against exploitation, against the bloated military budget. We must fight for the people that are not being served by the system — the Blacks, the Hispanics, the elderly, the women." UAW president Douglas Fraser told the meeting that "we are on a collision course with the Democratic Party and they ought to be put on notice about that," and that the Carter administration was pursuing "the politics of personality and not the politics of principle." While there seemed to be little follow-up to this particular meeting, nationally it wasn't the only one of its kind during that period, and the sentiment it expressed was by no means an isolated one. That it happened at all showed that the social turbulence of the time involved not only the grass roots and a broad array of rank-and-file individuals but also the leaders of the country's social movements as well as older, established movement institutions. Nevertheless, the trouble that was to descend in the next decade could already be seen in the results of that year's midterm elections, in which Democrats lost fifteen House seats and two Senate seats.

It seems clear now that many of us that were involved in social struggles during these years did not see ourselves as taking a defensive stance. Although we were aware of the looming right-wing threat and fought against it energetically, the depth, comprehensiveness, and effectiveness of the coming assault on people's rights and living standards was impossible to foresee. The right-wing threat was seen as primarily political, not economic. Carter was handling the economy badly, with inflation and the oil crisis serving as shocks. He made some signature moves as a statesman, but by the end of his presidency even those would be threatened. However, with auto sales booming (1979 would be a record sales year in the industry), it seemed that the UAW leadership, and the region's political leadership more broadly, had no idea of the gravity of the employer offensive that was about to engulf the Midwest, and especially Detroit and its African American community.

But the early signs came soon enough. In late May 1979, Chrysler Corporation announced that it would close its Hamtramck Assembly plant, also known as Dodge Main, throwing three thousand workers out of their jobs. Dodge Main had been a significant institution in the region's automobile culture for nearly seventy years. Hamtramck, the home of the plant, is, like Highland Park, an administratively separate city within the borders of Detroit, and it had been a primarily Polish American city since the World War I. A decade earlier, African American workers had formed the Dodge Revolutionary Union Movement (DRUM) at the plant, marking it in modern times as a locus of working-class radical militancy. DRUM went on to become the core of the League of Revolutionary Black Workers, some of whose members, including DRUM leader General Baker, would become part of the group around the Communist Labor Party. Given this history, it's hard to believe the company could have thought they'd be able to pull this off without a fight.

The fight to save Dodge Main was citywide. The day after the company announced its plans, and as headlines about the proposed closing blazed across the daily newspapers, the front-page story in the *Daily World* talked about Dodge workers springing into action to save the plant. The story related how the local union leadership was already reaching out to a broad range of public figures and politicians—the beginnings of what would become a citywide effort to force Chrysler to change its mind.

At the center of this effort was Lee Cain, a member of the local union executive board who had worked at Dodge Main for thirty-five years and who was a state committee member of the Communist Party of Michigan. Cain was an African American who had fled his native Mississippi in the late 1930s or early 1940s with the Ku Klux Klan nipping at his heels. He was an important figure in the workers' movement in Detroit, although he'd spent almost his entire life as a rank-and-file worker. For decades, he'd written a column for the in-plant union newsletter, and Billy Allan would occasionally quote from the newsletter in the *Daily Worker* and, later, in the *Daily World*. Cain had run for the state legislature in 1952 on the Progressive Party ticket. As a rank-and-file leader of UAW Local 3 for decades, he had served as chief steward and Fair Employment Practices Committee chairman, and, of course, had been a well-known activist in the civil rights and citywide labor movements. He was a strong-bodied, box-jawed man of medium height who wore dark, square-framed glasses and whose accent still carried the sound of his rural Mississippi roots. Until he started to speak, he seemed like a quiet, unimposing man. (In a recent conversation, a friend, Keith Mickens, a retired Chrysler worker and UAW official who had been active with the city's Marxist study groups during the early 1970s and who was a leader of a rank-and-file group called Autoworkers for a Better Contract during those years, remembered that Cain could get the attention of any crowd by the sheer volume of his voice.) He wasn't prone to long speeches, but when he talked, it was as if all the air had been sucked out of the room. He could cut through the most complex political and economic problems, not by reducing their complexity, but by reframing their context. For Cain, the context was always the working class's interest in a given question. Anyone who was skeptical about the Communist Party's claims of being the political party of the working class had only to spend fifteen minutes in Lee's company. Listening to him talk — he often would have the last word on a given topic, even before Tommy Dennis had given his version of the last word — was to hear a real working-class leader and a true partisan of his class. And this was saying something, given that the Party at that time was full of such people.

There soon emerged a citywide rank-and-file autoworkers committee aimed at building public support to save Dodge Main, similar to an earlier committee that spearheaded a successful fight to save another Chrysler assembly plant in the city. Lee Cain was part of this committee, as were several other people I knew, including friends that worked at other Chrysler plants in the city. Included also was Cain's own Communist Party club of auto and other industrial workers, some of whom were union officials. The fight to save Dodge Main, along with the fight to stop the closing of a major city hospital, was among the major working-class struggles in Detroit in the summer of 1979.

It was in the midst of these struggles that the Party held its Twenty-Second National Convention in Detroit. This was planned as a big affair and a contribution to the citywide initiatives then underway. The centerpiece of this effort was a mass rally at Cobo Hall, the city's main convention arena, with Gus Hall and Angela Davis as the main speakers. In the run-up to the convention and rally (dubbed "People before Profits"), Henry Winston came to town and placed before us what seemed like an impossible task. Communist Party clubs from across the city were to go door-to-door in their working-class neighborhoods and sell ten thousand tickets to the rally at a dollar each. It must be remembered that Detroit at that time was, more or less, in between depressions, a condition that would come to characterize the city from that point forward. Unemployment was sky high, and the various attempts at economic comeback that city governments, including the progressive Young administration, had attempted over the years foundered between the rock of good intentions and the hard place of the economic and political realities of the day. Detroit was in the middle of what one might call a strike of Capital against the city, a circumstance that gradually become clearer, as businesses increasingly fled the city in the wake of the auto companies' abrogation of the "Treaty of Detroit," the name given to the labor-relations regime derived from the 1950 industry-wide "pattern bargaining" scheme negotiated between Walter Reuther and the auto barons.[2] This setup had been the terms under which Detroit's workforce had lived for nearly thirty years. It was now about to come apart, and the closing of Dodge Main was just the first sign.

The Party's campaign swept the city that summer, with people brought in from other parts of the country to help. This was how

2 "Pattern bargaining" is the term for the practice by which the contract agreement reached with one company would set the pattern for collective bargaining agreements for the industry as a whole.

I met Carl Bloice, the editor of the Party's West Coast weekly, the *People's World,* for the first time, and where I came to find myself in meetings with Angela and others. While I vaguely remember these meetings and activities, in general, much of that summer is a hectic blur in my memory. We went door-to-door, as Winnie instructed, and the results were almost never anything but gratifying. There are some stories in the *Daily World* about the people we met, and while these might seem almost apocryphal to the casual reader, they are nevertheless true, and they show the deep wellspring of attraction to radical thought within the Detroit population.

As it happened, that we billed the Communist Party rally as also a rally against the closing of Dodge Main helped sell tickets and build momentum. (A kind of humorous aside: All summer long Winston insisted that we bill the event not as an "Angela Davis rally," but as a rally with "Gus Hall and Angela Davis"; we were told that we must include both names in any pitch we made. However, Gus didn't show up. He was reportedly in the hospital with a back injury, a point duly noted, not only in the *Daily World* but also in the coverage the convention and rally got in the local press.) Angela made several appearances in Detroit in advance of the rally, also garnering wide publicity. At the end of it all, I have no idea how many tickets were actually sold. By the end of August, when the convention finally arrived and the rally actually took place, I was exhausted. It didn't help that this was the precise moment when I and the woman I'd been living with for the previous two years broke up, just as that summer's work was coming to fruition, with me moving out of the house we'd shared.

It is unclear whether we made it to ten thousand attendees, though we likely sold that many or more tickets. Estimates from the commercial press gave seven thousand as the crowd's size. The *Daily World* said it was eight thousand. Both figures might be a little short. Whatever the case, crowds packed the hall. People were constantly milling in and out. Besides, we kept loose tabs on whether everybody that came was a ticket holder. Angela gave a rousing speech, but, as I remember, before the crowd heard her, they had to endure George Meyers, the Party's labor secretary (and the pre-Taft–Hartley head of the Maryland CIO), read Gus's speech. That part of the rally sits in my mind somewhere between faux formality and vaudevillian travesty. Nobody was listening. On the other hand, the atmosphere was festive, and whenever other speakers mentioned the idea that got the media's attention, that the workers themselves should take over Dodge Main (and, by implication, the whole of Chrysler) and run it for the benefit of the people, the line would get cheers and applause.

The CPUSA rally in Detroit in late summer of 1979 was easily the biggest public meeting called by the Party in its own name, at least in Detroit, since at least the World War II years. It may have been the largest CP rally in the history of the city. It was certainly one of the biggest rallies the Party had held in the country since the onset of the Cold War three decades earlier. It was an inspiring event. Henry Winston, speaking before the 369 convention delegates and 250 guests, including many from around the world (leaders from Communist parties abroad were granted visas for the first time in decades), submitted that the Party had set the stage for "rapid growth."[3] At that moment, it really did seem possible.

A couple of months before Chrysler announced its plans to close Dodge Main, the national Party reassigned Tommy Dennis from Michigan to New York City, where he took up a number of posts until his death in 1991. He had served as Party leader in Michigan for eighteen years. At his going-away dinner, at which I was honored to speak, city council president Erma Henderson presented Tommy with a "Spirit of Detroit" award. I was sorry to see him go. By the time he left, not only had he been a mentor and teacher but we had even been neighbors for a few months. Tommy had a joyful personality that showed through even when he was engaging in politically complicated topics.

---

3 The convention was held at Detroit's Cobo Hall, then the city's main convention center.

Yet, with all my admiration of and proximity to Tommy, I never got to know him as well as I would have liked. As open hearted as he was, he was also a private person. But he had a decisive impact on my life as a political colleague. Perhaps because when I was in its milieu the Communist Party in Michigan was clearly a working class–led organization with a primarily working-class membership, the local CPers wore the language of theory lightly, while at the same time giving the impression that Marxist-Leninist theory was in their marrow. Tommy's smile, which was witty rather than gregarious, is the biggest thing I remember about him. But nobody I'd ever met in the movement was better than Tommy at discussing politics tactically. Of course, he knew Detroit politics intimately, primarily because he was friends with and had been comrades of many of the important movers and shakers in that world. Tommy was an autoworker and leader in his UAW local in the 1940s who apparently lost his job as a result of the Taft–Hartley law, which drove many Communists out of basic industries and deprived workers of the right to elect leaders of their own choosing to union office. When the government arrested him under the Smith Act, as one of the Michigan Six in 1953, he was the Michigan Party's organization secretary. Their trial, and Tommy's role in the Party, was front-page news throughout the mid-1950s.

That he and Billy Allan won 1,100 votes in their 1974 run for governor and lieutenant governor can be looked at two ways. On the one hand, it is a negligible number of votes. But if we remember that the Cold War was still raging, even though the defeat of US imperialism in Vietnam was at hand, then 1,100 people pulling the lever for an openly Communist gubernatorial ticket of an African American man and his white running mate—well, those thousand people making that statement as Communist voters was no small thing. Add to this the fact that Peggy Goldman, the Party's organizational secretary in the state, won some 7,000 votes in her bid for a seat on the state board of education, and the significance of the Communist vote was a thing worth studying. At least, this was my impression of the matter.

Like Tommy, Peggy Goldman stands out in my memory as someone whose outstanding quality as a Communist had a lot to do with how she conducted her life and her work in the movement without pretense. Peggy was married to an autoworker, and their children, during the period of which I'm writing, were still in elementary school. She and her family lived in a typical one-family home of the type common on Detroit's Northwest side, in what was still at that time a racially integrated neighborhood. Perhaps I'm resorting to clichés, but what I remember about Peggy is similar to what I remember about Tommy: They both seemed to be quite happy people.

One reason I mention this is that joy was not a quality one always found among left-wing people. Joy seemed to be a quality reserved for counterculture people and artists and their friends. Before encountering the Communists, at least the ones in Michigan, I'd known far too many radical political people in both the white New Left and the Black radical and nationalist communities who seemed eager to live up to the caricature of the revolutionary as stern and sour, driven by the work and given up wholly to it. This was not the case with these people. Maybe the horrors of McCarthyism had vanquished the performative revolutionaries, leaving behind a cohort of everyday people with families to raise while carrying on the work. Whatever the case, the Communists threw good parties and picnics. I should know. I attended as many as I could, and event organizers sometimes tagged me to give a formal speech of the type that always accompanied these occasions.

Peggy had grown up in a Communist family, so the Party was a kind of heritage thing for her. It was in the Communist milieu that I learned the degree to which radical politics can run in families. This was one of that milieu's more attractive features, but at the same time, it was a mixed blessing, as the Party's often familial atmosphere made it difficult for newcomers. For a time, I felt this difficulty myself. But what stands out is the degree to which people strove to make me comfortable, and the degree to which the sort of patronizing, tokenizing relationships that have always been a feature of my work in liberal milieus were minimized in this context. The leadership of the Party was mixed, in terms of nationalities, colors, and ethnicities, yet the organization was a majority white one. I don't know the gender balance of the Party during this time, but Peggy's leadership was just as widely respected as Tommy's was, and since she was our chief organizer, that meant her authority was respected as well. It's hard to convey just how novel all this was, even in the late 1970s and early 1980s. At the time that I'm writing about, there were only two female US governors; before that, there'd only been three in the entire history of the country. And, of course, there were no Black governors, though the story was more mixed in both the national and state legislatures. That the second and third highest elective offices in the City of Detroit at that time were both held by women, one Black, one white, both "Old Left" progressives, said more about the uniqueness of the politics of the city than it did about the status of rights in the country when it came to either "race" or gender.

Sam Webb was sent from the New York headquarters to replace Tommy as the local Party leader, and we saw the title change from the old one of district organizer, borrowed, I think, from the trade-union movement, to executive director, a nod to the emergence of the nonprofit civic organization as the mainstay of nonpolitical social-reform organizations. Sam seemed at first like a radically incongruous fit. It wasn't just that he was a tall, lanky white guy with an on again–off again mustache and a Maine accent that one associated with North Atlantic fishermen. Not to stretch comparisons too far, but his vocal tone reminded one of the nicknames given to jazz singer Mel Tormé, the "velvet fog." Michigan has its own particular accent among the sons and daughters of Irish and Polish immigrants, characterized in part by a ringing tonal flatness. Sam wore his rural New England origins on his sleeve, and we weren't all that used to white people with country manners that hadn't come from the same part of the country as had the Black people with their own country manners. He was hard working and eager. It was Sam who insisted that we drive to Flint once a week, rain or shine, hot or cold, to pass out copies of the *Daily World* at the auto plants there. Like many such exercises, it seemed like an isolated, tactically detached gesture. We never knew how many people actually subscribed to the paper because of our efforts. I'm still not sure I understand why the CP leaders were so hesitant to see opportunities for organizational growth in such things as subscriptions to the *Daily World* and vote totals for CP candidates. This seemed at odds with the public pronouncements of Gus Hall and other Party leaders. I've long suspected it was because of McCarthyism's festering wounds. Nevertheless, I enjoyed Sam's company on these excursions. He had a happy and warm disposition that soon put one at ease. Yet, even though he was a quick study, there was an air of dogmatism about him that would more fully come into play later, during the Party crisis that came with the end of the Cold War. The resulting effects were largely negative. However, that all came later. In the long run, Sam came to regret some aspects of his role in the Party's crisis. Nevertheless, that role—he was a firm partisan of the Gus Hall–led faction—led to him becoming Gus's successor as Party leader. But he quit the leadership, and the Party itself, a few years ago, from what I take to be his frustration at the sectarianism that Gus's victory in the crisis legitimized. Eventually, in 2016, after a long silence, Sam drove from his home in the Catskills to Detroit to help my wife Sherri Barnes and me move into the vacation home we'd bought in the city—the city that finally, in the second and third decades of this century, seems to be making something of an economic and cultural comeback. And while he's grown older, as have we all, Sam has lost none of his lankiness, his Maine accent, or his analytical self-awareness, though he has lost the tendency toward political rigidity, much to his own relief and that of his longtime friends.

During the late 1970s and early 1980s, Detroit mayor Coleman Young was facing a host of stressors at this time as well. Young had championed the Carter administration and was critical to the president's election. Yet, just as Carter was neither inclined to fight nor, to some extent, able to withstand the rising tide of the right wing, neither was Young, or Detroit, able to successfully push back against the gathering war against the cities that the right wing and the Republican Party would wage in those years. Nevertheless, the basic progressive character of the Young administration remained intact during the early 1980s. You could see this in all sorts of initiatives, including the way his administration involved ordinary citizens and activists in the city's governance. Another factor was that the Young administration, and city government generally, included in positions of responsibility many people that had first involved themselves in left-wing politics in the 1940s and early 1950s, and this gave the administration its particular flavor. This analysis was not peculiar to me. These were conclusions that the Party had drawn, and my chronicling of the Young administration and the activities around it only reflected the fact that the Party's analysis was based in reality. Yet, in some ways, that analysis was unique within the Left in Detroit at that time. I would sometimes find myself at odds over this with friends, but soon many of them came around to our point of view. One of these was my longtime friend Pat Fry, who had been active in local movement politics since the early days of the anti–Vietnam War movement. She had been an early participant in the Venceremos Brigade (a grassroots group of US citizens in solidarity with Cuba) and therefore was something of a legend among us. Our friendship went back to the middle 1970s, and she had always been a wonderful conversation partner. In any event, she had been an important figure in the Marxist study group circles in Detroit but was becoming increasingly frustrated at the sectarianism that seemed rife among those groups by the early 1980s. At my invitation, she came to a discussion the Party hosted in April 1983 at which the topic was the Young administration. Carl Winter and others, including myself, spoke. Pat says that our presentation convinced her to join the Party. (I had long lost my copy of the report I'd delivered at that event, but I had given one to Pat, who years later let me have a copy, and soon after I moved to New York City she became my successor as the *Daily World* Michigan reporter, a post in which she served with distinction.)

Midway through Reagan's first term, I was growing tired of living in Detroit and wanted to change my circumstances. My work at the *Daily World* had coincided with both the transition to and the first term of the Reagan administration and the first two terms of the Young administration in Detroit, a confluence of circumstances that made for significant social turbulence and a time that witnessed a host of massive and historic struggles. While it would be convenient to conclude this essay by saying that the 1979 Communist Party Convention was the high point of my experience in the CPUSA and as a *Daily World* correspondent, such a conclusion could also be misleading.

About a year after moving to New York City in 1983, my time as a *Daily World* reporter came to an end. I was ready for new challenges and began a decade-long career as a labor organizer and trade-union journalist. I had seen the maturation of the trends that the 1979 CPUSA Detroit convention helped mobilize resistance against. The crisis around the closure of Dodge Main was only a harbinger. The next half-decade would see a speedup in decline of industrial unionism in this country, triggered by the unilateral abrogation of the Treaty of Detroit by the big auto companies. A complete accounting of this process would take another full essay, but suffice it to say that much of our contemporary political landscape can be traced back to events like those in Detroit and Southeast Michigan in the period between the spring of 1979, starting from Chrysler's Dodge Main closure announcement, and the fall of 1984, when Ronald Reagan was elected to a second term, winning nearly 60 percent of the vote in Michigan and all but four of the state's counties. (Wayne County, with its many auto and other manufacturing facilities, was the only one in the southeast of the state that Reagan didn't win.) By that time, Detroit was in the throes of a massive rise in crime and social disorder, a circumstance that can be laid squarely at the feet of the auto companies and the rest of the region's capitalists, who abandoned the city in a rout and with a haste so dramatic that the term "capital strike" seems more than appropriate. In Detroit, the working-class population resisted bravely as the auto barons pressed down hard on the UAW to give up a significant percentage of the hard-earned gains of the previous four decades.

One event of lasting importance that I reported on was the founding convention of the Democratic Socialists of America, which met in Detroit in March 1982. I had long been a reader of DSA founder Michael Harrington's work (his 1973 autobiography, *Fragments of the Century,* was a favorite), and I was interested to see him at work. Left-wing anticommunism had always seemed to me a waste of energy, and this was, of course, the least attractive feature of Harrington and his project. Yet one had to admire the group's attempt at an otherwise nondogmatic approach. In this convention the anticommunism was muted, and this was a new feature for social democrats in this country. As a theoretician, Harrington has always been, to my mind, underrated, and so I found his attempt to carve a kind of radicalism out of the existing trade-union and Democratic Party leadership interesting, despite its limitations. One of those limitations was the organization's approach to the fight against racism. It has seemed typical for social democrats to want to avoid any assertive action in the fight against racism, preferring instead to play a supportive, rather than creative and generative, role in Black people's struggle. Relative to the Communists, the socialists always seemed less militant in such matters. The DSA founding convention reflected this. While it had a number of Black speakers, the overall participation was overwhelmingly white. This was a far cry from my CPUSA experience of national gatherings, and even though, in recent years, my attitude toward DSA has changed as it has taken on the character of a mass socialist organization, it is clear that it still has work to do to overcome this less than attractive inheritance.

The early spring of 1982 was the fiftieth anniversary of the Ford Hunger March, an event that has come to be widely seen as a turning point in the efforts to organize a union at the auto giant. In the midst of that Depression winter of 1932, with about half the Detroit population out of work, a group of reporters had allegedly asked Henry Ford what someone would have to do to get a job in one of his factories. Legend has it that Ford answered, "There are plenty of jobs. Just come on down" to his factory. Whatever the prompt, the Young Communist League and the Unemployed Councils decided to take Ford up on his offer. The legend might just be a dramatic fiction, but it is true that some five thousand unemployed workers gathered in the March winds to march to and demonstrate in front of the big Ford Rouge plant. Police tried to disperse the crowd with tear gas. This proved fruitless. When marchers got to the plant gates, they faced Ford private security chief Harry Bennett, who was rumored to have been an associate of the Purple Gang, the local bootlegging syndicate. Bennett drove through the factory gate, Frank Sykes remembered, "in a new Ford and started shooting with a machine gun." As the smoke cleared, marchers discovered dozens wounded and five young men dead. The "Ford Hunger March," as the event became known, thereby became a milestone in local labor history.

Chris Alston was there along with Sykes. I interviewed both of them for the commemorative booklet that my friend and UAW public relations staffer Reg McGhee and I put together for the banquet celebrating the anniversary, held at the UAW Local 600 union hall. By then, I'd been hearing the stories of the March from Alston for years. He was proud to show anyone he could that photograph of him standing as pall bearer, next to a banner-sized photograph of Lenin, at the funeral of the fallen.

This was the first official commemoration of the Hunger March, and in tribute, a whole swath of the local labor movement and other luminaries turned out. Speakers included George Crockett, newly elected to Congress, and Dave Moore, a Local 600 veteran who had been a leader of the Communists at the Rouge plant in the 1940s and who at this point was one of Rep. Crockett's top staffers.

Most of the time, I kept the various aspects of my life pretty compartmentalized. Rarely did my artistic interests become part of my life in the Party or at the paper. One reason for this was that political communities tend to see and utilize artists largely as entertainers for events. At least this had been my experience, and I didn't want to be known as the Communist "house poet," primarily featured as the warm-up for the main speaker at fundraisers. Nevertheless, those efforts at compartmentalization weren't absolute. In 1982, the paper published two obituary tributes I'd read over the radio, to Thelonious Monk, who died in February, and jazz saxophonist Sonny Stitt, who died early in the summer. The tributes were also published in the journal *Solid Ground*, edited by Kofi Natambu, one of the more significant poets to come out of Detroit. *Solid Ground* was an important literary, cultural, and political journal of the 1980s. Those that want a glimpse into Detroit culture of those years would do well to study this short-lived but groundbreaking journal.

There were a few other instances in which my artistic and political lives came together. One of these was a pamphlet I wrote for the US Peace Council on Black leadership in the US peace movement. My interest in the peace movement has always been a cornerstone of my politics, and the way that the Communist Party wove the fight for peace together with defense of the USSR and socialism as it then existed was an appealing part of CP politics. I was not one of those who had a hagiographic approach to then-existing socialism. Its flaws and weaknesses were readily apparent and always seemed the logical outcome of how those societies came into being. None of this seemed controversial, except to those who traded in the myopia of anticommunism, an ideology that seemed more a defense of imperialism than of democracy. In any case, in the early 1980s, the Cold War threat coming from our own government had reached monstrous proportions, but what was missing in the enormous peace movement that responded to that threat was an accounting of the movement's own history. Especially missing was the story of the role African Americans played in the original movement against atomic warfare. The pamphlet I wrote, "To Save the Soul of America: Black Leadership of the US Peace Movement" (1982), was my small contribution to knowledge in this area. It was also the first stand-alone work published in my name. I decided to open the pamphlet with a poem, whose topic might still resonate today.

For Charlotta Bass[4]

they were burning babies on those lonely hills along the parallel
& it was treason to believe that radioactive immolation was anything but a holy act
in those dark days the jails filled with those that spoke and acted so children could live

as we dig through the rubble of another winter
very few remember the brave woman of color who would be vice president for peace
but the object of her desire, frail and lanky, still stands with banner unfurled

The year 1982 was particularly stressful for the thousands who worked in the auto industry and their communities. It was also stressful for me personally. The struggles of the previous few years had begun to take their personal toll. Living on Party wages was difficult, even in a low-rent town like Detroit, and my occasional freelance work still wasn't enough to keep my little apartment warm. Besides, my freelance opportunities were drying up, just like everything else seemed to be. My mother had died in May of that year, after several years in a mental hospital for what the doctors may have misdiagnosed as schizophrenia and what might truthfully have been depression. I remain grateful for the nice condolence the *Daily World* staff published while I mourned. Despite the fact that I would soon leave Detroit for new opportunities, I remained a committed chronicler of the struggles against the efforts of the auto companies to rescind all that workers had won over a generation. In 1982, while the country was in the midst of a recession, the companies ramped up their insistence on wage and benefit concessions from workers. Union members would reject one concession agreement

4 Geoffrey Jacques, "For Charlotta Bass," in *To Save the Soul of America: Black Leadership of the US Peace Movement* (US Peace Council, 1982).

negotiated by their elected leadership, only to have another brought before them for a vote, this time with marginally fewer concessions, but concessions nevertheless.

The auto barons were brazen. During the early 1980s, General Motors, then in the midst of a $40 billion worldwide "capital investment program," announced that it would close its famed Cadillac Assembly plant on the city's southwest side. It held the city for ransom demanding tax concessions before it would even say publicly that it would keep the factory open. Frank Runnels, the president of UAW Local 22, spoke out consistently against the company's plans. Runnels, who had just a few years earlier hosted the optimistic twenty-five-union conference for a shorter workweek, which I covered as my first front-page *Daily World* story, was now on the defensive, trying to save four thousand jobs. The leadership of the city council at that time included not only Henderson and Maryann Mahaffey but also Kenneth Cockrel Sr., elected in 1978 after campaigning vigorously against tax breaks to corporations. Cockrel was a radical lawyer who had been a leader of the League of Revolutionary Black Workers and a defense attorney in some high-profile movement cases, including that of workplace shooter James Johnson, who, in Cockrel's successful telling, had been driven mad by working conditions in one of the city's Chrysler plants and ended up shooting a foreman and a couple of others. He also defended community activists that had gone on trial for their part in the New Bethel incident of a few years earlier. Cockrel also brought into the council the entire consciousness of late-1960s New Left–Black Power radicalism that was embodied in the League of Revolutionary Black Workers, which, though its own official lifespan was little more than two and one-half years (from its founding in July 1969 to its fading by the beginning of 1972), had left a legacy that is still alive in the city. Indeed, the closing of Dodge Main was also widely seen as a frontal attack on the Black worker militancy that the League represented, given that the movement got its start in a series of 1968 wildcat strikes at that factory. At a city-council meeting where GM executives were presenting their ultimatum, council member Mahaffey tried to negotiate with one particularly belligerent corporate type, who, after she asked him some question about whether the company would take less than a full tax abatement, responded sharply, "We need everything from everybody right now." In the end, the city council gave GM what it wanted. The company still ended up closing the plant.

During this time I would often joke that it seemed that in order to serve in a trusted position in the Young administration you had to have a background in either the Communist Party, the Progressive Party, the Socialist Party, or, in a rare case, the old Proletarian Party; and this seemed true not only of senior elected officials like Henderson but also of people who held positions of responsibility throughout the government.

One of these was Jack White, a former Teamster official who at the time I knew him was a leader of the city's advocacy group for seniors, the Area Agency on Aging. White was fond of telling the story of how he, as a young white worker, was steeped in racist ideology. One day there was a strike at his job. The union organizer, a Communist, insisted that White work with the Black workers on the job, or he couldn't be in the union. Faced with the choice between his union and his racism, White said, he gave up one and embraced the other, joining the Communist Party along the way, and never looked back. Jack was one of those white Communists who also refused white flight and lived in a very nice house in a working class–middle class neighborhood on the city's northwest side, where he would give, each year, a Fourth of July party that was famous throughout the city as a gathering place for everybody who was anybody in the town's civic and trade-union worlds. The highlight of those parties was the moment when Mayor Young would show up to glad-hand and eat barbecue with the rest of us. For years, the Fourth of July parties at the homes of Jack White and his neighbors (they took down the fences between their backyards to make room for the celebration) were the only Independence Day celebration I attended.

Among the peculiarities of the time was the mixed response of Democratic Party liberals to the rise of the right wing and the election of Ronald Reagan to the presidency. In Michigan, this peculiarity came in the 1982 governor's race, in which I came to play a small part. Leading in the Democratic primary was Congressman James Blanchard, a leading member of the cohort of those liberals who were increasingly being labeled "Reagan Democrats"—officials who did not look askance at the Republican president's economic and social retrenchment programs but instead sought to reconcile their (usually rather weak) liberalism with his initiatives. My freelance writing during this time included several articles for the *Detroit Metro Times,* the latest of the city's alternative newspapers. The *Metro Times* (it long ago dropped "Detroit" from its name) still publishes. A front-page article over my byline published during the primary contest profiled Blanchard, who as congressman had voted for the first Reagan budget. While this move that did not endear him to the traditional liberal-labor coalition that had governed Democratic Party politics since New Deal days, it did position him to become the first Democrat to win the governor's office in twenty years. Michigan had always been a conservative state, with liberal pockets like Detroit and Ann Arbor; in 1980, Reagan won the state by six and a half points. My article, which highlighted Blanchard's record as a "Reagan Democrat," caused something of a minor sensation in the governor's race. Blanchard's primary opponents included Zoltan Ferency, a former three-term state Democratic Party chair and Michigan State University law professor who was running as an open socialist. Ferency won third place, which was something of a milestone. During the contest, the Ferency forces used my article on Blanchard as part of their campaign literature. Blanchard campaign officials, some of whom I'd known personally from my Wayne State University student days, red-baited me in an attempt to discredit the article. This did them little good, since I was already publicly known as the *Daily World* correspondent and also had some name recognition through my radio show. Further vindication came when, after the campaign, my article received an honorable mention in the contest for one of the state's most prestigious journalism awards.

The end of 1982 found me in New York City, probably on a combination vacation and work trip. While I was there, news came on Christmas Eve of the death of French poet Louis Aragon. He had been among the founders of the Surrealist movement and was a renowned poet in his home country but barely known in this one. He was also a leader of the Communist Party of France. While I've already pointed out that I usually compartmentalized the artistic and political sides of my life, the news prompted one exception. The poem I wrote in honor of Aragon was the only one I've published in the *Daily World:*

For Louis Aragon[5]

so strange a Christmas without blankets without heavy
 breath
so strange a Christmas without you
without these sounds which pierced the nocturne of long
 knives
which gorged deep into the cowboy's diaphanous wounds

as dawn breaks over your four score shoulders
bringing its boat full of sweet flowers
bringing the gaping mouths of children into view

as dawn brings its announcement of windswept withering
 bodies
its announcement of garlands of births
its chimes of white teeth and saliva full of three colored
 tomorrows
our palms become sweaty leaves in your absence

in this moment so full of wet streets and sirens
— the first of your existence as memory —
your dream infects us
a contagious dream filled with rough hands and roses

5 Geoffrey Jacques, "For Louis Aragon," *Daily World,* December 30, 1982, 21.

Sometime after I'd returned to Detroit, I was at some social event or other and had a conversation with Carl Winter, who was living with his family in Michigan. Carl had been Party leader in the state during the 1940s and 1950s and was one of the original Smith Act defendants. He and Helen (his wife, and one of the Michigan Six) had moved back to the city, presumably to be with family and so that Carl could begin what turned out to be a short-lived retirement. (He would soon return to New York City to take up the post of editor of the *Daily World.*) What I remember about this event — I can't for the life of me remember the occasion — is that Carl upbraided me for my poem. After a kind of grudging compliment (he liked the poem but didn't understand it), he said something to the effect that I had my hands in too many pies, and that I would have to choose. Now, I liked Carl, and often sought his counsel on various matters. Besides, he could be as jovial as he could be stern. Maybe it was just that I liked being around a legend and wanted to soak up whatever he could give me. But on this occasion, I took his caution as a thing to ignore, at least in the way that he intended. Instead, I took the moment to renew my desire to leave Detroit and seek another future. At this point I was approaching thirty and had spent my entire life in Detroit, except for my two terms in Ann Arbor during my first year in college. I rarely traveled, except on trips to the East Coast or elsewhere for the paper (and I've not here chronicled all of those trips, including a very funny moment covering a UAW convention in Dallas with Billy Allan), through which I did manage to see a bit of the country. I'd been to Canada and Cuba but otherwise had never left the country. Sometime in either 1982 or 1983, on a trip to the West Coast, I'd spent some time visiting the *People's World* newspaper in San Francisco and wrote an article or two for it. Carl Bloice asked if I would consider moving to the Bay Area to work for the paper there, and I said I was interested. When word got back to him, Mike Zagarell, editor of the *Daily World,* said he'd prefer that I move to New York. I accepted the offer. The truth is that I was also looking for a way to move to New York; for a couple of years I had been romantically involved with an artist I'd known in Detroit progressive and artistic circles who had moved to the city in the late 1970s. Cheryl Hanna was a graphic designer as well as a gallery artist and, in the summer of 1981, had drawn a cover for *Freedomways*, much to my delight and surprise, as we had lost touch with each other. My own involvement with *Freedomways* had begun around this time, and it was through the journal that I got Cheryl's contact information. So, my reasons for moving to New York were personal as well as professional. I'd also wanted to pursue my career as a poet and thought I needed the creative juices of New York to make that happen.

The eight years I spent in New York before the Party crisis of 1991 were also years of adventure, but are outside the scope of this essay, which is limiting itself to my Detroit years in the movement. These were foundational years for not only my political but also my artistic and cultural outlook. Much of what I'd learned in those years helped me understand politics and culture in ways that shaped my life to come, for both good and ill. In the ensuing years, I would spend over a decade working in the labor movement as an organizer, a journalist, and an editor of an academic journal devoted to labor studies. These jobs put me at the center of some significant historical developments. My *Daily World* experiences, and those that prepared me for my job there as a Communist labor and political reporter, comprised an excellent education. The movement in Detroit was a good school of politics and struggle—as good as any, and perhaps better than most.

2

Flashback to My Long-Ago Communist Youth

Leon Wofsy[1]

Though sorrow lay deep on our souls
Though tears welled in our eyes
We gathered new courage from the grave
Where our brave comrade lies

Recently my wife and I went to the San Francisco Ballet for a performance of the company's *Shostakovich Trilogy.* Gail had thrilled to this program a year ago and made sure I wouldn't miss the repeat. At one point in the marvelous performance, my tears poured out. At intermission, I tried to sing to Gail the words of a song that Shostakovich used as a theme in the Chamber Symphony. I couldn't because sobs choked me again and again. The Chamber Symphony is based on his String Quartet no. 8, dedicated to his friends who died in World War II and to all the lives lost in the Holocaust. The theme (words above) was

1 An earlier version of this essay was published as "Flashback to My Long Ago Communist Youth," *Leon's OpEd,* May 26, 2015, https://leonsoped.blogspot.com/2015/05/flashback-to-my-long-ago-communist-youth.htm, and used with permission of the author for this collection. Leon Wofsy died August 25, 2019 at age 97.

a workers' funeral dirge dating back to revolutionary struggles in czarist Russia.

Can I understand the tears? Can I explain the unquenchable emotion that still beats inside me from a childhood and youth such a long, long time ago? The tears were for remembered heroes and martyrs of the twentieth century. They were for slaughtered millions on millions whose lives were known only to their loved ones and acquaintances. But the images that overwhelmed me were distinct and personal, especially vivid as they marked my memory of childhood.

There was Harry Hersh Simms, his murdered body carried home on the train that paused in Stamford, Connecticut, as my family came to pay respects. A young Communist, he was shot by hired thugs in West Virginia where he had gone to help miners organize. There was DeWitt Parker, family friend, who died in Spain fighting fascism as a volunteer in the Abraham Lincoln Brigade.

When I was eleven, I heard of Angelo Herndon, an African American labor organizer arrested and convicted for insurrection after attempting to organize Black and white industrial workers together in 1932 in Atlanta, Georgia. When I was even younger, there was Maurice Fitch, a Black man beaten most brutally in the Stamford police station where my father and eleven of his comrades were assaulted because they had demonstrated for unemployment insurance.

I note here only a few distant memories of events that moved me deeply when I was very young. But that's just a narrow window on a concern that has deepened so much from the vantage point of my tenth decade: The simplistic and distorted "history" of Communism that prevails today, especially in our country.

The history of the last century, so vital to our understanding of the world of today, is buried under a largely unchallenged, establishment version that equates Communist with Stalinist and Stalin with Hitler. That version allows for nothing other than recounting the devastating crimes associated with Stalin and acolytes who replicated his tyrannical methods.

Socialist movements in general, and the Communist current especially, became very influential in the first half of the twentieth century because they challenged an imperialist system that was generating global catastrophe. There were two unimaginably devastating world wars within little over twenty years and the unparalleled global economic depression of the 1930s. Moreover, Western capitalism sustained colonialism and the lingering legacy of recent slavery.

In 1917, during the chaos of World War I, the brutal and backward regime of czarist Russia was overturned and, after a fierce civil war, the Soviet Union was established. Many people everywhere saw this as the dawning of a new social system, socialism, based on the interests and power of working people, the majority, as opposed to the interests of a small superrich ruling class.

In the aftermath of a devastating war and the successful Soviet revolution, there was an upsurge of Communist, socialist, labor, progressive, and anticolonialist movements all over the world. Their influence grew through their response to the deep depression of the 1930s, the rise of fascism, and the defeat of fascism in World War II. Over the course of decades, several additional revolutions overthrew oppressive capitalist governments, most notably in China, Cuba, Vietnam, and South Africa. Also, much of the traditional system of colonial rule by Europe's major powers collapsed following World War II.

The history of Communist movements in the twentieth century is really two (or more) vastly contrasting stories, each highly relevant to the world at present. From one perspective — the one that pseudohistory wants to erase — Communists showed remarkable courage and foresight in struggles for social justice everywhere. In the United States, where the Communist movement was never large, it played an outsize role in building industrial unions, supporting legislation for unemployment insurance and social security, and combatting lynching and Jim Crow. Internationally, Communists were the first to recognize the nature of fascism and to fight it in the "belly of the beast" in Italy and Germany. No surprise that a first goal of the Nazis, signaled in the famous Reichstag fire frame-up, was extermination of the Communists. Enemy number one in Hitler's *Mein Kampf* was the Soviet Union.

As for the Soviet Union, it was pivotal in turning the tide of World War II against Hitler's armies, at enormous cost in human life. The Soviet Union, along with emerging Communist China, was a major catalyst in the collapse of the colonial system. Its support and the role played by South African Communists were credited by Nelson Mandela as vital to the victory of the African National Congress over apartheid.

As we remember the millions of Jews, homosexuals, trade unionists, and victims of many nationalities who were murdered in the Nazi Holocaust, we should remember that the blood of countless Communist and socialist revolutionaries is spread to the far reaches of the earth.

From another perspective, there is tragic paradox. The greatest and most obvious is that Stalin's rule was responsible for myriads of deaths and that he murdered thousands of Communists in the name of "Communism." The governments formed in Eastern Europe, within the USSR's sphere of influence after World War II, instituted methods of autocratic rule, extensive surveillance, and harsh suppression of opposition.

As in the Soviet Union itself, wherever Communist-led or influenced governments gained power, there were major advances in literacy and in implementation of basic rights to education, health care, and social welfare. Formerly very backward countries saw significant improvement in the place of women in society. But the contradiction between advancing social progress and the suppression of dissent only hardened over time. Antisemitism, rooted deeply in czarist Russia and declared illegal in the early years of the USSR, rose strongly again after World War II.

Another tragic aspect of the paradox between the great good and undeniable evil that marks twentieth-century Communist history is that it took so long for most Communists to recognize the one side of the contradiction. For me, it wasn't until it was exposed by then Soviet premier Nikita Khrushchev in 1956. I explored this to some extent in my 1995 memoir, *Looking for the Future.*

Why come back to this now? Because the contrasting stories remain both unfinished and of no small importance today. It is not simply a matter of doing nostalgic justice to the idealism and hope of earlier socialist movements and to the heroism and self-sacrifice of individual Communists. The imperialist system that plagued the planet and called forth the historic revolutionary challenge of the twentieth century remains a menace today. Capitalism continues to generate inequality, now at an exponential rate. It plows on, fueled by an inherent and insatiable greed that subverts any serious effort to deal with climate change and environmental crises. Profit and markets take precedence over the existential need for cooperation among nations to eliminate cascading wars and the ultimate threat of nuclear disaster.

It is an oppressive system that favors oligarchy over democracy wherever it is dominant. Every movement for social change in our country confronts the obstructive power of huge financial interests. Significant reforms have been and can be won. There isn't a major issue where that's not possible, domestic problems and even foreign policy included. But though reform is not revolution, the struggle is all the more effective to the extent that movements recognize the system they're up against.

We're just coming through an impressive learning experience during the two-term presidency of Barack Obama. One can speculate over what President Obama should or shouldn't have done, but any positive step evokes the fiercest opposition from the Republican Party and its obscene billionaire sponsors, the Koch brothers and the Adelsons (not to ignore some Wall Street–friendly Democrats and all the racists who want to make the White House "white" again). Obama, backed by two strong electoral majorities, came head-on against the system, even though he tried hard to gain its confidence.

The battles to change society for the better continue in various forms in every part of the globe. Given the precarious state of today's world, that's a dire necessity, not simply an expression of idealism and hope. Both the achievements and the failures of revolutionary movements of the last century impact the prospects for social change and survival in this one. Much is still to be answered concerning why the revolutionary challenge to imperialism fell short, why efforts to create socialist societies proved so difficult, why grotesque distortions undermined noble aspirations. The questions are many, the answers still to be developed through new experience and new thinking.

My purpose in this reflection on the past is simply to advocate for an honest and necessary look at a whole history. It's not only with regard to Communism that history has to register dramatically contradictory realities. That's reflected in the evolution of most social movements and certainly in the history of nations, a primary example being our United States. What is harmful and shameful is to bury the history of movements for a better society under an anti-red cloak of denial.

As I write this, Shostakovich's powerful tribute is with me again. And I remember many gentle and idealistic folk, now gone, whose daily lives were selflessly committed to a decent and humane future of full equality. Among them were my parents. I remember with pride.

3

My Experience in Freedom Summer

Marian Gordon[1]

This is very personal, talking about *my* experiences, and generalizing as much as I feel is appropriate from there. Also, I am speaking not only from the perspective of how Communists related to the Civil Rights Movement, but how the Civil Rights Movement affected at least one Communist.

My participation in the movement ranged from local actions in Philadelphia starting in junior high school, to going to Mississippi in the summer of 1965 and participating in local activities in Los Angeles and other places. My comments will reflect on how being part of a large group of people with shared values and beliefs, with an ideology that encompasses those values and beliefs, informs one's actions. I will definitely be commenting on the Communist Party (CP) in particular, but much of this relates to revolutionary and Left organizations in general.

First of all, I want to clarify my status now. I am no longer a "Communist" in the Party, but I am a member of a socialist

1 Unlike other narratives in this collection, the following is based on questions posed to Gordon and other participants in a panel discussion at the conference "Communists in the Civil Rights Movement," hosted by the Tamiment Library, New York City, April 29–30, 2016. Gordon revised her remarks in December 2019. This essay was originally written while the author was a CCDS member. She is presently an active member of Democratic Socialists of America (DSA).

organization, the Committees of Correspondence for Democracy and Socialism (CCDS), and still believe in the same ideals that I did for my thirty years in the CP. My reasons for leaving are not relevant to this particular discussion.

As far as I knew then and lately, the Party totally supported the freedom movement. Sometimes there were internal discussions about various organizations that were part of that movement, but they were over specific issues, not about support or no support.

Did being a Communist limit my participation in the Civil Rights Movement? Not at all; the values and ideals of the Party made it almost automatic that I would participate and gave a sense of support and backup to what I was doing.

Another question: Did coactivists know my Party affiliation? I don't believe that I ever talked about it when I was in the South. In Los Angeles, I probably only mentioned it to a few people—basically those whom I might have been trying to bring closer to the CP (including, by the way, Kendra Alexander, who became a Party leader). I probably more often identified myself as a socialist. But I talked about, and acted on, the components of what being a Communist meant to me: building relationships with people, and constantly educating folks about how the various issues related to each other and how living under capitalism causes so many of the ills of our society.

Did the Party leadership (local or national) react to my activity? I don't think a big deal was made about it, but as implied above, I felt supported in all activities that I participated in.

This perspective relates mostly to how being a part of a "revolutionary" culture informs what we do, or at least what I did. And I say *culture* in this context, not party, because at least in my case, that is where I come from. I am speaking not just as an individual who was a Communist, but also as a member of a Communist family, a Communist community. Culture matters, maybe as much as politics.

I grew up in a neighborhood that changed from predominantly white to predominantly African American. For many years into my adulthood, I referred to my elementary school as racially integrated. In fact, years later when I found an old picture of my sixth grade class, I was surprised to see that the class was overwhelmingly Black. I believe that I had not been aware of that as I was growing up because of my family's teachings that race "does not matter."

In fact, it wasn't until I was in my mid-twenties, on a trip to Cuba with the Venceremos Brigade (a series of US-organized volunteer work projects in Cuba), that I accepted that there really is such a thing as cultural differences between peoples. I grew up saying that "people are all the same." Yes, sometimes even Communists can be simplistic. But the point is, living in a very integrated community is part of the material base on which my values were formed.

As an aside: I saw this fact in another way during the campaign of Dick Gregory and Dr. Benjamin Spock for president and vice president in 1968. I was precinct-walking in an area of Pittsburgh near the steel mills, a very mixed community. The support for this ticket was significantly stronger than in any other area that we worked, and I had no doubt that the increased support was due to decreased racism. Generally, if you live and work with people, you end up relating as human beings.

* * *

My family was working class: My father worked in a factory and my mother was an office worker. They were in a Communist Party club that was working class. This is also part of what forms a person's consciousness.

There was a saying that arose, I think in the early 1970s: "The personal is political, and the political is personal." I think that is true, in a very deep and broad way. To sum up the above: As a child, I developed a perspective, a way of viewing people and the world, which included equality and fairness, and also activism and struggle.

My first memory of an action that I engaged in is from junior high school, when I circulated petitions to integrate the schools in the South. While I was doing this in the lunchroom, the vice principal came up to me and told me to stop. I would not have been doing that if not for being part of a Communist family.

I remember walking a picket line in Philadelphia in support of integrating Woolworth's in the South. I would not have been doing that if it were not for being part of a Communist family.

Another early memory regarding civil rights is of a young Communist woman named Norma, probably in her late teens, newly returned from a Freedom Ride (a massive protest campaign against segregation) in the summer of 1961, who came to speak at my high school

I will be honest here. Not every individual who calls themselves Communist (or socialist) is pure, or applies their so-called principles to their daily lives. I remember a friend of my sister whose Communist parents cut her off when she married an African American man. So let's be real. People, no matter what they say they believe, do not always live up to the ideals that they profess.

All that I've said so far reflects on the values I learned from my Communist parents and older sister. It all took place before I was old enough to be in the Party myself. I joined the Party as a senior in high school, in 1962.

And then off I went to college, with a scholarship — Antioch College, in the very small town of Yellow Springs, Ohio. We had a Party club there — three people, including me. Of course there was not a whole lot to do on a very liberal campus, in a very liberal small town in southern Ohio. But there was a Congress of Racial Equality (CORE) chapter, and we heard about a skating rink in one of the nearby towns (maybe Xenia, maybe Dayton, I don't recall), that did not allow Black folks to skate. So off went us CORE folks, including the commies, to integrate the skating rink. I was kind of fearful — I'd never learned to skate, and was petrified to go out on the ice! But I did it for the cause! And so did everyone else in our group, including the African Americans, and guess what — nothing happened. No muss, no fuss. Back to campus we went, and I never learned to skate. But on the serious side: It did not surprise us that there might be a segregated skating rink in southern Ohio.

And a year or two later, as three friends and I were driving from Antioch to California, in December 1964, we got off the highway to get something to eat in Missouri. It was a few days before Christmas, and as we approached the door I saw some red and white lettering on the door, I thought it said Merry Christmas. But surprise — when we got to the door, oops, it didn't say Merry Christmas, it said "WHITES ONLY." Turn around, get back on the road, and look for another place to eat. Even in the early to mid-1960s, there was blatant, out front racism.

* * *

So I moved to Los Angeles. And why I left Antioch also related to my background and values. Because Antioch was on a beautiful, rural campus, with lots of liberal-progressive people, even lots of radicals. But how much did it relate to the real world? The world where there was poverty, racism, struggle to survive. Not much, and I was frustrated.

So I transferred to California State College and got involved in the CP and civil rights groups in LA. And in early 1965 the voting-rights marches from Selma to Montgomery, Alabama, took place. Los Angeles saw the largest mobilizations in support of civil rights up to that point. And the CP was there. There were two days of demonstrations in front of the Federal Building. I don't clearly remember what happened on the first day, but those of us who were there decided to leave and come back again the next day. What I personally did was to go to Cal State, where we had a rally, and I spoke. It was the first ever time I spoke publicly. I was actually a pretty shy person, and did not think of myself as much of a speaker. Except when angry. And I was angry. So we had our rally, and got *a lot more folks* to come to the Federal Building the next day. That speech was inspired, at least partly, by my upbringing and training in the Party.

And that second day, 101 people were arrested. It was the largest mass arrest ever in Los Angeles, up to that time. And we were in jail for three days. That was an experience, an experience that again showed the differences that being a Communist can make.

The fifty or so women were in a large dormitory-type cell. I can't complain — we were relatively comfortable. But the Communists and other leftists were still angry, and felt the need to keep morale up. We engaged in singing, in meetings, and activities to make us feel our strength. And we were told by the guards to *Shut up!* (A close friend from that era, who was the first to hear this narrative when I tried it out last week, remembered that we got rolls of toilet paper and unrolled them around the big room, under the beds). But there were those who were intimidated and felt we should do just as we were told — be quiet, not cause problems. The Communists did not shut up, but kept on with our protest. After three days, we were bailed out.

Sometime later that year (1965), I decided to go to the South. "Freedom Summer" had taken place the year before, and Communists had participated since the start of the struggle, including the initial Freedom Rides. People from all around the country responded by volunteering to put their bodies on the line. And Communists were among them. As I recall, I didn't think too hard about it. Youth and all that, you know. It's a fact: Young people tend to think they're going to live forever.

My mother, however, was afraid. She asked me, maybe even begged me — I don't remember for sure — not to go. But as a red-diaper baby (a term for those of us whose parents were Communists[2]) it was easy to respond to her. I wrote my mother a letter, in which I talked about all that she had taught me about standing up for others and for one's principles, and that was what I was doing. After that, I had my mother's support.

Along with many other volunteers, I was sent to a training school. And then we all went to different areas. Friends and comrades were sent to Alabama and Mississippi. I was sent to Jackson, Mississippi.

---

2 The term, "red-diaper baby," was attributed to then Alameda County, CA Supervisor Kent D. Pursel, and first appeared in print in the spring of 1965 in California newspaper articles reporting on the Berkeley Free Speech Movement.

I retain vivid images of being there. This was one year after civil rights activists James Chaney, Andrew Goodman, and Michael Schwerner were killed by the Ku Klux Klan. There had been terrible, unspeakable violence against African Americans — shooting up of homes, beatings, and jailings. You all know the story. And during this summer, the violence continued. As volunteers, we participated in extremely moving church meetings and rallies, which is where I gained my immense love for freedom music. I remember picketing Piggly Wiggly stores — at least they were called something like that — I had never heard of the chain before. In Jackson, we were part of a coalition group called the Council of Federated Organizations (COFO), which was organized by CORE, the Student Nonviolent Coordinating Committee (SNCC), and the NAACP. I remember being in the statewide office sometimes, and at other times in a very small community-based office. Voter registration took place. I stayed with an African American family that was very poor. Their contribution, and that of others like them, was enormous, because as most of you know, local people, African American people, who showed any support for the freedom movement were in danger.

Specific experiences that I recall: Although I myself was not directly subjected to violence, one day I was crossing a street with two Black children in tow. A car was coming down the street, and the driver deliberately sped up when he saw us crossing in front of him, and I was disgusted to see that there were children in the car with this white driver. (Some things never fail to shock us.)

But even more shocking was one day when I found out that some of the Northern white volunteers in Jackson, tired of the heat, were sometimes going into a whites-only restaurant because of the air conditioning! I think I can safely say that a Communist would not do such a thing!

Let me be clear about one thing — there have always been, and always will be, huge numbers of people who do good work, who are staunch fighters in the struggle for a better world, who organize, who educate, who mobilize, and who are not Communists. And there are many socialists and Communists who were not born to it. Actually, I have special admiration for those who come to the affiliation on their own, sometimes even breaking from their families to do so.

So what's my point? What does all of this have to do with the CP? Well, I think being in the CP (and since then, CCDS) taught me not only the principles of justice and equality, and not only the idea of building toward a classless society. The Party also taught the importance of being with the people in the trenches, of building a movement, and of organizing. And the difference between being present, and mobilizing, and *organizing*. I learned the importance of having a class approach to movements. I learned the necessity of always fighting to bring the various movements together, and teaching the concept of a united front. And the importance of having a vision, because having a vision can give one the strength to go on.

Sometimes the Party was slow on some issues: There was a definite slowness to see the importance of the women's movement, as the CP had a very limited, archaic approach to that question. There was a very long and painful fight to get the Party to see even the validity, let alone the importance, of the gay rights movement. And in hindsight, I can say that the CP took a very wrong position on the creation of Israel as a Jewish state, and in not seeing that the whole concept of Zionism, of a specifically Jewish state, is a racist idea. And as far as having a vision, I feel that many, if not most, people in the Party had a vision that was so strong that it blinded them to the need for developing and changing ideas as knowledge increased. In other words, we were too often like religious fundamentalists in our beliefs, especially about the Soviet Union. Nevertheless, I have never felt sorry about the years I spent in the CP.

So back to what I said at the start. The topic of the panel discussion at the Tamiment, "Communists in the Civil Rights Movement," is probably more readily interpreted as what affect Communists had on the Civil Rights Movement. But I have to at least comment on what effect the Civil Rights Movement had on the CP, and especially on this Communist. The Civil Rights

Movement started taking off in the early to mid-1960s, and the Party was coming out of McCarthyism, desperately wounded and weak. The Party had pretty much been banished from the labor movement at that time. I believe that the growth of the Civil Rights Movement helped to revitalize the Party, gave it grounds on which to be active, to nourish itself, in addition to contributing to the movement. In the Civil Rights Movement, if many were fearful of the label of Communism, or fearful of associating with Communists, there were others who basically said that the struggle needed whatever allies it could find, and if Communists were fighting for the rights of Black folk, then that would be fine with them. And for me, being part of the Civil Rights Movement was the most moving, extraordinary, fulfilling thing I have done in my life.

Fig. 5. W.E.B. Du Bois Clubs members gather for a march in Harlem, New York City, on March 14, 1965, in solidarity with civil rights marchers in Selma to Montgomery, Alabama, whose actions that month had drawn national attention. (Photo by Ted Reich)

Fig. 6. May Day march in New York City. A sign calling for "Freedom for the Dominican people" refers to the 1965 US military intervention in the Dominican Republic against the rebel forces that supported the democratically elected president Juan Bosch, a progressive leader who was toppled by a military coup in 1963. (Photo by Ted Reich)

Fig. 7. Henry Winston, national chair of the CPUSA, addresses the 1971 May Day rally in New York City's Union Square, one of the first public gatherings of Communists and their allies after the end of McCarthyism. The rally was organized by the United May Day Committee.

Fig. 8. The U.S. Steel Company's South Works plant had been a fixture on the south side of Chicago since the late 1800s, employing upwards of 20,000 workers into the 1970s at eleven blast furnaces, eight electric furnaces, and twelve rolling mills and on more than six hundred acres. The plant began downsizing in the late seventies, and by the end of the decade the workforce had dropped to 10,000. In 1983, the company, soon to be known as USX, announced that it would close South Works, which still employed 3,900 people, and in 1992 the plant, then employing fewer than 700, was finally shuttered. Steel workers from the plant and from surrounding mills, together with the larger South Chicago community, struggled relentlessly to keep the plant open. Pictured here is a demonstration with former workers at the plant, including James Williams, marching in the center in the long black coat. (Photo courtesy of James Williams)

PART II

GROWING UP COMMUNIST DURING THE COLD WAR

4

Born Red: Pages from a Socialist's Life

Jay Schaffner[1]

My parents immigrated to the United States from the Ukraine after World War I. Like many other Jewish families, they left a Europe that was war-torn, fleeing from the plague and antisemitism. At that time, Russia and the Ukraine were in the midst of a civil war, and the Ukraine was not yet a part of what would become the Union of Soviet Socialist Republics (USSR). I don't think my grandparents were supporters of the new government in Russia, nor were they opponents of the world's first socialist state. They just were fleeing a bleak, oppressive environment in which they saw no hope for change.

My mother was born in Vinnytsia, in the western part of the Ukraine near the border with Romania. Growing up, I would hear stories about how, as a young girl traveling with her parents in the mid-1920s, she was hidden from the Romanian Iron Guard storm troopers in a villager's barn, where she heard the soldiers say they "could smell that Jews were present." Traveling from the Ukraine, the family went through Romania, and then up to France, where they embarked on a ship to the United

1 Originally written in 2013 as a presentation to a political science class at Lafayette College, Easton, PA; revised August 2020.

States — a new land where they hoped for economic opportunities, free of antisemitism.

My father was born in Narodychi, a town in the Ukraine that is now part of the Chernobyl Exclusion Zone, established after the 1986 nuclear reactor disaster. His father was the Jewish ritual butcher for the town and ghetto; his mother was the ghetto's midwife. My father was the youngest of thirteen children, only eight of whom survived past infancy. His family was extremely religious, very Orthodox. At the end of World War I, much of Europe was impacted by an influenza epidemic. My grandfather died from the flu. The Ukraine was in the midst of a civil war: Cossacks would regularly sweep through my father's village rounding up Jews, attacking and murdering them. Somewhere around then they decided to emigrate to the United States, but it was no easy matter. There were quotas for the number of immigrants who could enter from eastern and southern Europe, and particularly on Jewish immigrants, just as today there are restrictions on immigrations from developing countries. My father and his next oldest brother traveled with their mother from the Ukraine to Germany, then to England, and then by themselves across the ocean to the United States. They were fourteen- and fifteen-year-old kids, just like today's young refugees from Latin America or from Syria.

Unlike my mother, who was enrolled in public schools, my father went to a Jewish school, the Jewish Peoples' Institute (JPI). My father left school at eighteen, becoming a milkman in 1926. At first, he drove a horse and buggy. My father and friends would tell of his having stared down gun thugs on both the milk route and in union meetings. The corrupt leadership of the Teamsters local utilized mob gun-thugs to quell dissent within the union and "keep the peace" at union meetings.

My father joined the Young Communist League as a teenager, within a year or two of arriving in Chicago, hiding this from his mother. He later recruited his brother and a cousin. When he was eighteen, he was a member of the then underground US Communist Party (CPUSA). During the Depression, my father was active in helping to move families back into apartments after their eviction for not paying rent. He was also part of a brigade that collected groceries from store owners, and milk from other milkmen, to distribute in community kitchens to those who were out of work.

My mother, being younger than my father, was radicalized during high school, as a teenager growing up in the Depression. Due to their economic situation — her father was an unemployed tailor and violinist, her mother an often unemployed restaurant cook — college was not an option. She went to work as a secretary. My mother told the story of her going to the far south side of Chicago in 1937 to join a demonstration of steel workers at Republic Steel who were fighting for the right to be union members. She got lost and was late, and in the meantime the police attacked the demonstration of unarmed union members, their families, and supporters. Ten strikers were killed and hundreds were beaten.

While my father had been a member of the Communist Party since the mid-twenties, I don't think my mother joined the Party until World War II and the fight against Hitler. Both were active in broad campaigns launched by the Party and others to buy Victory Bonds to support the war effort; demonstrations to open a second western front in the fight against Nazi Germany to launch an allied offensive on Germany, as well as Italy; and for desegregation of Chicago's two baseball teams, a campaign led by Paul Robeson, the great African American singer, actor, and social activist.

My parents met in 1950 during a mutual friend's campaign for the Chicago city council on the Progressive Party ticket. They married during the middle of the McCarthy period. It was the second marriage for both. Being immigrants, they were terrified that they would be deported because of their political beliefs. Even though they were naturalized citizens, they still felt vulnerable, since friends who were also naturalized citizens were deported. My mother lost many a job. During this period the Communist Party went underground to avoid persecution and attacks; members who felt susceptible to attack were encouraged to leave the Party. Party offices were closed; leaders became “unavailable,” disappearing from both public and their families’ view, to become “available” once the political situation had improved, to then help “rebuild” the Party and the progressive movement. Laws were passed in Congress making it illegal to be a member of the CP or to hold union office if you were a member, and requiring the labeling of all publications and leaflets from the Party, or organizations designated as “Party front” groups, as coming from a “terrorist organization.”

During this period, my parents left the Communist Party. They were encouraged to do so for their protection as naturalized citizens, because it was felt that they were vulnerable, and for the protection of the Party as well. However, through the rest of the decade the FBI would visit places where my mother worked as a secretary or assistant bookkeeper, and the result was always the same — she would lose her job. The aim was to strike fear in the population over association with the Communist Party, and the effort even targeted those who had been members previously. The objective was to try to get those who had left the Party to testify and “name names” of those they might have associated with in the past. My father, on the other hand, was self-employed as a milkman since the early forties, when he refused to work for a dairy that was a haven for German Nazis.

Moving to Skokie

My parents, like so many others, saved to buy a house in a neighborhood with good schools for their children. We moved to Skokie, one of the suburbs on the north side of Chicago, and a town with a large concentration of thousands of Jewish Holocaust survivors. Imagine my parents’ surprise to learn that the part of Skokie they moved to was the old German part. The first year living there we constantly had “For Sale” signs posted on the lawn. My parents hosted open-housing meetings, to which neighbors would be invited in an effort to get them to commit to “opening up” Skokie to African American families.

Even in their new house, they still got harassed by the FBI. I can remember answering the door and telling my mother there were two men who wanted to talk to her. She picked up a knife from the kitchen counter, went to the door shaking, and said she had nothing to say to the FBI. She just assumed that two men, dressed in suits and hats, knocking on the door in the middle of the afternoon were FBI agents.

Growing up, I discovered that books were kept in two places—there were the bookcases in the living room, with the *World Book Encyclopedia,* and later *Encyclopedia Britannica,* and other books and records. And then there were the books hidden on the top shelves of the clothes closet in the bedroom. That's where the leftist and Marxist books were kept. I remember that some magazines came through the mail, while others were delivered by friends who would visit. These came in brown paper bags and would only be looked at with the drapes drawn, at night. I later learned these were *The Worker,* the Communist Party newspaper, and *Freiheit,* the Jewish Communist newspaper.

I remember family discussions about the nuclear bomb, the Civil Rights Movement, the Kennedy-Nixon election, the capture of Adolf Eichmann (the Nazi leader who was the architect of the Nazi death camps), the kibbutzim in Israel, and the ultra-right John Birch Society. My brother and I went to a progressive Jewish Sunday school, the North Shore School of Jewish Studies. After graduating from eighth grade, I became the librarian at the school, and when I was seventeen was hired to lead the new ninth-grade seminar class.

My brother and I would often join our mom on the weekly Women for Peace picket line in downtown Chicago—at first to demand an end to all nuclear testing, and later to demand withdrawal of US troops from Vietnam.

When I was ten years old and in fourth grade, I wrote a poem about the atom bomb that the school principal had published in national education publications. It also appeared in many different national, local, union, and Jewish periodicals.

The Bomb and Tom

If I had a plane,
I'd fly it down a green lane.
I'd see the presidents,
At their residence.
I'd talk to them about the bomb
That might save the life of Tom.

It would be nice for children
to grow up,
Not BLOW UP!
And try to read books, try!
And sigh when the tests begin,
Just wonder why?
And save little Tom, just save Tom
From the mighty atom bomb

I was greatly affected by the assassination of President Kennedy in 1963, as was the whole country, and wrote another poem, expressing the horror and grief of an eleven-year-old; I sent it to members of the Kennedy family and still have the personal responses I got back from Jackie and Ted Kennedy.

At other times I would help my father on his milk route. I was fourteen in 1966, a freshman in high school, and was reading different leftist publications. I had subscribed to *The Worker* in my own name, over the fear of my parents. I also read the pacifist journal *Liberation; The Nation;* the Trotskyist paper *The Militant;* and the Students for a Democratic Society (SDS) paper, *New Left Notes.* We formed a small student action group in high school, the Liberal Youth of Niles Township (LYNT), and were bold and audacious enough to say that if recruiters from the military services were to continue to come to our suburban high school, we could not prevent student demonstrations and disruptions similar to those taking place on college campuses across the country. I earned my first school suspension for this, along with visits to the school from the FBI, the Chicago "Red

Squad," and Army Intelligence.[2] That year I also attended my first national peace demonstration, going with my mother to Washington, DC.

The next year, now with a driver's permit, I would eagerly wait for Saturday so I could take over my father's milk route, with him in the truck telling me what to do. I would get a few dollars for this and also give my dad a little break. I remember talking with my father one day about social change, and arguing that the key force for change was the student movement, not, as he believed, the working class. I told him that students and the poor, along with the Black liberation movement, were the real radicals. When we got home, I asked him if he wasn't forgetting something. He asked me what I was talking about. I told him that he usually gave me a few dollars after helping him on the route. He responded, not anymore — he did not want to corrupt me by making me part of the working class. Boy, did I learn my lesson. I no longer thought that being part of the working class made one a sellout.

The Sixties: A Time of Hope and Social Unrest

My political view of the world is a product of two generations: my own, the political generation of the 1960s, and that of my immigrant parents, who were radicalized in the 1920s, 1930s, and 1940s.

The sixties were a time of hope. The aspirations and struggles of people shaped the consciousness of society, of our country and of the world. I think the common understanding today is that the Vietnam War was a colossal mistake, although back then many thought the anti–Vietnam War movement was wrong. I believe that nothing could be further from the truth. The growing and massive antiwar movement, from those who marched, to the GIs who refused to continue fighting, to those

2 The Red Squad was a unit within the Chicago Police Department known alternately as the Industrial Unit of the Intelligence Division or the Radical Squad.

who resisted the draft, to people like former secretary of state John Kerry, who threw away his war medals—together with the relentless desire of the Vietnamese people for peace, freedom, and independence—forced an end to the war in Vietnam. The victory of the people in Vietnam inspired people, especially young people, around the world, with the perception that militarism, particularly the US military-industrial complex, was not invincible.

The sixties were a time of social unrest, a time that made our country what it is today:

This was a period when the African American people of the United States were able to win a nearly century-long fight against segregation and Jim Crow inequality.

It was a period when teenagers were faced with the draft and the prospect of dying in a war half-way around the world that increasing numbers felt was wrong. The antidraft and antiwar movement was in its ascendancy.

Coming of age in the early sixties, young people really had to wonder if the end of the world was around the corner, if the world would be destroyed by a nuclear war. Antinuclear organizations coalesced with the antiwar movement.

When you read the papers, you would learn about newly independent countries in Africa and Asia. Starting in the mid-fifties, one third of the world would become independent of colonial rule.

Growing up at this time, one would wonder about what was happening in that part of the world which had an economic, political, and social system entirely different from that of our country. No matter what the Cold War threw against the Soviet Union, it was still there, and it was the country that put the first human being into space orbit.

This was a time before the Internet, before social media, a time when the only national television stations were those of the CBS, NBC, and ABC networks, perhaps a local television station in some parts of the country, and the new thing called public television. News broadcasts were in the evening and were a big thing. Those newscasts covered events such as the Birmingham, Alabama, police using water cannons and dogs against young people demonstrating for the right to vote; open housing marches led by Dr. Martin Luther King Jr. in Chicago; demonstrations against the war in Vietnam; horrific photos of US planes dropping napalm bombs on Vietnamese civilians; student demonstrations against curfews; demonstrations against the House Un-American Activities Committee; space flights of our country and of the Soviet Union; and pictures of the massive May Day and November 7 parades in the Soviet Union (November 7 marks the anniversary of the 1917 Bolshevik Revolution).

My generation was shaped by these events: African Americans being brutalized and murdered by white sheriffs and the Ku Klux Klan; daily images of caskets coming back from Vietnam; the assassinations of President Kennedy, Martin Luther King Jr., and Robert Kennedy; the vicious attacks on the Black freedom movement and, in Chicago, the brutal police murder of Black Panther leaders Fred Hampton and Mark Clark; the attack and murder of peaceful student demonstrators at Kent State and Jackson State; and then on 9/11 — September 11, 1973 — the CIA's toppling of the democratically elected government of Salvador Allende in Chile. These events helped shape the consciousness of the generation of the sixties and seventies.

Student Years and the W.E.B. Du Bois Clubs

I was active in the student movement both at my school and in the larger Chicago-area high school student antiwar movement, which became part of the Student Mobilization Committee to End the War in Vietnam. I was also involved in the local reform Democratic club, Politics for Peace, and the Liberal Democrats, which ran delegates pledged to Eugene McCarthy in the 1968 US presidential campaign. From my own activities, and from the publications that I read, I realized that no matter how strong your local student or peace group was, it was limited unless it was part of a larger group. That is why I then joined High School

SDS and started going to the office and activities of the Chicago area antiwar coalition, the Chicago Peace Council.

At a demonstration against Dow Chemical, maker of napalm, that I went to with my mother on the far southwest side of Chicago, someone gave or sold me a publication called *Insurgent*. I really liked it; the articles were easy to read. I learned about the United Farm Workers in California, the peace delegations that went to North Vietnam, and the GIs imprisoned for refusing service in Vietnam, the Fort Hood Three. *Insurgent* was put out by an organization called the W.E.B. Du Bois Clubs of America, named after the pioneer civil rights figure and author. This was an organization that was both Black and white and was much different from SDS, which was predominantly white. This really impressed me. Soon I met and talked with a local leader and signed up. I was now a member of a socialist youth organization. However, I would soon learn that the Du Bois Club in Chicago was not a very strong organization.

I felt that I needed help and advice from others about how to build the most effective student movement in my high school and in other Chicago area high schools. I talked with people in the local Politics for Peace and the Chicago Peace Council. These were people who seemed to have their heads screwed on right. They were focused on building the most massive, diverse, unified movement to end the war in Vietnam. Some of these people were friends of my parents. Wow! What a surprise to find that many of the people who I worked with and was most impressed by, the ones who made the most sense at coalition meetings, were in the Communist Party.

The party that I was attracted to — the Communist Party — worked first and foremost to build the broadest possible front for struggle against the war; against racism; for equality for African Americans, Chicanos, Puerto Ricans, Native Americans, and Asian Americans; and for increased political independence. If anything, it downplayed building its own organization. What was important was the mass movement — enlarging it, building it, and deepening its political perspective.

That summer of 1967, I worked in a local office of Vietnam Summer, a nationwide effort to reach the grassroots of the country and talk about the war. Many days I would go door-to-door in nearby Evanston, after working in a coffee shop in the morning. Later that summer I planned to go to the national Du Bois Clubs convention in New York, after the New Politics convention, which might nominate Martin Luther King Jr. and Benjamin Spock (the famous pediatrician) for US president and vice president (which did not happen).

The New Politics convention fell apart because of both the presence of police agents in the ranks and the inability of many of the white participants to respond to demands made by the Black caucus. I would not, as it turned out, go to the Du Bois Clubs convention because I came down with mononucleosis and would be out of school for weeks.

Later, after recovering, I was asked to be a part of the local Du Bois Clubs executive committee. The efforts of the Du Bois Clubs at this point were focused on a campaign to prevent being cited by the attorney general as a subversive organization under the McCarran Act, which created the Subversive Activities Control Board (SACB). Organizations so cited would have to identify themselves in their publications, or when their spokesperson spoke in public, as subversive. We organized to talk with other groups and organizations, to get them to go on record against such an SACB ruling, and circulated petitions. On my sixteenth birthday, in 1968, I spoke at a press conference representing the Chicago Area Du Bois Clubs, along with a Chicago alderman, clergy, and antiwar activists, against the SACB.

One of our other campaigns was to mobilize support for Muhammad Ali, who was being stripped of his world boxing title and threatened with prison for refusing military induction. If not for Du Bois Club members, enamored with Ali, raising this issue in the Chicago Peace Council, I don't think this coalition and its member organizations would have seen the importance of both supporting him and using the matter to link the issues of the war and racism.

During the rest of that year, I struggled to keep up with classes in high school, continued my involvement in the peace movement, participated in demonstrations and memorials when Dr. King was murdered, and helped plan for the massive peace demonstration at the Democratic Party convention. We brought car loads of students from our suburban school down to Lincoln Park and Grant Park.

That year three teachers were fired for "deviating from the approved curriculum" and for being the faculty advisers to our student group, now embracing all three Niles high schools, called the Niles Township Student Coalition (NTSC). Unlike many of my generation, I was convinced that we needed the broadest, most encompassing name, to help mobilize the largest numbers of our fellow students, not the most left-sounding name. We consciously decided against calling ourselves SDS, even though we participated in the citywide high school SDS. We organized among students, parents, and in the community, and were able to save the jobs of two of the teachers. We also opened up an alternative coffee shop, the Poison Cookie Hole, for students from north side and suburban high schools. I think it lasted about six months — only so much you can do with no licenses to serve anything and with no ability to bring in live bands.

Joining the Communist Party

That summer, at age sixteen, I joined the Communist Party. I also attended my first socialist school, the national school of the Du Bois Clubs at the World Fellowship camp, near Conway, New Hampshire, and was an observer at my first Communist Party national convention.

While I was in high school, the FBI, the Chicago police Red Squad, and various military intelligence agencies spied on me. They visited my high school, illegally obtained both my academic and disciplinary records, visited neighbors, and even took to calling the parents of girls I would ask out or talk with on the phone (this is way before Twitter, Facebook, and text messages). To continue to ask girls out would put them in the position of having FBI files. I could stop my political activities, or I could continue my activities and talk with girls in school and at social events but not on the phone. I chose the latter.

My junior year would be my last in high school. Because I had enough credits to graduate academically but insufficient physical education credits, the school board and my parents worked out an agreement that I would graduate with a full degree, leaving school in November 1969. However, for one month I would add additional phys ed classes each day (and not cut any of them) and an independent seminar, and I would attend the first-period meetings of student government. (I was in pretty good shape back then.)

Before leaving school, I worked with our student government to secure student-senate support for a food drive for food kitchens for Puerto Ricans and African Americans in Chicago. The kitchens were run by the Young Lords (a radical Puerto Rican organization) and the Black Panther Party. We collected food for a number of weeks and then delivered carloads of boxes to the Young Lords and the Panthers. I, along with two other students, accompanied by my parents, dropped boxes off at the West Side office of the Black Panther Party, and to our surprise, the leader of the Panthers, Fred Hampton, came down to talk with us and invite us upstairs. This was less than two months before he, along with Mark Clark, would be murdered by the Chicago police, in their apartment, while asleep.

To collect food in the suburbs of Chicago for African American and Puerto Rican communities — to convince the student senate to conduct this schoolwide food drive — required lots of persuasion and argument. Looking back, I don't think this would have happened if I had not been in the midst of it, and a member of the Du Bois Clubs and the Communist Party. Both organizations, composed of Black and white members, instilled in their white membership the need to constantly fight for equality and against racism, in their communities where their individual members lived and in the organizations to which they belonged. I lived in Skokie, and my organization was my high school, and convincing my fellow students of the need to take up the struggle for equality and against racism concretely by conducting the food drive was my way of bringing the issues of equality and the fight against racism to my fellow students. The fight for equality, the fight against racism, was something instilled in my consciousness by my parents and then by my membership in the Du Bois Clubs and the Communist Party.

We organized a massive high school presence for the Moratorium Against the War at Northwestern University, and by agreement of all concerned, I left high school in November, after completion of the independent study. (The independent study was a review of ten books on African American history and thought, starting with Du Bois's *The Souls of Black Folk.*) Throughout high school I was elected to student government by my homeroom and there helped change some school policies (getting rid of the school dress code, for example) and succeeded in getting the student government to oppose the war in Vietnam. That year we organized an alternative prom in the nearby forest preserve, attracting hundreds of kids from all three affiliated high schools, with local bands performing. It went off without a hitch, even with the presence of pot and beer. With that many in attendance, the cops turned a blind eye.

Organizing the YWLL

Upon leaving high school, I went to work for the Chicago Area Temporary Organizing Committee for a Marxist-Leninist Youth Organization (ChiTOC). I earned a grand total of twenty dollars per week (the same wage as those working for the United Farmworkers). The Du Bois Clubs were in decline, and there were also a lot of people around the country, mainly African American youth, who wanted to work with the socialist youth of the Party, but on equal footing from the ground up. A new youth organization was what was called for. So, I helped organize the founding convention of what would become the Young Workers Liberation League (YWLL). This new organization solved that problem; it would have open, public ties with the Communist

Party USA (CPUSA) and would declare its allegiance to the "science of Marxism-Leninism." This was not unique to the youth of the CPUSA: Young people all over the world were inspired by Cuba, Vietnam, Che, Ho Chi Minh, and the staying power of the socialist countries, both those that were Moscow-oriented and those supporting Mao and China.

Years later I would come to the conclusion that the Party really was trying to better control and direct a youth organization, instead of supporting an independent socialist or socialist-minded youth organization. This was also happening in other countries around the world. The Connolly Youth Union was formed in Ireland; KNE, or the Communist Youth League, was formed in Greece; organizations similar to the YWLL were formed in Cyprus, West Germany, and throughout the Caribbean. While Lenin had written that each generation needed to come to socialism in its own way, through its own experiences and understanding and through their own organizations, in fact, Communist parties throughout the world, including the CPUSA, were fearful of the independence of youth organizations and of the massive youth revolts that shook the world in 1968, especially in France, Germany, Italy, and Mexico — the last ending in the student massacre prior to the start of the Olympics — and indeed on many campuses and communities in the United States. This was a time when young people were in motion — in different organizations, on campuses and in communities across the country. While many of these sixties organizations would fade, the next year a new youth upsurge took place, this time within the ranks of the Democratic Party and around the antiwar campaign of George McGovern, first for the nomination and then in the 1972 general presidential election. A decade later, a new youth involvement appeared in the presidential campaigns of Jesse Jackson. Given the limited resources and membership, would it not have been better to immerse Party youth in these movements, rather than isolate ourselves in our "own" Marxist-Leninist youth organization?

Young people then were drawing the conclusion that a world based on private hoarding, racism, sexism, class exploitation, and imperialism was not working and that there needed to be an alternative. I think that many young people got caught up in the "self-expression" of their politics and lost sight of the reality that politics is based on moving real masses to change society and that change happens when those masses are ready and prepared to move. Many lost sight of the fact that there would be no revolutionary change until those masses felt that no other change was possible. Because "revolution was in the air," or so many thought, we didn't see the need to constantly fight for democracy, for democratic rights — to fight against every effort to limit democracy and continuously expand democracy and democratic rights. We considered this to be "bourgeois democracy," and the movement we were part of was revolutionary. We failed to see that there can be no change whatsoever without democracy and that a future socialist society would, in fact, have to be democratic as well as socialist.

Today young people and others are drawing the same conclusion and looking for an alternative. Today there is again a new interest in socialism; it is no longer a dirty word. In the past two years, the most looked-up word in the Merriam-Webster online dictionary is *socialism*.

It was easy to feel that you were part of something big. The new organization, the YWLL, was at the time of its founding much larger than the old Du Bois Clubs. In the Chicago area, we were really much larger. We had seven chapters, all engaged in different types of activities and work. Soon after our founding came the massive response to the invasion of Cambodia and the bombing of Laos, and then the murders of the protestors at Kent State and Jackson State. We helped mobilize as many young people as possible to participate in the demonstrations.

Going to Vietnam

In June of 1970, the national office of the YWLL asked me to be part of a three-member delegation to Vietnam — North Vietnam — invited by the Ho Chi Minh Working Youth Union. At eighteen, I was the youngest US citizen to visit North Vietnam.

Our two-week trip was extended because of the renewed bombing by our government, and the Vietnamese did not feel that it would be safe for members of the CPUSA to travel back from Vietnam through China, given the split in the world Communist movement between China and the Soviet Union. (A split we would later learn, based on the Pentagon Papers, that was used to time escalations of the war.) So, on the day I would have graduated from high school I was in the northernmost provinces of Vietnam. Ours was the first US delegation to visit that part of Vietnam since the end of World War II. I will always remember that trip to Vietnam: meeting with leaders of the Vietnamese government; learning about the wars of liberation, first against the French, now against my own government; meeting with Vietnamese youth, and leaders of trade unions, women's organizations, and the All-People's Front; witnessing the destruction that the war had brought down on their country by my country; appreciating the greetings that people everywhere gave us when they learned we were from the United States; and seeing the resourcefulness of the people. When I returned, I spoke all over — at protest meetings, teach-ins, in colleges and high schools — and I gave radio and television interviews.

Free Angela Movement

For two years, I continued to work full time for the YWLL, participating in coalitions against the war; in support of the people of Chile, whose government was overthrown by the CIA; for the freedom of Angela Davis, a wrongly arrested young African American comrade; for the youth vote (until 1972, you had to be twenty-one to vote); and against South African apartheid and Portuguese colonialism.

Helping to build the Chicago-area movement for the freedom of Angela Davis was an incredible experience. We took the fight to all different organizations. Initially our demand was for bail, for an end to Angela's being held in solitary confinement, and for her freedom and that of all political prisoners. We also linked her struggle to that of the Puerto Ricans being held for fighting for independence against US colonialism and to that of Native Americans. While we demanded her freedom and release, the initial demand was for bail and for justice, a demand that people who were not yet convinced of her innocence could join and participate in. In this way, we were building the broadest front of struggle possible, at the level that people were initially ready to support. How to talk to others, how to convince them, and how to work with non-Communists and those who were not even radicals, were the skills that were taught by the local leaders of the Free Angela movement, Sylvia Woods and Ben Green, an African American Communist and a Jewish Communist, both of whom were friends of my parents. The building of the massive Chicago-area movement for the freedom of Angela Davis was also aided and nurtured by local Communist Party leaders Claude Lightfoot and Ishmael Flory.

The fight for the freedom of Angela transformed both the YWLL and the Communist Party. Across the country large numbers of young African Americans joined. Many joined the already existing collectives and study groups. They were radical, and they wanted to be a part of Angela's organization, the Communist Party, and its youth organization, the YWLL.

Communist Party Ticket on the Ballot

Instead of being a part of the massive movement to change the Democratic Party and the way elections take place, in 1972, we were involved in the first campaign of Communist Party chairman Gus Hall, running for US president, with Jarvis Tyner, chairman of the YWLL, as his running mate. We argued that placing the Communist Party on the ballot was the most important election issue of the time. This was a fight for real democracy, against undemocratic election laws that keep third parties off the ballot, and against the undemocratic anticommunist laws of the country. In concert with the campaign to free Angela Davis, which was later won due to the massive support of many, many organizations and people, the YWLL jumped into the campaign to put the CP ticket on the ballot. We collected thousands and thousands of signatures in support of the right of the Communist Party to be on the ballot.

During this period, I went to work in a small machine shop. After a couple of months, I was elected to be part of the local union's political action committee. I was able to get many in this shop of Black and Polish workers to wear Angela Davis buttons. I also was active in the young voters' movement, which was spurred by the reform movement growing out of the McGovern campaign. The Party and YWLL were for the youth vote, but since the Party had relatively few younger members, the numbers involved in the young voters' movement was limited. I was elected one of the three Illinois cochairs of the young voters' campaign by a conference of hundreds of delegates from across the state.

Running for Office

I left the machine shop at the beginning of 1974 when I ran for the University of Illinois Board of Trustees on the Communist Party ticket. (In Illinois, in order for a political party to be on the ballot, it would have to run candidates for all statewide offices, including those of university trustee, who were elected, not appointed.) We ran on a platform calling for open admissions and a rollback in tuition. While the ticket of Gus Hall and Jarvis Tyner received just over five thousand votes in Illinois, the three Communist candidates for university trustee got many times more. One of our candidates polled nearly thirty-five thousand votes; I received over twenty thousand. This was the first statewide election in which eighteen-year-olds had the vote. During the campaign I spoke at nearly every college campus downstate and in the Chicago area, and the three of us were "recommended" by a number of college daily newspapers. On some campuses the recommendation was for the "Youth Rights Candidates" — one of the three Communist candidates, a candidate from Barry Commoner's Citizens Party, and one of the official Democratic Party candidates — a real coalition effort.

Was it important to get the Party on the ballot? Yes! We helped to break down numerous antidemocratic laws, remnants of the McCarthy period, and especially antidemocratic election laws aimed at keeping third parties off the ballot. We helped counter anticommunism in the country. Coming out of the McCarthy period, there were still anticommunist laws on the books, laws that prevented the Party from running for office, from being on the ballot. But I think on the part of the national leadership of the Party, the ballot campaign also reflected a combination of leftism and syndicalism (an avoidance of participation in the electoral process as it really existed). It was a go-it-aloneism that would only manifest itself more sharply in later years. And it pitted the Party as an organization against its own members and the mass work they were doing as Communists in non-Communist organizations and coalitions. The task of collecting thousands of signatures every two years to put the Communist slate on the ballot required the full mobilization of the entire Party membership, and it exhausted the Party, preventing its members from doing any other political work. It also separated and isolated the Party and Party members from what was taking place within the Democratic Party—the increase in the number of elected African Americans to public office, from town and city councils, to mayoralties, to state legislatures and the US Congress; and the increased influence of the peace movement, which in 1972 was able to capture the Democratic Party nomination. If the Left, including Communists, had stayed with this, would the course of events have been different after 1972? Probably not. The politics of the country were too unfavorable and the alignment of forces too weak to prevent the reelection of Richard Nixon. But a peace movement composed of both electoral and nonelectoral (street-action based), with full Left and Communist involvement, would have been a much stronger peace movement coming out of the elections in 1972.

Moving to New York

At the Third National Convention of the YWLL, in December 1974, I was elected to the national leadership, as national education secretary. I moved to New York City in January 1975 and have lived here ever since.

From 1969 until 1975, when I left Chicago, I was a member of both the Illinois District Committee of the CPUSA and of the district board. I was elected as a delegate to the national convention from Illinois in 1972, 1975, and even after I left the state, I was elected from there as a national delegate in 1979, 1983, and 1987. In 1991 I was elected as a delegate to the national convention from New York.

From 1975 until 1981, I was part of the national leadership of the YWLL, first as national education secretary, then as national organization secretary, and lastly as chairman of the New York Section of the YWLL. I was also a member of the National Committee or Central Committee of the CPUSA from 1975 until 1991, when I left the Party.

As part of the national YWLL leadership I traveled to thirty out of the fifty states in the country. This was for work on campaigns for youth employment, for a youth salute to Paul Robeson, for the 11th World Festival of Youth and Students, and for youth rights. It involved public speaking, being on radio programs, and working in the election campaigns of the Communist Party. In 1975 I helped organize more than twenty-five hundred people to travel to Chicago for the Bicentennial Celebration for Jobs, Freedom and Peace, at which time the candidates of the CP, Gus Hall and Jarvis Tyner, were nominated. Earlier that year I testified before Congress on behalf of the YWLL in support of the Hawkins Jobs Bill (a national jobs creation bill introduced repeatedly in Congress by Rep. Augustus Hawkins of Los Angeles) and to promote special steps to create youth jobs. In 1978 I helped organize for a national Youth March for Jobs in Washington, DC, a march whose demands were endorsed by over one hundred youth organizations from around the country and whose leadership met with staff of Vice President Walter Mondale.

That same year I was part of the leadership of the US Preparatory Committee for the 11th World Festival of Youth and Students that was held in Havana, Cuba. In preparation for the festival, I headed the first organizing delegation to Cuba, and I would later be a liaison with Cuban and international youth organizations. More than four hundred US youth and students attended that 1978 festival—the largest, broadest, and most diverse US delegation ever to attend a world youth festival. It included young elected officials, young trade-union officers, student government presidents, and representatives of national church and civil rights organizations.

In 1978 I met Judith Eisenscher; we started dating and got married the next year. For forty years, Judith has been my closest friend, confidant, lover, and comrade. And she is the mother of our two children. At the time of our marriage, Judith was the women's issues reporter for the *Daily World,* a copy editor, and a member of its editorial board. Judith left full-time work at the *Daily World* when our youngest started kindergarten; we had reached the point in our lives where we could no longer both work full-time on Party wages. Judith then went to work as a public-school librarian. I could not have continued my activities without the support of my wife and the sacrifices that she made in raising our kids, often when I was absent, traveling in this country or abroad.

From the sixties to the seventies, I helped organize mass demonstrations against the war, racism, political repression, and apartheid in South Africa. I also participated in Congressional lobbying against the war, against US involvement in Chile and US support for the apartheid government, for youth jobs and free universal public education, and against attempts to reinstitute the draft for military service. Some of these demonstrations were very peaceful; some were attacked by the police. Like many others, I was arrested a number of times.

A Peace Movement versus an Anti-Imperialist Movement

With the end of the war in Vietnam in 1975 and the growing antiapartheid movement and movements for solidarity with Chile and Cuba, there was real pressure to turn what was the antiwar movement into an anti-imperialist movement. The Left in the peace movement wanted this, and the Party also moved in this direction. I went along and advocated for it. There were some in the Party who had misgivings. Looking back, I think they were right. What was needed was the continuation of the largest, most massive and diverse peace movement that was possible, a movement that would have been able to mobilize against Reagan's Star Wars and the increase in nuclear weapons, a movement that would have been able to organize against the ever-increasing military budget, which today is the largest ever — a $717 billion military defense budget, at a time when the government is slashing every form of social welfare.

When we built the Chile solidarity movement in Chicago, we did so initially both in solidarity and against our government's complicity in the fascist Pinochet military junta. The US government was instrumental in overthrowing the democratically elected government of Salvador Allende, a socialist, as became clear years later during the Senate's Church Committee hearings. The Chicago peace and solidarity movement later combined our support for the people of Chile with support for the people of Cuba, who suffered from the US blockade and continue to suffer from the efforts of our government to economically strangle their country.

A broad massive peace movement is not the same as an anti-imperialist movement or a solidarity movement. An anti-imperialist movement requires a more advanced and higher level of political consciousness than a peace movement. Both are necessary and needed, but the lack of a broad peace movement limits and impacts all struggles for progress and democracy. Some of us lost sight of what my mother's generation knew only too well: The struggle for peace and against nuclear weapons is the overriding struggle of our time.

In 1976, I represented the YWLL at the First Congress of the Young Communist League of Greece, held just months after the fascist junta there fell. Imagine my surprise when landing in Athens to be greeted by machine-gun toting troops in the airport! I later learned that these same troops, like the police and judges in most Greek cities, were the very same that had been in place under the fascist dictatorship.

Voices of the Future and Anniversary Tours

Beginning in 1981, I headed Voices of the Future, a program started by the YWLL to organize travel to different socialist countries and arrange for cultural exchange. Voices sent a number of youth tourist groups to the Soviet Union, Cuba, the German Democratic Republic (GDR), and Czechoslovakia. Voices helped pioneer what is known today as people-to-people travel: It was based around encounters with young people and visits to schools, work sites, and cultural institutions, along with visits to traditional tourist sites. (Today, "people-to-people" travel means staying in people's homes and working alongside or going to school with those whose country you are visiting.) Voices also organized a US speaking tour for the leadership of the African National Congress, years before the fall of apartheid in South Africa.

These trips were organized through Anniversary Tours, a travel bureau started in 1972 that had extensive experience in travel to the Soviet Union. Anniversary also had an unofficial—not public—relationship with the Party. In 1983, I was asked by the board of directors at Anniversary to be its general manager, and a year later its president. Voices at that time became the youth tourism division of Anniversary. Anniversary Tours became the third largest US travel agency sending tourists to the Soviet Union. By the late eighties, it was sending upwards of four to five thousand tourists each year to the various socialist countries. Working with Promoting Enduring Peace and the Soviet Peace Committee, Anniversary organized annual peace cruises down the Volga River, where US tourists would travel and speak with Soviets along the river route. These later became biennial trips, with a trip down the Mississippi on the Delta Queen in between. Here, Soviet tourists had the opportunity to join with US peace activists and meet with US citizens up and down the Mississippi.

I would make annual trips to the Soviet Union, to the German Democratic Republic, Czechoslovakia, and for a few years to Cuba, to plan Anniversary's tourist program for the coming year. During the ten years that I was with Voices and Anniversary, I also traveled to Bulgaria, Hungary, Poland, Romania, Austria, Finland, France, West Germany, Greece, Ireland, Jamaica, and the Democratic People's Republic of Korea (North Korea, or DPRK).

The trips were necessary in order to see the sights and facilities that our tour groups would be using and visiting, so that we could better describe them and sell the tours. Our arrangements were with the official tourist bureaus in the Soviet Union and Eastern European countries, and with counterparts like Anniversary Tours that were committed to social tourism in the other countries. Once a year all of these youth social-travel bureaus and tourist organizations would meet in Prague to better get to know our partners, exchange offers, and plan future programs. Some of these plans included multicountry peace or music tours. During this period there was no such thing as independent or private travel bureaus in the Soviet Union and Eastern Europe. There were the official government travel bureaus, the official youth agencies, and the official trade union bureaus. All had their own facilities. For our general tours we used either the official or trade union facilities; for our youth and student tours we used the youth facilities. Some of the youth facilities could not really be sold on the US market. Instead of hotels, or even hostels, they were dormitories or summer camps—not what students paying $1,500 or more, back in the eighties, would be willing to accept.

Social tourism would include visits and meetings with trade unionists, women's organizations, student associations, youth groups, peace organizations, and friendship societies, all of which had to be organized individually, after first making the travel and accommodations arrangements. With each organization we needed to "state our case," asking that they, for instance, set up a meeting with a women's peace organization from Minnesota, or a group of auto workers, or a Black student association. This was necessary since all such meetings would involve a tour of facilities, a formal presentation of what the organization did, questions, give-and-take, and socializing with food and drink. All of this required such requests be included in the official plan and budget of the organization involved.

Meeting every year, often with the same people, enabled me to develop friendships and to have a unique perspective on what was happening in what we referred to as "real existing socialism" in the Soviet Union, Eastern Europe, Cuba, and the DPRK. I was also able to participate in peace marches and demonstrations in Western Europe, and at times to speak as a representative of the US youth movement or peace movement.

Observations of "Real Existing Socialism"

This perspective that I developed on "real existing socialism" helped my own development, and it brought me into conflict with the top national leadership of the Party. For roughly ten years, I would spend a total of three to six weeks every year in different socialist countries, an opportunity that few members of the CPUSA had. Every trip that I made, until the last year, I would report back to Gus Hall, the general secretary of the CPUSA. Initially, these were cordial conversations and discussions. Toward the end, the last two to three years, Gus's response was that I was making things up, that I was lying about what I was seeing and hearing. In 1989, we even ended up screaming at each other. What were some of these observations?

We wanted to organize a bus peace tour in the Soviet Union between the two major cities of Moscow and Leningrad. We were put off again, and again. Finally, Intourist (the national travel bureau of the Soviet Union) told us that there was no adequate highway between the two cities, and the trip would take too long. Until then we would use the overnight train, which took eight hours. Since we kept pushing this, Alla Komplektova, the head of the capitalist countries department of Intourist, asked to speak to me in private. She told me that this was just not possible, and again that the road was inadequate.

I told her that I didn't believe that there was not a major highway between the two largest Soviet cities. She finally said, Jay, as one comrade to another, and this is secret, there are two highways, a not-so-good two-lane highway, and a military highway. We then talked about the duality that existed, a secret military this or that, and the public version of the same. This was a concrete example of the drain that defense spending was causing the Soviet Union, similar to, though not as extensive as, the drain of military spending on the US economy. (Alla's husband was Viktor Georgievich Komplektov, a candidate member of the Soviet Politburo.)

My visit to the DPRK was at the insistence of the top leadership of the Party because they understood that there was an enormous tourist potential there, and that Anniversary would be given very favorable financial conditions. On my way to Korea, I met (as I often did) with Carl Bloice, the Moscow correspondent of the *Daily People's World,* a fellow member of the National Committee of the CPUSA, and a longtime friend. He urged me to look behind the wall on the main street in Pyongyang, as we were coming in from the airport. The main road was well-maintained and clean, but behind the street wall, one could see impoverishment, crowded living conditions, and street cooking. The Pyongyang New Otani Hotel (Ryugyong Hotel or Yu-Kyung Hotel) is a 105-story pyramid-shaped skyscraper over 1,000 feet high. Construction started in 1987, and it was reported to be opening in 2018. When I was in Korea, concrete was being brought floor-by-floor, not by hydraulic concrete machinery but manually, in small wooden boxes. There was no way that such a project could be finished with such technology.

In all of my visits to the Soviet Union a similar observation struck me. I did not see large-scale construction trucks in Moscow, Leningrad, or Kyiv. What I saw would be the equivalent of large pickup trucks. There was just no way that major construction projects could be completed on time when the vehicles hauling raw materials and equipment were this size. Again, I am sure there were larger trucks and transport vehicles (I would see pictures of them in the annual November 7 and May Day parades), but obviously they were reserved for the military, not the domestic economy.

In 1987 or 1988, I was having dinner in the GDR with my interpreter. This was the interpreter provided to me by the US-GDR Friendship League ("der Liga"), with whom we would arrange the friendship component of our trips to the country. I asked what projects the Free German Youth (the Communist youth organization) were working on. She proudly told me that in Berlin they were repairing, fixing, and painting the city's Jewish cemetery. I responded by asking if there was that much vandalism, desecration, and painting of Nazi swastikas at the cemetery? Her response was: "Who told you? That is a state secret." I responded that she told me — that as a Jewish Communist from the United States, I knew only too well that repair of Jewish cemeteries, around the world, in any country, including the United States, only took place when they were desecrated and destroyed. She begged me not to tell anyone. I told her I wouldn't.

We wanted to arrange a program in the GDR for African American law students and their professors and kept trying to have a lecture from the university law faculty to show how "racism had been eradicated in the GDR." We kept being stonewalled. Finally, Reiseburo (the official GDR travel bureau) and the Friendship League arranged for a meeting with a legal scholar, a judge who was also a member of the Central Committee of the Socialist Unity Party, the GDR's Communist Party. Speaking as one Central Committee member to another, he told me this was not possible. I kept pressing him. I told him that the materials we have in the United States say that racism had been eradicated. He said those were not materials from the GDR, but materials that were issued by the CPUSA. He said that in the GDR they did not say that racism was eradicated. So, I asked, what do you say? His response: "We just don't say. If we don't refer to it, it no longer exists." This helps explain why the rise of neo-Nazis and the alt-Right has been so extensive in the former socialist half of the country.

In Prague, in 1988 or 1989, while real existing socialism was still in power, I was meeting a friend who had worked for one of the tourist organizations and been posted to the United States for different periods of time. We worked with this organization in sending tour groups to Czechoslovakia. When in the United States, he and his wife had dinner in our apartment, and our families went on picnics together (within the allowed fifty-mile perimeter from Columbus Circle). Now we wanted to have dinner in Prague. We went to at least a dozen restaurants, all of which were empty, but we were told that there were no available tables. Finally, he blew up and started shouting, asking how much of a bribe he had to pay, and if that would be in Czech *koruna* or US dollars? His wife asked him not to make a scene, and he said that someone had to make a scene, that this was just not right.

At the annual meeting of the youth and student travel bureaus, at which Voices of the Future and Anniversary Tours were for many years the sole US representatives, you would meet the same representatives year-in, year-out, and friendships would form. In the mid-eighties, representatives from a number of countries were having dinner, and we at one point made toasts to our children. When it came my turn, I toasted my daughter, Michelle, and then my son, Joshua. The reaction to Michelle's name was to ask if we were French, otherwise why would we name our daughter with a French name? The reaction to Joshua's name was, "What kind of name is that?" I responded that it was a traditional name, even a biblical name. Representatives from the GDR said that it was a very unusual name, they had never heard of such a name, and that there were no such names for children in their country. There was silence from those of us from the Western countries.

In one of our annual meetings with Intourist to discuss what our rates would be for the following year, I had objected to the proposal that was presented to us. The response from the Intourist side, in English, was that we expected you to try and "Jew us down."

I would often be away for two, three, and four weeks at a time. Looking back, it was really unfair to put such a burden on my wife—for her to have sole responsibility for our two young children while she was working and for me to be literally unreachable except by telex.

Throughout this period, both Judith and I were paid "Party wages," initially $100 per week, later increased to $125. I think that after twenty years, we were each making $150 per week, with two small children. We were only able to get by—pay rent and purchase food and clothes for our family—with the help of both of our parents. We were part of a like-minded community of friends, many of whom also had children the ages of ours. Together we supported one another, shared common values, and tried to bring our children up in an atmosphere that valued friendship and equality, not material possessions.

For ten years, roughly from the time I went to Voices, until 1991, I remained part of the Party's national leadership committee, but for all intents and purposes I was not part of the day-to-day activities of the Party. My Party assignment was to help organize as many people as possible for friendship tours, peace delegations, people-to-people travel programs (essentially a part of the peace movement), and the effort to stop the ever-spiraling nuclear arms race. I also had a special responsibility, that of helping to raise as much money for the Party as possible.

I would participate in the meetings of the Central Committee, but in essence I had taken myself out of the "life and activities of the Party." My travels had opened up my mind to what the reality of "actually existing socialism" was and was not; what the shortcomings were in the process of building socialism in the Soviet Union and other countries; and what the level of support was for the socialism that existed and for the leadership of those countries. These were conclusions that were in direct conflict with most of the top leadership of the CPUSA. Like a number of other comrades in the leadership who had developed questions, which later turned into disagreements, I kept quiet and stayed in the leadership, hoping that changes which were brewing in some of the socialist countries would make an impact in our Party. We were inspired by reforms that were being introduced in the Soviet Union by Mikhail Gorbachev. We embraced and identified with the campaign there of glasnost — opening up, reviewing, reassessing, admitting to incorrect past policies and programs. We were inspired by perestroika, the practice of restructuring and reforming the economic and political system. We were wrong. The leadership of the CPUSA was unmoving, and it became one of the steadfast opponents of change in the international Communist movement.

Speaking Out for Change

Beginning in 1988, a number of members of the Central Committee, at first eight, then twelve, and later twenty-two (if I remember correctly there were about eighty-five to one hundred total members of the Central Committee at that time) began to speak out for change — change in the way the CPUSA worked, its basic organizational principles, and the line and policies of the Party. We asked to be able to give a minority report at a Central Committee. This was unheard of since the mid-sixties, even though this had been a fundamental feature of the Party and the international Communist movement before then — the notion that there should be the fullest possible debate and discussion before a position is adopted, and that this could only happen with contending views in play, as opposed to a consensus presentation that was to be enriched and elaborated on. Contending views were definitely not part of the norm after 1968 and Czechoslovakia.

The Czechoslovakia "Intervention" Revisited

In 1968, I was sixteen years old, a member of the Communist Party for only a few months, an activist in the peace movement, and a leader in the high school student movement. How on earth could I defend the Warsaw Pact countries' intervention in Czechoslovakia—an "intervention" and, ostensibly, not an invasion to overthrow the Czech experiment in "socialism with a human face." But I did, and so did thousands of other young Communists in the United States and thousands more around the world. How so? We believed that the primary internationalist responsibility of socialists was to support and defend the land of the first successful socialist revolution—the Soviet Union—and to defend and support the other socialist countries. Even if we had misgivings about sending troops into Czechoslovakia, we felt that the socialist countries were only doing this because the very existence of socialism in Czechoslovakia was being threatened and undermined by US imperialism and NATO and West German attempts to recover Germany's pre–World War II power. And it was not only the Soviet Union and the Warsaw Pact countries and their respective Communist Parties that defended this action. It was supported and defended by revolutionary leaders and their new socialist societies that the whole world looked up to: Fidel Castro and Ho Chi Minh, Cuba and Vietnam.

Boy, were we wrong! The experiments of the Czechoslovak Communist Party under the leadership of Alexander Dubcek were bold, and they could have inspired a new and different perspective on what kind of socialist society was being built in Eastern Europe, what was wrong with the socialist economy then in place, and what might be needed to salvage it. In 1993, after I had left the Party, I read Dubcek's autobiography, *Hope Dies Last*, published after his death the year before. I wish, back in 1968, this could have been available to the world Communist movement to consider and study.

After the invasion, the National Committee of the CPUSA met and adopted a report and resolution in support of the Warsaw Pact action. There were, I believe, five dissenting votes and a number of abstentions, and the vote was publicized. Because we felt the Party was based on collective action (we forgot that in order to reach any collective action, there had to be full discussion), many of us were shocked that there were dissenting votes.

One of those was Gil Green, then the chairman of the New York District and a longtime friend of my parents from his days in Chicago. In fact, Gil and my father joined the YCL in Chicago at the same time. Another dissenter was Earl Durham, a leader of the Party in Chicago.

The information from this National Committee meeting was presented to all the districts in the country, and there would then be a vote of the respective district committees to support the resolution of the National Committee. In Illinois, and in most other places, in addition to the members of the district (or state) committee, the entire active membership of the Party was invited to the meeting. This was called an "actives" meeting, and it was the quickest way to get information and policy to the largest number of members. In reality, this was for the entire membership of the district who could afford to be seen and have their picture taken by the FBI and Chicago Red Squad, who were perched outside of the meeting location, taking names and photos. Looking back, I now find it interesting that the report back was not given by the district chairman, Claude Lightfoot, nor the district organizer, Jack Kling, but instead was given by another member of the National Committee from Chicago, Lou Diskin, the district educational director. He spoke for about an hour, citing the reasons why the Soviet action was necessary in order to prevent the rollback of socialism in Czechoslovakia. Maybe this was done to enable Claude and Jack to more fully participate in the discussion, to back up the report that was given. Maybe it was felt that Lou could make a better presentation, I don't know.

But what I will always remember is what happened after Lou finished. David Engelstein, a member of both the state committee and the district education commission (and who taught the classes in Marxist political economy and dialectical and historical materialism for most of the younger members of the Party), got up and asked for equal time to give a minority report, in which he said, unlike the previous report, he would only cite sources from the international Communist movement, not from the bourgeois press. Wow, did this create a shit-storm! New members of the Party, like myself, were thinking, how can you have a minority report, once the national leadership has adopted the policy for the Party as a whole? Jim West, another member of the National Committee from Illinois, and the future head of the Party's Review and Control Commission, got up declaring that David was out of order, that this was anti-Party activity and a gross violation of democratic centralism and Party discipline. Different members got up to debate David's request for a minority report, most denouncing it. Then both Claude and Jack got up to speak in support of a minority report, not equal time, but half the time of the original report — thirty minutes. Claude specifically said that many of the younger comrades do not understand this, and many of the older comrades seem to have forgotten, but this is how we do things in the Communist Party. We discuss outright, fully; when there are different positions, we present them, and then we come to a collective conclusion. Wow! I can still picture this discussion, this scene. It was never repeated until the year before the 1991 convention and the split in the Party.

Not only did the Warsaw Pact countries trample another socialist country, but internationally the Soviet leadership trampled the internal life of parties around the world. The Soviets were able to get away with this in regard to different Communist parties because the international movement was based on the premise that the international duty of all Communist parties and their members was to support and defend the first socialist country to successfully throw off the yoke of capitalism, the Soviet Union. The prestige of the Soviet Union was further built by the sacrifice and suffering of the Soviet people in their decisive actions to defeat the Nazi armies in World War II. This principle of defense of the Soviet Union was one of the nineteen principles for membership in the Communist International, as it existed from 1919 to 1943. Just as the Soviet Union contributed to the defeat of Nazi fascism, it would later give political, military, and financial support to liberation movements around the world struggling to free themselves from colonialism. And it would give political and financial support to its brother and sister Communist parties throughout the world. In the aftermath of World War II, with the international reaction of imperialism to the worldwide revolutionary upsurge, including the active role the CIA played in undermining trade unions and leftist political parties and liberation movements, many of these groups became increasingly reliant on financial support from the Soviet Union, and to disagree with Soviet policies meant to "bite the hand feeds you."

Tiananmen Square

The 1989 crushing of the Chinese democracy movement in Tiananmen Square angered many of us in the ranks of the CPUSA, but we were not able to organize against the lavish support which the Gus Hall leadership gave to the Chinese Communist Party. I can remember the annual New York *Daily World* picnic on the grounds of Arrow Park (owned by a cooperative of progressive Ukrainians) in Monroe County, just north of the city, at which Gus Hall heaped praise on the crushing of the rebellion in Tiananmen Square. What did I do? I, along with the two other leading comrades I was talking with, could only turn our backs on the general secretary and national chair of our Party and walk away from the speaker's stage, in anger and disgust.

In the CPUSA, the movement within the ranks for openness and a change in policy, direction, and leadership grew, leading up to the 1991 convention. Again, this drew strength and encouragement from what was happening in the international Communist movement, specifically in the Soviet Union. In the year and a half before the convention, there was a minority report to the National Committee; there were numerous discussions and discussion bulletins. Most of the discussion focused on differences with the national leadership around Gus Hall and on the lack of collectivity, a deviation from socialist principles of organization. Alternative perspectives were put forward on international questions, the nature of socialism, the electoral policy of the Party (the Party did not support the 1984 presidential candidacy of Jesse Jackson, running Gus Hall and Angela

Davis instead), trade union questions, and how the Party should be organized. There was, however, no unified political position put forward by those in opposition. The closest was a call for dialogue and initiative, for renewed discussion in the ranks of the Party, that was publicly signed by more than twelve hundred individual members, more than one third of the membership.

The outcome of the convention in December 1991 was a foregone conclusion, even though many in the opposition held out hope that some change was possible. The leadership brought in members of the Cleveland police to guard the podium against members of their own party! After the convention, roughly one third of the membership of the Communist Party left. The two largest district organizations, New York and Northern California, voted in membership meetings to leave the national Party organization. In other districts, like Illinois, Southern California, Michigan, Ohio, and Western Pennsylvania, those who asked even the least question were literally run out of the organization, including former members of the National Committee, longtime Communists, and some charter (founding) members (those who had joined in the first decade, like my father).

Leaving the Communist Party

What were the political reasons for my departure from an organization that I had literally dedicated more than half my life to—more than two decades? I had come to these core beliefs:

- There needs to be greater commitment to democracy and the struggle for democratic rights—to the fullest expansion of democratic rights, both in our country and throughout the world, including the then socialist countries. This had to be a pillar of both the organization and the struggles that it engaged in.
- Socialism is a political and economic process, and not a finished product that can be declared achieved. Further, there needed to be recognition that both socialist democracy and a socialist economy require pluralism and a multitiered

economy. I am very happy that Cuba is now in the process of moving in this direction.

— The preservation of the earth has to be a primary focus for everyone: dealing with climate change; getting rid of nuclear energy and nuclear weapons; preserving the food we eat, limiting Monsanto, Nestle, and the fossil-fuel extraction industries; and not turning over the national forests to those who ravage the earth and hasten more devastating climate change.

— The working class is changing and not static. The Communist Party narrowly viewed the working class as primarily those industrial workers who had the power to shut down the system, and often these were primarily white. The working class is multinational and multiracial. Industry was in decline, and modern technology was on the cusp. Today, the scientific and technological revolution — the changes in how we communicate, how we could treat illnesses, how we organize work and leisure time — is an even bigger change than the Industrial Revolution was. The working class clearly works in all sectors of the economy. For instance, today the largest employer in the country is Walmart.

— Peace and the prevention of nuclear war is not a tactical issue, but a basic issue that should underlie everything we do.

— Democracy has to be extended to the Communist Party itself — full discussion and debate, full disclosure of how finances are raised and used, not secret control by only one or two people. I came to reject democratic centralism, one of the bedrock principles of the world Communist movement, as it was practiced. It has no place in today's world, in the struggle to expand and develop full democratic rights. Democratic centralism was supposed to mean the fullest discussion in the ranks of the membership, with the elected leadership at all levels then making decisions based on such discussion, including full debate of positions and alternatives, which would then be binding on all members. In reality, the membership did not have access to information, knowledge of events in other places, or knowledge of what resources might be available to carry out policies and decisions, and therefore could not really fully participate in the discussion of policy and programs. Instead of resolutions being put forward that could be debated in leadership bodies, omnibus reports were presented and a "general line" was voted on. Thereby, the membership, including members of those leading bodies, never really knew what the actual differences were.

— I rejected the notion that there is a "science of Marxism-Leninism." The ideas of Marx, Engels, and Lenin were wonderful in their time, but the world has changed. We can learn from their contributions, discard what is wrong and maybe should never have been considered, and consider the thinking, contributions, and practice of so many others. A "science" is something that can be proved, not something that is proclaimed. In their lifetimes, Marx and Engels said they did not want to be referred to as "Marxists."

— I joined the Communist Party to help build and expand the people's movement. Over the years, the Party leadership developed a political position that counterposed the building of the mass movement with the building of the Communist Party. I believe the primary catalyst for change is the broad mass people's democratic movement, whatever form it takes, with the socialist movement being a component, perhaps agitating for more advanced positions.

Committees of Correspondence for Democracy and Socialism

After the 1991 convention, some members organized themselves into the Committees of Correspondence for Democracy and Socialism (CCDS). Other members, upon leaving the Party, went about their lives, continuing their involvement in the trade union movement or in building electoral coalitions, devoting themselves to their jobs and professions, or giving all of their time and energy to their families.

Initially those of us who formed the CCDS hoped for a realignment of the Left in the United States, with those of us coming out of the CP being one of the streams of such a new political amalgam. For a while the CCDS grew, reaching over three thousand members in the first two years, nearly three times the number that had left the CP. However, people began to drift away. There was no clear program, activity, or direction, and it soon became obvious that some of those who had left the ranks of the CP had not abandoned the politics and style of work that they had learned and practiced. The CCDS is still in existence, along with a number of other socialist groups that come from a similar tradition (Communist, Trotskyist, Maoist). There are some remnants of different Left political currents, but there is no one grand Left or socialist organization.

At the same time there are many more people — thousands, even millions, in our country — who consider themselves socialists but are not part of any socialist organization. The Democratic Socialists of America (DSA) has grown to a membership of more than sixty thousand nationally, as of this writing, from around six thousand just two years previously. While this is the largest socialist membership organization in our country in decades, that number still does not touch the many more who see no future in capitalism, the many more who consider themselves socialist. The task before today's and tomorrow's socialists is to build a new movement, one that is broad, diverse, bold, and inclusive of different perspectives and tendencies within its ranks. This movement has to do what socialists inside and outside of DSA are now doing: presenting alternative electoral slates — sometimes as socialists, often in coalition with others — challenging at the ballot box, and winning office — locally, for the US Congress, and ultimately for the presidency.

The reality that there is not one umbrella socialist organization holds not just for our country alone; it is a worldwide phenomenon. The mass response to the Bernie Sanders campaign in our country, the development of groups like Podemos in Spain (which received the second largest number of votes in recent elections), the Left campaign of Jeremy Corbyn and the Labour Party in England, the initial election of the Syriza government in Greece (with all its problems and vacillations), and the numerous progressive governments in Latin America, including Mexico, all show that in the world today there is a new openness to alternatives to the government and economy that exists, and millions are exploring socialism.

Working at the Musicians Union

After leaving the CP, I was without a political reference point, without a political organization (I had been a member of the CP for twenty-three years), and without a job. I lacked confidence in my abilities, but I had underestimated the organizational and political skills I had learned in those years. I became a clerk-secretary at Local 802 of the American Federation of Musicians in New York and after one year was promoted to head of the recording department.

While I had taken music lessons, I was not a musician. After many years of piano lessons, I gave up hope of ever playing an instrument, having tried the piano, flute, and guitar. Now I had to learn the bylaws of the union, learn to distinguish musical instruments, what types of instruments made sense on a recording, the composition of different sizes of orchestras, the terms and conditions of twenty-three different recording contracts, and how the union operated at both the local and the international level. I was at the union for twenty years, becoming part of the national negotiating committee for recording contracts, and was elected to the executive board of Local 802 twice and was a delegate to the international union convention and the Central Labor Council (AFL-CIO). During those twenty years, we began to process grievances against the major recording companies, television networks, ad agencies, and cable television programs on which there was live music. For the last ten years, the recording department at the local was able to win grievances for back pay, work that had not been paid, and for pension and health benefits totaling over two million dollars per year. I took great pleasure in taking money from CBS and NBC, from Sony and

Universal — money they never intended to pay — and getting it to musicians.

In 2009 I was defeated in the election campaign, and it was clear that the new leadership no longer wanted my services. I took early retirement at the beginning of 2010.

Portside: A Left News Service

Starting in 1998 a number of us in the leadership of the CCDS thought it was possible to work with others in the creation of a listserv that potentially could go to many more than those who were then in the ranks of the organization. It took us two years of preparation, and in October 2000 we launched *Portside,* a Left news service that initially posted five articles daily.[3] Those of us working on *Portside* plunged ahead. We expanded our ranks, and today most of the twenty-five moderators are not members of the CCDS, but all are socialists in one way or another. *Portside* now reaches upwards of seventy-five thousand readers daily, with individual emails to subscribers of *Portside, Portside Labor, Portside Culture,* and our daily digest, P*ortside Snapshot.* Thousands read *Portside* via Twitter, RSS, and Facebook, and the Portside website is visited by thousands daily.

Portside is part of a growing new movement for change in our country — a Left and socialist movement, just as the port side is the left side of a boat.

A New Socialist Movement

I think there is a "change gonna come." I think that it is blowing in the wind. I have no idea what form this change is going to take, but I also know that it will be extremely difficult to put the lid on the box of the 99 percent who are fighting against the 1 percent who are hoarding all of the wealth and resources of our country. A few years ago, I would not have thought that the

3 *Portside,* https://portside.org.

notion of the 99 percent would become a mass concept worldwide. But it has.

I think there will be bumps, ups and downs, but there will be change. I think that people around the world are beginning to fight against the imposed right-wing austerity drives. I am not sure how long the people of our country will tolerate the nightmare of Trumpism and the divisions it is sowing amongst us. I am not sure how long the people of our country will allow the public education system to be privatized, an example being the closing of existing schools in cities like Philadelphia, Chicago, and New York while diverting public tax dollars toward new charter schools. Empty schools now dot community after community. Nearly two hundred years ago, and in the years afterward, working people campaigned for the expansion of all forms of public services: public education, public libraries, public hospitals, and public spaces. Now, when so much more is possible, the elected leadership of our country is dismantling public institutions. It is no wonder that both Bernie Sanders's and Elizabeth Warren's campaign demands of free public education, an expansion of Social Security, and a national public healthcare-for-all plan have resonated so powerfully across the country.

Who would have thought that marriage equality would become a reality? But it did. However, there is a real danger that other gains and victories, for more than half the population, will be taken away. The assault on Planned Parenthood and women's right to choose is an attack on the whole country. The erosion and weakening of the Voting Rights Act, the restrictions on who can vote and where they can vote, the reintroduction of gerrymandering on an unprecedented scale, is the reimposing of de facto political segregation. The election campaigns of Donald Trump show that racism has not been overcome and that politics based on fear and hatred is still with us. I worry about future actions in Iran, or the possibility that the US will support an Israeli attack on Iran. I am cheered by what is happening in Latin America, especially the election of Andrés Manuel López Obrador (AMLO) in Mexico. The opening under President

Obama of relations between our government and the people of Cuba was long overdue. As I write this, restoring that opening and removing the embargo against Cuba that has been in place since 1963 is necessary for peace and the well-being of the peoples of our two countries.

I think that radical consciousness will grow and develop, and as part of that there will also be a growth in a new socialist movement. In 1848 when Marx and Engels wrote the *Communist Manifesto,* there was no large socialist movement, no socialist countries, and no Communist parties. In the early part of the twentieth century, socialists were elected to city and state offices across the country and to Congress. Eugene Debs received 6 percent of all votes cast for president. This was when there were no socialist countries or Communist parties.

So again, I think that a new Left movement will come into existence. It will be based in part on mass support for the ideas that were thrust into public consciousness by the Occupy movement,[4] by Bernie Sanders, and now by a whole new wave of progressive and socialist candidates. It will work on different levels, in different forms, in community after community. Out of this new Left will also come a new socialist movement. I am not sure what it will be called, what it will look like, but I know that I will be a part of it.

4 Occupy Wall Street was a two-month long protest movement that emerged in lower Manhattan in the fall of 2011 when activists set up camp in Zuccotti Park in Manhattan's financial district. The movement focused on economic inequality, corporate influence in politics, and other issues. Its decentralized, networked organization and its social movement strategy set the template for protest, social, and electoral movements in the years that followed, both in the United States and around the world, popularizing the 99% vs. 1% concept.

5

From China to the United States

Peter Hodes[1]

I was born the youngest of three children in New Orleans in 1950. I always liked how easy it was to know how old I was at the time of any particular event. (You've probably already calculated my age — see what I mean?)

In 1953 (yes, I was three years old), my father, Dr. Robert Hodes, was fired from his job at Tulane University, where he had been a physiology professor and researcher. The administration never admitted that the reason they fired him was because of his Communist beliefs and activities, although undoubtedly that was the case. As this book went to press, my family is asking Tulane for an apology.

After being fired, my father was unable to find another job in his profession, because there was a (secret) blacklist of fired Communists and those accused by Joe McCarthy's witch-hunters of being Communists. Yes, what a blight on US history was this era of persecution based on political beliefs!

1 Originally written September 2015; revised March 2021.

Living in China for Five Years

My father eventually decided to accept an offer from the People's Republic of China to teach neurophysiology to Chinese graduate students in Beijing. We called it Peking at the time.

So, in 1954 my family moved to China, where we lived for five years. At four years old, I quickly learned Chinese and became somewhat rusty in English, because everybody around me except my parents was speaking Chinese. I was completely immersed in another language and culture. There were no signs in English and certainly no McDonald's or other fast food chains until many, many years later.

In December 1959 we returned to the United States, where it was no longer technically illegal to be a Communist Party member. The Smith Act had been ruled partially unconstitutional by the Supreme Court. The effects of the McCarthy era, however, were still deeply ingrained in the culture, as they are to this day.

On the way from the airport into New York City, nine-year-old me spotted billboards advertising competing car companies. I asked my mother why there was such a thing. Why not simply build the best possible car? I reasoned that then there would be no need for competition, which brought with it wasteful advertising and other public-relations expenses.

This was the Communist philosophy that I had absorbed as a child growing up in China: cooperation instead of competition. If the people focused on a goal, the society would "overcome obstacles" and everyone would enjoy the benefits of having achieved the societal goal.

I remember the joy of banging pots on my balcony as part of the campaign to rid the country of sparrows, which were eating too much of the grain being cultivated to feed the population. Another campaign I participated in was to stop the practice of spitting in public places. We circled the offending spit with chalk, in an effort to educate about the public-health threat and to publicly shame the person who had committed the offense.

At one point in the late 1950s in China I experienced international solidarity with the national liberation struggles via my diet. Suddenly I was encouraged to eat lots of dates, where previously I didn't even know what they were. I think it was to support the people of Afghanistan in their struggle for national liberation.

During those years in China I was routinely mistaken for being a kid from the Soviet Union. This meant that I was treated with extra friendliness because the Soviet Union and China were close friends at the time. When I explained that I was actually from the United States, I learned to quickly add that I did not like the policies of the US government. I don't remember anybody specifically asking if my parents were Communists, but that must have been the assumption, because at that time a US citizen in China had to be an invited guest of the Chinese government.

I learned about discrimination against African Americans in school as well as at home. When I returned to the United States, I was a little surprised to find that there were African Americans who were middle class, which was contrary to the impression I got from the Communist news in China, that every African American was poverty stricken.

I entered fourth grade in the neighborhood public school in New York City at the end of 1959. Within days I had my first ever schoolyard fight. A kid came up to me during recess, and in an almost friendly way asked, "You want to fight?" In China, there was no such thing as fighting among school kids. So, I was more bewildered than anything else when I was asked if I wanted to fight. Needless to say, within minutes, I had suffered a beating, complete with a chipped tooth.

My parents talked to the school administrators, who asked another fourth grader to befriend me and, hopefully, function as my protector. Or maybe they expected that he would teach me how to fight. When he approached me in the cafeteria the next day and asked if I was Peter, I immediately expected my second fight, asking him why he wanted to know my name. Clifford and I became good friends for fourth, fifth, and sixth grades. One time when he was absent, the same kid accosted me on the playground, but this time I was at least prepared and managed to do some damage to him as well. It was considered a draw, and I never had any more fights.

Joining the Party

It was mostly to please my parents, both lifetime Communist Party members, that I joined the Party. I joined in 1966 or 1967, when I was sixteen or seventeen. I don't think there was a strict age requirement, but I joined more or less as soon as I was allowed to.

It was all quite natural, in that it was expected of me. It reminds me of how a fish is not aware of being in the water.

My mother was mighty proud of me. (My father had died when I was fifteen.) At the time, there were plenty of other Left organizations, but they were all on the wrong path! Either they were "Trots" (followers of Leon Trotsky) or "ultra-leftists" or "reformists" or "social democrats." These were practically curse words in my household; so, for me, there was never a question of joining any of these other Left organizations.

Before I joined the Party, my parents would sometimes bring me to rallies and pickets for various progressive causes. For some reason, I particularly remember a picket line in front of the United Nations building in New York, around 1962. Maybe it was a protest or maybe it was in favor of peaceful coexistence with the Soviet Union. In any case, there were counterprotesters, and it was kind of scary for me.

At that picket line, as at so many other political activities, there were plenty of family friends, many of whom were Party members, although mostly that was not made explicitly clear. So these activities were a mix of the political and the social. Angela Davis, in her autobiography, makes clear how there was not a big separation between political and social activities. It was just my life — political and social interwoven.

It was much later in my life that I felt some discomfort with the separation of the political and the social. This was when I was working in a factory, and upon returning to work after a weekend of Party meetings, I couldn't easily explain to my coworkers who didn't know I was a Party member, how I had spent the weekend. I longed for more time just socializing/relaxing — more like what I understood they had in their lives.

A Special Comrade

A special person in the Party was Irving Potash.

I was in ninth grade and was harassed by some kids to give them money, walking to the subway station after school. When I told my mother about it, she devised a plan which featured Irving Potash. The next time I saw the kids waiting for me, I was to go in the public phone booth (remember those?) and dial Irving's number.

When he answered, I told the kids that my uncle, a judge, wanted to talk to them. I don't know why they agreed to take the phone from me and talk to Irving, but they did! And he gave them a stern warning to leave me alone. And it worked!!

Weird, huh?

The Socialist World

The socialist world, which included one-third of the total, was a big influence on me. Both China, where I had grown up from age four until age nine, and the Soviet Union were shining examples for me of all that was good in the world. I also loved the GDR (German Democratic Republic), specifically because it was so successful on the international athletic stage. It was a powerhouse at the Olympics, disproportionate to its size.

Industrial Concentration

Most of the time that I was in the Party, I was engaged in "industrial concentration." Later, when I had been active in the labor movement for many years, I came to think of this as similar, although broader in scope, to "organizing the organized." In both cases, we focused on those workers who were already unionized — "organized" — and worked to develop them to become the leadership of the entire progressive movement. And of course one of the important progressive movements was, and still is, to unionize the labor force generally.

Because employers and their government allies have made unionization so difficult in this country, the obvious strategy has been to concentrate our efforts where we would get the biggest "bang for our buck." This has meant focusing on large, basic industries where the organization of the work by the employer has already made it easier to unionize, as compared to trying to unionize innumerable small workplaces.

We would "salt" a workplace that we wanted to organize. This meant that a union staffer or union activist would get a job at the targeted worksite. That worksite had then been "salted" and the chances of organizing it were, at least theoretically, greatly increased. Organizing for the Party followed a similar policy, in that we were concentrating our efforts, to bring left-wing awareness to specifically targeted groups of industrial workers. In the Party, instead of "salting," we called it "colonizing." Wow, what a poor choice of words!

For me and my comrades in the Boston area, the large General Electric (GE) factory in Lynn, Massachusetts, was the clear choice for "colonization." Looking back after all these years, I think it was the correct policy (minus the terminology). I worked there for seventeen years (a "colonizer"), always active in the union. I helped to bring the union local to endorse Rev. Jesse Jackson for president in 1984. Yes, it was overturned pretty quickly by the more mainstream majority of the union leadership. But the discussion that it raised was a positive and lasting achievement in itself. Another campaign in that period was to get GE to divest from apartheid South Africa. Again, the fundamental questions of working-class solidarity we raised in this effort were effectively presented, regardless of the success or failure of the campaign goals. I was active in the plant on issues of health and safety. We held management's feet to the fire, which would often result in improved health and safety measures in the factory.

After many years of being a steward and rank-and-file leader, I was elected to full-time union officer in the mid-1980s. In that role, my activities were similar, although I would spend more time directly negotiating with management. This sharpened my negotiating skills, which I would later use in negotiating union contracts after I had left GE and become a full-time organizer/representative for various labor unions.

The most disappointing aspect of being a union officer or union staffer was always that I spent so much time on discipline cases. Even though defending union members from (oftentimes excessive/unfair) discipline is important, I would so much have preferred to spend my time on more general union issues which affect more than the handful of members who find themselves "in trouble" with management.

That said, the most important structural change that the union achieved while I was at GE involved disciplinary action meted out against union members. For as long as anybody could remember, management would, "on the spot," without pay, suspend or fire a union member who was thought to have committed some act which violated company rules. After a member was suspended or fired, the union would file a grievance and then meet with management to argue that the discipline was unjust. While these meetings went on, the member continued to be without pay; sometimes for an extended period of time. If management reversed itself or was forced to reverse itself by an arbitrator, the member would be "made whole" and provided with back pay. The problem, of course, is that "justice delayed is justice denied." When a union member has been unjustly fired and then reinstated after a year with full back pay, in no way is that person truly "made whole." It's impossible to undo the damage that has been done.

In the mid-1980s, when a number of progressives, including me, were elected to serve as union officers on the local union executive board, the union confronted this situation and ultimately won a change in management's handling of union members' discipline. While the company claimed that it was their unilateral decision to change their policy, there is no doubt that our struggle, which included a long strike, forced them to change. Shortly after this historic strike, the company changed its policy to one of paying a union member who was suspended or fired while the supposed infraction was investigated by higher-level management. In addition, the company was thenceforth more cautious in suspending or firing a union steward, having learned from the strike that the union was prone to be more militant in protecting union stewards than nonstewards.

Federal law recognizes a higher threshold for justification in disciplining a union steward, because they are considered to be equal in stature to management if the steward is engaged in union activity. For example, if a steward, while representing another worker, uses curse words, the law recognizes that as different than a nonsteward using curse words and thereby violating company rules.

Many years later, when I moved to California, I found that this policy of paying a worker while his or her discipline is being investigated is law for public-sector workers, part of the Weingarten rules. Instead of being called a "suspension" or "discharge," it is called "paid administrative leave." It works, to some extent, as a disincentive for management to be too quick to discipline workers, because there is the danger of paying them for sitting at home while the investigation is ongoing. And even worse, if it is found that the worker did nothing wrong, the whole process of discipline would have been for nothing.

At the GE plant, in terms of the bigger picture of building democracy in the workplace, every success we had helped to build confidence among the union membership that, when united and militant, we could win. This confidence, in an upward spiral, could then lead to greater chance of other concrete successes.

My Activities

All of my political activities were the result of my being a Party member. The Party didn't instruct me to do X, Y, and Z. No, my activities were the result of decisions arrived at through discussion and debate. Usually, the top leadership of the Party would start things going by specifying a policy direction they believed in, but it was not implemented simply because it was announced by the leadership.

One example of implementing a Party policy comes to mind, from when I lived in St. Louis. I might not have been as bold if I had not been a Party member. In the early 1970s, while I was working in a factory in the city (again, a "colonizer"), the movement to make Martin Luther King Jr.'s birthday a national holiday was gaining momentum. This campaign to honor Dr. King was significant in several areas, because he was not only a civil rights leader but also an antiwar activist. Although this was a nonunion shop, management asked the workers for their opinion as to what should be the additional paid holiday to be celebrated.

If not for the support I felt from my fellow Communists, I might not have been bold enough to publicly campaign for the holiday to be in honor of Dr. King. St. Louis, after all, had a long history of virulent and even violent racism, going back to the Civil War and earlier.

Worldwide Socialism

With the breakup of the Soviet Union and the downfall of socialist governments in Eastern Europe, I suffered discouragement about the likelihood of a socialist world or socialism in the United States in the near future. I still believe, however, that in the long term it will happen.

Mostly I have the same positive view of socialism as when I joined the Party. Over the years, I've come to appreciate more the difficulty of balancing democracy with the "centralism" that is needed for a planned economy and planned society (as opposed to the "free market" idea of capitalism). We were taught the theory and practice of democratic centralism as an important component of Marxism-Leninism. I still think that it's a valid way for an organization or a society to function. It takes into account the need for leadership and at the same time a method of selecting that leadership.

In practice, I was pretty well satisfied that the Party got it right during the time that I was a member. If there was too much emphasis on one or the other, it was almost always too much centralism and not enough democracy. We were functioning in a very difficult environment, and so the tendency to emphasize "top down" centralism was understandable. We wanted to replace capitalism with socialism while living in the most sophisticated and highly developed capitalist country the world had ever seen. As an organization, great discipline was required if we were to accomplish the task at hand.

To this day, the requirements for replacing capitalism with socialism remain more or less the same.

The Struggle to Expand Democracy

The great majority of my efforts and those of my comrades in the Party was in promoting and expanding democracy in our society. That is, not as much effort was put into building the Party itself. I think that is as it should be, right up to the present-day political movement for radical change.

For me, there was a constant tension in finding the best balance at any moment in history—to not be lagging behind popular desire for democratic reforms and at the same time not too far in advance of that sentiment by constantly screaming about the need for socialist revolution now. That tension continues today, and I saw it well balanced in the recent Occupy movement.[2] It was not calling for socialist revolution per se, but there were demands for radical reform that would help lead to revolutionary change.

2 See footnote on page 173.

Leaving the Party

In the late eighties, I drifted away from the Party, rather than experiencing a decided break. I didn't feel enough concrete benefit from Party membership for my political work. On the contrary, I felt that I was sometimes hampered simply by the number of hours I spent in Party organizational meetings.

I have continued with approximately the same political work since I left the Party. However, being in the Party provided a solid foundation for me to understand the complexities of our modern world. The Party's clear-minded approach to fighting racism has been particularly helpful throughout my life.

6

My Parents Were Communists

Naomi Chesman Smith[1]

My parents were activists. They met in the struggles of the 1930s and 1940s, undertaken so we could have Social Security benefits, unemployment benefits, maybe even a better world. That's when they met. So, my parents were activists, and they were Communists, and I was born in 1949. The next year, a man named Joe McCarthy made a speech that ushered in the infamous period that carries his name—the period when progressive people, people trying to make the world better, were restricted, lost their jobs, or even were jailed. That was the time that I grew up. When I was one year old, we moved into a New York City public housing project that had just been built. When we got there, we learned that there was an agreement that the project would only admit people who matched the community in the midst of which it was built. So that meant I grew up in a nearly all white housing project.

As I said, my parents were activists. My mother became the head of the grievance committee and my father headed the tenant newspaper. When I was about three or four, my father, who was a New York City public-school teacher and a member of

1 Transcribed March 2021 from Showcase Schools, "StoryLab with Principal Naomi Smith," *Facebook,* July 24, 2017, https://www.facebook.com/watch/?v=1235784919864544; edited August 2023.

the teachers union, was blacklisted. He lost his job. So there we were. He had to retrain himself to be an accountant.

So life went on — I became four and five. All I really wanted was friends. That's what I wanted, but that was hard. Somehow people were not kind to me. People called me names. They wanted to fight with me, and I just didn't know what was wrong with me.

At five, I decided I had to do something about this. I climbed into the cupboard, where my mother kept her money, and I took a single large bill. Of course we had limited money, because my father had lost his job. So there I was with that single large bill and I crossed Williamsbridge Road (I asked an adult to cross me, of course) and I marched to the bakery, went in, handed the money to the bakery lady, and said "I want two of these, and four of these, and ten of these," and then I went back to my project with two bags of goodies for my soon-to-be friends. I put out a blanket, put out the cakes. You cannot believe how many friends I had. Everybody in all the buildings in the project around wanted to be my friend ... until my mother found out. "Naomi! What are you doing?" I just wanted to have friends.

Well, it didn't work, in case you were thinking of trying that strategy. As I went up in the elementary grades I still had these issues where people we're picking fights with me and calling me names. They weren't kind and I just knew there was something wrong with me.

One day one of the names that someone called me was Comrade Chesman (my maiden name.) I thought that this had something to do with being a Communist — maybe people don't like me because my parents were Communist. I went home and I said, "Mom, maybe people don't like me because you and Daddy are Communists". She replied, "Ridiculous, impossible," so I went to my default of thinking that something was wrong with me. I got older and I became an activist myself, and I was active in the Civil Rights Movement and the peace movement, and that brought me to City College. I was sitting at a table collecting signatures on a petition to end the war in Vietnam, and next to me was Susan Grayson, who had lived in the next building over in our project. She was one of the kids who really wasn't very kind to me. In college, we were friends. She turned to me during a lull and said, "I'm really sorry, Naomi."

"Sorry about what"?

"My sister and I were talking last night and we feel so bad about how poorly we treated you, growing up."

"What are you talking about"?

Susan replied, "Everyone was told, 'Don't play with Naomi. She's a Communist.'"

I said, "You must be kidding me. You have to come home and tell my mother."

I became a teacher, I became a principal, and I really knew what it meant to not belong, and now I make it a priority to make sure that in my school there's no child who feels like they don't belong.

7

We Were *Movement* Organizations — People's Organizations, Not Puppets of Anyone

Joseph Harris[1]

Childhood

I was born in 1944. Until I was nine years old, I lived in Queens, New York. My mother was the chair of a community Communist Party club in Flushing, Queens. My father was a tool-and-die maker, an open Communist, and chief shop steward at Sperry Gyroscope, a defense-industry factory of about twenty thousand workers in Lake Success, New York. He and a group of other Communists had organized a union there during the late 1930s, or perhaps during World War II.

In 1951, during the Cold War with the Soviet Union, Sperry fired my father, supposedly for being a security risk. His union, United Electrical Workers Local 424, under severe right-wing attack, failed to back him up. Afterwards, he was unable to hold a steady job, as every company that hired him soon fired him after he refused to sign the government's loyalty oath saying that he was not a member of the Communist Party (because sign-

1 Originally written August 2020; revised August 2022.

ing the oath could have led to a perjury charge and a prison sentence).

A couple of years later, in 1953, right after the government executed Julius and Ethel Rosenberg as atomic spies for the Soviet Union, my family left New York and settled in the Los Angeles area, where my father's life of short-term employment continued. Eventually, he started his own little machine shop, where he bid for subcontracting work from North American, Lockheed, and other large aerospace companies — and did not have to sign a loyalty oath.

High School Senior Year: 1960–1961

In the spring of 1960, my older sister, who was a student at UCLA, participated in demonstrations at a Woolworth's five-and-dime store in support of sit-ins by southern Black students for the right to be seated at lunch counters. I was very proud of her activism, although I had no thoughts of joining her.

In the fall of 1960, John F. Kennedy was elected president. My friends and I, in our conservative, almost all white, almost all Christian high school in Manhattan Beach (a seaside town in Los Angeles County), hotly debated JFK's and Richard Nixon's political positions. The school even organized a mock presidential election among the seniors, in which I actively participated.

I began to speak out publicly on my deepening political beliefs. My first "public" speech occurred during "religious appreciation week" (perhaps it was in October 1960). All the kids were gathered in the school cafeteria to listen to a Jewish rabbi, a Catholic priest, and a Protestant minister talk about their religions. After the rabbi spoke, I raised my hand and told the assembled students that I was Jewish too, but that in contradistinction to what the rabbi had said, Jews believed that all human beings were their brothers and sisters — not that non-Jews were the "cousins" of Jews. My closest friends were Christians, and I didn't appreciate the rabbi isolating me from them.

In the spring of 1961, my second "public" speech — and my first detention — occurred when I called the teacher of my Senior Problems class a liar after he told our class that Marx wanted all women to be public property. I blame this incident on the fact that at the beginning of my senior year, my father had suggested that together we study Volume One of Marx's *Capital*—and we did, one chapter each week for thirty-three weeks. Then we read Vladimir Lenin's *State and Revolution* and *What Is to Be Done?* Marx, of course, never wrote that under Communism women would be public property. What he wrote was that under Communism the working class would own and control the means of production that capitalists previously had owned and controlled. My dad had explained that since I soon would be studying in college, it would be good if I knew at least one theory of the world, so that I would have something to bounce other ideas against.

Another transforming event was my attendance, with my best friend, at a huge rally of the Christian Anti-Communist Crusade at the Los Angeles Coliseum. He had obtained tickets to the rally through his uncle, who was a member of the fascist John Birch Society. I felt like a spy at a mass Hitler rally. It was fascinating and frightening.

Finally, I entered the world of work. In the summer before my last year in high school, I worked in a plastics factory as a "sealer," which meant that I operated a machine that sealed the edges of plastic sheets, making plastic bags. During my senior year, I started a little business, using a homemade stencil set and spray paint to paint house addresses on curbs. And I worked a drill press for my father in his little shop in our expanded garage.

I was growing up.

College

In spring 1962, while I was a freshman at the University of California, Berkeley, I organized my first political event. I lived in a big student co-op called Cloyne Court, and because of political discussions I got involved in, I invited the editor of the *People's World,* Al Richmond, to come and speak, which he did, and after which he answered questions. I had no thought of follow-up or further organizational activities.

That summer, I worked as a firefighter in the foothills below Yosemite National Park, a brand-new working and living experience for me. It included my first encounter with hostile antisemitism. I was badly picked on at our firehouse in the little town of Raymond (population about 150), and as a result, I challenged one of the two antisemitic bullies to a fight on a Saturday, when we would be off duty and could fight away from the work site (and not get fired). I knew my ass was going to be seriously beaten, so the evening before the fight I mentally prepared myself to use every dirty trick I could think of to hurt him. But then the foreman came to me, told me to pack my suitcase, and drove me to another firehouse in another small town, called Ahwahnee, where I spent the rest of the summer in peace. It turned out the foreman was the bully's uncle, and a World War II vet, and a decent guy. Weeks later, the bully came to me one day during a lull when we were fighting a big brush fire in scrub oak country and apologized to me. And he told me that after I had left, the other bully had turned his attention to him.

During my sophomore, junior, and senior years, I partially supported myself doing odd jobs. I remember three of them, aside from donating blood and being a subject for psych tests. First, I worked as a pot washer in a local restaurant for one morning. I quit at noon, figuring the work was too hard for me. Second, I worked as a "hasher," serving meals to young ladies (rich UC Berkeley students) who lived in a fancy boarding house. In exchange for my work, I received free meals. That job ended when, on a Friday night, the young ladies were sitting at their dining-room tables, dressed in their low-cut gowns for their evening dates. When I leaned over to place a bowl of hot soup on one young lady's place setting, I became entranced by her breasts, prominently displayed before me. You can guess what happened: I spilled the soup all over her gown — and was promptly fired. Third, I worked as a plumber's assistant for quite a while, going around with him to various houses. It was good work, with good pay.

In October 1962, during my sophomore year, the Cuban Missile Crisis happened, and the world almost came to an end. A group of political activists, including my girlfriend, held a demonstration on campus calling for an end to the US military blockade of Cuba. I remember seeing them on campus and being asked to join — and saying no. I explained to myself that I had three interests — school, sports, and girls — and demonstrating was not something I did.

Activism and Civil Rights

In spring 1963, I finally became an activist. This came about because my (new) girlfriend's siblings included two mixed-race children, so racism had become a personal issue for me. After debating and debating within myself, I joined a demonstration against racist hiring practices at a Mel's Drive-In restaurant.

In early 1964, I participated in "shop-ins" at Lucky's Supermarket on Telegraph Avenue in Berkeley. What fun, and what a creative tactic![2] Fifty students who supported the efforts by the Congress of Racial Equality (CORE) to integrate the supermarket staff, entered the store en masse, obtained grocery carts, filled them with the most perishable foods, and then went to the checkout lines. After the foods were bagged and it was time to pay, we discovered we had no money to pay for our groceries. In a short while, all the store's carts were filled with unsold foods, many of them quite perishable. When the fraternities heard about the shop-in, their members came to the store and helped return the food to the shelves. Meanwhile, other students continued their shop-in activities. In the end, we won, and Lucky's started hiring Black workers.

About this time, I joined the Berkeley W.E.B. Du Bois Club, which described itself as a "socialist-oriented youth organization." In reality, it was the youth organization of the Communist Party. Through the Du Bois Club, I participated in study groups

---

2 See "CORE 'Shop-in at S.F. Supermarket," *San Francisco Chronicle*, February 20, 1964, 4.

or classes on historical materialism and Marxist economics. These had a huge impact on me. Marxism was no longer a private father-son conversation; now it was a conversation with my peers.

As a Du Bois Club member, I eagerly participated in the Civil Rights Movement. Soon after I joined, I was arrested with fifty others while quietly picketing on a Sunday morning outside San Francisco's Sheraton Palace Hotel against its unfair hiring practices. The demonstration was sponsored by the Ad Hoc Committee against Discrimination. While we were picketing, the hotel obtained a court order telling us to disperse, which we refused to do. Later, while we were crowded together in the drunk tank, the comedian Dick Gregory heard about our arrests and came to the jail, demanding that he too be arrested. The police accommodated him, and he joined us. Another incident stands out in my memory: Another member of the Du Bois Club approached me while we were in the drunk tank and whispered, "How would you like to join a study and action group?" He meant the Communist Party, of course. I told him not to talk to me about that in such a place, and that ended the conversation. However, his initiative started a conversation in my head that lasted two years while I mulled over my future.

We beat the Sheraton Palace and the San Francisco Hotel Association, forcing them to sign a nondiscrimination hiring agreement, after a sit-in at the hotel that led to the arrest of about three hundred of us. To put this struggle in some perspective, remember that until July 1964 discrimination in employment was still legal in the United States. I should mention that while I was sitting on the lobby floor, who should pass by on her way upstairs for some swanky event? The young woman whose dress I had spilled soup on just a few months before.

I'll never forget how I became the chairperson of Berkeley Students for Fair Housing (SFH), which was fighting against Proposition 14, a state ballot proposition to amend the state constitution to relegalize discrimination in housing. I had gone to a Du Bois Club meeting in the spring of 1964, was assigned (with my permission) to attend a meeting of SFH, went to the meeting and was nominated by another Du Bois Club member to be chair, and was duly elected. What a surprise for me, and what a mistake! I was totally unprepared for the responsibility, and, naturally, did a poor job.

The Du Bois Clubs provided the militant, activist atmosphere that encouraged me to join the Mississippi Summer Project in 1964, led by the Student Nonviolent Coordinating Committee (SNCC). Since I was underage, SNCC required me to present my parents' written permission before they would accept my application. My father opposed my participation unless I brought a firearm with me for protection. (My father was a volunteer in the Abraham Lincoln Brigade who had fought in the Spanish Civil War against fascist Franco in Spain in 1937, where he was wounded twice.) But a woman comrade whom he especially respected convinced him to sign the consent form, and I worked for SNCC in Mississippi. While I was there, my mother and father actively supported SNCC's work along with other California parents of SNCC volunteers, raising money, lobbying public officials, and getting valuable public relations items out for us.

I left for Mississippi right after attending the founding convention of the national W.E.B. Du Bois Clubs in San Francisco in June 1964. I drove a Willys Jeep that had been donated to SNCC. Leaders of the Berkeley Friends of SNCC and I went to pick up the Jeep the night before I left. We couldn't find it and took another Jeep that was parked nearby with the keys on the floor (as they were supposed to be). This mistakenly stolen jalopy, stuffed with clerical supplies for SNCC, broke down several times, but I finally dropped it off in Memphis, Tennessee, where SNCC women mechanics readied it for use in Mississippi (after getting permission from the owners of the Jeep!).

Along the way, I stopped in Oxford, Ohio, where SNCC had its main training school, at the Western College for Women. There I witnessed SNCC leader and Summer Project director Bob Moses giving a good-bye speech to a busload of volunteers who were about to leave for Mississippi. With everyone holding hands outside the bus, Moses told them (and me) that three civil rights workers (James Chaney, Andrew Goodman, and Mickey

Schwerner) were missing and likely dead, and that it was not too late for volunteers to turn back. No one did; they boarded the bus and headed to Jackson. I continued driving the Jeep to Memphis, Tennessee, where I underwent training in nonviolence.

I'll never forget traveling from Memphis to Jackson. A group of northern white students who had been trained in nonviolence in Memphis were told to exercise care on the bus trip. We were to sit apart from one another and blend in with other Greyhound passengers...Then, when we arrived in Jackson, we were to call a Black-owned cab company for rides to the SNCC office on Lynch Street (!). We did that, and then a bunch of white kids got in together in Black-driven cabs. Wow, did we fool the White Citizens Council! The good thing, of course, was that we made the trip safely and without incident.

I spent the summer of 1964 in Jackson, "Freedom Registering" residents in the Black neighborhood (Twenty-Second, Twenty-Third, and Twenty-Fourth Precincts) where Medgar Evers, the state chair of the NAACP, had been assassinated in front of his home one year before. Luckily, I experienced no violence. However, I was stopped once, supposedly for a driving violation, but really because the car I was driving had both Black and white passengers. And, a car swerved at me and my African-American date one evening as we walked along the street.

Every morning, I would leave the Freedom House where I (and others) slept on the floor. I would be met outside the door by a group of local Black teenagers, male and female, who would accompany me the entire day and deposit me back to my door at the end of the day. My bodyguards would stand on the sidewalk next to each house and wait for me as I knocked on the door and gave my pitch to whoever answered. I don't know how these students happened to adopt me; I assume SNCC organized them.

SNCC had set three goals for those of us who were assigned to Freedom Registering. First, we were to persuade each person who answered the door to fill out and sign a Freedom Registration voting form. That form was based on the New York State voter registration form, which was a reasonable voter registration form — in contrast to the official Mississippi form. If we succeeded with this first task, our second task was to ask the person to accept a few forms to take to relatives and friends to complete and sign. We would explain that we would return the following week to collect the completed forms. Third, if that organizing task worked out, we would ask the person to hold a small meeting in their home to talk about the Mississippi Freedom Democratic Party, which SNCC and other civil rights groups were organizing to challenge the official, racist Mississippi Democratic Party. Through this work, I met Mrs. Hazel T. Palmer, a wonderful Jackson resident who at the end of the summer traveled to Atlantic City, New Jersey, as a representative of the Mississippi Freedom Democratic Party (MFDP) and still later became a leader in the MFDP.

During the summer, SNCC workers helped seventy to eighty thousand Black Mississippi residents fill out Freedom Registration forms — a form of mass political education. And the thousands of completed forms provided invaluable proof that Black citizens would register to vote in huge numbers if a safe and reasonable voter registration process existed. I like to think that my daily work in this project helped the freedom movement in some small way.

The MFDP conducted a tremendous but unsuccessful struggle at the 1964 Democratic National Convention in Atlantic City to oust and replace the official racist Mississippi Democratic Party delegation. My little part in this effort was picketing on the boardwalk outside the convention hall. However, proving that Black Americans would register to vote if they were allowed to do so, and struggling to build and seat the MFDP, led significantly to the passage of the 1965 Voting Rights Act, which enabled mass Black voter registration in the apartheid-like South.

I owe a tremendous debt to SNCC. The Mississippi Summer Project profoundly affected me. It was an incredible learning experience. I was already used to being in the minority and sticking up for myself and my beliefs — after all, I was a nonreligious Jew and a budding "Red" who had been raised in a white, conservative, Christian neighborhood. Now, for the first time in my life, I lived and worked with Black people. I had a Black girlfriend. I took political leadership from and was protected on a personal level by Black people. And, I participated in democratic militant grassroots organizing in one of its finest manifestations.

Weeks after I returned from Mississippi to Berkeley for my senior year in college, the massive Free Speech Movement (FSM), led by SNCC Summer Project volunteer Mario Savio, engulfed me. Most people don't know that it began because the administration at the University of California stopped allowing the Civil Rights Movement to collect money and organize support at the entrance gates to the university. As a Du Bois Club member, I became involved in the successful FSM, first participating in a sit-down that trapped a police car with an arrested student activist in it. I engaged in class debates, a giant march, and a campus strike that shut the university down. I was arrested along with eight hundred others in a sit-in in Sproul Hall, the administration building.

In January 1966 (I think), I received my draft notice. I didn't want to go to Vietnam, but I didn't know what to do. I knew Canada would do as a place of refuge for me, but I was not eager to make that move. I did know, however, that I wasn't going into the army. So, I went to doctors and got notes saying I was asthmatic, which I was…a little. Then, before going to the Oakland induction center, I breathed in feather dust in my closet. When I was wheezing badly, I went to the center. I gave them my doctors' notes and wheezed in their faces, and they didn't care. I passed the physical with flying colors. A perfect specimen. I was shocked and didn't know what to do. Then they gave me the loyalty oath to sign, saying I was loyal to the US government. I didn't even know about this step in the induction process.

To make a short story very, very short, I refused to sign, and they took me out of line and basically kicked me out of the building, giving me a "1Y" classification. At the time, I was told that 1Y meant "mentally or morally unfit." Yippee! I supported the antidraft movement, but the loyalty oath gimmick was new to me.[3]

I was very lucky. If I had not received the 1Y classification, my life would have taken a very different, and more difficult, turn.

Becoming a Communist

When I was getting ready to graduate, in June 1965, and leave the University of California with a Bachelor of Arts in economics, I faced big decisions about my future. I didn't know what to do with my life, what career to pursue, where to live. The one thing I was certain about was that I didn't want to become a liberal — that loathed word to a Berkeley radical. And, I was afraid that after I left the radical surroundings of the Berkeley student protest movement, I would become a liberal and a talker, not a doer.

I joined the Communist Party shortly before I graduated. Basically, I joined because I believed that belonging to a disciplined, "study and action" Marxist organization would help me remain an activist and radical no matter where I lived or what job I held. I respected and liked the young Communists I worked with, so this made joining the Party an easy decision.

I spent the summer of 1965 working as a Du Bois Club community organizer in the ghetto on the west side of Chicago. It was another great organizing experience, this time in semi-leadership. Again, I was woefully unprepared, but I grew.

Two events stand out in my memory. First, we organized a boycott of a major supermarket, because of its racist hiring practices. The boycott was exhilarating, as the Black neighborhood supported it one hundred percent. The store stood empty of customers. After three days, management came to us and begged for the boycott to end, promising to immediately hire local resi-

3 Wikipedia now says that a 1Y classification, which ended in 1972, was for someone who had a mild physical disability, used drugs, or was married, and so forth, but that a 1Y classification would not keep you out of the service in a declared war or national emergency. *Wikipedia,* s.v. "Selective Service System," https://en.wikipedia.org/wiki/Selective_Service_System.

dents. A glorious victory! On the other hand, what organization did we leave behind at the end of the summer? Zero! That fact speaks volumes to the shortcomings of short-term organizing efforts led by outsiders.

Second, sometime during the summer, Illinois CP district organizer Claude Lightfoot asked me to meet with him so we could talk about how our organizing was going. During the conversation, he gently tried to educate me about some white, paternalistic attitudes he saw in me. Fifty-seven year later, I cannot remember any details of the conversation, but what I still carry with me is gratitude to him for trying to help me be a better person.

After the summer ended, our Chicago group and similar organizing teams from other cities gathered at Claude's family farm in Indiana for a week-long Marxist school. It was a wonderful session, but fascists burned the farmhouse down right after we left. (The same thing happened the next year at a summer school in New York State.)

In late 1965, Mickey Lima, the Communist Party district organizer for Northern California, called me to a private meeting with him. He asked if I would like to attend a secret three-month Party school, to be held in Toronto, as a joint effort of the Canadian and US parties. It was to be the first such joint effort. I eagerly said yes. (I was unemployed and had no big financial obligations, so I could afford to go.) He told me that I should tell no one, including my girlfriend, about it — that I was just to disappear. He gave me money for a train ticket to Chicago and bus fare from Chicago to Toronto. So, I disappeared, but I did tell my girlfriend (who was also in the Party) some bare details.

I secretly took the train to Chicago and then the bus to Toronto, but I was turned back at the border. The guard asked why I was going to Toronto and how much money I had, and I answered: "tourism" and "twenty dollars." My answers didn't suffice, but the twenty dollars did get me back to Chicago, where I called Lou Diskin, who ran the Party's bookstore. I told him I needed a couple of hundred dollars, and I couldn't tell him why! He kindly gave me the money, and I did better at another border crossing. When I reached Toronto, I called the phone number I had been given, and I was told my call was twenty-four hours late, and how could they know I was who I claimed to be? Nonetheless, they came and picked me up. (As I look back, I am struck by the amateurism of "the movement" regarding "security.")

We had a great school for six weeks, until one morning the organizers told the US folks to get across the border ASAP, before the Canadian government deported us as personae non grata. We left, and we had our own school for six more weeks in New York City, in a storefront on the Lower East Side. A great school, and a huge service to young Marxists. In these schools, we studied political economy, the national question (characteristics and rights of a nation versus a national minority), and other subjects.

I spent 1965 to 1969 in Berkeley and San Francisco. I held various jobs: ironworker apprentice (three months); warehouseman (three months); longshoreman (one day); export document clerk (three months); computer operator (nine months); and computer programmer (six months). I also worked full-time for the organizing committee for what would become the Young Workers Liberation League (YWLL), and I helped staff the Party's bookstore in San Francisco. (The YWLL was founded in February 1970, and it became the youth affiliate of the Communist Party USA [CPUSA].)

The varied work experience was invaluable for my personal and political development. For example, work as an ironworker apprentice in construction was hard and dangerous. One day on my way to work, I stopped my car on the side of a rainy road, asked myself what I was doing, concluded that I probably would be injured or killed on the job, called the boss and told him I was quitting, and went home. (A few weeks later, I learned that the foreman who pushed us to do dangerous things had fallen, done a somersault in the air and landed on his feet, destroying his brain. I guess I should have felt sorry for him, but I didn't.) Another lesson from that job was that I determined I would never again run on a job. Ever since then, whenever I see a young person running on a job, I stop them and tell them: Never run on a job!

During my one day on the waterfront as a longshoreman, I was nearly killed when I got caught between a big swinging load and a wood retaining fence. As the load came at me, I jumped backward into the fence, thrusting my legs at the load. Luckily, I crashed through the fence to safety.

My work as a fruit-export document clerk taught me about office politics as well as a little about the fruit-export business. My work as a warehouseman taught me how to cooperate with other workers to make work last as long as possible, when that tactic will ensure another day's work (and pay).

My work as a computer operator taught me how employers would pit workers against one another, each month firing the least efficient ten percent of the keypunch operators. (In those days, keypunch operators entered all the data and program instructions for computers onto keypunch cards, which in turn were fed by operators into the computers.)

I wish that I could better remember my political activities from 1965 to 1969, the four years between obtaining my BA and going back to school for my MA and then PhD. I do remember that they were busy, but not very successful. Looking back, I feel that I/we lacked direction. (I am referring to youth work. That was the only thing I knew anything about.)

I faintly remember a few initiatives/activities. In 1966, I participated in organizing and running a freedom school in an Oakland church for students at Oakland High School who were conducting a boycott, protesting racism. In 1967 or so, I led the formation of a group called Citizens against the Tactical Squad. It went nowhere, but it held a couple of forums. The only things I remember are that I had a meeting one night at Black Panther Party leader Bobby Seale's home in Oakland to discuss our activities, and that Panther leader Kathleen Cleaver later spoke at one of our forums. She was an excellent speaker. Also, in 1968 or so, I spent a lot of time in the Party's bookstore in San Francisco, assisting Hank, who ran the store — a very interesting experience. All day long, I would talk with customers who were looking at left-wing books and trying to puzzle out their views. A storefront bookstore is an excellent aid to recruitment. I led several study groups during this period. I can't remember anything about them — I only remember that I did this because in the past three years two of my ex-students mentioned the classes to me. Lastly, in June 1969, I took a trip to Los Angeles to attend a special meeting of young Communists in the Los Angeles area. The purpose was to discuss a public hearing that the US Senate's Subversive Activities Control Board (SACB; established under the McCarren Internal Security Act) had scheduled for the next day in Los Angeles. The SACB's reason for being was to threaten and intimidate Communists and like-minded people by inducing them to testify against themselves and name others — and then blare their names to the public in newspaper headlines. The SACB was empowered to order the registration of organizations that it found to be "Communist fronts," "Communist action" groups, or "Communist infiltrated" groups:

> (e) It shall be the duty of the Board-
>
> (1) upon application made by the Attorney General under section 13(a) of this title, or by any organization under section 13(b) of this title, to determine whether any organization is a *Communist-action organization* within the meaning of paragraph (3) of section 3 of this title, or a *Communist-front organization* within the meaning of paragraph (4) of section 3 of this title; and
>
> (2) upon application made by the Attorney General under section 13(a) of this title, or by any individual under section 13(b) of this title, to determine whether any individual is a member of any Communist-action organization registered, or by final order of the Board required to be registered, under section 7(a) of this title.[4]

4 *Wikipedia,* s.v. "Subversive Activities Control Board," https://en.wikipedia.org/wiki/Subversive_Activities_Control_Board.

We had heard that there was to be a surprise witness, and the rumor was accurate. Bill Divale, a UCLA student who had sat in the room with us the night before and who was a leader in the YWLL and a CP member, took the stand to "out" two of his comrades. Divale, who went on to become a professor at York College in New York City, testified that Angela Davis, who was applying for a professorship at UCLA, was a Communist. Soon after she was hired, she was fired! And, Divale outed Clifford Fried, who was a leader in the large American Federation of State, County and Municipal Employees (AFSCME) staff union-organizing drive at UCLA. Shortly afterward, Fried received a six-month jail term for a sit-in, a much harsher sentence than any of the other sit-in participants received.

I have barely touched on the activities of the FBI, police departments, and numerous other government "security" organizations and special operations in disrupting/damaging the work of movement organizations and harming the lives of individual members and their families. This topic deserves special attention.

Maturation

In 1969, I had a conversation with Victor Perlo, who headed up the Party's Economics Commission. We discussed the Labor Research Association (LRA), which was located in New York City and published a monthly economics newsletter, *Economic Notes*. I expressed interest in working for it, and he told me that I needed to study more economics before LRA would be interested in me.

The conversation influenced me, and I moved to San Francisco and spent one year at San Francisco State College obtaining an MA in economics. Then I moved to Riverside, California, to the east of Los Angeles, where I worked toward my PhD in economics at UC Riverside. I studied under Howard Sherman, who was the first university-faculty Marxist economist I had encountered. Professor Sherman was a fine role model. I owe him a great debt of gratitude, not least because he encouraged me to stick up for my opinions, including when he and I did not agree.

I lived in Riverside for one school year. The only thing I remember about my Party work in Riverside is that our Party club and YWLL helped a local of the International Association of Machinists in a bitter strike against Rohr Industries, which assembled suburban rail cars. I participated in organizing a prayer service with local clergy at the picket line. The leader of the local commented to me that he was glad to get our help, saying that we were using the local and the local was using us. From his perspective, "using" each other had both positive and negative connotations, although the positive outweighed the negative. His union needed our outside help for the strike, but he was leery of his union developing ties with a bunch of lefties — perhaps partly because of how we might influence his members. From my perspective, we were doing a good deed by helping his union win a strike. I don't remember expecting the YWLL to get anything out of our activities except for building a reputation as a good organization.

I lived in Norwalk, an integrated working-class suburb of Los Angeles, from 1972 to 1974, where I was as an active member of our local YWLL chapter. I have three distinct memories of my time there. First, our chapter was a well-integrated organization, with Black, Chicano, Native American, and white members. We were workers and students, with creative, bold leadership. Second, we were active in fighting to free Angela Davis, who had been charged with "aggravated kidnapping and first-degree murder" in 1970 and who was acquitted in 1972. The national campaign, as I recall, was called "Free Angela by Christmas." Our part in this was collecting mistletoe in the desert (an hour from where we lived) and making and selling many, many little plastic bags filled with mistletoe and a slip of paper with the message "Free Angela by Christmas" written on it. We sold these bags widely, but I can't remember where. It was fun, creative, youth work. Third, our YWLL ran a candidate for Congress in 1972 under the aegis of the statewide Peace and Freedom Party (P&F). They chose me to run, and I did. What fun! And a great political education. P&F ran candidates around the state, and most of us received about 5 percent of the vote, wherever we ran and no matter how effectively we ran. Seven thousand five hundred people voted for me. Basically, P&F's vote across the state was a form of antiwar protest.

A few words about the campaign. Our artist members designed and made silk-screened posters, and we plastered them up around the district. For glue, we used a mixture of flour and water — very effective glue. We distributed thousands of leaflets. I debated the incumbent Democrat (Chet Holifield) in a big church and hammered him on the Vietnam War issue. Our total budget was $1,100, but that was the best a group of youth could do. One of our volunteers was a middle-aged white woman comrade from somewhere in our district who was active in Women Strike for Peace; she handled press relations for us. At that time, the Party was against the proposed Equal Rights Amendment (ERA) to the US Constitution that the House of Representatives passed in 1971 and the Senate passed in 1972 (and later was passed by thirty-five of the required thirty-eight state legislatures). The Party and many labor feminists opposed the ERA on the grounds that it would undermine the legal basis for special protective programs for women workers, such as forbidding overtime at night. Somewhere, I was asked my opinion about the ERA, and I gave the Party's position. Well, that was a disaster. The Party was wrong, and our press director was right, and she was mad — and I was stuck. I don't remember how we got through that, but we did.

In this instance, running a third-party campaign was not divisive, and it did not cause a defeat for the more progressive candidate. Our experience proved to me that blanket injunctions against third-party campaigns are as dogmatically wrong as their opposite — that is, "Don't work within the Democratic Party." Our members grew from the experience, and we conducted valuable antiwar activities.

La Lucha Continua (The Struggle Continues)

I've used all this ink to get across the idea that in the 1960s and early 1970s, my local Party organizations—and my local Du Bois Club, my SNCC, my FSM, my YWLL, and so on—were *movement* organizations. By that I mean that we were *people's* organizations, not puppets of anyone, either foreign or domestic. We were grassroots, low-budget, no-budget, by-the-seat-of-the-pants, amateurish, eager, audacious, bold, and often short-sighted and naïve and arrogant. We thought we had the answers. We thought we were at the cusp of revolutionary change. History has proven that we did not have all the answers, and we were not at the cusp of revolutionary change. We accomplished wonderful things for peace and justice, but we fell far short of achieving our ultimate goals.

During the 1960s, 1970s, and 1980s, I actively participated in Party life and mass work in a variety of political arenas, especially civil rights, peace, and labor. However, by the mid- to late 1980s, my participation had fallen away to almost nothing. I left the CPUSA in about 1990. I'm not going to describe my experiences in the Party after 1973, but suffice it to say that they were both good and bad. Overall, we all did the best we could in fighting against war, against racism and other forms of discrimination, for workers, against imperialism, and for socialism. I would join a disciplined socialist party again if it seemed as though I would be a decent fit within it. I still believe democratic centralism is the best form of organization for a revolutionary political party, but we, from top to bottom, did not appreciate the importance of democratic procedures and a democratic ethos in movement organizations, nor did we have an adequate understanding of how best to implement democratic centralism.

With hindsight, it's easy to criticize. Unfortunately, it's a lot easier to analyze past political situations than present ones. Some of the positions we then took now seem so obviously wrong. Here are three examples: First, we said that the existence of socialism as a world system was irreversible, which certainly was not a Marxist analysis and was just plain wrong.

When the United States won the Cold War at the end of the 1980s, capitalists regained their dominant position in all the newly formed countries that had made up the Union of Soviet Socialist Republics (USSR) and in all the other countries in Eastern Europe: Bulgaria, Czechoslovakia, East Germany, Hungary, Poland, Romania, and Yugoslavia. Essentially, all that was left of the former world socialist system was China, Vietnam, and Cuba, and these poor, developing countries were struggling to survive and to develop new and more workable models of socialist development within a world economic system ruled by the United States and its junior partners in the North Atlantic Treaty Organization (NATO).

Second, we said that our strategy for winning socialism was to first build an antimonopoly coalition consisting of the working class and many small business owners, the self-employed, and small farmers. At the same time, we defended the idea of socialism as a political-economic system that had no or a very small place for small business. Given this stance, what small business owner, or "wannabe," would want to ally with forces whose goal was to win socialism? The essence of an "antimonopoly coalition" is that people with different ideological views need to work together against a common oppressor to successfully defend their own varied interests. Naturally, dreams and plans of how to escape exploitation and oppression include dreams of becoming one's own boss—of owning one's own business. An antimonopoly coalition that ignores these dreams will never succeed. Two important factors need to be addressed here. First, a person's class position does not *determine* their ideology; class position *influences* a person's ideology. Being a member of the working class does not mean that one has a working-class ideology. In fact, the working class includes many millions of small business "wannabes" and self-employed "wannabes" who want to escape from the working class, not "rise with it" (Eugene V. Debs), as well as the many millions of workers who cannot find regular jobs and are forced to work as "casuals" or supposedly "self-employed," without legal rights under labor and employment laws. Workers in these situations tend to develop ideologies different from those in classic employment relationships. Second, there are no strict boundaries between classes. Thus, many millions of people belong to two classes, in that they have at least two sources of income: as employees and also as self-employed or small business owners, or as employees or contract workers and also owners of small farms.

Third, we were so ignorant as to think that tiny and small and medium-sized businesses are not viable economic formations that bring benefits to society — and that outperform government ownership in many situations. Unfortunately, the CPUSA uncritically copied the existing formulas — formulas that did not work well — of the Soviet Union and elsewhere. All we had to do was look around us, in our own country, to see the viability of small businesses — even in the face of unfair monopoly competition and domination that included control over government contracting practices. I could add other errors, including the basic mis-estimate that revolution in the United States was around the corner.

This essay, like the others gathered in this volume, is comprised of recollections. At some other time, in another context, I would be eager to discuss questions of Marxist theory. We need to discuss socialism as a socioeconomic system in human history (not a brief transitory period), advanced state monopoly capitalism as a world system, relationships between vanguard political parties and mass organizations, democracy under socialism, and the organizational structures of parties that are fighting to win or build socialism in the pre-internet and internet eras, and many more questions.

Fig. 9. Demonstration by Advance Youth Organization calling for nuclear disarmament and no nuclear arms for West Germany, before the White House, January 15, 1962. (Photo by Ted Reich)

Fig. 10. Free Speech Movement leader Bettina Aptheker (front left) together with Bob Starobin, Jerry Harawitz, and Leni Siegel (FSM activists), University of California, Berkeley, November 9, 1965. (Photo by Howard Harawitz; © 2014 by Howard Harawitz; used with permission)

Fig. 11. Eighteenth National Convention of the Communist Party USA, Webster Hall, New York City, June 22–26, 1966. This was the first convention in seven years, after a hiatus due to stepped-up enforcement by both the Eisenhower and Kennedy administrations of the McCarran Act of 1952 and the Communist Control Act of 1954, and the CPUSA's litigation and other resistance against these laws. These laws criminalized membership in the Communist Party, though the Supreme Court later nullified such restrictions. At the podium is Henry Winston, national chairman of the CPUSA. (Photo by Ted Reich)

Fig. 12. In September 1960, eighteen months after the Cuban Revolution, Fidel Castro led a Cuban delegation to the annual meeting of the United Nations General Assembly. Many of the worlds' delegations were staying at the Waldorf Astoria Hotel; however contrary to established custom, the manager of the hotel refused to allow the Cuban flag to be flown outside and refused to allow the Cubans to eat in the hotel dining room. Castro moved the delegation uptown, to Harlem and the Hotel Theresa, the "Waldorf of Harlem." There Castro met with world leaders: Soviet prime minister Nikita Khrushchev, Egyptian president Gamal Abdel Nasser, and Indian leader Jawaharlal Nehru. There he also met with Malcolm X, Harlem leaders of the Civil Rights Movement, independistas from Puerto Rico and New York, and socialists and Communists from the United States. New Yorkers welcomed the Cubans, bringing food to the hotel, sharing music, and dancing in the streets with their revolutionary friends. Fidel Castro had put the Eisenhower Administration on display—racism was not just a regional matter, confined to the South, but a vast problem throughout the United States, including in the liberal North and New York City. On display for the world was Manhattan and Harlem — crumbling tenement buildings; garbage-strewn streets; high rates of asthma and tuberculosis; soaring crime rates; poorly funded, overcrowded, and segregated schools; and police brutality. Local NAACP leader Joe Overton called Harlem a "police state." The button here was put out by a coalition of the community and political groups that welcomed Fidel to Harlem and New York. (Button courtesy of Cindy Hawes)

PART III

THE WORLD OF WORK AND THE PARTY OF THE WORKING CLASS

8

The Work We Do to Broaden Workers' Thinking Is Important

Dave Cohen[1]

I was born in Quincy, Massachusetts, on March 30, 1951. I had one older sister, Nancy. My father, Abraham Cohen, was also born in Quincy, on September 22, 1916. His parents, Hyman Cohen and Fannie Cohen (Guberman) also lived in Quincy, on Glenn Terrace. My mother Madeline Cohen (Sivachek) was born in 1918 and raised in Dorchester. We rented an apartment on Hancock Court in Quincy. My father's parents were Russian Jews and my father spoke Russian and Yiddish before he spoke English. Both his parents were socialists. My mother's parents were Slovakian. Nana was a cook and seamstress and Grandpa John was a plumber. My mother and father met when they were young, both working at a radical Jewish camp, Camp Nitgedaiget. My father was a counselor and my mother was a cook.

We moved from Hancock Court when I was three. My folks had bought a three-family house on 77 Bigelow Street in Quincy. The earliest thing I remember about the new house was that in the living room there was a large walk-in closet. On the wall were buttons that used to ring bells in every room in the house. It previously had been a rooming house, and the bells were used

1 Originally written October 2015; revised February 2020.

to call people to dinner. The location of our house was considered downtown Quincy, but we went to school in the section of Quincy called the Point.

There was a brook running through the city, several houses down from us. In the spring, herring would leave the ocean and swim up brook to spawn. There were so many that you could grab them out of the water by hand. Over the years, pollution killed off the herring.

There were lots of kids in the neighborhood, so it was a good place. When I was five, I think, it was time for me to go to kindergarten. My mother walked me to the Daniel Webster School in the Point, the same grade school my father had attended. It was about one-half mile to school, and there were always a lot of kids walking to school. My first day in kindergarten I was very excited because there were so many kids there. I was a bit of a wild child and had to sit in the corner, because I was yelling to other kids when we were supposed to be listening. Kindergarten was only half the day, so my mother came to get me at lunchtime. She asked me how was school and I replied that it was great, and I was really going to like it. Of course, I didn't tell her that I had to sit in the corner.

At that time, my father was a part-time optometrist, and he had his office in the front room of our house. He mainly gave eye exams at night after he came home from his main job. After World War II, he and some friends bought a company that made gravestones. Quincy was very famous for its granite quarries, although the last one shut down soon after the end of the war. There were still many small shops, usually called granite sheds, that made gravestones. My mother was the bookkeeper and all around businessperson, ordering supplies and paying bills. My father ended up owning the shop after one of the partners and the secretary left the area together. It was a little messy as both were married to other people. One of the other partners left to set up his own shop.

When I was young it was mainly my father, my mother, my father's friend, Ideal Frabrizio, and his cousin Tony Salvucci who worked there. Sometimes a fellow called Yank (because he was an "American") worked there. Yank drank pretty heavy. It was a union shop, part of the granite-cutters union. Tony's father, who lived across the street from the shop, had been the local union president for many years. He only spoke Italian. Tony lived with his parents and had very bad epileptic seizures, often three or four times a day. When he felt one coming on, he would go to his house across the street. Tony spoke fluent English but had a bad stutter, so he didn't talk much. Ideal had been friends with my father since high school. He was born in this country but lived in Italy when he was young. He spoke very bad English because, he told me once, most Americans were too stupid to talk to. Ideal was a member of the Socialist Party but read the *Daily Worker*, the Communist Party newspaper, and was usually an "elector" for the Communist Party when they ran presidential candidates in Massachusetts. I believe Mr. Salvucci was also a member of the Socialist Party.

I worked in the shop during the summer from the time I was about eleven or twelve until I was twenty years old. I started as a "lumper," which meant I did any odd job that was needed. Ideal shaped the pieces of granite into the finished gravestones, which created lots of big chips of granite. He used a hammer and various chisels to do the shaping. I had to make sure his work area was clean of chips, drag them out of the shed with a rake, put them in a wheelbarrow and bring them out back of the shop to dump them. I also had to hold a straight edge or a curved edge against the granite so Ideal could chip a straight or curved edge. Woe be to me if I let the guide slip out of place. I often would get small cuts on my face when a chip would fly up and hit me.

Another job was cleaning the finished stones. To cut the letters into the stone, the stone was covered with a glued-on sheet of rubber. The lettering and any designs were then traced onto the rubber from a full-scale drawing of the stone. The letters were then cut out and the stone put in the sandblasting booth. Here, sand was shot out of a "gun" that was held by the sandblaster and it ate away the granite where it was not covered by rubber. By adding rubber and putting it back on at times, designs like flowers with curved petals could be created. When the stone was finished, it was my job to clean it. This meant pulling off the rubber, but saving every piece possible, to be used again. Then the stone was washed with a mild acid to remove the glue. Basically, I would fill up a bucket of water, take a handful of the acid powder out of a big bin and mix it in the water. Then I used a big scrub brush to rub the stone until all the glue was off.

Once, when I was about eleven, I was cleaning a marker. Markers are the small gravestones that lie flat on the ground, usually about twenty-four inches by fifteen inches. They weighed about one hundred pounds. It was on a big cart, propped up on pieces of wood, so it was about level with my head. I was scrubbing it and pulled it by accident, so it started to fall off the cart. I tried to stop it but couldn't, and it hit my face as it was falling. The whole side of my face was scraped and bleeding. They took me in the front office to clean me up. I was feeling sort of faint. Mr. Salvucci brought me a cup of expresso to drink. This was a break-time ritual — he brought over expresso and everyone drank it out of very small and dainty cups. I had never had coffee, let alone expresso, but they were urging me to drink it. I took a sip and it tasted so bad that I fainted. When I came to, my father said I could go home. So, I rode my bike home.

Eventually I moved up to doing the layout on the stones and sandblasting them. The process of sandblasting was very dirty. Not only would the sand fly around, but as the granite was blasted away it created a fine dust. Sometimes we would wear handkerchiefs across our face, but not usually. Granite has a lot of silica, an inert mineral, in it. Sandblasters would breathe this in and get a disease called silicosis from it. Basically it was like the black lung disease coal miners would get. The silica would just build up in the lungs; it never dissolved, and it turned the lungs to stone. There were many old-timers who would stop by the shop to kibitz, and they all had trouble breathing and were always coughing up stuff.

The scariest part of working at the shop was unloading the granite slabs off of the delivery trucks. The slabs were about five feet wide and fifteen feet long and eight inches thick. The shop had a huge, very old derrick. It was the largest derrick in Quincy.

Fig. 13. The author's co-worker, Ideal Frabrizio, working on a large gravestone. Photo by Madeline Cohen; courtesy of David Cohen.

It had a vertical wooden beam about thirty feet high and an equal size wooden beam that lifted the granite. The whole thing was centered on a huge metal wheel that rotated. Originally it was run by donkeys, but it had been "modernized" so there were big cables that ran to the power shop. A big motor moved the wheels in the power shop to move the cables that made the derrick rotate, move the beam up and down or just lower the cables from the end of the derrick. The controls were big levers and foot pedals in the powerhouse.

My father ran the derrick, and my job, or my mother's job, or Ideal's job would be to hook ropes or chains around the granite slab and hook those ropes to the chain on the derrick. Using hand signals, we would let my father know how to move the derrick. They would be lifted off the truck and carried over to a pile of other slabs and placed on top, or just placed in front of Ideal's workplace so he could split the slabs up for different size gravestones. The scary part was that the derrick was very old and often times the cables would slip, or when you signaled to stop moving the stone it wouldn't, and you had to duck and not get hit by the several-ton piece of granite.

Some Other Thoughts on Growing Up

In many ways I had a normal childhood, I suppose. I went to school, was bored a lot, and got in trouble (in school). In grade school I received a failing grade in "conduct" for three out of four terms a year. That pretty much continued throughout my school career. The non-normal part was that my father was a member of the Communist Party, and in the 1950s that meant trouble. My parents shielded my sister and me from it most of the time. Later on, as I got older, I was able to put together things that happened to me with things that were happening to my parents. In 1956, my father was brought before the Massachusetts State Anti-Communist Commission and accused of being a Communist. That was in the newspapers. Around that time, I remember being told I couldn't go to a friend's house on Saturday mornings to watch cartoons and the Three Stooges. We didn't have a television at that time. I later figured out that the neighbor's parents didn't want me in their house.

During the Cuban missile crisis, I got in trouble in school because I said (probably mimicking something I heard my father say) that it was no big deal that the Russians were putting missiles in Cuba, because we (the United States) had missiles on the Russian border.

I entered high school in 1966. A big issue at the time was the segregation of the Boston school system. Schools were either all Black or all white, and the Boston school committee worked very hard to keep it that way. Of course, the all-Black schools were in the worst condition, and students received a worse education. One of the proposed solutions was to have Black students from Boston attend schools in the cities surrounding Boston, which like Quincy were basically all white. This was called the Metco program, and it was voluntary on the part of the white cities. In Quincy, the politicians were opposed. In 1967 or 1968 someone in Quincy High School decided there should be a debate on whether or not Quincy should join the Metco program. It would be held in front of the entire school body. I was a member of the debate club and was selected to present the "pro Metco" side. I did a lot of research, and when the debate was over the winner was decided by who received the most clapping from the audience. The "pro Metco" side won the debate. I felt pretty good that the students were convinced that integrating our schools would be a good thing. Of course, the politicians never gave in and took part in the Metco program. Some years later, after I had left home, my mother and father were part of a small group, the South Shore Coalition for Human Rights, that sued the City of Quincy and the Commonwealth of Massachusetts over the way they handled public housing. The methods used helped ensure that all white cities remained that way. With the victory the group won, the racial composition of Quincy began to change, as African Americans and Asians moved to the town.

In September of 1969 I began college at the University of Massachusetts in Amherst. In most ways I did not want to go to college, since I disliked high school, but there wasn't much choice. If I didn't go to college my choices were to be drafted to go to fight in Vietnam, elect to flee to Canada, or go to prison. College seemed like the lesser of the evils. I was an anarchist, mainly I read works by Peter Kropotkin, but because our house was filled with works by Marx, Engels and, Lenin I had read some of them also.

School didn't start out that well. I had longish hair and a beard, so most of the men on my dorm floor considered me a hippie. It turned out that most of them weren't happy that I was also Jewish, so I didn't talk to many of them. My roommate was in his second year and was a business major, so we didn't have much to discuss either. UMass was in the midst of a cultural change. At every dorm and all over campus there were tables signing up freshman and giving them "freshmen beanies" to wear. I wasn't going to do that. I noticed there were many Vietnam vets who were just out of combat; some were released to go to college if they had less than one month of service left and came directly from Vietnam to the university. They were in no mood to wear freshman beanies and undergo hazing from "upper classmen." It was a clash between the old ideas of college and the reality of life for young people in 1969.

I soon hooked up with people in the radical movement and the antiwar movement. By the end of my first semester I met people who were members of the Communist Party (CP) on campus. My father had asked the Party to have people look me up. I was still an anarchist and a hippie, but I was friends with the people in the CP and some people who were in the Progressive Labor Party. I have to admit that I didn't attend many classes and spent most of my time on radical activities and sometimes partying with pot and various other drugs.

After about a month, life changed somewhat on my dorm floor. There was an influx of three or four Vietnam vets, just out of combat. To the men on my floor, who all supported the war, they were just as weird as I was. One night there was a banging on my door. I asked who it was, and a voice yelled out that they wanted to meet with the "Jew hippie commie bastard." I opened the door figuring I was going to get a beating, and the vets came in. I asked what they wanted, and one guy said they were told by people on the floor to stay away from the Jew hippie commie bastard, so again I asked what they wanted. Their reply was that they wanted to get high, smoke some dope, and they figured I was the best guy to see. I did have some pot, so we smoked some and had a jolly good time. I became friends with most of them, and while they were around, I was never bothered by the "pro-war" men on the corridor.

I spent a lot of time listening to their stories of what the war was like, and they appreciated that. Later, when I was recounting these experiences to my father, a World War II veteran, he noted a big difference in how the war ended for soldiers in Europe. He said that they spent weeks traveling from place to place to be processed for return to civilian life. Then they had a long boat ride home across the Atlantic. During that time, all they talked about was their war experiences. He felt that time spent talking with each other helped them talk out the horrors they had seen or committed. He was shocked that soldiers could be in Vietnam one day and several days later they would be on a college campus.

The vets knew I was active in organizing against the war, and they respected that. I didn't preach to them or attack them, and they knew I was concerned about my friends who were in Vietnam. When I told them that my father had said to me that the war in Vietnam was a rich man's war fought by workers, they all wished that they had a father like mine.

One fellow had served three tours of duty. He was from Chelsea, Massachusetts, not far from my hometown of Quincy. He had been placed under arrest shortly before his last tour was ending for having the troops under him read a book on the history of Vietnam. He suffered from what probably would now be called posttraumatic stress syndrome. If woken by any noise while he was sleeping, he would automatically attack that person. He really couldn't have any roommates. When he got drunk, he would get violent. One night he was drunk and roaming the dorm corridor with a large knife. Everyone was afraid to approach him. I went to talk with him, and after a while he gave up the knife and went to sleep. That happened several times, once or twice he beat on me a bit, but usually he recognized me as a friend and would calm down. His fiancé was a nurse, and she got him some help.

In the spring of 1970, there was a large rally called for in New Haven, Connecticut, to support members of the Black Panther Party who were on trial in that city. I went to that rally. Unknown to me, my future wife and comrade Judy was also at the rally. The night before, thousands of people were in the streets marching. Soon we came to an intersection with National Guard troops on the other side. I expected them to shoot tear gas at us, which was the norm by then. Instead, we heard them given the order to fix bayonets, which they did. This was a new twist. Then they were ordered to take a step forward with bayonets pointed towards us. They then began to march forward, with our side falling back, as no one wanted to get bayoneted.

The next day the rally took place, and then there was a meeting of college students. At that meeting it was proposed that we go back to our colleges and organize a student strike. The issues were to be an end to the war in Vietnam, an end to racism, and an end to repression. When I got back to UMass there were already notices posted for a big meeting to organize the strike. At the meeting there was heavy debate over the intent of being against war, racism, and repression. There were some leaders of the antiwar movement on campus who only wanted to organize against the war. They thought that white people would be alienated by the focus on racism. Most of those people were affiliated with the Socialist Workers Party. The debate ended with the majority of people present voting to endorse the demands of ending war, racism and repression. I was asked by some folks to serve on the steering committee of the strike, but being an anarchist, I refused, not wanting a "leadership" position. Instead, I volunteered to work on getting the engineering and science departments to join the strike. They were considered the toughest parts of campus to organize.

I would spend all day outside the engineering and science departments leafleting and talking to students. Many were sympathetic but scared. In the engineering department, missing a lecture meant your final grade was lowered! I would also explain why I was an anarchist, which was less understandable to most students. Most of the students in the engineering and science departments were very job-oriented. Soon I started going into the classes and politely but firmly saying I needed a few minutes to address the class. I would explain the strike and why it was important for the students to join or support it, then I would thank the professor and leave.

These interactions began to have an effect on my anarchist beliefs. I had been debating with my Communist friends the difference between anarchy and socialism. I wanted to immediately create a new society, without a government, based upon mutual aid and cooperation. My Communist friends were not opposed to my end vision of society but felt you could not jump from a capitalist state to no state without workers having time to develop their skills at running the country and their workplaces. They called this period "socialism." I soon became convinced that they were right and began to call myself a socialist, although I always had respect for anarchists like Kropotkin, as well as the working-class anarchists I had met.

The school year came to an end, with a victory for the student strike. The administration agreed that for that semester, students would be marked on a pass/fail system, instead of the normal grades. Grade-wise, that was my best semester in college.

One other thing became clear to me. Towards the end of the strike there were rock concerts organized out by the campus pond. After a hard day working on the strike, it was fun to relax and listen to music. I soon noticed an interesting thing. There were police all around the edge of the campus, but around the pond, drugs were freely being distributed. People with shopping bags were giving away all sorts of drugs, without the police interfering. I don't know if the police organized the free drugs (which I helped myself to) or just felt that a stoned crowd was less trouble then a riled-up crowd. As the semester ended and students went home, the strike came to an end.

I left for home and spent the summer working with my father and mother making gravestones. That summer the government held lotteries to see when young men would be drafted to fight in Vietnam. It was broadcast on the radio and everyone at work was listening. They would draw birthdays and that was the order you would be drafted. The first drawn was number one, and therefore the first group to be drafted. I was working on a stone and my birthday was drawn, giving me a draft number of fifty-six. Ideal came up to me, cuffed me on the head and said, "Stupid American." I had seriously been thinking of dropping out of college, but with a number so low I knew I would have to return to UMass to keep my student deferment. Later on that summer I had some political discussions with Ideal, and he thought what I said was stupid. The next day when I came to work, there were books sitting on the stone I was working on. It was four or five volumes of writings by Lenin. Ideal came to me and said that he wouldn't speak to me unless I read Lenin. Ideal was the person I went to when I had work related questions, so I knew I had to read Lenin. I started that night, so that the next day I could prove to Ideal that I was following his instructions. I still have some of those books.

In September 1970 I returned to UMass, but I spent most of my time engaged in political work. I barely attended any classes my second semester. I again returned home in the summer of 1971 and worked making gravestones. By this time, I was very active in the Young Workers Liberation League (YWLL), the youth group of the Communist Party. That summer the YWLL in Boston had decided to run a candidate for the Boston School Committee. The schools in Boston were some of the most racially segregated in the country. The committee would make up school districts that stretched across the city with many twists and turns just to maintain separate Black and white schools. Open racists dominated the committee.

The person the YWLL chose to be a candidate was a young Jamaican woman, Pat Bonner-Lyons. She was, I believe, the first Black woman to ever run for the School Committee. The campaign material said that she was a socialist. I became involved in the campaign, so every day after work I would go to Boston and help collect signatures to secure her position on the ballot. A local newspaper described her as, "a young articulate Black woman.... She attacks institutional racism of the school system, the inferior quality of education, and the lack of concern on the part of many school administrators and not a few teachers."[2] Most of the signatures we collected for Pat were in the Black community. The level of racism was extremely high in many parts of Boston. There were a few people from South Boston who wanted to campaign for Pat but were very afraid. They wanted to take Pat's picture off the literature. We had long debates about that and of course reached the decision that it would be giving into racism to remove her photo. A few of us went to the outskirts of South Boston and handed out campaign material.

2 "Neanderthals, Hacks, and Racists," *The Heights (Boston College Newspaper)*, November 5, 1973, 5.

Being new, I was not in the leadership of the campaign. I remember there being various issues that caused tension in the campaign. Support was growing for Pat in the Black community and among white progressives. They looked at the issues she raised and the proposed solutions and tended to ignore the fact that she was a member of the YWLL. It was becoming a community campaign. Some people in the YWLL seemed to me to resent this and were reluctant to share leadership of the campaign with others. There was also tension with the older folks in the CP who felt they were not being consulted enough by the YWLL.

There was a primary for the School Committee race; only the top ten vote getters would make the final election. Amazingly, Pat finished in the top ten! This set off shock waves throughout Boston. I was not there for the final election, but as I remember Pat was the first runner up for a seat on the School Committee.

Angela Davis Campaign

I returned to the Amherst area sometime in September 1971, even though I wasn't going to school anymore. I had many friends out there. I spent most of my time involved in building a campaign on campus for the freedom of Angela Davis. She was a Black woman professor in California, a member of the Communist Party, and active in the prisoner-rights movement. Ronald Reagan, governor of California, had tried to get her fired but failed. I won't go into the whole story here, but she was arrested and framed on a murder charge, based upon an incident involving the attempt to free George Jackson, a Black political prisoner. The movement to free her became a nationwide effort. At this time, the demand was that Angela should be released from prison on bail while awaiting her trial.

This campaign to me became another lesson in how Communists should work with people who supported the issues but were not ready to accept socialism as the goal. On campus it was the YWLL chapter that started having a table in the Campus Center with information on the case and with a petition for people to sign. Soon other students began to join in, and there was considerable support from the African American students on campus.

There was an ongoing movement to develop an African American studies department, led by a group of African American professors. They had fought hard to set up a lecture series on African American history in honor of W.E.B. Du Bois, the famous Black intellectual who was born in Western Massachusetts. The lecture series was to be given by Herbert Aptheker, a white member of the Communist Party who was a professor of African American history and a coworker and the literary executor of Du Bois. The professors won the battle with the administration to fund the lecture series by Aptheker. The lectures were held in a very large auditorium, and most of them had overflow crowds. His final lecture was on current history and focused on the campaign to free Angela Davis. The lecture hall was packed, and the university had to set up speakers in the Campus Center auditorium so other people could hear.

Instead of just regular petitions, we had people sign onto the call to free Angela on large, rolled paper. The chancellor of the UMass campus, Randolph Bromery, who I believe was the first African American chancellor, signed the petition with a large signature. We then started planning for a rally, to be held in the Campus Center auditorium on January 3, 1972. The speakers list included the professors who had fought to bring Herbert Aptheker to campus and who had started the African American Studies Department. I was the last speaker, representing the YWLL. I must say it was an honor to do that, but by the time I got up to speak many people were leaving the room, which had been packed.

After the rally a man came up to talk to me; his name was Mike. It turned out that he was from Quincy also. He was about eight or nine years older than me and was working at a factory in nearby Easthampton, Massachusetts, called Paragon Rubber. It seems that they were hiring for the night shift, so I applied for a job there. I needed a job, but also some people in the Communist Party said that if we wanted to have a working-class revolu-

Fig. 14. Paragon Rubber molder removing dies from the press, 1930s. Photo from the National Archives and Records Administration, catalog identifier NAID 518343.

tion we needed to be in the working class. That made sense to me.

Paragon Rubber was a rubber-molding factory. There was a section where the rubber was made, according to what products were to be produced. I worked in the molding section on second shift. Although the accompanying photo is from the 1930s, it shows what it looked like when I worked there. The other part of the plant was kick presses that would trim off the excess rubber from the molded pieces. In the molding area it was often over one hundred degrees, and when you leaned into the presses, it was much hotter, especially during the summer. There were overhead water pipes that you could open to drench yourself when the heat was too much.

Paragon operated on a piecework system. You were guaranteed minimum wage for each hour worked. Each time you unloaded a machine, that mold would have a set price of, say, 25 cents. At the end of the night if the "pieces" you produced added up to more than the minimum wage, you got the higher amount of money. On a good night you could make about $4.25 an hour, which was better than the minimum wage of $1.60 per hour. Being low on the seniority list I didn't always get presses with jobs that had cycles that synced with each other. The most senior operators got the best picks of presses. Each mold had a different curing time. Usually, you ran two presses a night, and hopefully you could sync the schedules so that while you were cutting up the molds you just took out of the press, the other press would be just finishing its curing time. There were big clocks hanging around the molding area, because you always had to watch the clock to make sure a mold didn't overcure. After working there for about a year and a half I developed a "tick" of looking for the clock every several minutes, which stuck with me even when not working. There was a union at Paragon Rubber, the International Union of Electrical, Radio and Machine Workers of America (IUE). We never heard much from them.

Besides the heat, there were other health threats at Paragon. After being there a while, I noticed that there were several male workers who were big strapping guys, but all they did was sweep up, all around the factory. I asked someone why, and they told me that their lungs had given out. The problem was twofold. In the rubber mixing department, a lot of talc powder was used to keep the rubber from sticking inside the Banburry machine. The Banburries mixed the various rubber compounds and then extruded it out in different shapes: flat about four inches wide, tubular of various circumferences, or whatever was needed to produce a particular product. That talc powder was always in the air and being breathed in. In the molding area operators breathed in the fumes of the rubber as it melted in the hot presses and then cured. After the molds were stripped of the finished product, they were placed back on the big dies, sprayed with a mixture of soap and silicon (so the rubber wouldn't stick) and then loaded with rubber, slid back into the press, and then the press was closed by steam pressure. The presses were heated to several hundred degrees, and when the soap and silicon were sprayed on them a cloud of vapor would fill the air. It took me a while to figure out that breathing in the silicon wasn't good for your lungs. It wasn't too much different from the stone cutters I had met who suffered from silicosis from cutting granite. Silicon is an inert substance, meaning once it got in your lungs it just stayed there.

The other problem was that everything in the molding room was run by steam. Steam heated the presses. Steam provided the power to open and close the presses. To operate the presses you had to reach in between the presses to move valves, and many times while pulling or pushing the valve you would brush your arm up against a hot steam pipe and get burned. This happened so frequently that every couple of months a man from the workers compensation insurance company would come by to measure and record new scars. I believe we got about $25 dollars per inch of scars, which was very good money.

I worked on the second shift along with Mike, who stopped working there after a while, but we remained friends, and he joined the CP for a time. Mike had a drinking problem. Before work he would pick up a pint of Thunderbird wine for each of us to drink. I stopped doing that, because Thunderbird was a very cheap wine and in the heat of the shop it gave me a horrible headache that lasted all night long.

Mike had told his mother, who still lived in Quincy, that he met me. She had been in high school with my father. She said she remembered him getting in trouble because he had a petition or something about some "Negro" kids who were arrested and were facing the death penalty in the South. This must have been the Scottsboro Boys case, involving a group of young African American boys who had been riding the rails looking for work in the midst of the Depression, the early 1930s. Two young white women were also riding the rails. They were all arrested, and the police charged the young men with raping the young women. One of the young women later recanted her testimony and said the police had forced her to say that. I told my father about this, but he didn't remember getting in trouble for that. He was in the Young Communist League as a boy.

A couple of months, maybe more, after I started working there, people began talking about not knowing what was going on with contract negotiations. The union contract was due to expire, and negotiations were being conducted in secret. The president of the Local was George, who worked in the Banburry department. I suggested we start a petition to the Union demanding a meeting to let the members know what was going on. This was widely agreed to, and we wrote up a petition and started circulating it. Many workers signed it. This type of action was in line with the policy of the Communist Party at that time. The late 1960s and 1970s were a time of great upheaval in the labor movement. Many unions were run top down, with little or no democracy. Many unions failed to represent women and African Americans. Young men were returning from the war in Vietnam and were in no mood to be pushed around at work.

There was a national movement of rank-and-file workers committees that had been organized in many unions to force changes and make the unions more militant and democratic. I read the newspaper of that movement, *Labor Today,* whenever it came out. One book by a CP leader stuck with me: *Rebellion in the Unions: A Hand-Book for Rank and File Action,* by George Morris. What resonated with me, being a young antiwar, antiracist radical, was its analysis of the current AFL-CIO. George pointed out the very conservative political nature of George Meany, the AFL-CIO president, who boasted that he had never been on strike and supported political conservatives. The book exposed the AFL-CIO International Affairs Department for its ties to the CIA and the help it gave the CIA in destroying left-wing unions in other countries. The book also discussed racism in the labor movement and the lack of democracy in most unions. It called for the formation of rank-and-file movements of workers within their unions to fight for militant, democratic unionism. George explained the need for a labor party based in the unions' membership, which would be democratic and militant. This call for militant action, for democratic unionism, struck a chord in me. How could we get to socialism if the working class wasn't organized into militant, democratic unions that the members ran?

Looking back at this book, I now also see some things I disagree with. While calling for a labor party, it argued, together with others on the Left, that organizing against the "Right" was the main tactical course that socialists should follow. This led the Party to continually see the Democratic Party as a party that could be won over to being "Left," despite it being dependent on corporate money. In the late 1980s and 1990s, when there was actual work being done to organize a Labor Party, the Communist Party opposed it. One of the reasons I left the CP in 1990 was its hostility to forces trying to organize political parties to the left of the Democratic Party. Another reason for leaving was the Party's total abandonment of the fight within unions for union democracy and militancy.

The Communist Party, along with other socialist organizations, had a policy of "industrial concentration." That meant that it was important to build the CP amongst workers in what were called "basic industries," that is, industries that created profits and that were the backbone of manufacturing in this country. These industries included auto, steel, electrical, transportation, shipping, and rubber, among others. Other sectors of the economy such as education, health care, public works and civil service, and the service industries, were not considered as important, even though there were many Communists who worked in them.

This led to many debates. In the Boston area, some people pointed out that the hospital sector, together with education, employed many more workers than manufacturing did. In many places the racial make-up of hospital workers was more diverse, with more African American workers than in basic manufacturing. So shouldn't our industrial concentration policy be the hospital industry? The argument to counter that was that hospitals were mainly nonprofit (at that time) and didn't produce surplus value (profits), so striking hospitals would not hurt the ruling class as much as striking manufacturing concerns such as General Electric, which was the largest employer in Massachusetts. Eventually, in Massachusetts the CP came to endorse both electrical manufacturing and hospitals as our industrial concentration.

I once tried to figure out where this policy originated and what role "industrial concentration" would actually play in the struggle for socialism. I didn't find many clear explanations in any CP literature, even looking at older material from the 1930s and 1940s. What was clearer is that this idea of identifying "key" industries came out of a time when manufacturing was the dominant sector of the economy. Sure, there were restaurant workers, teachers, and nurses, but manufacturing was king. Factories of the largest corporations employed tens of thousands of workers in one place. When a General Motors plant was shut down due to a strike, the whole local economy was affected. When workers won extra holidays from General Electric, many of the small manufacturing companies followed suit and so did many nonmanufacturing employers. So, one could see that, especially in the struggle for reforms, basing a political party in the manufacturing workplaces of the biggest corporations that ran the country made absolute sense. The industrial concentration policy also fit in well with a hierarchical approach to making socialism. The Communist Party was the vanguard of the industrial working class. The industrial proletariat was the vanguard of the entire working class.

How did this fit in with making a revolution? Most revolutionary theory that dismissed the idea that we could vote in socialism harkened back to the concept of the mass strike. All workers would go on strike and bring the country to a standstill; we would then storm the political centers and take power, much in the same way the Bolsheviks did in 1917. Of course, this theory came about when manufacturing was the majority of the working class. Recently I read transcripts of the Comintern debates in the 1920s, which advocate "industrial concentration" policies reflecting such lines of thinking.

By the 1970s and especially the 1980s, the landscape was changing. Manufacturing was still important, but corporations were moving work out of the United States. Imperialism was changing from mainly exploiting resources of other countries to also exploiting workers in other countries, on a massive scale. In the United States, the service and public sectors are huge, vastly outnumbering manufacturing in numbers of workers.

If we think that transformation to a socialist society (however that comes about) requires the support of the majority of workers, then "industrial concentration" is not as key a policy as it once was. If we reject the hierarchical approach to building socialism, then we see that organizing the majority of workers is key to making a transformation to socialism.

Back to Paragon Rubber

Within two days of circulating the petition, a notice was hung up that announced a membership meeting was to be held the next day at the town hall in Easthampton, Massachusetts, where we would vote on the contract. The next day we all went to the town hall before work started. The first shift left work early. We sat in the auditorium and George introduced the IUE organizer. He then said he would read a list of the changes to the contract and that there could be no changes to that list. He then very quickly read through the items; immediately upon finishing he said, "Everyone who wants to vote no and go on strike and lose your jobs go stand against the wall, everyone in favor of accepting the contract stay seated, the yes votes win. The contract is accepted." Then he left. We were all shocked. It happened so fast that no one had time to react or think about what was on the list. We then went back to work. People weren't even sure if we had gotten a pay raise.

A couple of weeks later there was an announcement that there would be a union meeting in the shop to elect the union officers. This was a yearly event. A bunch of us went to the meeting. Out of the 150 members of the local, about twenty showed up. When it came time to nominate and elect someone to be chief steward (the person who handled member grievances against the company), I was nominated and elected. The fellow who nominated me was a UMass English student who was working his way through college. He had seen me collecting signatures to put the Communist Party candidate on the ballot for the presidential elections, so he knew my politics. We used to argue about Ezra Pound, the poet. He loved his poetry even though Pound had sided with the Italian Fascists during World War II. I was aghast that he could like poetry by a fascist. He basically nominated me to piss off the union leadership, but other people voted for me because I had started the petition around negotiations.

I must say that I had no idea what to do as chief steward, and George, the local president, was not going to help. It took me several months before I found out that I was also supposed to represent workers in the two other businesses in the building. One day one of the bosses came to me and wanted me to sign a warning the boss was going to give a worker. I asked him why he wanted me to sign the warning. He said that according to the contract (which I didn't have a copy of) the chief steward had to authorize all warnings given to workers by the company. I didn't know much, but I knew that I wasn't going to sign warnings given to workers, so I refused to sign it. He got mad and left. Other workers told me I did good by not signing it. So, from then on, I refused to sign any warnings.

Most of the time things were quiet at work. The company was owned by a Jewish fellow from New York. About every couple of months, he would come to Easthampton and wander around the factory. Often times he would loan workers money, and then the company would deduct ten dollars per week out of your paycheck to pay him back. While I was there, a new hire asked him for a loan of several hundred dollars and then never came back to work. People figured that he must have heard the boss was an easy touch and got hired just to get the money. After that, the owner stopped lending money.

On second shift there was one young worker who was a speed (amphetamine) addict. He would shoot up at the beginning of his shift and work a hundred miles per hour while he was high. He was always getting arrested for stealing stuff to pay for his habit. Mostly he robbed the gas station he lived next door to, so the police knew where to find him. He was basically on parole to the company. He worked weekdays and then on Friday nights one of us would drive him to the jail in Northampton, drop him off, and he would serve his sentence in jail for the weekend.

All in all, Paragon Rubber was a pretty bad and unhealthy place to work, but the pay wasn't bad for basically unskilled work. The idea that workers were entitled to a healthy workplace had not occurred to us yet, so we put up with the bad conditions.

While working there I was introduced to Leon Massa, the business agent for a UE local in neighboring Holyoke. I was introduced to him by Harold Williams. Harold was an African American worker who worked at Monsanto Chemical Company in Springfield, Massachusetts, and he was a member of the Communist Party. He had been a member of the United Electrical, Radio and Machine Workers of America (UE) when UE represented the workers at Monsanto. UE was an original CIO union, the second largest, but during the McCarthy period the UE was voted out of Monsanto and the IUE became the union there. I didn't know much about the UE then, but I was soon to learn more. Harold Williams was the one who taught me. He told me how right before World War II, his older brother, also a member of the Communist Party, told him he should try to get a job at Monsanto. The pay was good, and they had a good union there. Harold didn't believe him. He told his brother that he wouldn't work the dirty jobs just because he was Black. Harold's brother assured him that the UE was different, and that Black workers had the same rights as white workers. Harold got a job there and found out it was true. Harold's brother had worked at Fisk Rubber Company in Chicopee, Massachusetts, home to a very militant local of the United Rubber Workers Union. They went on strike every contract, until the plant closed in the 1980s.

If you worked at Fisk Rubber, you had to have a savings account that you put money into every week. The Union checked on this. The purpose was to make sure each worker had their own strike fund, since every two or three years there was a strike. Another member of the Party also worked there, Al Thiemy, a German American. He had the honor of having two lockers, one for his clothes and one for his "library," where he kept Communist literature. Every worker was free to stop by and borrow something to read. The company had tried to shut down the library, but the union defended Al having two lockers.

Leon Massa had been active in the labor movement in Western Massachusetts since the mid-1920s, when he had been an organizer for the Trade Union Unity League, a left-wing union formation. He was the business agent of UE Local 259 in Holyoke, which basically represented workers at Worthington Compressor Company. One day Leon called me up and said he wanted me to meet a fellow at a bar in Holyoke after work one night. The fellow I was to meet, Ed H., worked second shift at Worthington Pump. I was to bring him some pamphlets from the Communist Party. I was a little nervous but didn't want to refuse Leon's request, so at 11:30 one night after work, I drove to the bar in Holyoke, went in, and soon met Ed. It turned out Ed had worked at Millers Falls Tool in Greenfield, helping to organize it, and then was on UE staff for several years. He then got a job at Worthington. He was enthusiastic about the pamphlets and took them to show some other workers.

I wrote earlier about the effect CP literature had on me concerning the trade union movement. I must say that, over time, the contact and discussions with the older comrades I met in the labor movement were what had the most effect. Harold Williams taught me a lot about being militant but not obnoxious at work. His stories of dealing with racism had a big impact. We used to have CP meetings every two weeks, so I got to see Harold and his wife Becky a lot. Leon Massa taught me a lot about how to handle grievances and build a fighting union. He knew the history of union organizing in every workplace in Western Massachusetts, going back to the 1920s. Leon had been expelled from the CP in 1956 for "economism," which turned out to mean he refused to break up the UE in 1956 and take the workers into the "mainstream" AFL-CIO unions. Despite that, he continued to be a Communist. Many of the old-time activists in UE were like Leon. They had been in the CP and were kicked out in 1956 but still believed in the need for a CP and promoted it, even if they didn't pay dues. It was from these people, like Don Tormey, a UE international representative, that I learned how to work in the labor movement and be a Communist. At times, their advice clashed with directives we got from the CP, and in time I came to realize that people like Don, Leon, and Harold were almost always right.

One of the things all the old-timers stressed was that as an elected officer of a union local, you had to maintain support from the membership and not use your elected position to advocate for something that had no support among the workers. What this meant was that if I, as president of my union local, wanted to endorse something political, I shouldn't do that without educating the membership why it was important and getting their support. Too often as a local union president, I would be asked by various groups or the CP to endorse some organization or struggle. They just wanted my name on a paper, showing the cause had support.

Here's how that got me into trouble once. I was president of the UE local at my shop, Holyoke Wire and Cable. There was a national campaign going on to support Rev. Ben Chavis, an African American minister who, along with some other activists in North Carolina, was facing a prison sentence for allegedly burning down a horse stable that refused to rent horses to African Americans. The CP was active in this campaign through the National Alliance against Racist and Political Repression (NAARPR), a group that was formed after the campaign to free Angela Davis was won. Another comrade in Springfield was active in the alliance. He asked me to endorse the campaign. I said that I would have to get the local membership to vote on it. He kept pressuring me and he explained that he was being pressured by the Party in New York. They started saying that it was racist for me not to endorse the campaign. Under this pressure, I decided to call a special union meeting to discuss the campaign around Rev. Chavis. I didn't consult with the other elected union officers or anyone else in the factory. The night of the meeting came, and no one showed up! The union was new in the shop (more on that later), and never had there been a union meeting without a good turnout. I felt horrible and knew I had screwed up big time.

The next morning I went to work, and a member came up to me. She had not voted for the union during the election and was a member of the John Birch Society. She asked me how the meeting went last night. I said not good. To that she replied, "Don't use the union to promote your own personal beliefs." No one else said anything to me about it. I realized that I should not have given into the pressure from the Party in New York; they didn't understand or care about union democracy or doing work that would help workers grow politically, they just wanted names on paper. I then started talking to the members of the union who I knew would be interested in the situation of Ben Chavis. I gave people some literature about the case. After about two months I knew there was enough support to bring it up at a regular local union meeting and ask for a resolution endorsing the campaign. It easily passed at the next meeting. The campaign around Ben Chavis was good to be involved in, I just had to work on it the right way, which may have been slower but got better results in the end.

By the end of the summer 1973 I was ready to quit Paragon Rubber. It was a small shop and I felt I could be more effective working in a larger shop. I left in late July and attended the World Youth Festival in Berlin, the German Democratic Republic. When I returned, I had to find a job. Leon Massa called me and said that the UE had recently lost a union election at a factory. He heard I was looking for work and asked if I would try to get a job at Holyoke Wire and Cable Company. It was owned by TRW Corporation, which at that time was among the fifty biggest corporations in the US. The factory had moved from the inner city of Holyoke to South Hadley, out in an industrial park where no people lived. This was a major trend with corporations in the 1960s and 1970s. They were moving out of cities that had growing populations of minority workers to industrial parks in basically all-white small towns.

I applied for a job there and got one. I was lucky. I had gone with another comrade and noticed that the secretary who was taking job applications was telling everyone that there were no openings, even though they had an ad in the paper. I noticed a man going in and out of an office, and when he came by, I jumped up and gave him the application and a pitch on why I needed a job. He turned out to be the personnel manager, and he hired me. Later, he told me that was the biggest mistake of his career.

TRW Holyoke Wire and Cable had about 450 workers at that time. A very large proportion of them were Polish who didn't speak English. There was a smaller group of African American women and some Puerto Rican workers also. Many of the other workers were of French-Canadian descent. That makeup was pretty reflective of the city of Holyoke. The other interesting point was that there was a union at the shop. It was an independent union (that is, it didn't belong to any national union) called the Holyoke Wire and Cable Employees Association (the Association), and it was basically controlled by the company. I later found out that TRW had such arrangements in many of its shops. There was a signed contract and the union had a lawyer who represented it.

The job I got was in the bare-wire department. Here, wire was made that would later be used in various products the company produced for other companies. We made the wiring systems for Ford cars, before circuit boards replaced them. In the bare-wire department, my job was to take bare copper wire of various gauges, and run the wire through a trough of liquid tin, through dies, and produce a copper wire that was smooth and tin-coated. Of course it was extremely hot working over liquid tin. The entire department was very hot, and there were no windows or air conditioning. Most of the workers were young men, Black, white, and Puerto Rican, and we all got along extremely well. We had to help each other, because some of the reels of wire that had to be put on and taken off machines weighed four hundred to five hundred pounds. The foreman was of course a jerk, who yelled at us if we sat down for a rest, even if our machines were running.

The heat was the worst part of the job. One day, a couple of months after I started working, it was very hot, and everyone was mad about the heat. I suggested that we stop work and demand the company do something about it. Everyone agreed, and we told the boss we wanted something done about the heat, and we would be in the warehouse waiting for an answer. Pretty quick the personnel manager, Bill Bernstein, was there, yelling at us to get back to work. We refused, and I told him what we wanted. He then agreed that the company's "safety expert" would come down, check the temperature and then figure out what to do. We agreed to that and went back to work. Soon the safety guy, Fred, came into the bare-wire department with a thermometer and a note pad. He started taking the temperature and writing it down for various parts of the room, then he left. We noticed that he only wrote down the temperature from areas of the room that were the farthest away from the machines. No one ever stood in the corners!

Soon he came back with Bill the personnel manager and announced the temperatures and said they were not too hot to work in. We objected and demanded he stand next to the tin pots and take the temperature. He did and of course it registered thirty degrees higher than he had reported. We said we would stop work again if something wasn't done. Bill then relented and said that he would have the maintenance department put in windows and bring fans into the room. We won. Shortly after that, the president of the Association came and told me that I was now the union steward for the bare-wire department. Of course, there was no election, but I figured being steward would give me some cover to raise hell. One of the workers told me that the company preferred that their foremen or forewomen first served as union stewards or officers. It created the atmosphere of cooperation. So, I knew that I had to be careful so that people wouldn't think I was just some guy on the make for a foreman's job.

Party School

I received a call from the district organizer (DO) of the Communist Party. He told me I was selected to attend a Party school that would be held in Toronto, Canada. I believe it was to run six weeks. The DO was Ed Teixeira (Tex), an old friend of my father's. Ed was of Cape Verdean descent and had been active in Boston in the struggle to desegregate the school system. I felt I couldn't refuse. This put me in a tough situation, I felt very bad about quitting Holyoke Wire and Cable and leaving the union organizing.

My instructions were to fly to Toronto, not to bring money with me, and I would be met at the airport by Canadian comrades. It was quite the adventure. I landed in Toronto, met my contacts, and was taken to the home I would stay in. They told me that since I was a hippie (I had shaved my beard, but had a mustache and longish hair) I would be staying with an old Canadian hippie. He turned out to be an older Jewish cartoonist who did cartoons for the Canadian Communist Party newspaper and had a younger wife and two young daughters. They were very welcoming. He had an older son who was part of a very well-known folk-rock band in the United States.

The school was held in the basement of a restaurant in Toronto, the owner being a "sympathizer" of the CP. There were maybe twenty-five "students." The lectures were given by leaders in both the US and Canadian parties. There were of course differences in the approaches of the two parties, and one problem of the school was that once differences appeared, they were generally ignored and not discussed. For example, in the Canadian labor movement many Communists were open about their membership in the Party and they didn't understand why that wasn't true in the United States. They disagreed with our focus on overthrowing "leadership" in US unions, and for our part, we thought they must be sellouts, because they didn't emphasize democracy and militancy in unions. After those differences came up, we just never talked about the labor movement again. There were also problems around the question of fighting racism, which was central to our thinking but less so for the Canadians, who did not have the same history.

For whatever reason, we had been told not to bring much money. Those of us who smoked were soon broke and desperate. We had a meeting with the organizers and demanded an allowance, which we finally got. The other problem was that the restaurant owner, who provided us with lunch and dinner, was only feeding us potato and pasta dishes — nary a vegetable in sight. After several weeks everyone was feeling ill and had gained a lot of weight. Again, we had a meeting with the school organizers and demanded a better diet, which we sort of got. By the end of the six weeks, people were being approached and questioned on the street by Canadian plainclothes police. All day long there were men sitting in the restaurant drinking coffee and staring at us as we came in and went into the basement.

Did I learn anything? I think I learned some things, but a lot of the economics and philosophy were still a mystery to me. I was glad to go home. I returned home broke and in need of a job. I went back to Holyoke Wire and Cable and begged for my job back. After a couple of weeks, they said they needed someone as a machine set-up person in one of the departments that assembled wire harnesses. Actually, this would be better for me, as I would now be out in the main production area and working with the women who made up the majority of the workers. Much to my surprise I was hired back. It was early 1973, and the UE was ready to get deeper into the organizing drive.

Soon after I was rehired at the shop, I received a call from someone in the Party who told me I owed Teixeira an apology. I asked why. They said I was supposed to have reported back to him immediately upon my return from Party school and then taken a position as a full-timer for the YWLL. I said that someone should have told me about reporting to Tex, and I was never talked to by anyone about working full time for the YWLL or the CP. I said that I was back to work and engaged in a union drive and I was going to stay there. They were disappointed.

At work I began to meet some of the women involved in the previous union drive. One woman, Stella, was very important.

She was in her fifties (I was 22 at the time) and spoke fluent Polish, which was key. We became friendly and worked well together. She eventually became the chief steward for the union.

Slowly we began to put together a good group of workers, young and old, English and non-English speaking, Black and white. Our big weakness was with the older male workers, mainly in the extruding department. Men my age were very supportive. One day I was informed that I was now the vice president of the Association. The former vice president had been promoted to foreman. After talking it over with union supporters in the shop and with the UE staff people, it was decided that I should keep the position for now. It gave me reasons to get around the shop and talk to people about their problems. There was a grievance procedure, and I made sure to use it. The company was in a fix. They didn't like solving grievances to the workers' satisfaction, but if they didn't, they were afraid the UE would use that as evidence that the company union was no good. Not all the other officers of the company union were openly "pro-company," they were just afraid to fight the company and were used to taking their lead on what to do from the "union" lawyer, who I had no doubt was in contact with the TRW corporation. He had quite a little business going. If we called him, he charged fifty dollars. If he came to the shop for a grievance or to meet with the company, it was one hundred dollars. For 1973, that wasn't bad money. Often times he would call the union and charge them fifty dollars. It turns out that he "represented" many other company unions in the area.

As our strength grew in the shop, we, the UE, tried several different tactics. One was to win over the other leaders of the Association to join in the move to get UE representation. That didn't work, and some of them grew more hostile to me. We went to the Association meetings and voted that the Association affiliate with the UE. They ignored that. One day I was called out to the cafeteria. There were the rest of the officers of the company union along with the union lawyer. I sat down and right away he began accusing me of violating my "fiduciary responsibility" to the Association and declared that if I didn't resign or stop organizing for UE I would be fined and jailed. He read from something he said was the law. I vigorously denied violating my fiduciary responsibilities and refused to resign as vice president or stop organizing for UE. After a while I demanded my right to make a phone call. I called the UE office and talked to Amy Newell, a UE field organizer from California who was working on this, her first organizing drive as a UE staff person. Amy went on to become the first woman UE national officer. I told her what was happening and then asked what "fiduciary" meant. I had no idea. She explained what it meant and told me to keep telling them to go to hell. I did that, and soon the meeting ended. I didn't hear any more about the matter. UE supporters were now acting out in the open. We were passing out UE leaflets in the shop. TRW Corporation was clearly getting worried.

Here's how the Association acted. One day, the company called a meeting with the union officers. They told us that they were hearing workers complaining about the pay. We still had five months or so to go until the contract expired. The personnel manager said that the company would be willing to think about giving workers an early raise if the Association asked for it. Clearly the company thought by giving an early raise it would kill the union drive, but since they had a contract with the Association, they could not just give a raise. The union had to ask for it and pretend to bargain for it. The other officers didn't get what the company wanted them to do. The personnel manager, Bill Bernstein, kept repeating himself and was getting frustrated, and I was laughing. Finally, Bill spurted out, "Just ask me for a goddamn raise." Finally, one of the officers got it and said, "Could we please get an early raise?" Bill responded, "Yes, we will give everybody a ten-cent raise." He left to post a notice to that effect, and the meeting was over.

I told Amy what happened, and she wrote up a leaflet saying ten cents wasn't enough and pointed out what happened at the meeting. The shop was in an uproar, with most people, even those who were opposed to joining the UE, mad about getting just ten cents. I was amazed that the company had conducted themselves the way they did with me being there. They should have known I would tell people how the ten cents came about.

A little while later, I was asked by the company to drive to Vermont to pick up some parts they needed for a machine. I agreed, as it was nice out, I'd never been to that part of Vermont before, and it would be a day away from work. I drove up to the place and picked up the part. I didn't have any money, so I had to borrow money from the boss at the Vermont factory to buy gas and lunch. I told him to add it to TRW's bill. Of course I got home too late to go back to work.

When I got to work the next morning, all hell had broken loose. People were asking what we were going to do. It took me awhile to find out what had happened. While I was gone from the shop, the company union officers had got together with their lawyer, all this at work, while being paid by the company. They decided to remove me as vice president of the union. They posted a notice saying I had been removed for being disloyal and supporting the UE. A group of us went to them and demanded an explanation, which they were very confused about, and they had a tough time explaining their actions. This only confirmed to us that the company was directing their actions.

The response of the workers was outrage. One of the former heads of the Association, an older woman named Jenny, started a petition to have me reinstated as VP. The overwhelming majority of the shop signed it. It was a funny position to be in. Many anti-UE people, like Jenny, wanted myself and other UE supporters to run the company union. They felt we would fight for them, but also, they wouldn't have to join an "outside union," which they were afraid of. We had to double our work in explaining that in the UE, the shop members ran the union, not the staff or other outsiders. We also had to explain the benefits of belonging to a national union, the support we would get from other workers and the help in negotiating our contract from the UE staff.

The Association refused to reinstate me as VP. We also took this opportunity to explain that in the UE officers and stewards were elected, and in the case of vacancies there would be an election to fill the opening. (Officers were elected in the Association, but vacancies were filled by appointment and stewards were appointed). This issue came up again, as the Association scheduled officer elections. The UE folks were under pressure from workers to run for the positions in the company union. We finally agreed to do so but explained that we were still for joining the UE. We put together a slate, with myself running for president, Stella running for chief steward, Rosa, an African American woman, running for secretary-treasurer, I believe, and one or two others. The election was held, and we won. Now we had a big problem. It was finally decided that we would refuse to take our offices and urge everyone to vote for UE. It was around this time that we filed with the National Labor Relations Board for an election. It was confusing to some people as to why we didn't take over the company union, and especially to those who felt that that was the way to avoid having to join UE.

The company and the Association ran a standard campaign against the UE: "They won't be able to get you anything more than the Association." "If you join UE there will be a strike." "UE dues are too expensive." Later on, after we won, I found out that there was a vicious underground campaign directed at the Polish workers concerning me. The basic pitch was that I was a Jewish Communist, and did they want a Jew to run their union? It basically relied on the anti-Semitism that was prevalent in Poland and therefore assumed present among the workers. At times I thought something was up as a few Polish workers made remarks to me that even though I was a Jew, I was their Jew, and they knew I would stick up for them. I remember one young woman of Polish descent telling me that in her Polish Catholic church (in Holyoke there were two Catholic churches, the Polish and the French-Canadian), the priest told them that if they could bring an African American (I'm sure that was not the language he used) to church they would have two venial sins removed. If they could bring a Jew into church, they would have five venial sins removed.

The election between the UE and the Association was scheduled for December, right before the shop normally shut down for the Christmas holiday. There were anti-UE posters throughout the shop and we passed out leaflets every day. One thing we did throughout the campaign was to fight hard over grievances workers had. This showed workers that the UE would be a fighting union that they were part of, not a do-nothing outfit like the Association.

Two weeks before the election, as we came to work one morning there were a bunch of television news crews outside the factory, and Bill Bernstein was giving a speech. It turned out that he was announcing that due to the slowness of the economy, the entire factory was to be closed and employees laid off, and they were not sure it would reopen. This was meant to be the final threat to workers: If you vote UE you will lose your jobs. Again, we put out a short leaflet at lunch time demanding that the company pay the workers through the New Year and demanding a guarantee that everyone would be recalled to work. That went over big.

Election day came and of course we were very nervous. The NLRB agent in charge of the election met with the UE committee and staff, the Association officers, and TRW bosses and went over the rules for the election. At one point he demanded that all UE people take off their "Vote UE" tee shirts. This was to ensure there was no "electioneering" near the polls in the cafeteria. We pointed out that outside the cafeteria the company had huge anti-UE posters posted, but that was ok with the NLRB agent. Again, he demanded we take off our UE shirts. One woman said ok and pulled off her tee shirt. There she stood in her bra. The NLRB agent almost fainted and quickly said we could wear our shirts. Direct action wins again.

The election took all day, and when the votes were counted, we had won, by about sixty votes out of 450. The next day at work, everyone's last before the layoff, no one worked. We drank and celebrated, while the Association folks drank and felt bad. We went out of our way to be friendly to them and say that we had to work together. A few days after Christmas the company announced that everyone would be recalled to work. Now we had to begin to negotiate a new union contract.

We achieved our first contract after six months, in June 1975. In September I went to my first UE convention. In 1976 I was elected president of UE Local 259, an amalgamated local that covered eight or nine shops. In 1978, I became a UE field organizer.

Some Thoughts on Work in the Labor Movement as a Socialist

One question that was raised at times is whether working in the labor movement is "Communist work," that is, whether we were doing anything that would help make a socialist revolution. Gus Hall, chairman of the CP, oftentimes said that people who spent their life working in the labor movement wasted their lives. The only way to really be a Communist was to work for the CP. He said that to my wife and me when he was trying to recruit us to work full time for the CP in 1987. He publicly said that about a longtime steel worker who was known as a Communist and who had played a major role in fighting racism in the steel workers union. I disagreed with that sectarian approach, and so did the old-timers I talked with, and so did the many other Communists who were my age and active in the labor movement.

When I was younger, and learning about Marxism, we were taught some very rigid ideas. Society progressed in stages, from barbarism, to primitive communism, to feudalism, to capitalism, to socialism, and finally to Communism. It was inevitable. Marxism was a science, and this was the way society worked. Of course, Marx and Engels would not have agreed with this crass interpretation of how they viewed human history.

As I got older, I began to realize that humans make human history, and if we want to build a new society that eliminates exploitation in all forms and allows every human to develop to their fullest, then humans must consciously do this. In our country the working class — in all its variations of race, color, nationality, language, sexual orientation, age, religion — is the class that has the most reason to build a new, better society. But it isn't inevitable that it will happen. Recognizing this means that the work we do to broaden workers' thinking about how our capitalist system works, how racism and other bigotry divides us, is important work. Building democratic unions that the workers themselves run is important because we need to learn how to run society in a new manner — collectively, honestly, compassionately. We also need to learn that there is not one special group of people who will run society for us; the entire working class must be involved. As Marxists, we learn from history, and recent history has shown us that a hierarchical approach to socialism — "The Party is the leader and the rest should follow orders" — failed miserably in the Soviet Union and Eastern Europe. Now is the time for new approaches.

Our job was to talk to people about this, about how to fight day-to-day against the boss, and also to talk about the bigger picture of how capitalism works and to talk about socialism. Did I do this perfectly all the time? Of course not. At times, the day-to-day work of fighting the boss overwhelmed the other "work." Following are some incidents that made this concept of changing how people think clearer to me.

Four or five years after our first contract at TRW Holyoke Wire and Cable, the company began announcing the movement of work out of our factory to different locations around the world. They were among the early companies that moved work to along the Mexico–US border. Work was also moved to Taiwan and Brazil (the latter under a military dictatorship at that time). A TRW VP came to the shop to meet with the union. He went into a long explanation of how the movement of work to Taiwan would benefit TRW. It meant the loss of work to about 150 women in our shop. He pointed out that in Taiwan the woman there would be paid five cents per hour. In our shop, women were making maybe five dollars an hour, which, while still not great, was a huge increase over the wages being paid before we joined UE. He asked for comments. Stella, the chief steward remarked something like this: "So, I'm going to lose my job, when after thirty years I'm finally making good money and benefits. Some poor woman in Taiwan is going to do my job but only be paid five cents per hour, and I'm supposed to feel good about all the extra profits TRW will make?" The boss stared at her and finally said, "I guess you're just not smart enough to see the big picture." We yelled at the boss and the negotiations ended for the day.

Stella understood the big picture. She understood what corporations did to people, she understood solidarity among workers and that our enemy was not the women workers in Taiwan but TRW. I liked to think I had something to do with that.

Or another example: After a tough negotiation and fight at one factory, especially over health insurance, the members voted in favor of the contract. We were all sitting around having a beer when I began to talk to one worker. I'd known him a long time and always thought he leaned to being politically conservative. We were talking and he said that he thought we were right when we said we needed national health care, that health care was a right of all people. He then went on to say he thought all necessities of life should be guaranteed to everyone and no business should be allowed to profit off of them. I asked what he meant, and he said…housing, food, transportation, health care, retirement. Years of talking about things like this seemed to pay off in the end.

I remember a union meeting we had when my shop was shutting down. It was a large meeting. One fellow who had always opposed the union — he had been an officer in the Association — stood up and asked me why this was happening. I felt a little overwhelmed, because I was still young, most of the people in the room were more than twice my age, and I knew they would have trouble finding work. I talked for about fifteen minutes about how corporations worked, about the difference between democracy and capitalism and how we needed something better than we had. He politely thanked me, and the meeting continued on. No one was upset that I was against capitalism.

Some twenty years later I was part of a warm-up act of speakers at a rally for Ralph Nader, who was beginning his run for president. I gave a little talk, and when I finished an older man stood up, thanked me, and asked if I recognized him. It took me a minute, but I did: His name was Clyde and he had been a union steward in my shop. He explained that after the shop closed, he went through a rough time, couldn't get a job, began drinking, and his marriage broke up. A familiar story around plant closings. It took him a while, but he got his act back together. He said he came to this rally, not knowing I would be there, but because he remembered that I had told him that workers had to be political, that what we won on the shop floor could be taken away from us by politicians. He thought Ralph Nader wouldn't be taking things away from workers.

Clyde was older than I was and had been active in organizing the union at Holyoke Wire and Cable. One time someone was writing racist slogans in one of the men's bathrooms. We figured out who it was. I got a group of white men together, Clyde being one of them, and we went to confront the racist guy. He was shocked that white men were telling him he was wrong, and not just me (because I was Jewish). It was "regular" white guys who were telling him to knock it off. It felt good that they got the idea that racism was wrong.

I think of other accomplishments. In 1984 Jesse Jackson began a run for the presidency, only the second African American to do so. Judy and I lived in Greenfield, Massachusetts, a UE stronghold in the western part of the state. Franklin County, where Greenfield was situated, was essentially an all-white rural community that also had some factories. The early 1980s was a time of intense struggle. Factories were shutting down or being sold. Major corporations that had bought basic manufacturing companies in the 1960s and 1970s were either moving them down South or to Mexico. Many were being sold to investment companies via "leveraged buyouts," that is, the purchasing companies had to borrow the entire cost at high interest rates. To pay these loans off, they tried to break the unions and cut wages and benefits. The major corporations had failed to make investments for many years in these businesses, so they were at a big disadvantage. Ronald Reagan had launched his Strategic Defense Initiative, commonly called Star Wars, and contracted companies were guaranteed 20 percent profit, so many sold or closed their unrelated manufacturing plants, where 5–7 percent profit had been considered good.

In this context, we thought it would be good to promote Jesse Jackson's primary campaign for the Democratic Party nomination. We were not supporters of the Democratic Party. We had a group of UE members and also members from the railroad unions that had been on strike. Jackson had supported railroad workers and paper workers who had been on strike in Maine. We contacted the Jackson campaign in Massachusetts, but they said it was a waste of time to run a campaign for Jesse in an all-white area. They were only going to run a campaign in the all African American districts in Boston and Springfield. We felt, because of all the work we had done over the years, that white workers would support an African American candidate. We didn't want to give in to racism. So, our small group put together our own leaflets and passed them out at worksites and at supermarkets. They were not just "vote for Jessie" leaflets. They explained his positions, which were very progressive. When the Democratic primary was held, Jackson won in Franklin County! He also won in the Roxbury section of Boston. While some leftists refused to have anything to do with the Democrats, we felt that an opportunity to fight racism was too important to pass up. This we had learned from the Communist Party.

The other issue we worked hard on over the years was the concept of single-payer health insurance — basically, a Canadian-style national health care system that removed insurance companies from the picture. In the late 1980s two doctors, Steffi Woolhandler and David Himmelstein wrote an article explaining how the Canadian system worked and advocating a similar system in the United States.[3] The UE had long supported the concept of national health care, so now there was a new way to promote and fight for it.

We also viewed this fight as an important step in the fight for socialism. Making ideas that are fundamental to socialism

---

3 David U. Himmelstein and Steffie Woolhandler, "A National Health Program for the United States," *The New England Journal of Medicine* 320, no. 2 (1989): 102–8.

become predominant among workers is an important part of the struggle for socialism. Making the idea that basic human needs should not be a vehicle for profit and promoting a way to eliminate capitalism (insurance companies) from health care, by adopting a single-payer system, was an important arena of struggle. In the UE we began to use the idea in campaigns to organize nonunion workers. As we and other unions attempted to build a Labor Party (something the CP and other Left groups opposed), fighting for single-payer insurance became a key demand.

Judy and I came up with the idea to put the idea of single-payer health insurance on the ballot, in the form of a nonbinding referendum question, something that the Massachusetts laws allowed. It became a Labor Party project. In Franklin County we put in a lot of work explaining what this idea meant. In November, the single-payer question won, getting about 65 percent of the vote. In subsequent years we won by even higher margins.

In the early 1990s, I left the CP, along with many other people. For me, the Party had become a non-Marxist cult around Gus Hall. He and his cronies had dismantled all work in the labor movement and refused to help organize the fight against corporations demanding concessions. I attended the CP convention in Cleveland where we tried to "reform" the Party, but to no avail. One incident was indicative to me of where the Party was headed. Many other Left groups were passing out literature outside the convention hall. One young man made a proposal to the convention that no one should read any literature that they were handed unless Gus Hall said it was all right to read it. This resolution passed. To me, this codified the CP as a caricature of Communists as created by J. Edgar Hoover — people too stupid to think for themselves, who had to be told what they could and could not read. It was a shame.

I remain a socialist, committed to fight on issues, to learn the lessons of the past and to find new ways and forms to create a socialist country and world.

9

CPUSA Trade-Union Club in Health Care, 1970s–1992

Marilyn Albert[1]

I am sixty-nine years old and a retired registered nurse with forty-five years of experience as a health-care worker. I was born in Cleveland, Ohio, to parents who belonged to the Communist Party USA (CPUSA) and who were both called before the House Un-American Activities Committee (HUAC) in the 1950s. Following this, employment for my parents became difficult, and we moved to Los Angeles in the late fifties. My parents began their political lives anew as civil rights and antiwar activists and as leaders in the progressive movement in California, in which they were very influential.

I was an antiwar activist from my teenage years until the end of the war in Vietnam. I joined the women's movement in 1969 in New York City but grew increasingly attracted to the Communist Party and Young Workers Liberation League (YWLL), the Party's youth division. At that time, many Party young people were either workers or made a choice to become workers in key industries, including the health-care industry. I became a hospital nurse and remained one for almost forty years.

1 Originally written August 2015; edited January 2020.

It was the culture in the Communist Party to be a worker and a rank-and-file activist. Young people who joined the Party at the time that I did, did so for several reasons: the impact of the movement to free Angela Davis, the Party's focus on the centrality of fighting for the equality of the African American people, the international anti-imperialist and socialist movement, the CPUSA's role in and relationship with them, and the Party's historical role in the labor movement in the United States. No other organization offered this historical experience to young people.

Other young people on the Left who were not in the Party also made a conscious choice to join the labor movement. At that time, organized labor was largely led by conservative, white males. African Americans, Latinos, and women had to struggle to have a voice in organized labor, and in response formed organizations such as the Coalition of Black Trade Unionists and the Coalition of Labor Union Women. There were fierce struggles for democracy in some unions, such as the United Mine Workers of America, the United Steel Workers, the United Auto Workers (UAW), and the Oil, Chemical and Atomic Workers, to name a few. Politically active young people seeking to be part of the labor movement wanted to democratize the unions, unite labor with the broader social justice movements in formation, and force the unions to oppose racism and male supremacy in their policies and practices. Some young people worked their way into local and national staff or even leadership positions during the 1970s, but some consciously chose to remain rank-and-file activists.

Some of us were attracted to health care because certain unions—in particular Local 1199 in New York City—had a very progressive history. Women activists were also interested in nursing from a feminist perspective. Lastly, there was a growing movement in the late 1970s to change the US health-care system, and many young nurses, doctors, social workers, and others became involved in that.

As I gained experience as a health-care worker, I was fortunate to be a member of two CPUSA clubs, one in Boston and, later, in New York City. Rank-and-file health-care workers and staff members of Local 1199 made up both of these clubs. Local 1199 also had locals in New England, in Baltimore and Philadelphia, and in New Jersey, Ohio, and West Virginia.

Communists were active in 1199 from its birth in the 1930s, and a Communist Party club, originally based among hospital and drugstore workers, existed for decades in New York City — until the 1990s, that is, when most members of the club, if not all, left the Party and helped form the Committees of Correspondence for Democracy and Socialism. It was the collectivity of the CPUSA hospital workers' club in the city that has left a lasting impression on me and was my best experience in the Party. Whether we were health-care workers or union staff members, we worked together as equals over a period of many years. We had a huge influence in the union, particularly during a crisis period.

The authors of a book that is considered a definitive history of 1199, *Upheaval in the Quiet Zone,* venture a completely erroneous opinion about whether a CPUSA club existed during the crisis period in the union, stating that the CPUSA would have been too weak to have had such a club during that time.[2] Another book, *Working-Class New York,* has a more accurate description of the Party's role in New York unions.[3]

The club probably erred in not working to retain an organized rank-and-file group in the union after the 1986 victory of the Save Our Union movement, which removed a union president who had become corrupt. In my opinion, we should have struggled to maintain an independent rank-and-file formation in 1199, which in the late 1990s was affiliated with the Service

2 Leon Fink and Brian Greenberg, *Upheaval in the Quiet Zone: 1199SEIU and the Politics of Health Care Unionism* (University of Illinois Press, 2009).

3 Joshua B. Freeman, in *Working-Class New York: Life and Labor Since World War II* (New Press, 2000), characterizes the Save Our Union coalition as "an amalgam of Communists (at this late date New York City might have been the only place in the country where Communist Party members could influence the internal life of a union), non-Communist leftists, and longtime militants" (316).

Employees International Union (SEIU) and lost some of its militant character. Had we done so, we might have even influenced the overall character of the SEIU International, which, in my opinion, became a very problematic international union, and remains so.

When the Soviet Union and other socialist countries collapsed in 1989–1991, it provoked an internal struggle in the Party around the nature of socialism, the Party's policies regarding the fight for African American equality, internal democracy, and other important issues. The months taken up in this struggle, prior to the formation of the Committees of Correspondence in 1992, were painful, but also exciting. Our hospital workers' club, in its entirety, stood with those who were openly criticizing the Party. The circulation of a document called "The Initiative," which outlined the issues being debated and was signed in a very open way by a large group of Party members, as well as the short-lived organized debate in some Party and Committees of Correspondence publications, led in 1992 to a very painful decision for many to ultimately leave the Communist Party. This brought the long experience of a CPUSA club in health care in New York City to an end.

Now, more than twenty-five years later, it is exciting to see a new socialist movement building in the United States and across the globe. Many former Party members have become active in the new movement and the new organizations that have emerged. We bring with us valuable experiences, and we hope to be able to share them with young people, while respecting their need to gain their own experiences and develop their own practice.[4]

4 Documents related to my history in the Party and the health-care workers movement are archived at Tamiment Library of New York University.

10

From Red-Diaper Baby to Union Leadership

Paul Friedman[1]

My Roots

My mother Lisa was born in 1918 at Manhattan Lying-In Hospital on Sixteenth Street and Second Avenue. My father Bill was born in 1920 in a small town near Lviv in the Ukraine. His birth name was Velvil, which translates to "Wolf."

My maternal grandparents Ben (Benzion) and Mary (Miriam) immigrated to the United States in the early days of World War I and met in New York City. They both came from Salonika, a city in Turkey that was known as "the Jerusalem of the Balkans," where many Sephardic Jews from Spain settled after fleeing from the Spanish Inquisition of 1492. The Ottoman Empire welcomed these Spanish Jews who refused to convert to Catholicism.

My grandmother was Sephardic and her maiden name was Soulom. My grandfather, Benzion Sevy (Zvi), was Ashkenazi, and his ancestors migrated to the Ottoman Empire from Germany. He was culturally assimilated into the dominant Sephardic community of Salonika and spoke Ladino. Ladino is the language that Jews from Spain and Portugal spoke. Ladino

1 Originally written May 2020; revised August 2020.

is a mixture of early second millennial (900–1500 CE) Spanish and Hebrew.

My grandmother told her grandchildren that when she was a little girl in Salonika, she was asked by striking workers at a tobacco factory to enter the factory and find out who was still working during the strike. She was chosen because no one would suspect a young girl of being so daring.

Her mother, my great-grandmother Delicia, was the revered head of the Soulom family. Her husband died at an early age. Unlike her children, she was deeply religious and always wore black clothes as a sign of mourning. During the Armenian genocide in Turkey, Delicia hid a young Armenian boy who was being pursued by Turkish authorities. They knocked on her door and asked if she had seen him. She convinced them she hadn't seen anyone. She had hidden the boy under my grandmother's bed.

My grandfather Ben was involved as a teenage youth in the Young Turks movement in 1908, which ushered in multiparty government and eliminated the Ottoman monarchy. My paternal grandfather, Joseph (Yusel) Friedman, married Mollie Ross and had four sons and one daughter. The infant girl died in a house fire. My grandparents left the Ukraine after my father was born and immigrated to Argentina. After a few years they came to the United States and settled with other family members in Waterbury, Connecticut. Yusel was a house painter, a member of Painters Union Local 9 in New York City, and a member of Workmen's Circle.

My mother, after graduating from high school, attended Lebanon Hospital's Nursing School on the Grand Concourse in the Bronx. My dad went to Morris High School in the Bronx. In his high school years, he was initially a member of the Young People's Socialist League (YPSL). He soon left YPSL and joined the Young Communist League (YCL) because, he told me, "YPSL just talked, but the YCL acted."

My parents met in 1937, when seventeen-year-old Bill was speaking at a street-corner rally in the Hunts Point section of the Bronx. The rally was called by the YCL in support of the

Spanish Republican effort to repel the Franco Fascist uprising. My mother, who was attending nursing school at the time, was invited to the rally by her cousin Manny Harriman, who soon joined the Abraham Lincoln Brigade, US volunteers who went to Spain to defend the Republican government. Bill Friedman, who was friends with Manny from the YCL, took notice of Lisa Sevy. One year later they were married.

A Red-Diaper Baby

I was born in 1947 at Jewish Memorial Hospital in Washington Heights, Manhattan, the youngest of three children. I was a red-diaper baby.[2] My father's favorite records were songs from the Soviet Red Army. The Communist Party (CP) was an extended family to me. Picnics, vacations, concerts, and Jewish secular education were infused with warmth, friendliness, and caring. And it was all generated from "the Party." My parents' close friends were Party members. When my parents spoke of people and mentioned their Party connection, it automatically meant that they were good people — people who cared. If there was something negative that was ascribed to a Party member — "That Joe, he was a philanderer" — it was an aberration from the model. You were of the highest moral character if you were a Communist.

By the time I was four, the repressive McCarthy era was in full swing. It was a total contradiction to this young boy that Communists, such a perfect, near utopian community, could be opposed, denigrated, hated. On the one hand, my dad would ask me to go to the corner store (Newman's candy store on Colgate Avenue in the Soundview section of the Bronx) to ask for the *Daily Worker.* Mr. Newman would hand me the paper and say, "You know, I read that paper, too." I would skip home feeling warm. On the other hand, when my dad was involved in an accident when his car hit a young neighborhood boy, before the police arrived to interview him, my family rushed through the house hiding books and copies of the *Daily Worker.*

2 See footnote on page 120.

My father was a Party section leader in our neighborhood. There was an effort to integrate the Parkchester apartments that were owned by Metropolitan Life Insurance, a whites-only development. Through some maneuvering, a Black family moved in, but when this happened, they were scheduled for speedy eviction. The Party was mobilized to help resist the eviction. My dad was part of a sit-in that blocked the family's apartment door. At 11:00 p.m., way past our bedtime, the story was on the television news, and we watched as my father and others were put into a paddy wagon.

I hold a first memory of being on a picket line at the age of four and discovering all that seemed pure and good to me had a strong counterforce. Willie McGee was an African American man from Mississippi who was executed on May 8, 1951, after being found guilty by an all-white jury of raping a white woman. A few days before his execution, I was with my dad at this demonstration. I remember chanting, "One, Two, Three, Free Willie McGee," and being excited to do so. At some point, three teenage white youths shouted back, "They should kill him, he should die." This innocent four-year-old was totally bewildered.

There was a special place that my family vacationed a few weeks each summer through my early years. It was a family resort in Upstate New York called Camp Unity, and it was run by Communists. To me, it was like going to Disneyland. We could only afford going because my mom worked there as a housekeeper and later as Camp Unity's nurse. I was with my parents and sisters every day, and I could go anywhere on its vast grounds and feel totally safe. I even watched my dad pitch in a softball game. I learned to swim there. The dining room was where the entire camp ate three meals a day. On weekends they needed two seatings, because Camp Unity was so full. There were cultural events almost every night. The resort's cultural director, for at least one season, was Harry Belafonte. There were family game nights, plays, and concerts in the "Rec Hall." I could climb trees whenever I wanted, and watch and play ping pong in front of the dining hall. On weekends there were lectures on various subjects. I didn't comprehend them, but loved to sit with my dad and listen to the grownups talk. *Red Adventure Land, Fantasy Land....* This was my childhood and it is no wonder it led me into the Communist Party and its allied groups.

My Evolution

When I turned nine my family moved to Flushing, Queens. My dad was no longer working full time as a "functionary." I have not heard this term, *functionary*, used except in Party circles. He started working at Korvette's department store as a salesman in the men's jewelry department (tie bars, cuff links, rings, etc.). My mother was working as a nurse at Flushing Hospital. With two incomes, we were able to move into a modest three-bedroom apartment in a cooperative development.

In seventh grade I started attending an Ethical Culture youth discussion group that met in the recreation room of a neighboring building. It was my first participation in anything that was "political" without my family. The adult leader was engaging and led the group of about ten kids in weekly discussions on challenging political and ethical topics. One evening he came with five small black-and-white photos of men's faces. He passed them around and asked each of us to make a list of who we thought was Jewish. Although we could not all agree, there was no one who chose less than three of the photos. After we did the exercise, our group leader identified Nazi SS officer Adolf Eichmann, Pope Pius XII, and three other famous individuals who were decidedly not Jewish. Lesson learned.

A short time later I was invited to a Queens Student SANE meeting. Student SANE was affiliated with the National Committee for a Sane Nuclear Policy. I was thrilled to be involved with kids my own age who were in the fight for peace. The small group decided to organize a local march to advocate for nuclear disarmament. We gathered about a dozen or so young people and marched with homemade signs from Flushing to Fort Totten army base in Bayside, Queens. After my initiation into demonstrations, I found my way to peace actions at Bryant Park in Manhattan and, most memorably, at Duffy Square just north of

Times Square, where we were attacked by police on horses and I escaped injury by climbing onto the statue of Father Duffy.

As I entered high school, I threw myself into the student boycotts for school integration. I made my first public speech at a pre-boycott rally across the street from my school, Bronx High School of Science. I had the honor of being censored by my friend Josh Muravcik, who was a leader of YPSL. He objected to my radical rhetoric and pulled me away from the microphone. Although we moved even further apart politically, we have remained friends.

It was in my junior year at Bronx Science that I began to attend the Center for Marxist Education in downtown Manhattan and took a class, Introduction to Marxism. At the center I was fortunate to listen to a debate between Norman Thomas, the leader of the Socialist Party, and Herbert Aptheker, a historian and author who spoke for the Communist Party. It was a surprisingly civil discussion given the history of rancor between these two Left competitors.

Moving closer to joining the CP, I began to attend activities sponsored by Advance Youth Organization, which was the Party-supported young people's organization in New York. I never joined Advance, but I went on the Advance bus to the 1963 March on Washington. I traveled from my home, taking a bus and two trains, to show up at 5:00 a.m. in front of the Advance headquarters on the Lower East Side. I hadn't reserved a seat, and by luck I got the last one. I was squeezed in the middle of the last row. After hearing Martin Luther King Jr.'s speech, marveling at the bravery of civil rights leader John Lewis speaking truth to power, hearing Peter, Paul and Mary sing Bob Dylan's "Blowin' in the Wind," and being surrounded by 250,000 dedicated demonstrators, this teenager resolved to devote his life to the cause.

The W.E.B. Du Bois Clubs

Advance dissolved in 1964, when a new socialist youth organization, the W.E.B. Du Bois Clubs, was founded. I graduated from high school that summer. I read all I could about the consolidation and growth of this new organization and was determined to join and build it. I began college at State University of New York (SUNY) New Paltz and quickly found a small group of socialist-minded friends. In the dining hall I noticed a student wearing a peace button. We immediately became friends and eventually comrades. We've remained friends our whole lives. He and I set out to build a New Paltz chapter of the Du Bois Clubs. Students for a Democratic Society (SDS) was not active on campus at that time. The school administration refused to recognize the Du Bois Club, and we were not allowed to meet on campus. We then formed a "front group" on campus called the Socialist Study Group, a caucus of the officially sanctioned Young Democrats. We had some serious, intelligent, dedicated faculty members who advised and supported us. Professor Martin J. Sklar was notable among them. Professor Sklar was an editor of the New Left magazine *Studies on the Left,* and he spoke at a Vietnam teach-in we organized where students packed a large room at the Student Union building. I vividly recall the standing ovation he received as he eviscerated US imperialism. Sklar later became an intellectual leader of the neoconservative tendency in the United States.

It was during my freshman year that I was asked to join the Communist Party, and I happily handed over my fifty-cent initiation dues. I remained at New Paltz for three semesters and then moved back home to New York City. I wanted to be closer to my political comrades in the Du Bois Clubs and the Party and closer to where the action was. I also was in trouble with the New Paltz administration, because I stupidly gave them the opportunity to suspend me for forging a signature on a form allowing the use of a meeting room in the Student Union building.

I transferred to New York University, where there was a large SDS chapter. I participated in protests there. I spoke at an anti–Vietnam War rally organized by SDS held in the main corridor of the university. The United States had just invaded the Dominican Republic (1965), and I made the connection between the imperialist policies of the war in Vietnam and the invasion of this independent Caribbean nation. In that same corridor I also participated in an all-night sit-in against a proposed increase in tuition. At 3:30 a.m. Richie Havens, the folksinger probably best known for singing "Freedom ... is a constant struggle" at Woodstock, showed up unannounced and entertained us for hours.

After one semester at NYU, despite vigorous disapproval from my parents, I stopped attending classes and devoted myself full time to the movement. I worked the summer of 1966 at the Du Bois Clubs' small storefront on Rivington Street on the Lower East Side, where we held meetings and dances sponsored by the Lower East Side chapter.

Student Mobe

In early 1967 I was asked to represent the Du Bois Clubs as a national coordinator of the Student Mobilization Committee against the War in Vietnam (Student Mobe). For reasons I believe were proven wrong, SDS was opposed to large national demonstrations. It argued that large mobilizations took away from the effort to build local movements. In reality, the larger national marches and coordinated demonstrations and student strikes enhanced local organizing. The publicity and recruitment efforts for these actions created opportunities to speak to hundreds of thousands, if not millions, of people. The peace movement and the Left grew steadily through the work of Student Mobe and its parent organization, the National Mobilization Committee to End the War in Vietnam.

Student Mobe was de facto a coalition of the Du Bois Clubs/CP young people, the Trotskyist Young Socialist Alliance/Socialist Workers Party (SWP, YSA's parent organization), and pacifists. The Du Bois Clubs and YSA had a few thousand committed activists all over the United States, and combined with various campus peace groups that were flourishing, we were able to organize many large and successful actions both in localities and nationwide.

When a call came out for a national student strike, a call originated by Bettina Aptheker, a Du Bois Clubs member and

Berkeley University Free Speech Movement leader, it quickly garnered wide support. Every day we would receive mail from campuses across the country with organizations endorsing the strike, and not just from the usual suspects; fraternities and sororities, Young Democrats and Young Republican clubs, religious clubs, YWCAs and YMCAs, Hillel clubs, student government leaders, and student newspapers all sent in their forms endorsing the strike.

Besides myself, Student Mobe's national coordinators were Kipp Dawson, representing YSA, and Linda Morse, an organizationally unaffiliated peace activist. Linda had the hardest job, because aside from all her tasks she was the mediator between these historic rivals of the Left, the Communists and Trotskyists. She did a marvelous job and kept us together for the two years I was at Student Mobe.

Policy Questions

Following my departure from New Paltz, I began to question the CP policy of having a separate youth organization, the Du Bois Clubs—which defined itself as a "broad based, socialist-oriented youth organization"—that vied for leadership of the upsurge among students. After my experience with Student Mobe, I started questioning the refusal to recognize other Left organizations as legitimate. Mine was a minority opinion in the Party. I came to the conclusion that it was a mistake to be separated from the large number of students in SDS and other campus groups. I believe that we needed to break out of a "fortress mentality" that was a by-product of McCarthyism. There was also a self-isolating outlook by which the Party was the vanguard of the working class, and all other Left organizations were inferior, at best, and enemies to be vanquished. In addition, any Left group that disagreed with the Soviet Union's positions was deemed anti-Soviet and not to be trusted by the Party.

I decided to take a symbolic, small step away from this by agreeing to participate in a Militant Labor Forum panel sponsored by the SWP on the next steps for the peace movement.

As far as I know, this was unprecedented. An openly identified CP member speaking on a panel discussion at SWP headquarters was shocking to some. I thought that a publicly advertised meeting would attract at least a few people who were not totally closed to considering ideas that the CP advocated. I was of the opinion that we should not fear "mixing it up" with others on the Left — or the Right, for that matter.

In the winter of 1967, I was working full time as youth director for the CP in New York. I worked closely with the youth clubs of the CP, the largest of which were active at City College and Brooklyn College, with smaller groups on the Lower East Side, Queens College, and Hunter College.

Organizing Hospital Workers

I returned to college in 1968, met the woman who was to become my wife in a children's literature class in 1969, and graduated from NYU in June of 1970. After graduation I got a job working in the Columbia University medical library at the Washington Heights campus, where the medical school and Presbyterian Hospital were located. I took this job to join an effort to unionize the workers at this giant nonunion medical complex in upper Manhattan. The Washington Heights Party organization had an extremely ambitious plan. The "Project," as we called it, involved building a movement in the community against the Vietnam War, enhancing the tenants rights activity that members were playing a major role in, organizing for child care in Washington Heights, and organizing over five thousand workers at Presbyterian Hospital and its affiliated medical research center and medical school, College of Physicians and Surgeons (P&S), into New York's health-care union, Local 1199. The Party had two clubs in the community, Upper Washington Heights/Inwood and Lower Washington Heights. A third club consisting of those who worked at the Columbia Presbyterian Hospital Medical Center was formed quickly after the Project began.

The Party clubs began to search for Party members who would seek jobs at the Medical Center. The main target of the union organizing drive was the hospital, but most of us got jobs at the physically contiguous P&S. Initially there were just three CP members working there. By getting about a dozen younger Party members to obtain jobs at the Medical Center and recruiting at least an equal number of already employed workers, we established a large Party club with members in a variety of departments at P&S and the hospital. The Medical Center club met every Monday at a member's home and invariably with a full agenda that had us meeting late into the night.

The Washington Heights Project was vibrant and multifaceted and deserves to have its story told. I will focus here only on the union organizing effort and my role during the time I was involved.

After a year working in the Medical Center library, I applied to the pediatric cardiology department and was transferred to a position as a research technician. I learned how to read electrograms, run a blood circulation machine for animal experiments, and monitor the electrogram machine in the open-heart operating room at the hospital. Although I remained on the P&S payroll in this research job, I was in the operating room at least twice a week during open-heart surgeries.

The main goal was to organize the two thousand service (blue-collar) workers at the hospital, but as a first step we focused on the smaller P&S, which had one thousand workers, mostly doing research work funded by grants. Local 1199 already represented a similar research and medical school at the Albert Einstein College of Medicine (AECOM). The union at AECOM was very active and successful and had a good reputation. At P&S we had what we characterized as a "company union," the Supporting Staff Association (SSA). During my time at the Medical Center we had two sets of elections at P&S. Both times there were three choices on the ballot, 1199, SSA, or "No Union." In the first round, no choice received a majority of votes. Local 1199 came in first, but when the runoff was held the "No" votes invariably went to the company union. With around one thousand eligible voters, 1199 lost by twenty-four votes the first time and by one vote the second time.

As a member of the organizing committee, my job was to keep in touch with sixty to eighty workers in my and adjacent departments. I used my breaks and lunch hours to do my "rounds." I kept a small pad with each worker's name, and checked off when I had spoken with them about the "issue of the week," such as health benefits or pensions. When the organizing committee was leafleting the entrances, I would arrive around a half hour before my shift.

In 1973, after the mass firing of African American food-service workers, union organizing exploded at our main target, the hospital. The workers were fired because they protested the disciplining of a coworker for wearing a colored tee shirt under his white uniform. When twenty-two of the workers came in with colored tee shirts, they were all fired on the spot. There was no union and no grievance procedure, and the fight for civil rights and union rights were merged.

All Party members at the hospital and P&S joined the union's organizing committee. Although I worked for P&S, I had access to the operating rooms of the hospital, and I took responsibility for covering the male orderlies who worked in them. I would go to their locker room before the shift began or during breaks. I organized twenty workers to sign union cards and attend meetings and rallies. One Party member, a Latina who worked in one of the hospital laboratories, was assigned to the laundry, where there were almost two hundred Spanish-speaking workers. We had no contacts there, and it was in a separate building. For months, efforts were unsuccessful, because these workers were so fearful of losing their jobs. After months of almost daily visits, a few of the women in the laundry began speaking to her. After that she made steady progress, and we carried the majority of votes from the laundry.

Local 1199 assigned its top organizer, Eddie Kay, to steer the organizing drive. He was a leader who inspired and agitated. He was a tough task master, and I witnessed him bringing workers to tears of joy and some to tears of exhaustion. I observed and studied his methods. Steve Kramer, who years later became an elected leader of 1199, was a worker in the hospital's mail department. That job gave him access to a wide area of the hospital. He was a ball of energy, and popular. The hospital fired Steve in the middle of the organizing campaign, and 1199 put him on staff as an organizer. He was in front of the hospital at 5:00 a.m. when the dietary workers would come in to prepare breakfast, and he was there at 11:00 p.m. when the nursing assistants were reporting for the night shift. In between he held small meetings with workers and filled in charts that listed every worker and assessed their support for the union. He was the recognized leader of the workers at Presbyterian Hospital, and after 1199 negotiated their first contract there, the hospital was forced to rehire him.

In 1974, just a few days prior to the union vote, Coretta Scott King spoke at a pre-vote rally where hundreds of workers gathered across the street from Presbyterian Hospital. The rally was held at the Audubon Ballroom, where Malcolm X had been assassinated in 1965.

The National Labor Relations Board conducted the vote at the armory across the street from the hospital. The whole block between Broadway and Fort Washington Avenue on 168th Street was packed with workers awaiting the results. When we got the word that the union had won, the workers in the street broke out in cheers and tears of joy.

It was soon after this victory that I was asked to join the staff of 1199 as an organizer in the white-collar division, the 1199 Guild of Professional, Technical and Office Employees (the Guild). I had been asked a year earlier but deferred my decision, at least partly due to pressure from those in the Party who felt that members should remain in the rank and file. But the lure of working full time at what I loved won the day. I have to admit that the pay was better. I went from $98 a week (1199's minimum wage) to $100 a week.

I was immediately assigned to a team that organized the technical, professional, and clerical staff at Roosevelt Hospital in Manhattan and then the technical and professional workers at Presbyterian Hospital. After six years, I was assigned by the union to the position of assistant director of organizing for

1199's National Union of Hospital and Healthcare Employees. I traveled around the country advising and supporting organizing and contract campaigns. I helped 1199 affiliate large groups of registered nurses who had organized independently but were attracted to 1199's militancy and member-driven model, as well as its support for progressive causes.

During this period, there were two internal fights in 1199 that I was deeply involved in. In the union, staff were (and are) dues-paying members with membership rights. I was involved in organizing and bringing in thousands of workers. I say this to explain why I felt that 1199 was *my* union. I was an elected vice president of 1199. When Leon Davis, the founding organizer of 1199, decided to move in the direction of merging with the Service Employees International Union (SEIU) in the early 1980s, a major internal battle took place. There was open opposition to the merger from a recognized longtime and popular African American leader, Doris Turner, as well as from the international union we were affiliated with, the Retail, Wholesale, and Department Store Union. Ultimately the merger failed.

During this open internal dispute, Leon Davis retired. Doris Turner was elected president of 1199 New York and Henry Nicholas, an African American leader and president of 1199 C (Pennsylvania and New Jersey), was elected president of 1199 National Union. Turner began a purge of those who opposed her and led staff and other supporters in a vicious and violent suppression of anyone she deemed disloyal. Democratic norms were thrown aside. Many courageous rank-and-file members and former staff withstood this and were able to field a slate that ran against Turner's incumbent slate when she ran for reelection. The "Save Our Union" (SOU) opposition slate was successful, and Party members in the rank and file and those recently fired from the union staff worked as equals with all those in 1199 who were committed to a social action–oriented, democratic union. The Party organization did not make a formal decision to support the opposition.

Although originally Turner's slate declared victory, the vote count was declared void because of ballot tampering. Dave

White, 1199 vice president and close Turner advisor, was on the Turner slate, but when he realized the disastrous and corrupt rule of the incumbents, he gave testimony to the Department of Labor that he personally witnessed and participated in massive vote tampering in the executive office of the union. In the rerun election, the SOU slate won. Almost all, if not all, Party members in our hospital club participated in this fight. The decisions of SOU were made independently, never by the Party organization. The Party members were fully integrated into SOU, and when decisions were made by the group, the Party members were equals, no more or less than anyone else. They did not come in with predetermined decisions on tactical or even strategic matters. That would have been viewed as manipulative.

Eventually, 1199 did merge with an international union, but during this years-long process there again emerged sharp internal disagreement—not over the need to merge but over with whom to merge. In 1199 New York, the leadership was evenly split between those who wanted to merge with SEIU (my strong preference) and the American Federation of State, County, and Municipal Employees (AFSCME). The 1199 New York president, Dennis Rivera, was in favor of AFSCME. When the vote of the union's executive board was held, it was tied, and Rivera decided to forego the merger at that time. The Party members on the executive board were divided on the issue as well. Some voted for SEIU, some for AFSCME, and at least one spoke out for staying independent.

I relay these instances to offer the suggestion that progressives and socialists have a right and obligation to bring their ideas and opinions to the organizations they participate in as equal members. There is no need, and it is probably counterproductive, to join an organization that functions as a unified body with previously decided positions. Even if motivated by the best of intentions, such a structure takes away from the democratic life of the organization and thwarts individuals' development by short-circuiting the process of thinking through a problem and coming to a democratic decision.

For a few years, in the early eighties, when my children were young, there came a time that my schedule, especially the traveling, became too stressful for my family. Although the union sometimes made accommodations for me, overall I couldn't do the traveling required, and I left 1199 for a period of time. I worked at a variety of New York/New Jersey–based unions at midlevel leadership. I then returned to 1199. For my whole adult life, I stayed in the union movement, specifically in the health-care sector. I *fully* retired (after two false starts) in 2019.

Leaving the Party

I was a member of the Party for almost a quarter of a century. I learned from listening to and working with some great mentors. I had the honor of traveling to Cuba and cutting sugar cane with Kendra Alexander and Angela Davis. I saw how gentle, committed people like Gil Green and Bob Heisler could argue and convince without rancor. I witnessed the remarkable insight coming from a mass leader like Bettina Aptheker. And I learned to comport myself with humor from Mike Zagarell and Mike Myerson.

I left the Party in 1991, along with one-third of the membership, after the twenty-fifth national convention in Cleveland. At this convention there came a time when I and many other delegates decided to leave. A large group of us stood up and someone began singing "We Shall Overcome." We clasped each other's hands and encircled the convention floor. When we finished singing, hundreds of delegates exited together. I had held out hope that the changes that President Mikhail Gorbachev had initiated in the Soviet Union would allow the CPUSA to transform into a democratic, nonsectarian socialist organization. Unfortunately, this would not be.

11

Another World Is Possible

Frank Emspak[1]

I have struggled with trying to put together a coherent analysis of how I came to the Communist Party (CP) and left it, and then participated again and again left. But in my case, and I suspect for many other people who found that they came from a Left background, the very experience of growing up and gradually gaining consciousness led inevitably to a point of decision: to join the Communist Party or not.

During the 1960s and early 1970s, thousands, if not millions, of people joined in both militant opposition to the war in Vietnam and tremendously brave challenges to racial segregation without becoming engaged in any Communist or Marxist formation, much less the Communist Party. So for those of us who did take that step, something further, political or personal, must have triggered the decision to join.

The Civil Rights Movement, which began to mobilize in 1955, was the motivating force and model for the upheavals of the sixties. It was central to the awakening of the white student movement and opposition to the war in Vietnam. It was the Civil Rights Movement that broke the back of McCarthyism. While

1 Originally written May 2016; revised January 2020. Frank died in Madison, Wisconsin, on June 14, 2024.

northern progressives trembled, Black people in the South challenged the status quo.

On the campuses it was support for the Civil Rights Movement, especially the Student Nonviolent Coordinating Committee (SNCC), that sparked the Free Speech Movement at the University of California, Berkeley. In turn, at least for me and I suspect many others, seeing Bettina Aptheker,[2] a Communist publicly involved in leading something like the Free Speech Movement was new. The big divide at that time was the question of willingness to work with individuals or organizations that were identified as or attacked as being "Communist." Here in Wisconsin, many of the people who were strong supporters of the Civil Rights Movement were also the first to oppose the war in Vietnam, and the decision of the students at Berkeley to directly challenge McCarthyism and the exclusion of Communists from the movement had a big impact.

Joining the Communist Party in the 1960s was no trivial matter. No matter what the official legal status of the Party, it is inconceivable to me that anyone joining accepted the notion that the Party was a legal entity just like any other party. The fifties were too close, the repression too recent, and the typical way that most of our fellow citizens felt about the Party too hostile.

I cannot separate the idea of a Communist Party from the concept of class consciousness. In hindsight, I realize that I came to a belief in that association in the sixties, when I understood the necessity for both if one is to have a trade union movement that actually takes up the interests of working people. And as contradictory to some as this may sound, the ability to have a Communist Party within the trade-union movement is central to the very notion of a democratic union movement and a democratic society.

2 Bettina Aptheker was the daughter of Herbert Aptheker, a leading and public intellectual of the CPUSA. She was one of the leaders of the Free Speech Movement at Berkeley.

Growing Up: Unconscious to Conscious

I did not know I was officially a red-diaper baby until 1964, when a right-wing newspaper columnist attacked Aptheker and called her a "red-diaper" baby.[3] By then I was twenty-one years old.

By 1964 I had been labeled a Communist and a troublemaker for years, starting in grade school (of all places) and then throughout high school and college. The labeling was a consequence of being born into my family. My father, Julius Emspak, was the secretary treasurer of the United Electrical Workers (UE). By the time I was conscious of politics, he was in the papers constantly, attacked as a red, indicted, jailed for a short time, and the subject of countless federal hearings.

The strain contributed to his premature death at the age of fifty-six in 1962, when I was a freshman at the University of Wisconsin (UW). I think his premature demise was caused not so much by the constant hounding but by the destruction of the union he helped build and by the concomitant betrayal of friends and coworkers as they left the UE and in many cases joined the International Union of Electrical Workers (IUE). Some who cooperated with the red-baiting had worked together for twenty-five years and grew up together in Schenectady, New York.

One consequence of the attacks was a strong desire on the part of my family that my brother and I find a path forward that did not involve political action. In my case that was supposed to be science. At the same time, however, my parents (like many left-wing parents) wanted their children to know something about what they did and what they believed in, and to be grounded in Marxist philosophy and thought.

3 See footnote on page 120. Emspak is probably referring to an unsigned article published in the *Redland Daily Facts,* April 29, 1965, 7: "Aptheker political views already known in print." Or he could have been referring to the source document the *Redland Daily Facts* article refers to: Calvin Trillin, "Letter from Berkeley," *The New Yorker,* March 13, 1965, 52–107.

The Westchester Discussion Group

The Westchester Discussion Group was a serious and innovative teaching and learning group. It provided members with an understanding of Marx and Marxism — but for me, most crucially, an understanding of things like the labor theory of value. It was taught by Morris Coleman, a Communist educator who had helped direct the CP's school in New York City. These discussions and our understanding went on in parallel, really in a separate universe, from what was going on in high school. The group itself, the classes and discussion, were a link to the social and political movements of the prior era. It was an attempt — partially successful — to make sure that the political idealism, cultural framework, and philosophical base of the upheavals of the thirties would not be lost. The message was clear: Change was possible. But it was possible only through direct involvement. Thus, one fundamental principle was to combine philosophical understanding with some sort of direct action. This belief was also one of the things that made the Communist Party attractive to me some years later.

Specifically, group members were encouraged to participate in the Civil Rights Movement — by going to New York and demonstrating in front of Woolworth's against segregation, for example — or in the ban-the-bomb organizations and demonstrations. (This got me suspended from high school for a couple of days). But the demonstrations (and the parties afterwards) also put me in touch with people my age who were trying to do something. That resulted in my participation in discussions, meetings, and journalism. I met Steve Max, a recent high school graduate, and active New York high school students who put out a paper, *Common Sense.* Many of the people associated with it became leaders of the Students for a Democratic Society (SDS), the Student Committee of the National Committee for a Sane Nuclear Policy (Student SANE), and, to a lesser extent, the CP.

All of this activity seemed to go on sort of under the radar. Something was beginning to happen, but it was certainly a surprise when four or five years later something did happen.

I also think one has to realize the huge influence of rock 'n' roll on "something" happening. Rock 'n' roll music brought to white people a Black universe. It was an energizing, powerful music — and initially an optimistic one.

An important objective of our parents was to build a safe place for the group members. Many were often isolated in high school, so the discussion group was a place to socialize and make friends. This notion of a collective and collective support was also a motivating factor for me later as regards the Communist Party.

Because our group members were politically involved and thinking about things outside of the usual high school concerns, we were distinct from most of our peers. In 1976, and again in 2001 when I spoke to people in my high school graduating class (Roosevelt High School class of 1961, Yonkers, NY), I found that they were almost completely untouched by the events of the sixties. Some were mildly inconvenienced by the draft — almost none served — and some participated in antiwar marches. But only one or two self-identified as activist. Some were openly hostile. Although many spoke highly of and honored my closest friend, who had retired as a lieutenant colonel in the US Air Force, when it counted, none of my classmates volunteered as he did to join the military. Likewise, with the possible exception of one person, I was the only male who gave up his draft deferment because of principled opposition to the war in Vietnam. Giving up my deferment indicated that I was not hiding behind some bureaucratic protection as I was protesting the war. As it turned out, when running for office in various unions this issue came up constantly, and people measured my commitment to principle in light of a willingness to sacrifice personal safety.

In the late fifties, because of all the red-baiting and undercurrents within the movements in New York City and its suburbs, no one was coming forward to discuss the Communist Party. It was for all practical purposes still underground. Every once in a while, I saw a copy of the *Daily Worker,* but while our discussion group learned about Marx and the labor theory of value, we did not learn specifically about the Communist Party.

As members of our discussion group graduated from high school and went on to college, starting in 1958 and '59, many became active in the Civil Rights Movement, moving down South. Some stayed for their whole lives. Others became initial leaders in SDS or, a bit later, in the anti–Vietnam War movement.

The Family

The political was one thing; my family was another. Growing up, there was simply no separation between the "family" and the union, the United Electrical Workers. My father's brothers all worked at General Electric (GE) in Schenectady. The family spent holidays in Schenectady. I went with my father on trips to local unions. So in my mind the union meant fighting for people and against corporations. Our local Yonkers paper, the *Herald-Statesman,* was a conservative rag, and whenever the opportunity arose there would be a front-page headline along the lines of "Reds called before HUAC ... Julius Emspak of 49 Cliffside Drive...." (In 1965, when I became chairman of the National Coordinating Committee to End the War in Vietnam, the paper printed almost identical headlines—just the name was changed).

In response to all of this my parents were torn between wanting me to be a politically principled and active person and wanting me to be safe from persecution. Their plan of action was very simple. I was to become a Nobel Prize–level scientist, and then I could comment on political matters. Nobel Prize winner Linus Pauling was their idol. I got into the University of Wisconsin, and with their enthusiastic support off I went. In fact, other lefties from New York were there, as were other sons and daughters of the UE. Of course Wisconsin was probably one of the last places on earth that would shelter me from the political and social upheavals that were upon us. Maybe they secretly knew that. I doubt it, but one never knows about parents.

When I was eighteen, in June of 1961, the issue was whether to register for the draft. My father urged me to do so, noting that if I did not, my ability to engage in any future political action would be compromised. So I went to downtown Yonkers and registered at the local board. It took almost twenty years for me to finally be finished with my local board, but who knew? But my father was right about the impact that registering would have on my future in the trade-union movement.

Another World Is Possible

Although almost no whites knew it, the movement for a new life — the Civil Rights Movement — was in full swing by 1960. The Black movement broke the back of McCarthyism, which had incapacitated the progressives of the North, marginalizing many of them. McCarthyism was supported by and enthusiastically carried out by leading liberal figures such as Hubert Humphrey. But down South, another world was being envisioned. And it is that feeling — that another world is possible, that we can have another vision of the future — that became a core motivation of the sixties. In some ways, it is the central thought that appeared to be missing among a new generation in 2015 — until the eruption of Black Lives Matter, the "Fight for $15" (that is, for a fifteen-dollar minimum wage), and the 2016 presidential campaign.

In the early 1960s, the UW Left was all white, as was the school, with less than 2 percent people of color enrolled. The organizational center of the Left was the Socialist Club, a regular meeting place for almost anyone who considered themselves Left. The Green Lantern Eating Co-op was another, off-campus, center for political activity. The intellectual arena was dominated by a group of graduate students centered in the History Department. They founded the journal *Studies on the Left,* an ideological and historical magazine, the first significant one since the fifties.[4] The notion of community-based mass movements was mostly a theoretical concept, but that was changing as a few members of the Socialist Club who had returned to UW from the South

4 A similar magazine, *New University Thought,* appeared soon after. *Studies on the Left* was published in 1959–1967.

shared their organizing experiences. Peace-movement activists in the club also knew community people, and the Communist Party knew people in the wider community, especially the small Black community in Madison and in Milwaukee. It was at this point that I became more conscious of the Communist Party.

It is hard now to appreciate how strait-laced the culture and the intellectual life of the University of Wisconsin were in 1961. The idea of a table in the Memorial Union student center to discuss issues was a big deal. It took an effort to get one in the main corridor, but once we did it always facilitated forceful debates. The chairman of the Socialist Club was expelled from school, never to return, because we had an unauthorized table. From an intellectual standpoint, UW undergrad for me was a great experience, once I realized that classes were an adjunct to the real intellectual work.

In 1963, Michael Eisenscher, a public Communist and friend, and I began to organize the Wisconsin Student Employees Association (WISEM). We wanted the federal minimum wage applied to UW student workers. As state workers we were making 75 cents per hour, while the federal minimum was $1.25. For those like me who were working to make it through the year, this was a huge issue. We eventually were able to bring in about three hundred students. UW appointed leading liberal professors to meet with us. But the university administration would never agree to recognize the union, and essentially we spent a year talking to a wall.

Meanwhile, UW moved to expel me. Nathan Feinsinger, the leading labor lawyer on the UW faculty and national mediator for General Motors and the UAW, called Fred Harvey Harrington, president of the university. In my presence, he indicated how much legal trouble he was going to cause his good friend Fred if the decision to expel me was carried out, so the issue was dropped. While I think Feinsinger acted out of principle, he was also doing it because of who I was, the son of a respected and distinguished labor leader.

We eventually won the $1.25 wage, after a rumor got started in May of 1964 that the Teamsters were not going to deliver toilet paper to the dormitories. We did not achieve recognition, and the organization disintegrated after the wage increase was announced. But the efforts we made with that small organization illustrated several things:

1. We had the sense under Michael's leadership to go outside UW and seek progressive trade unions and individuals to help us — and the International Brotherhood of Teamsters was a progressive group at that time.
2. The liberals were the people fighting us on campus.
3. It was possible to win.
4. The established labor unions — meaning the unions located at the then new Labor Temple — would have nothing to do with us, even refusing to give us official NLRB union sign-up cards.

A good number of the undergraduates who were active in the WISEM became the people who helped organize the Teaching Assistants Association a few years later.

The Antiwar Movement Comes to Madison

By autumn of 1964 I was the chairman of the Socialist Club, and the Vietnam War opposition was heating up nationally. A big change of consciousness began to make itself felt when students, led in part by Bettina Aptheker, launched the Free Speech Movement (FSM) in October 1964.

Students at the University of California, Berkeley, were raising money for the Congress of Racial Equality. The head of UC Berkeley, a nice cold-war liberal, banned the activity. Jack Weinberg, a recent graduate, was at the table collecting money when the police arrested him and placed him in a police car. The students refused to give in, and thousands surrounded the car. A huge upheaval began, one that ultimately shook the student world. Students saw their peers fighting the university and began to think of "student power" and the right of students to direct the university. These ideas led directly to the big campus-based antiwar demonstrations.

The Socialist Club and others invited the FSM people to come to UW and tell us about what had happened, and in November 1964 they did so. Aside from the scope of the actions at Berkeley, one thing stood out in the minds of many leftists and future Communists: The FSM students said that anyone, no matter what their political views, could participate in the movement. No red-baiting. A public Communist was one of the leaders.

During the time preceding the FSM, things were moving along at UW. A peace movement based on the ban-the-bomb group formed and published a national magazine, *Sanity,* that took on the anticommunist and exclusionary politics of the dominant group of the time, the National Committee for a Sane Nuclear Policy (SANE).

Students like me participated in and helped turn Student SANE away from its anticommunist fixation and toward concentrating on banning the bomb. The result was that Student SANE was expelled from the national organization, led in large part by Norman Thomas, leader of the Socialist Party.

To break out of the repression and destruction of the fifties, and recognizing that young people were in motion for social change, the CP set up the W.E.B. Du Bois Clubs — essentially their youth organization. At UW the CP had grown, the Du Bois Clubs were functioning, and there were serious efforts to work with welfare-rights people and the Black community. CP people and their friends — like me — were the only ones on campus doing this. In Madison, while SDS was a presence, the CP and friends seemed to me more prominent. From my point of view, it was more ideologically coherent and also more organically connected to radical Black movements in New York City and Los Angeles.

In Madison it also had some meaningful connections to the white working class. For example, in spring of 1963 the Du Bois Clubs sent a delegation to help miners on strike in Harlan County and Hazard, Kentucky. I was asked to accompany them. Arriving with food and money in Hazard, we were promptly arrested (it was never clear why) and had a chance to discuss philosophy with the jailers. I defended evolution. (I was told it was a fad, and that we were in the buckle of the Bible Belt).We spent all night in the Hazard city jail sitting on sacks of dynamite. The police told us that in the morning they were going to formally charge us with blowing up the Louisville and Nashville Railroad bridge, but they never did. Very early in the morning, the town intellectual, a graduate of Harvard University, came by to continue the debate over evolution. The police chief arrived and, after he determined that we were on the side of the miners, told us that the city of Hazard was prounion — and then let us go. But he also said that we would have a police escort when we wanted to go around talking to people. The tapes and material we gathered are now in the Wisconsin Historical Society Social Action Collection.

Overall, in terms of Madison and politics, there was growing interest in the world outside of UW. But essentially the world of the 1950s was intact as 1963 ended and 1964 began. By the end of 1964 and the defeat of Barry Goldwater and election of Lyndon Johnson, all was basically quiet, despite the FSM rumblings. That was to change in 1965.

While there was some opposition to Johnson's bombing of Vietnam, almost the entire country was silent until his escalation of the war in early January 1965, when students, longtime pacifists, and some in the Civil Rights Movement began to question the war and the nation's priorities. Madison became one center of that movement, which eventually took two forms. One was a university intellectual–based movement of professors, graduate students, and basically liberal people who believed — at that time — that it was lack of knowledge that fueled the administration's war policy. They believed that if the policy makers only knew the real history they would back off. This became the teach-in movement, which in itself helped break the hold of McCarthyism and self-censorship on university campuses. But it was essentially an elite movement, and it was also wrong in its assumptions about US interests in Indochina. Many (but not all) of its leaders were frightened by or opposed to independent activity, demonstrations, sit-ins, and direct actions of students, who increasingly challenged the assumptions of the war and who, because of the draft, faced real personal consequences. The second form was that of the more radical, action movements of draft resistance, civil disobedience, and an intellectually independent general opposition to the ideology of the Cold War. It included the growing number of those sympathetic to or actively supporting various national liberation movements alongside their support of the Vietnamese. It was also strongly antiexclusionary; anyone opposed to the war could join. The class-conscious Left and the pacifist organizations were the leadership of this wing. In Madison, the Madison Committee to End the War in Vietnam exemplified it.

In 1965 I made the transition from student to full time movement activist. Over the next thirty years, no matter what type of job I had, I always considered myself to be an activist and organizer. Sometimes, as when I worked in hospitals or in large factories like United Shoe Machine or GE, it was easy to be involved. At other times, in professional jobs in the state of Massachusetts or as a university professor, activism took a different path. But throughout, my sense of myself was as an activist, in terms of both physical organizing and also intellectually challenging the status quo. In looking around at the political world, I saw the CP as a potentially unifying force, with dedicated people doing good work.

I graduated from UW in January 1965. When the student leadership of the Madison Committee to End the War in Vietnam (CEWVN) went on to graduate school, I did not. I went on to full-time antiwar work. In retrospect, it was the experience of the Westchester Discussion Group—that of combining action with ideology—that helped move me in this direction. But it was the experience of the family—in my father's case, leaving graduate school in 1935 and reentering the workforce—that made the decision to stay out of school and join the movement an obvious one.

In the spring of 1965 I became editor of *Crisis,* the journal of the CEWVN. We made specific efforts to develop community distribution. On April 1, 1965, UW participated in the teach-in movement, but it was a campus-based, intellectual affair without much wider participation and a distinct hierarchy. On May 21–22, the Vietnam Day Committee in Berkeley held their teach-in, calling it Vietnam Day. It was of an entirely different character than those in UW, Michigan, or elsewhere. It was a mass-education exercise, involving big outdoor crowds and music. It had an air of celebration and mobilization — the beginning of a movement. The event culminated with a call for an international day of protest against the war.

In Madison, we received the news and decided to act in support of the call from Berkeley. Our CEWVN was still centered on the campus and still trying to educate, and we had only begun to realize that some sort of direct-action demonstrations were needed. But by mid-June 1965 I was writing to people all over the country and advocating along with Berkeley for some sort of protest. Simultaneously, Staughton Lynd and Bob Moses of Student Nonviolent Coordinating Committee (SNCC) decided to call for an event, the Congress of Unrepresented People, in Washington for August 6–9.[5] In keeping with the nonviolent activist beliefs of Moses and Lynd, we sought ways to confront the war. Our assertion was that the majority of people were against the war, and so the logical thing was to take over our House of Representatives and declare peace. Just as patriots had assembled 250 years earlier in their Continental Congress, so would we, and, like them, take direct action.

Many of the leaders of the antiwar movement were in contact with each other and decided to use the Congress of Unrepresented People as the setting to discuss how we could coordinate protests and make them a national event. After two days of meetings we decided several important things:

5 Those days were chosen to commemorate the dropping of the atomic bomb on Hiroshima by the United States. It was a traditional day of anti-nuclear war demonstrations.

1. Direct action was needed against a war that was not simply a result of lack of knowledge on the part of the elites.
2. Anyone who was opposed to the war, on any grounds, should be invited to participate in actions.
3. We should support and organize for International Days of Protest on October 15–16, 1965.
4. We should seek a decentralized, locally based series of initiatives that would happen all over the country, rather than try to bring people to one or two central places (New York, Washington, or San Francisco).
5. We needed some sort of coordinating committee that was not SDS or any other specific group and was open to encouraging anyone who was against the war, on any grounds, to do something.

In the end, delegates decided to launch the National Coordinating Committee to End the War in Vietnam (NCC). It was decided to locate it in Madison, because of the strong support of Madison people at the Congress and because it was not in New York (left-wing factionalism), Chicago (SDS), or the West Coast (too remote). I was chosen to be "chairman."

On August 6, 1965, with the encouragement of Staughton Lynd and Bob Moses, we also decided to enter the House of Representatives to declare peace. After all, it was *our* House of Representatives. Needless to say, we were unable to declare peace. And by the end of the day about five hundred people had been arrested. In my case, a federal judge had to order my release, as the DC police refused to grant me bail. I never did find out why, in spite of Freedom of Information Act (FOIA) requests.

After I arrived back in Madison I resigned from my job as a researcher at University of Wisconsin Hospitals. I notified my draft board that I was going to work full-time as the chairperson of the NCC and thus gave up my draft deferment.

The NCC was an attempt to build an all-inclusive, locally driven antiwar movement. My view then, and the view of the majority of participants, was that anyone opposed to the war could and should join a local antiwar group and do something to oppose the war — no one should be excluded. We called this "nonexclusion." The first question was, "Are you against the war?" And if so, great! Not, "Are you against Communism, or are you a Communist?" The difference was exemplified by the liberal anticommunist editor of the Madison *Capital Times,* Miles McMillan, who interviewed me upon my return from Washington in August 1965. His first question was, "Are you a Communist?" And my answer, which could have been "No," was instead, "None of your business. The issue is the war."

During the next three months of intense activities we opened an office, which was trashed repeatedly. I informed the police that we would shoot the next person who invaded the office, after which there was not even a bubble gum wrapper on the sidewalk.

The idea of the protest caught on nationwide and internationally, and was aided by the anti–Vietnam War and pro–National Liberation Front (NLF) support network that the NLF had been building with the help of various Communist parties and anticolonial movements. At this point my respect for the CP began to grow, based on what I saw that it brought to the various antiwar formations. Party people that I met or could identify did all they could to bring about forms of agreement or unity. They reached out to old friends in the trade-union movement and were an integral part of the Black community

The October 15–16 International Days of Protest were a huge success, with hundreds of thousands demonstrating for the first time in the United States, joined by huge numbers in other cities around the world. Internally, however, the NCC could not survive divisions and sectarianism, and it dissolved a year later. The Young Socialist Alliance (YSA), associated with the Socialist Workers Party (SWP), insisted that members of the antiwar coalition take a position for immediate withdrawal from Vietnam. Others, like myself, said that all who opposed the war on any grounds were welcome into our antiwar coalition. The disintegration of the NCC was profoundly depressing, especially as the idea we had of locally based, nationally coordinated activities could involve the greatest number of people acting in their own communities. Another aspect of the sectarianism and disintegration was a distancing of the movement from the Black student movements, especially those in the South.

Back to the UW Campus

During the spring of 1967, my father's close friends urged me to consider going back to school and getting a PhD. Carl Marzani and Russ Nixon pointed out that "one never knew" when it might come in handy. At the same time, at the urging of a leader of the United Steel Workers, I had applied for a job and was hired at the not-yet-opened Hennepin, Illinois, plant of the Jones and Laughlin Steel Company. The union wanted me to be their in-plant organizer. But before I could actually start work, I was notified that I was no longer employed. An old enemy of the UE and leader of the USW in Pittsburgh saw my name. He contacted the district director and that was the end of my career at Jones and Laughlin. The mill was closed in the early 2000s.

In June 1967 I was accepted into the UW History Department as a special student. In September I was officially accepted to the graduate program in history. At more or less the same time, I was hired by Maurice Zeitlin, then a professor in the Sociology Department of UW and a leader of the antiwar movement. My hiring was a terrific decision on his part as far as I was concerned, and because of his studies of Latin America it was also an opportunity for me to develop an understanding of what was happening in the world.

In September 1967 he and several progressive businesspeople launched Madison Citizens for a Vote on Vietnam (CVV), the "referendum committee." I became the ward and precinct coordinator, essentially the director of organization for the referendum effort and a member of the five-person steering committee. We barely lost the vote in April 1968 on a referendum calling for an immediate withdrawal of US troops from Vietnam. However, in order to get on the ballot we needed to get ten thousand notarized signatures, which required building a robust ward and precinct organization. We also won the right of students to vote in municipal elections in the cities where they resided. Those efforts transformed the political life of the city. The 1968 election campaign also started Paul Soglin, who won an election as alderman, on his way to becoming mayor four years later. Gene Parks, the first Black alderman, was also elected. During this campaign the work of CP members was exemplary. It was their work that helped me determine to join the CP.

The Communist Party

Throughout my political life I have been called a Communist. Organizationally, however, that was not the case most of the time. Over nearly fifty years of political activity, I was in the Party for a relatively short time in the late sixties and late seventies.

Two issues made me open to the Party, aside from its commitment to the antiwar movement. The first was its principled fight against racism and its ability to work with community and political leaders in Black neighborhoods in many places in the United States. The second was the need that I felt for some sort of organization that could help lead the fight against the war and against racism in a principled way — while respecting others, in other words, and not being the dogmatists I found in the student and antiwar movements.

I joined the Party in the autumn of 1967, however, *not* as a public spokesperson — and in fact not in public at all. There was simply no way that I or the Party could see for me to become a public Communist and still maintain a high community profile and level of leadership. (Later, that applied in the trade-union movement, too.) This decision meant that I was not as open as I wanted to be with close associates in the antiwar movement, especially the steering committee of Madison Citizens for a Vote on Vietnam (CVV).

When I joined the Party the organization was undergoing huge upheaval. It was brought on by the commitment to fight racism and reinforced by the militancy of other, more or less Marxist and revolutionary Black organizations. The upheaval was also a consequence of the need and desire for renewal and the question of what that would look like, as well as the democratic upsurge among students and student organizations. A new generation of red-diaper babies had ideas that were more democratic than those of the old guard.

And if that were not enough to cause upheavals within the Party, there was a shift in attitudes toward the Soviet Union, not only by some older Communist leaders but also among many younger members. Younger people, and veteran Communists as well, were becoming aware that all was not well in the USSR and that increasingly US Communists had to have a more independent attitude toward the Soviet Union (USSR) and its Communist Party. The fact that China had already declared its independence was also a major factor.

Of course all these issues were being discussed in an atmosphere of intense political activity and with the realization that some of the discussions and most leaders, public or not, were subjects of FBI surveillance, as was later substantiated by various FOIA documents. We did not know that the US government, in the form of the COINTELPRO program, also orchestrated some actions that seemed particularly disruptive at the time.

We had a vigorous Party organization in Madison, including students, working people, and community activists. Within the antiwar movement, CP activists contributed significantly to the success of Madison CVV, especially in reaching out to the working class of the city. Likewise, when it came to the issue of racism, Party people played a major role in the Black student strike that commenced in February 1969. Another comrade and I were the teaching assistants in the Black history class and were also members of the strike committee.

The significant role played by the Madison Party in the CP at large was in raising the issues of internal, organizational democracy, proper relations with the Soviets, and how best to fight racism. But the Madison Party did not act alone. We were in agreement with the more working-class Milwaukee Party when it came to issues of how to reach out to white workers and the question of what we called the "labor aristocracy." In each of these areas we challenged the analysis of the national CP. The relationship with Milwaukee was important because it meant that issues raised by Madison could not be dismissed simply because the club was primarily "just students."

Although it sounds dated now, the Madison Party collective called itself the Fanshen Collective, referencing the book by William Hinton about China and the renewal of their society brought about by the Chinese Revolution. His work described what the revolution meant in a Chinese village. Our naming ourselves was one way of saying that we opposed the increasing attacks on the Chinese CP.

In mid-August 1968 I was driving to Milwaukee for a meeting of the state committee of the CP called to discuss the Soviet intervention in Czechoslovakia. I was thinking that the CPUSA would either have its shining moment or become a relic, depending on how we handled the Czech crisis. Our group was looking forward to having a debate on the matter, even though the New York–based leadership had already taken a position without consultation. My feeling then was that 1968 would be a turning point for the Party. In my view, the Party needed discussion and vision to recognize that something was wrong in Eastern Europe. If it did, the CP would have a chance of becoming politically and culturally a much greater part of the wider social movements than we were. Failing that, we would be in trouble sooner or later. My feeling today is that this assessment was fundamentally correct.

The Wisconsin state committee did take a critical position regarding the Czech issue and did criticize the way in which the decisions were taken. The state committee also began preparations for the upcoming nineteenth convention of the CP. The Madison club participated actively in the discussions about racism, China, the role of the working class, and the functioning of the Party.

During this period, November 1968 through the winter of 1969, in accordance with Party procedure we submitted papers for the preconvention discussions and for presentation at the 1969 conference. Our key points were as follows:

1. Regarding racism and white privilege and how to fight it: We noted that white privilege exists and must be dealt with directly.
2. Regarding the Soviet intervention in Czechoslovakia: We did not support it.
3. Regarding democracy in the Party: We thought that the way in which the US Party made its decisions regarding Czechoslovakia violated Party rules.

Internal democracy is key to the commitment of people to any political organization, especially one that demands all kinds of sacrifice. If one does not think one is being heard or respected, one leaves. The issue for the Party was its long-term political survival as a meaningful force. Could it arise from the destruction of the forties and fifties and become a part of the leadership of the political movements of the sixties and seventies? The discussions over racism and the role of the USSR, especially how they were dealt with internally had, therefore, a bigger impact than they would have had as political disagreements only. A consequence of a failure to address more directly some of these issues was the loss of many committed people who felt that their views were disrespected. Many felt that the functioning of the Party was at considerable variance with its rules.

The Nineteenth National Convention (April 30–May 4, 1969) showed the limitations of the Party. It was demoralizing to us, as from our point of view we never had the chance to air our differences in some positive way. We found the papers that we had written and submitted as part of the preconvention discussion in a closet, not distributed. Even so, we were encouraged by many people we met, people like Charlene Mitchell from New York and the Alexander family from Los Angeles, as well as some older people like Will Weinstone, Dorothy Healey, and others.

Overall, our assessment was that the Party was playing a significant role in the fight against racism in many communities and in some unions. Our faith was confirmed a year later by the principled fight to free Angela Davis. In my view, now and then, the relationship with the Black revolutionary movements and people could have been the basis for the type of resurgent Party that was clearly needed. Nor would this be in conflict with a working-class base, as most Black people were in the working class.

In addition to writing papers and initiating discussion, which was a recognized part of the preconvention process, we also continued a high level of activity. In early 1969 the Black students at UW Madison went out on strike and occupied a building. They had thirteen demands, focused on recruiting more Black students, support for those that were already at the university, creation of a Black History department (not just a course), and the hiring of Black faculty. Party people had organized a white support group, People Against Racism, which sought to bring the issues to the white community. As noted, two of us were the teaching assistants for the Black history course, which had just held its first class. I was on the steering committee of the strike.

In the middle of the Black strike, the front page of the *Wisconsin State Journal* detailed the meeting of the state Party committee the day before, outlining my views on what should be done concerning the strike. It was clearly written from information provided by someone at the meeting, suggesting that a member of the state committee of the Wisconsin Party was a police agent, which of course turned out to be true. While embarrassing, the revelations did not change much; the campus was already divided, with many students supporting the Black students but many others opposed or oblivious. The governor had called out the National Guard to occupy the campus, and there were numerous arrests. In the end, the university agreed to establish a Black Studies Department, recruit at least 250 Black students from the state of Wisconsin, establish a Black student center, and hire more diverse faculty. The History Department however, did not really forgive those students, like me, who were, in their view, telling them what to do as regards curriculum and faculty.

After the Black strike and the convention, the Madison Club remained active in efforts to organize the Teaching Assistants

Association, among other projects. I, however, decided to take graduate school seriously and finished up my master's degree, took my prelims, and did the research for my PhD thesis, entitled "The Break-Up of the CIO."

Dolores and I had our first child in June 1969.[6] So it was a busy year. Dolores and I and our young son left for Paris in February 1970, where she studied the work of the French Communist writer Louis Aragon and I wrote the first draft of my dissertation. I also provided analysis of events in the US for staff of the National Liberation Front associated with the Paris Peace Talks, spoke extensively about the war in Vietnam, and studied the US political efforts to influence the peace talks.

When we returned to the United States in the autumn of 1970, the Party in Madison was just about nonfunctional. Several members had left the city, and the campus movement was in a lull. My wife and I moved to Boston in January 1972.

Boston: A New World Outside of the University

The Party organization in Boston was alive and trying to do work in packinghouses, hospitals, and in the electrical industry. It was a leader in the fight against racism, *the* defining issue in Boston at that time. The focus was also clear. Aside from the emphasis on community organizing and racism, the Party was trying to assemble resources to pursue an industrial concentration model, targeting health care and, to a lesser extent, manufacturing.

In the North Shore region of Massachusetts, then a major manufacturing area, the focus was on industry—specifically the electrical and machine industries and even more specifically the General Electric plant in Lynn. GE was the target for every Left organization, not only the CP.

I had a job at the Harvard Hospitals and was trying to organize a local of 1199, then independent. However, still thinking of

6 Frank Emspak and Dolores Fox married in 1964. They had two children, and Dr. Dolores Emspak has built a career as an OB-GYN physician.

a career as a college professor in history, I arranged interviews with leading Communist, progressive, and former Communist leaders of the trade-union movement of the thirties and forties. The same questions we had in the seventies and eighties were also of concern to the earlier generation of activists: What should their role be in the trade unions? Should they be public? What was the effect of the Party's decision in the mid-fifties to mainstream — that is, to take its activists out of the Left unions and bring them and their supporters (often significant local unions) into the rival anticommunist unions of the Congress of Industrial Organizations. (Transcripts of the interviews are at the Wisconsin Historical Society but are not online as of this writing.) This history is important to our thinking about the future, but it is beyond the scope of this essay. Suffice it to say that in the early seventies, bitterness over this policy lingered, as many of the people involved were still in union office or on staff in the UE and other previously Left unions.

In November 1972 I started at United Shoe Machine Company (USM) in Beverley. At the time, the USM was the largest and most profitable manufacturer of shoe machines in the world, with a monopoly on production and twelve hundred employees, including management. It was one of the largest integrated factories in New England — meaning it had a foundry, a stamping operation, machining, assembly, and design and development all in one place. It was also a large, stable local of the United Electrical Workers.

At that time there was no CP on the North Shore; it had been destroyed during the anticommunist union purges. But because USM was a UE shop, old CP people were still there, and I had a chance to meet them. During 1972–1975, when I was at USM, the only real Party work I remember doing was keeping my act together in the union and participating as best I could in supporting Angela Davis. Just wearing a pin was a big deal in this all-white plant, where no one even went to Boston except for a ball game. Living as I did in Dorchester was considered by my workmates strange and life threatening. (Dorchester in 1972 was in transition from white — mostly Irish — to Black, complete with block busting and newspaper emphasis on crime and disruption and unrest.) Since the Party always talked about working in the union, and since I was raised with that and believed strongly in the idea that progressive Party people should help lead, I ran for office. I did not win on my initial try. The business agent, Jerry Steinberg, really wanted me to take over and supported my efforts to contribute to the union. I did help with the union paper, called *Blue Sheet.* I was also concerned about health and safety and urged the formation of a pension committee. I was becoming a competent machinist. I was not great, but people saw that I did my job and made an effort. Everyone knew that I had an education, and since the name was associated with the union, the assumption was that I was sent there by the union. That was not the case. I did make lifelong friends, starting with a co-worker who explained to me how to avoid the foreman. They initially thought that I was lucky to survive my first few months there.

The idea of independent Left leadership — that is, someone from the Party who might be elected to leadership in the local UE — turned out to be an issue. There is a difference between being a staff person and an elected person. In my entire trade-union career, in three different unions, I always served in elected positions. Thus, I was dependent on and loyal to the membership — at least as I understood it. I believed as a Communist that one's first loyalty is to the members, within the framework of a class-conscious vision of society.

In the spring of 1974, the business agent arranged for me to meet the UE director of organizing. I went assuming that he, as an ex-Communist, would be happy to see that I was busily working away in the conservative UE local 271. Such was not the case. He told me in no uncertain terms that I was rocking the boat in a trusted, secure local and wanted to know why I was there. He claimed the national office had received anonymous letters from members of the local complaining about me.

Actually, aside from the idea of industrial concentration, USM was the best job one could get. It paid more than my senior lab-tech job at Harvard Hospitals, had excellent insurance, and I was able to have a garden in what had been the "victory gardens" adjacent to the plant. The garden proved to be a great way to meet an older cohort of active Italian union members, most of them in maintenance. So when I ran for office, I had tremendous support from a group that had access to all workers in the plant.

I reacted by attacking the official, saying his red-baiting was no different than what had destroyed the Left in the past. Anyone in the office could have heard the discussion. This was almost like a family fight, and terribly upsetting. But as it turned out, within the UE there were officers, friends of my father, who saw the need for a renewal and the need for class-conscious people in the union, at the grass roots, as a legitimate force for change. The irony, of course, was that it was these very people who had resisted the call to mainstream and who had been expelled from the CP in the mid-fifties.

Another result of that meeting was that within the shop, everyone seemed to know what had happened and know that the union in fact had not asked me to come to work at USM and somehow become an officer of the local. My personal stock went up. Later that summer the company attempted to fire me for allegedly assaulting the foreman. My department stood firm for me, refusing to continue work until the issue was resolved. Later that same day the company backed down, and the president of the local appointed me the shop steward. A couple of months later I won election to the executive board of the local. I was laid off from USM in 1975. In late 1976 I was hired at the General Electric aircraft instrument plant in Wilmington, Massachusetts, a division of IUE local 201.

Meanwhile, I had begun to take a more active role in trying to build a Party on the North Shore. However, my work schedule, as well as the Party's focus on the city of Boston and on electoral work, which seemed pretty distant, limited my efforts. The tension between industrial work and the demands of political action on behalf of the Party was a constant, from the time the Party started functioning on the North Shore until it essentially dissolved in 1986.

The issue was not only one of time. On the North Shore, General Electric was the dominant employer, and IUE Local 201 was the leading industrial union. The tension with Boston had to do with how public the Party and its members could be, given the anticommunist nature of GE, in particular, and its union, IUE Local 201. After all, the local had split from the UE on the basis of anticommunism. Of the three big GE plants in the United States, the North Shore location was the only one where union members voted (just barely) for the IUE.[7] So the issue of how public one would be, given the anticommunist clause in the local union's constitution, was a real one in the early seventies. And in the local, as at USM in the UE, many of the protagonists were still employed or in office. Nonetheless, in the community and in the factory, where there were still workers who self-identified as reds, there was no interest in rejoining a Communist Party. Outside of the Left unions, the ex-Communists who went in to the IUE, the USW, or elsewhere soon disappeared into the bureaucracy, retired, or left the movement entirely.

All of the older generation of Party leaders were quite aware of the relations between people like me and the issue of mainstreaming — even if I and maybe others of my generation did not know about it. I think the distrust by older CP Central Committee members of people coming to the CP from the trade-union movement, the freedom movement, or the women's movement — maybe even the antiwar movement — derives in part from a question of loyalties. Would these people be loyal

7 The International Union of Electrical Workers was launched by the Congress of Industrial Organizations (CIO) in September 1949 to replace the United Electrical Workers, which it had just expelled. (The UE had also voted to leave.) The UE was anti–Cold War and believed workers should decide who the officers should be, and hence Communists were in leadership. The support by the UE for Vice President Henry Wallace and the Progressive Party challenged the CIO's relationship with the Democrats. So the CIO, with the support of the Roman Catholic Church, and more covertly of GE, launched the new union, essentially destroying the unity of the industry. In 1949 the UE had about 500,000 members. By 1960 it had perhaps 100,000, while the IUE counted 325,000.

to the Party if certain decisions had to be made, or would they remain loyal to the movements from whence they came?

Gradually, we built a significant Party club on the North Shore. The Party functioned from the midseventies until 1986. It was built around fighting the company at GE and building meaningful community support for other unions, like the United Farm Workers. The Party attracted people because it did practical work to strengthen the union against the company. It was coherent. There was a social and support aspect that helped give each member a sense of belonging. The types of big policy debates that occurred in the late sixties were by and large absent. There was general agreement on the fight against racism and the need for industrial concentration.

In a way, workers at GE or USM were the "aristocracy of labor," with pensions, decent jobs, and health insurance. But we sure didn't feel that way, and as time has proven, many of those attributes, such as pensions, could be taken away. But what ultimately did the Party in was the issue of internal democracy, especially when it came to the relationship between the national Party leadership in New York and shop organizations such as existed at GE.

The first time we had a difference of opinion was during contract negotiations with GE in 1979. Progressives, including Communists, had formed an organization within the local called WAGE (Win Against GE). Hundreds of union members signed a letter opposing concessions. Aside from individual members, many stewards and some elected executive board members of the local, including me, helped build this movement. Our goal was "no concessions" and a mobilization to achieve certain contractual benefits.

While the progressive coalition was busy organizing and trying to win a majority within the local and elsewhere, the CP, through the *Daily World,* endorsed the new proposed contract. No one in Lynn was consulted before the article was handed out at the plant gate. The progressive coalition was stunned, and within it Party members were asked to explain. All Party members opposed the contract and continued their agitation and leadership of WAGE.

The repercussions within the union were such that the local leadership was now convinced that the Communists within the local were with the union membership and thus could become an effective and powerful rank-and-file opposition. This was indeed what happened. Red-baiting didn't work, since the Party appeared to be endorsing the contract, but the people in the shop identified as reds were opposed to the contract. It was never clear to me why the Party endorsed the contract without consulting with the largest shop clubs in GE. At the time, we were told that the Party took its cue from the UE, which had agreed to the contact pending membership approval.

In the Party there was considerable tension and an unresolved disagreement which morphed into a general discussion of the political demands of the organization versus what we perceived as the needs — both political and in terms of the security, particularly the public security — of those in industry. Endorsement of the Party's candidates for office or signing election petitions was sure to cause attacks on individuals working at GE. It was one thing to be "known" as a Communist, but it was something else for someone to have documented evidence that the person really was a Communist. We felt that given the political situation and the fact that GE was also a defense plant, some caution was needed. Our perspective was not necessarily shared by the Boston leadership.

The final break occurred with the contract of 1986. This was another bruiser of a negotiation. The firm was clearly looking to close plants. The union was seeking to find ways to ameliorate the closures. Liberal Democrats were proposing legislation that would socialize the costs of plant closures but at least give those laid off some additional income and training opportunities. Essentially, the Democratic Party proposed that the state would pay for extended unemployment insurance and training programs. Within local 201, a progressive slate (including the business agent) had been elected for the first time since 1950. Party people were engaged in the fight against the contract in increasingly public ways. And then history repeated itself. Without any discussion with the Party activists in GE, the Party came out in support of the GE-IUE and GE-UE national contract. Our attempts to meet with leaders in New York came to naught. The result was the complete demoralization of our group. Given the risks involved in staying in the Party (politically and employment-wise) what was the point? The group dissolved.

Summing Up

In the years after 1960, the Party was not able to overcome deep political, racial, and class divisions and establish itself on a new footing that would have encompassed the social movements of the sixties and seventies. But it remains clear that a party or some formation based on a commitment to the working class is absolutely needed. Its character must be based on a willingness to confront rulers with direct action and political mobilization in support of that action, as well as more traditional electoral efforts. The basis for such an organization must be the practice of internal democracy, combined with a sense that those who produce the wealth have every right to possess a majority of it.

12

We Had a Big Victory, One That Many Thought We Couldn't Win

Sharon Stewart[1]

In 1946 I was born into a working-class family in the small, predominately African American community of Okemah, an unincorporated area of Maricopa County, Arizona. Huge dust storms would sweep across our valley, dumping grit into our not-so-tightly sealed home. The dirt drove my mother crazy — at least that was how it seemed to me and my two sisters when she would wake us up at two or three in the morning on a weekend, shouting, "We are cleaning this house today!"

I am the second oldest of three girls, and our mother knew how to squeeze every penny to give her girls opportunities that she didn't have as a child. As the sixth child in a family of ten children that lived to adulthood, my mother was denied the opportunity of attending high school. She was born just three years before the Great Depression, and she and her younger siblings were familiar with actual hunger.

My father, who could troubleshoot and repair almost any malfunctioning machine at his workplace, was classified as a

1 Originally written January 2016; revised January 2020. Sharon Stewart died in Phoenix, Arizona, on October 28, 2021

laborer in the nonunion cotton-oil processing plant where he worked in Phoenix. The workers were paid low wages, and the paltry benefits allowed them did not include sick time, and so my father received no pay for a couple of months after he was severely burned on the job.

I knew at the time that my father was being taken advantage of, and I didn't like it. Despite my father's addiction to nicotine, I believe his inhalation of cotton fibers and dust for more than thirty-five on the job years contributed to his early death from emphysema in 1986. Arizona was and remains a "right-to-work" state. Workers, especially workers of color, are not valued.

As a teenager, I couldn't put my finger on why my family and my people seemed economically near the bottom of the ladder. (I realized, of course, that Indigenous people were at the very bottom.) I struggled with questions about racial, political, social, and income inequality. But even back then, I knew we led the culture thing; we dominated the charts at the Stax, Atlantic, and Motown record labels.

But music didn't blind me to the injustices of racism and economic disparity. Occasional glimpses of a homeless man lying on a sidewalk in downtown Phoenix actually made me sick to my stomach with anxiety, and seeing young children with runny noses and cracked lips, especially, pitched me into depression. I tried to escape by burying myself in books, reading uplifting stories about plucky girls and women who overcame obstacles despite the complexity of the challenges.

While most African Americans in Phoenix went to segregated schools until long after the Supreme Court finding that "separate but equal" was unconstitutional, those of us who lived east of Fortieth Street at what is now University Drive went to Tempe schools, which were predominately white. I was a serious student, and after high school I went to Arizona State University (ASU), where I majored in speech communication. I married my first husband too young, but after the divorce I eventually went back to ASU, and while there I cofounded the Cross-Cultural Discussion Group. Membership included Africans from the diaspora and people from the Caribbean and sub-Saharan Africa, as well as African Americans.

As a study group we shared information about the Black liberation movement that in the 1970s was sweeping across the nation and the world. We read and discussed works by Walter Rodney, Frantz Fanon, and G.W.F. Hegel. Topics like colonialism, slavery, and capitalism in the context of dialectical and historical materialism generated conversation that would go into the early morning hours. We were filled with the possibility of our capacity to contribute to changing the world in which we lived. The group disbanded when one of our leaders returned to Zambia.

Several years later, I was selected to attend the summer program for minority journalists at University of California, Berkeley. The program guaranteed graduates jobs at major daily newspapers. In September 1980, I was hired by the *Rocky Mountain News,* a daily with a circulation of over 400,000 published in Denver, Colorado. While teaching a journalism class at University of Colorado Boulder, I met my first card-carrying member of the Communist Party USA (CPUSA), Paul Krehbiel. In the past, I had met and argued with members of the Revolutionary Communist Party, Socialist Workers Party, and Freedom Socialist Party, none of which met my need to belong to an organization that best exemplified a multinational, racially diverse workers' party grounded in the principles of Marxism-Leninism.

Working with the CPUSA and a group of like-minded, committed people freed me intellectually and emotionally. I joined the Party because I agreed with its program and the work it was doing. As members of the Paul Robeson Club, Krehbiel and I were active in a number of organizations, like the Urban League, the labor union-led Coors Boycott Coalition, and a number of community-based neighborhood organizations. We fought rate hikes proposed by the public utilities commission, and we fought for the release of a young African American man who had been sentenced to life in prison, despite the fact that he was an after-the-fact accomplice to a murder, while his white friend, the actual murderer, was given a much lighter sentence.

One of the big issues our club was involved in was a fight to save my job at the *Rocky Mountain News*. My personal struggle against racism and sexism at the *News* ended in victory because I wasn't alone. Once informed about the *News*' actions against me, leaders of the NAACP, the Urban League, and other Black organizations began meeting with *News* publisher Ralph Looney and his team. I was the paper's only Black reporter, and thus community members were able to point out how the lack of diversity in the editorial department was a problem that needed correction.

News management targeted me after I wrote an article covering CP general secretary Gus Hall's visit to Denver, where he called for the impeachment of President Ronald Reagan. I had let the weekend editor know that Hall, a former presidential candidate, was in town. The editor explained that she was short-staffed and asked me to cover the story even though it was my day off. I interviewed Hall at CPUSA district organizer Rob Prince's home, and the resulting transcript appeared on the front page of the Metro section under a banner headline. Hall called for President Ronald Reagan's impeachment, blasting the president for his antilabor, racist, and war-mongering policies and behavior. He urged the continual building of the people's movement to stop Reagan and the right-wing corporate forces behind him and strengthen the movements for social justice.

When *News* managing editor Ben Blackburn arrived Monday morning and saw the newspaper, he was furious. "I come in and read my goddamn newspaper and it reads like the *Communist Manifesto*," he foamed. I was called into his office and grilled. "Was I a member of the Communist Party?" he angrily demanded. Blackburn was a known racist, a sexist, and political reactionary. I recounted how I became the reporter on the story, adding that my reporting had nothing to do with my political beliefs. He continued the grilling. How did I know that Hall was going to be in town? Why did I interview him? He was steaming. I answered that I heard Hall was giving a public speech in Denver and I thought it was newsworthy.

The witch hunt began. Sources at the rural communities on my beat reported that Blackburn's henchman, Al Knight, had called asking how they felt about my reporting. They were asked how often I visited the county supervisor's office and the various city offices of the four or five rural cities on my beat. At one point, a nurse at my Kaiser Permanente doctor's office told me that someone from the *News* called to see if I had really visited the doctor on a day that I took a sick day.

I didn't get fired, but Blackburn made my life hell. When an engine blew out on a company car, he wrote a nasty warning, saying that if my misuse of cars continued, I would be disciplined up to and including termination. When I pointed out in writing that reporters were not responsible for maintenance of cars, including putting gas in them, he dropped the matter, but even after a grievance hearing, refused to take the letter out of my file.

Management scrutinized everything I did. It was clear that they were working to build a case against me. After I couldn't find an agenda for a Northglenn city council meeting, I got a letter suspending me without pay for one week, saying this was the result of my lack of candor on when I had picked up the agenda — not that I had failed to pick up the agenda but that I picked it up at a different time, contrary to my having stated that the agenda was at my home. Without a doubt, I was on a fast track for termination.

The Party was deeply involved in putting together a fightback plan. Club leaders made my case their top priority. Filing a grievance challenging the suspension through the union was our first step. The union administrative officer was a strong defender who stood up for me when a few of my colleagues had asked me to resign from the bargaining committee, alleging that my personal problems with management could interfere with our unit getting a good contract. At the time, I was vice president of Local 37074 of the Denver Newspaper Guild; I told the group what they could do to get me kicked off the bargaining committee. The group decided not to come to the next union meeting, even though I advised them how to officially submit a petition with lots of signatures calling for my ouster.

A number of my fellow workers told me privately that they disagreed with what management had done, but they were afraid of retaliation if they spoke out in my defense. I was disappointed, believing that if everyone spoke up everyone would be protected. After all, Blackburn and Knight liked nothing better than pitting reporters against one another, and I wasn't the only person the duo regularly tried to humiliate.

Fear was in the air. My suspension happened not long after Reagan fired twelve thousand air traffic controllers in the Professional Air Traffic Controllers Organization, which spread fear throughout the labor movement. Party members fought back by getting the community involved, especially the African American community. The *News* already had a reputation of either ignoring the Black community or depicting it in racist ways in news articles and editorials. And as I was the only news reporter of color at the paper, the community rallied to support me, and in the process supported themselves as well. They understood that the attack on me was one in a long line of egregious slights against the community. The Black churches, community organizations, and elected Black political leaders spoke out on my behalf. There was talk of a boycott of the *News,* and this at a time when the *News* was in an intense circulation war with the rival *Denver Post.* The Party was instrumental in initiating all of these activities. I returned to work after my one-week suspension. Going to work every day was excruciating, and it took several months more for management to cave.

A local community newspaper did a feature on my case, including in the article the fact that Blackburn had commented that he wanted his coffee the color of Lena Horne's backside. There was also a rumor that he wanted coffee as black as my nipples. It was reported that he made jokes comparing women to mushrooms—"Keep them in the dark, feed them a lot of s&*t, and they grow real well." The American Civil Liberties Union agreed to take my case, and a lawsuit was filed. Finally, the pressure became so great on the *News* that the parent E.W. Scripps

Howard Company sent a team of lawyers from Cincinnati to make me an offer to settle the lawsuit.

As part of a settlement, I received back pay for the suspension and was given the Denver city and county court beat. Corporate management let Blackburn keep his title as managing editor, but he no longer had job duties; he was without portfolio. Henchman Al Knight, who was assistant managing editor, left the paper, since he too was left with no job duties. I think he went to work for the *Denver Post.* Dave Butler was hired as the new city editor, and he asked me which beat I preferred. Butler later told me that he had expected me to fail but was pleased when I regularly scooped the two *Denver Post* court reporters.

In return I dropped the union grievance and the lawsuit. The *News* was taking a beating in the community over this case and knew they had to settle before they lost more circulation, profits, and reputation. They had been so stung by the community response that they didn't want to do anything to reignite it. After ongoing discussion within the Party, I had agreed to accept the settlement. The main goals had been accomplished. Community leaders and comrades saw this as a very big victory, a victory that many thought we couldn't win. Coworkers told me that I was now the most protected worker at the *News.* And it was true: Management stayed clear of me and left me alone. I was given one of the toughest beats on the paper. Lawyers from corporate advised local management to desist racist and sexist practices. They forced local management to hire an affirmative-action officer as well as several more Black reporters and the company's first Hispanic reporters. Local management was told that a lawsuit that could have been in the six-figure range had just been settled.

I suspect that some of those involved wondered about my political leanings, but it was never voiced. It wasn't an issue. We lived in a society where the capitalist ruling class worked hard to demonize Communists. We didn't want to allow them to make that the issue. We wanted to make sure that racism and sexism were at the heart of the matter, thereby helping the community organize to stop them — at least in this case. And we were successful. The community—the Black community, progressives and leftists, and many other groups—saw this as a victory.

Without the support of CP members, on my own, I don't know how I would have withstood this attack. When one co-worker advised me to go to management and offer to quit if they would give me a solid recommendation, I was devastated. I thought she was my friend, but she said I was going to go down and take her down with me, since it was known she gave me some of the information about Blackburn's racist and sexist comments. The Party gave me the energy to withstand management's attempts to turn my coworkers against me.

The Party was also involved in the 1984 Jesse Jackson campaign for president. As a matter of fact, our club's strategizing around the Jackson campaign led to my election as an alternate Jackson delegate at the 1984 Democratic Party Convention in San Francisco.

The lessons learned from these campaigns were that active, committed fighters who had a good ideological analysis of the problem and a well thought-out organizing plan—the principles of the Communist Party at its core—could win against powerful corporate interests. The Party's understanding of the importance of combating racism and of how to do it was central to the struggle.

13

Party Time

Rafael Pizarro[1]

I never met Henry Winston, nor was I aware of him in his lifetime. What little I know about him is from comrades who did know him, and that's in bits and pieces. In my poem, Winston — or Winnie, as people fondly called him — is a stand-in for the many Communists I met who impressed me deeply, simply by the kind of people they were. Each, within their own personality, was principled, smart, strategic, brave, and hard-working. At the same time, they were full human beings who joked, argued, cooked, danced — not at all the stereotype of the over-serious intellectual or slimy schemer I had been made to believe that Communists conformed to.

I was a blue-diaper baby, son of a member of Local 1199. The powerful health-care workers union in New York wasn't Communist-run, but the leadership was very Left and tolerant of Communists, who were known as often the best union organizers. Republican coal-miners union president John L. Lewis said, when asked by a congressional committee why he turned a blind eye to Communist organizers within his union, "If you're going to build a house, you need carpenters."

I first saw Communists in action in the Left's struggle to recapture the leadership of 1199. Communists were among the

1 Originally written October 2019.

best, most stalwart leaders of that movement. The first I met was Marcial Garcia — or the first I met knowingly, as he was the only fully open Party member. He was a Cuban American organizer who became executive vice president (EVP) of the union. I was a new, young, organizer that had much to learn, and Marcial was my supervisor and willing mentor. He taught me that one of the most important jobs of an organizer was to find and train their replacement. This made it clear to me not just that education and mentorship was important but also that I was expendable. Whatever my abilities or talent, I was useless by myself and should always be looking to build a movement, to train future organizers, not just to win better conditions for workers, though it was hard to do the former without being seen to do the latter.

Marcial had been thoroughly trained in Marxist-Leninist economic and political theory and didn't mind sharing it with me. But he also had a passion for history. He often told me about the Spanish Civil War, and once, when I complained about not being recognized for good work I'd done, he said, "Do you know how many comrades were killed in Spain fighting fascism and there's not so much as a plaque on a wall to commemorate them?"

But he didn't mind revealing his limitations. In those first days of new leadership of 1199, Marcial was an EVP for the first time, just as I was an organizer for the first time. Often I would come across a question I didn't know the answer to. When I brought it to Marcial, he would sometimes say to me, rising from his desk, "I don't know; let's go find out."

But what I liked most about Marcial was his sense of humor, which was coupled with the confidence of knowing his beliefs were strong enough, had such deep foundation in theory and history, that they wouldn't be easily challenged. The losers of the election appealed, naturally, and at a hearing at the Department of Labor, Marcial was asked how he felt firing so many staff loyal to the old regime after the elections. In his sworn testimony, he said, "I felt like Robespierre." After we won the leadership and I asked Marcial about a job, he said, "I can't help you. I'm on the firing committee — I can get someone fired if you want — but you need someone on the hiring committee." He was only half joking, as another Communist spoke to me about work, and eventually I was hired as an organizer.

But there were many other leaders who weren't Party members and never would be. I remember one who complained out loud that you had to be a member of the Party to become an officer of the union, less than a week before she was promoted to vice president.

The brilliant strategy, hard work, and bravery I saw during the election campaign carried into running the union. The Communists were the most dedicated organizers, as if they carried a fire within them that wouldn't go out, no matter the storm. One thing that was drilled into me was the need for discipline. We were an army in battle, even if it was without firearms. So everything — events, organizing efforts — was prepared with the utmost care and attention, like a battle plan.

I was impressed enough to eventually join the Party. In those days, you had to have a card signed by two members to be considered. Marcial signed mine, then took me to the office of another member, joking, "Would you sign Rafael's card? No one else wants to."

I became active in the Party as well as the union. One day I got a phone call from Charlene Mitchell to ask if I would volunteer to help on her campaign for the US Senate. It was the first contact I ever had with her. I learned that she had headed up Angela Davis's defense committee and had been a Communist fighter and organizer since she was a teenager. Later, I learned that she had been the first African American woman to run for president of the United States.

The trait that most came through to me was her no-nonsense approach to everything. "If you're not meeting, you don't exist," she said. I made the mistake of calling her once when Bill Clinton was giving his first State of the Union address. She answered the phone: "Who's calling me while my president is speaking on television?" But it was her organizing skills and leadership that I admired most. So it was natural that she led the movement first to reform the Party (1989–1991) and then to create a new organization, the Committees of Correspondence for Democracy and Socialism, in 1992. Charlene anticipated every step of the way, every which way we could turn, every place we'd be blocked. We broke away from the Party, taking hundreds of members with us.

It was in the Committees of Correspondence that I met Carl Bloice. He had been the *People's World* correspondent in Moscow, and I like to imagine him, a tall Black man, walking around Moscow and ordering food in Russian. We became friends less on a political level and more on a cultural one. We both enjoyed sports. We both enjoyed popular music and we both enjoyed the other's company. I looked forward to meetings not so much for the substance but for afterward, when Carl and I and a couple of other friends would head to his place to watch the Knicks or the Giants. I'd take him to task for enjoying mainstream country music, and he called me "the bull of the mosh pits," because of my passion for punk rock. Naturally, this was all around political work and building a new organization, but it's telling that what I remember mostly is the fun we had together, not all the news articles he clipped for me and the creative writing I sent him for his approval.

Carl passed away a couple of years ago, Marcial about ten, and Charlene is in a nursing home, having suffered a debilitating stroke. But other comrades from those days are still friends and I cherish them for who they are, not just for what they do.

I recently rejoined the Party. I thought that in a time of imminent fascism, I wanted to stand in solidarity with those who were historically the last bulwark against reaction and fascism. I believe we'll need the discipline and clear vision of a disciplined, Leninist organization again, even if I don't agree with all of the decisions made.

The thing I hope I've gained through all of this isn't so much what I've learned a lot about politics, economics, and organizing, but that I've become a full person, able to learn about and practice those things, but also someone a new activist may look to and say, "That guy's a Communist, but he's cool. I don't mind talking socialism with him, because he's not a robot and doesn't take himself as seriously as he does the struggle." And these Communists I knew were the role models I needed to become that person.

Henry Winston's Laugh[2]

A Poem in Salute to the Communist Party of the United States of America, on the Occasion of Its 100th Anniversary in Struggle

Henry Winston paces his cell.
Five steps and back, five steps and back.
How do you not run into the wall, his cell mate asks,
"Three steps forward, two steps back," he jokes.

The boy with bad teeth and little education doesn't get it,
but he loves how Winston laughs.
It makes him laugh too.

At night, the boy cries — he's
too young to be here.
What can Henry do?

He tells the boy stories, stories
of life and struggles.
He knows not to make speeches, polemics,
for what would that mean
to this boy, far from home,
jailed for crimes of poverty.

He knows the boy likes a joke
but he knows not to make one

2 Rafael Pizarro, "Henry Winston's Laugh: A Poem in Salute to the Communist Party of the United States of America, on the Occasion of Its 100th Anniversary in Struggle," *Blue Collar Review* 22, no. 3 (2019): 55. Republished as "Henry Winston's Laugh," *People's World*, October 2, 2019, https://www.peoplesworld.org/article/henry-winstons-laugh/.

when the boy is in his bunk,
humming songs of rural Georgia.
Better be silent then and let him
work through his suffering.
There's time for laughter in the morning.

But in the morning, the guard says,
the one that would be kind if his job allowed it,
You have a visitor, Winston, be ready in ten.
Who could it be, the boy asks.

It's a reporter from a small newspaper;
he didn't want this assignment
but he does need his paycheck
and so does his family.

The boy lies on his bunk, face to the wall,
and only listens. The reporter asks,
Do you regret your crime?
What crime?
Being a red.

A man can't help what he thinks.
But is it worth losing your freedom, the reporter asks.
Henry lifts his head,
I don't know what you mean, I haven't
lost my freedom.

The reporter looks lost, confused—
but you're in jail for who knows how long.
I see, says Henry,
I see your error:

The man who works day and night and still doesn't have enough to feed his family, that man is not free; The woman who must accept the abuse of her employers' children, lest she lose her job—

she is not free;
The child forced to go to work at an early age
rather than get an education, that child is not free;
The men who are torn from their homes to kill men in far off lands who offend God no more than they, those men are not free;
The woman, bereft of everything a woman should have except her body, which she gives so she may live, she is not free;
The men who have been stripped of their souls and fill the space with sweet poison that only kills them slowly — those men certainly could be said to have lost their freedom.

Henry leans back and laces his fingers
behind his head and says,
Me, I'm perfectly comfortable.

The boy snickers, knowing when
Henry is having a little joke. The reporter stands up abruptly,
thinks he's been had, calls the guard —
None of this will appear in his article.

When he leaves, Henry and the boy burst out laughing.

The guards don't like this.
Tomorrow he'll be moved to another cell,
alone, where he cannot make friends,
where there will be no one to read the papers to him.

In the morning Henry is told to take his blanket
and the gate clanks open. He embraces the boy,
ignores his tears as he knows this will embarrass him.
Henry says no words, they would hurt and he is determined
that his jailers will not hurt him.

The gate slams shut behind him and
as he's led away by the arm he hears the boy call out one last time,

so that everyone can hear,
as if grasping for a round buoy—
Henry, Henry, wait!—what's the name of that book you told me about?

14

Building the Left in the Labor Movement

James Williams[1]

I come from a blue-collar family—factory workers, construction workers, and small farmers. For much of my upbringing, my dad was unemployed, and times were tough. I come from Kentucky and from a time when segregation ruled the land. I started out in a one-room schoolhouse but had moved to Louisville schools by the second grade. My folks moved around a lot, and it wasn't really until the sixth grade that I was in one school for the whole term. Having had polio from the sixth through the eighth grade, I was in special education.

My dad was a bricklayer and a socialist. I don't mean in the sense of having belonged to any particular party or being a socialist activist, but he did vote for Norman Thomas, the Socialist Party candidate, on occasion. He would talk to me about socialism pretty much as it existed through the British Labour Party. He taught me about the class struggle. My mother came from a Republican family, which meant, in that part of Kentucky, that your family supported the Union during the Civil War. In the 1930s and '40s and '50s, Republicans were actually the liberals

1 Originally written June 2016; revised June 2022.

in the South, being more inclined to support civil rights and fair treatment for African Americans.

Although my folks weren't especially religious, they raised me in the Christian tradition. There were parts of the bible that greatly influenced me — the Hebrew prophets, especially, who railed against the rich who abused the poor, those who upheld justice:

> God has taken his place in the divine council;
> in the midst of the gods he holds judgement:
> "How long will you judge unjustly
> and show partiality to the wicked? Selah
> Give justice to the weak and the orphan;
> maintain the right of the lowly and the destitute.
> Rescue the weak and the needy;
> deliver them from the hand of the wicked."
> They have neither knowledge nor understanding,
> they walk around in darkness;
> all the foundations of the earth are shaken.
>
> (Psalm 82: 1–5)[2]

> When an alien resides with you in your land, you shall not oppress the alien. The alien who resides with you shall be to you as the citizen among you; you shall love the alien as yourself, for you were aliens in the land of Egypt.
>
> (Leviticus 19: 33–34)[3]

Also important was the New Testament, with its Sermon on the Mount and, of course, Luke 4:18:

> The spirit of the Lord is upon me,
> because he has anointed me

2 Michael Coogan, Marc Brettler, Carol Newsom, and Pheme Perkins, eds., *The New Oxford Annotated Bible with Apocrypha, New Revised Standard Version, Fifth Edition* (Oxford University Press, 2018), 851.

3 Ibid., 174.

to bring good news to the poor.
He has sent me to proclaim release to the captives
and recovery of sight to the blind,
to let the oppressed go free...

(Luke 4:18)[4]

At the age of fourteen, I worked in the tobacco fields, harvesting Burley tobacco for four dollars a day. My folks couldn't afford schoolbooks or fancy clothes, so I made my own way. Somehow or other I managed to enroll in college with a scholarship. I got a job working in the library shelving books. That was my downfall. Our library had quite a few radical and labor books, and I managed to read most of them. I was particularly drawn to Karl Marx. Karl Marx seemed like the Old Testament prophets that I read about in the Bible.

When in college, I was caught up in the spirit of student activism. I joined the Students for a Democratic Society (SDS; I was one of the founders, actually), was a member of Friends of the Student Nonviolent Coordinating Committee (SNCC), and was active in the formation of the Southern Student Organizing Committee (SSOC). *Esquire* magazine wrote me up in an article about campus radicals.

This activism was fostered by my mentors, Carl and Anne Braden, two courageous white civil rights supporters who gained notoriety in Louisville when they bought a house for a Black family. A far-right prosecutor actually prosecuted them for sedition for this act. Carl served time in prison until the Supreme Court ruled state sedition laws unconstitutional.

Anne and Carl were journalists by trade, and they taught me the fundamentals of how to write. I wrote for the *Southern Patriot*, the organ of the Southern Conference Education Fund (SCEF), which they edited. Their home was also a way station for activists from the North and the South. I think the first Communist I met was Alva Buxenbaum, who was traveling for the Progressive Youth Organizing Committee (PYOC). These travel-

4 Ibid., 1875.

ers comprised the antiracist left spectrum: socialists, Communists, progressives, and pacifists.

The journalistic skills I learned from the Bradens served me well as editor of *IUE L761 News* at the General Electric plant in Louisville, Kentucky, where I worked while still in college. I also learned how to weld at the plant, which, together with my journalistic experience, helped me find jobs later in life.

In my final year in college, I was active in both SDS (to whose national council I was elected) and SSOC. In the summer of 1964, I moved to New York City to work for SDS as head of its Political Education Project (PEP). The faction I was associated with, along with SDS member Steve Max, used a book by Gilbert Green called *The Enemy Forgotten.* Green advocated for a broad coalition comprised of labor, the Civil Rights Movement, and the peace movement to affect change. The Max family was a Communist Party (CP) family that had severed ties with the Party after the Khrushchev revelations about Stalin and the Soviet invasion of Hungary. Steve's father, Alan Max, had been managing editor of the *Daily Worker.* Steve had been chair of the New York high school chapter of the Labor Youth League, the CP's youth organization. Steve and I joined a study group run by Dr. Albert E. Blumberg and his wife, Dorothy Rose Blumberg. Both were former CP activists and had served prison terms under the anticommunist Smith Act.

After 1964, as the Democratic Party sold out the Mississippi Freedom Democrats and President Johnson escalated the Vietnam War, working with the Democratic Party was no longer very popular in SDS. So I went to work for a union, the International Union of Electrical Workers (IUE), where I wrote for the newspaper and assisted field organizing campaigns. I became a member of the Greater Washington AFL-CIO Labor Council and a member of the board of the Newspaper Guild Local 35. My biggest experience was the Memphis RCA drive. We helped hundreds of RCA workers to have a union, over furious opposition from the establishment and the Ku Klux Klan.

I got itchy feet after this campaign, so in 1967 I went to work for the West Virginia AFL-CIO, where I met local members of the

Communist Party. They seemed downright sensible to me, but I did not join the Party at the time, largely because I opposed the Soviet invasion of Czechoslovakia. I met the Communist Party labor secretary, George Meyers, and we became friends and stayed in contact. I also met legendary Southern activist Don West, who was forming an educational and cultural center in West Virginia. In 1968 the West Virginia AFL-CIO ran its own candidate for governor. Naturally, I was drafted to work on his campaign. We won the primary, and suddenly I was press secretary of the West Virginia Democratic Party. I found myself with itchy feet again.

I moved back to Washington, DC, to work for the Newspaper Guild as assistant editor of the *Guild Reporter* and assistant research director. In my free time I helped build Washington Labor for Peace, labor people against the Vietnam War. My work at the Guild was praised until I signed an ad against the war in the *Washington Post*. Suddenly the Guild decided that I was incompetent (!) and fired me. The leadership of the Newspaper Guild at that time was vociferously anticommunist and, in fact, it was revealed that they actively collaborated with the Central Intelligence Agency (CIA). I wonder if my frequent lunches with George Meyers played a role.

Well, I was blacklisted. Not a good place to be. After a period of unemployment, I went to work for the National Education Association as an organizer in their higher education department. From 1970 to 1974 I ran a number of collective bargaining elections and participated in collective bargaining sessions. I helped win elections for fifteen thousand faculty at the State University of New York (SUNY) and eight thousand in the Pennsylvania State College system. This was strenuous work because I was on the road practically all the time with few breaks in between.

George Meyers suggested that I move to Chicago and edit a newspaper called *Labor Today*. By this time I had joined the Communist Party, in 1973. I joined largely because of the Party's opposition to racism and its support of trade unionism. On a campaign in Philadelphia, I met several Party members and found them to be honest and hard working. Back in Washington, a severe rift had developed between white and African American activists following the death of Dr. Martin Luther King Jr. and the subsequent riots. Friends of mine were no longer even talking to each other. The rift was heartbreaking to me, but I found in the Communist Party a culture of solidarity between white and Black that encouraged me a great deal. So, when George Meyers asked me to move to Chicago, I was ready.

Labor Today was an exciting and at the same time frustrating experience. I got to meet a lot of good, solid, active trade unionists from around the country who were waging amazing fights in their unions for democracy and rank-and-file control. I was placed under the direction of Fred Gaboury, who was director of the National Committee for Trade Union Action and Democracy. Fred was a logger from Washington State and brought with him a culture of militancy and trade unionism that reflected that state's Industrial Workers of the World heritage. (I thought I knew how to cuss until I met Fred.) Fred was very close with Gus Hall, the general secretary of the Communist Party, and was in frequent contact with him. Fred was given to barking out orders and expecting them to be followed. I thought his orders were often sectarian and ran counter to our work. I was told when I was hired that they wanted me to use all my trade union contacts to further the work of the paper. Once in place, however, they told me that such-and-such people were "social democrats" and that I was to have nothing to do with them. I had a great staff at *Labor Today*, all volunteers, and among them was Andrea Shapiro, who was probably the only one among us who could spell and who knew grammar.

In 1975 I was sent to a national Party school in New York City. The school lasted nine weeks and was taught by James Jackson, the Party's education director at that time. I met a number of comrades I stayed in touch with over the years. The best thing about Party school was that I met Sandy Patrinos, and that led to our marriage and her moving to Chicago. Sandy moved from her job as district organizer of Eastern Pennsylvania and Delaware to a position in Chicago as director of a new women's organization called Women for Racial and Economic Equality (WREE). She also became a leader in the Illinois Party as well as a Central Committee member. She worked for a union, for the YWCA, and later became administrator of an innovative medical program at Cook County Hospital. She died of cancer in 2000. Her archives are at the Tamiment Library at New York University.

In Chicago, I belonged to several Party clubs over the years. One was called the Red Flash, and it consisted mostly of Party members who were delegates to the Central Labor Council, trade unionists elected by their respective unions, but not known as members of the Communist Party, because anticommunist restrictions were still in place in most unions. Later, I was in an electrical workers club, a steel workers club, and finally a South Chicago community club.

My tenure at *Labor Today* was stormy at times. It was a stressful job to begin with, putting out a monthly newspaper on a shoestring, but I had lots of conflicts about content. I wrote some things I wish I hadn't and didn't write some things I wish I had. But Fred Gaboury and Gus Hall always had the final say. Word would come down to write an article about such and such that seemed irrelevant to me. A tipping point was an interview I got with Victor Reuther. I knew Reuther from my work in Washington Labor for Peace, of which he was an active supporter. Reuther was the brother of Walter Reuther, the president of the United Auto Workers. To put it mildly, the CP and the Reuther brothers did not get along.

My interview with Reuther was about the anti–Vietnam War movement in the labor movement. For me, as a journalist, the piece was a coup. I thought it was a great article—and more importantly, that it might broaden *Labor Today*'s appeal. I was afraid we had become just another CP house organ and too sectarian. Fred and Gus Hall hit the roof! They were stuck in the 1930s. As I look back, it seems that most of the Party's trade-union policies were retreads of failed policies of the past: the use of "colonizers" in industry (yes, we used that unfortunate term); the setting up of various "front" organizations rather than working within existing organizations; running Communist electoral campaigns that went nowhere.

Finally, after Gus Hall dismissed my complaints, I just couldn't take it anymore and resigned from the paper. *Labor Today* continued without a hiccup and folded in the mid-1980s when the Soviet subsidy ceased. (See the chapter "Solidarity, Support, Friendship, Money," by Jay Schaffner, in Volume 3 for more information.)

When I left *Labor Today,* I needed a job. The United Electrical Workers found me one in a steel yard, where I became shop steward. It was an interesting place to work because they mostly hired ex-offenders. It was at this time that we started an electrical workers club that consisted of about three members. It later dissolved when the remaining members left for other activities.

It seemed like the rank-and-file rebellion in the steel workers union was the place to be. I asked my friends in steel if they could help me find a job there. Steel was a major concentration industry for the Party, and there was a vibrant rank-and file-movement for change in the union. At U.S. Steel, I took an apprenticeship test, passed somehow, and was hired as an apprentice millwright. There was a lively Party club at U.S. Steel, and many of its members held union positions. We had a rank-and-file caucus and regularly published leaflets and newsletters. I liked working in the steel mill; I was a millwright and had an interesting, skilled job. There was a certain cachet or prestige in the Party for steel workers.

Working in industry was the highlight of my time in the Party, because I felt like I was doing something useful. It was hard, dirty, dangerous work, with constantly changing shifts, but for some reason I really liked it. I was a member of the state committee of the Illinois district of the Communist Party. I also attended some national Central Committee meetings as well.

Just a note on these state committee and Central Committee meetings: They seemed strange and unlike any other meetings I attended in my life. The chair would give a report on the current state-national-world situation. Then members would get up and give a sort of show-and-tell comment on their situation. There would be no comment or debate about the content of the main report, except maybe to compliment the chair on the fine report. A couple of resolutions might be offered, and these usually passed without comment. An exception was in the Illinois state committee, when a group of us proposed a resolution supporting passage of the Equal Rights Amendment. A heated debate ensued, and the resolution was voted down.

Chicago is a town with a vibrant independent politics. Independent in this case meant Democrats who were independent of the Democratic Party machine. Active movements began within the African American community and the Latino community to replace the machine. This culminated in the victory of Harold Washington for mayor in 1983. The Washington movement enjoyed great popularity in the African American community and among Latinos and labor and liberal folks. It was a real breakthrough in Chicago politics, but the machine, although battered, continued to resist progressive change. We steel workers worked very hard for Harold Washington and a number of independent candidates, including Rudy Lozano, who ran for alderman.

Harold Washington was not only Chicago's first Black mayor but a solid progressive as well. Tragically, Rudy Lozano was murdered soon after the election. The gunman was a young gang member. Who paid the gunman is still unknown, but I cannot banish the notion that somehow the Daley Democratic Party machine was involved.

The steel industry took a turn for the worse, and I was out of a job at U.S. Steel, along with several other comrades in various other mills. For a while I managed the Party bookstore, and we scraped along on Sandy's salary. Then I went to work for Imported Publications, a company that imported books from the Soviet Union and other socialist countries. I was their Midwest sales representative, and this meant pretty constant travel. It was a tiring job, and I made up my mind to leave when certain important decisions were taken without my input. I studied substance-abuse counseling at Harold Washington College, and

I landed a job at a hospital which specialized in substance-abuse treatment.

I had a serious alcohol problem, particularly after I lost my job in the steel mill. Like most steel workers, I was heavily invested in my job and my identity as a skilled worker. It was then that I began to drink heavily, eventually being hospitalized after a suicide attempt. I got help, got sober, and am still sober after over thirty years. I also confronted major depression, which no doubt colored my thinking at times. One, of course, did not discuss these things in Party circles.

The 1980s started out as a pretty active and robust time for the movement in Chicago. We had the Harold Washington mayoral campaign, and the Party seemed well grounded in many areas of the city's political life. By this time, I was in a community club and participated as best I could, while holding down a demanding job and bulling through a PhD program. Sandy also was a leader in the community club as well as education director of the Illinois district of the Party. We had a lot of interesting classes and visiting teachers, including Edward Boorstein, a US economist and author who worked for the Popular Unity government in Chile and had advised the Cuban government.

In 1980 I was sent to Moscow to attend classes at the Lenin School of the International Department of the CPSU. These classes were supposed to cement our support of the Soviet Union and its achievements. Some of the instructors were very frank and critical of the Soviet situation. I don't know how my fellow students felt about this, but it reinforced my feelings that something was definitely wrong.

But by the mid-1980s, when Mikhail Gorbachev came to power, things there began to change, in a good way, I thought. It seemed that the Soviet Union was on its way to a more open and democratic society. This was appealing to me as well as to Sandy, and we began to think about these changes in terms of our own Party. About that time the national Party leadership in New York threw out our Illinois district leadership and replaced it with another! This was a shocking experience, and we began to think seriously about how the Party could be changed. Leaders of the Illinois district were called into an emergency meeting and were informed that we had a new leadership and the old leadership was out! We had no inkling that a change was afoot or that there was any reason for a change. Some of the new leaders were open Stalinists. These unanticipated and uncalled for (in my opinion) changes cemented my feelings that something was desperately wrong in the Party, at the highest levels.

Meanwhile, change was happening in the Party nationally: There was a feeling that the Gus Hall leadership had led us down a dead end and would isolate us from our constituencies. At the national level also, African Americans in the leadership felt that they were being disrespected by Gus Hall. Eventually, about one-third of the membership left the Party in 1990–1991, including me and Sandy.

A friend suggested that I apply for a job in a new jail diversion program at the Cook County courts called pretrial services. At the same time, I enrolled in a master of social work program at the University of Illinois. Sandy had enrolled in a master of public administration program at Roosevelt University. She became administrator of the mobile mammography program at Cook County Hospital, while I became a supervisor at the adult probation department mental health unit. For reasons that escape me now, I entered the PhD program in social work at the University of Illinois.

Leaving the Party, even with all its faults, was a wrenching experience for us. Most of our friends were Party members, and they, too, began to divide along political lines, and the internal fights sometimes became very bitter and hurtful. Our lives, both political and social, had centered around the Party for decades. A number of members who left the Party began a new organization called the Committees of Correspondence for Democracy and Socialism. Sandy became very active in this and served on its national board.

In 1995 Sandy developed a rare brain cancer, and my political work and my studies were put on hold until after she died in 2000. I was fortunate to find a new partner, Andrea Shapiro, a comrade who was a red-diaper baby. We were married in 2001.

After I got my PhD, I took a job teaching social work at Savannah State University in Savannah, Georgia, a historically Black institution. Later we moved to Tacoma, Washington, where I taught at the University of Washington Tacoma campus. Now I am retired.

I have been involved in various community organizations since we arrived in Tacoma, and recently became active in forming a chapter of the Democratic Socialists of America. I am still a paper member of the Committees of Correspondence.

What can I make of all this history? Though it was not always a pleasant experience, I am grateful for my years in the CP. I learned an awful lot and met a lot of really interesting people. I had experiences such as trips to the Soviet Union that I couldn't have had any other way. Although I would like to have accomplished more, I don't regret joining the CP at all, although I'm not totally happy with my experience.

That doesn't mean I'm bitter — it just means I had hoped that things would work out differently. I still feel the United States needs socialism and that it is people like us who will make a contribution to that end.

15

Taking Organizing Seriously

Judy Atkins[1]

I went to high school in Northport, New York, and attended Wheaton College in Norton, Massachusetts. In high school I was aware of the voter registration drive in the South and the involvement of college students in the voter registration summer. In college I was an active leader in the antiwar movement. I think I was educated about the world by the Vietnam War. Opposition to the war convinced me that US foreign policy had changed since World War II, and now its role was to defeat Communism and, in particular, the national liberation movements of the so-called third-world countries.

Our campus antiwar committee invited speakers, read a lot about the war, and attended demonstrations in other cities, such as New Haven and Boston. We lectured our professors. I think the teach-in strategy was very important, as well as the antidraft movement. I met some pacifists—I think we actually met A.J. Muste in Connecticut just before his death, but I didn't know who he was at the time. (Muste was a leader of the early anti-Vietnam War movement, a lifelong pacifist, and an organizer of the 1934 Congress of Industrial Organizations [CIO] Toledo auto strike.)

1 Originally written February 2021; revised March 2021.

The split with our parents' generation was that they still saw the United States as the champion of democracy in the victory over fascism during World War II. And they said that you had to trust that the government in Washington knew what it was doing. I began to understand class divisions, as working-class males, and in particular African Americans, were the most likely to be drafted and to serve in the military, while the sons of the wealthy always found deferments. On the global scale, it was the wealthy nations against the poor nations. My interest in Marxism was rooted in these realizations. I took a class on Hegel to have a deeper grasp of dialectics and to understand the difference between idealism and materialism.

On April 4, 1968, Martin Luther King Jr. was assassinated. One year previously, a few of us had driven down to Brown University in Providence, Rhode Island, to hear him give an Easter sermon. We were devastated by his murder, and we watched as people in city after city demonstrated their grief and rage. The depth of US racism came to the fore, and the sadness that a brilliant, nonviolent leader was murdered drove home the realization that the fight for equality was nowhere close to finished.

All of this helped me decide what to do after college — not just how to make a living or what profession I might like, but how to end the war, fight for women's rights, and end the oppression of Black people. I did love the study of history and had some idea of attending grad school at New York University (NYU). I also wanted to continue studying dance. I was involved in the women's movement in college and in New York.

New York

I moved to New York City in 1969, after a summer of cross-country travel and Woodstock! I moved into a sixth-floor walkup on Thompson Street, thanks to a friend who wanted to hold on to it while she was traveling. It was a rent-controlled apartment. I got a job at the Brentano's bookstore on Eighth Street.

In New York I took dance lessons at the Merce Cunningham studio and pondered whether to go to NYU to study history. I found a Marxist studies/New Left hangout place where I joined a women's group and some discussion groups. I don't remember what it was called. I was in New York for the national student strike against the war and attended a large support meeting of workers and students. My other memories are of the 1970 postal workers' strike and watching the National Guard march by a little store on Bleecker Street, where I was working, in their failed attempt to bust the strike. I took part in a lively demonstration in support of the Black Panther women in the Women's House of Detention. A friend and I went to New Haven for a demonstration in support of the Black Panthers and heard French novelist, playwright, and political activist Jean Genet speak.

Meanwhile, the scene was getting pretty scary in New York with the 1970 townhouse bombing, where several members of the Weather Underground died. So later that summer a bunch of us bought an old van and moved to Western Massachusetts.

The next few years were survival years. I kept up my dance and looked for meaningful political work. The scene in the Amherst, Massachusetts, area was mostly rock and roll and drugs. I was not interested in the drug scene. I worked as a waitress at the Lord Jeffrey Inn and got my first horse.

The Move to Vermont

The FBI was around, looking for fugitives. At the time, a number of antiwar activists had arrest warrants out on them, based on evidence from FBI informants. Two people were arrested, and we formed a support group to help them with their upcoming trials. This support group became Brattleboro Political Action. We formed a study group and several of us got factory jobs. We concentrated our work on the public ownership of the electric power company in Vermont and we called for public ownership of all utilities. Instead of opposing nuclear power plants, and particularly construction of the Seabrook nuclear power plant in New Hampshire, we maintained that if there were public ownership, we would be able to control how power was produced and distributed. It was a great group of people.

1976

I got a job at a precision machine shop in Brattleboro. They made very specialized parts for industry, on Swiss screw machines. It was very precise work. It was nonunion, of course. My pay was just above minimum wage, yet we were expected to put in ten- to twelve-hour days and work on Saturdays. I hated overtime work.

There's a good story about why, all at once, everyone got fed up with the company and decided that I should get in touch with a union. I looked up machine unions in the telephone book. The Machinists Union didn't answer their phone, but the United Electrical, Radio and Machine Workers (UE) did, and I met David Cohen and John Case, two of the UE organizers. I won't include the story of the organizing drive, but after we failed to get enough support for a union election, I decided it was best to move on. At the union's suggestion, I applied for a job at Millers Falls Tool Company, owned by Ingersoll Rand, in Greenfield, Massachusetts. I believe the personnel manager hired me because we talked about horses. I was now a member of UE Local 274. I didn't have any idea how this would change my life. I feel so fortunate that these steps led me to the UE.

I moved to Greenfield. David and I began living together. It was through the UE that I came in contact with Party members. The UE gave me the real experience that through rank-and-file democracy the working class could in fact run society.

Joining the Party

The Massachusetts Party was composed of outstanding comrades—dedicated, down-to-earth, and working with other progressive organizations. There was respect for each other and each other's work. Sometimes the old timers could be a bit overwhelming, but their experience was respected. They had been real leaders in their younger years.

Our Western Massachusetts club was made up of individuals of different ages and backgrounds. Harold Williams from

Springfield was the chair — a well-known figure in the labor and African American community. He had worked at Monsanto during the fifties and sixties, when the International Union of Electrical Workers (IUE) and the Machinists were raiding UE shops. We often met at his house. His wife, Becky, gave advice to the younger comrades about how they should take care of themselves. At the time he was the chair of our club and an open member of the Party.

The club consisted of grad and undergrad students from the University of Massachusetts, peace and international activists from Northampton, and union members from Greenfield and Holyoke. We took our club work seriously, handing out the *Daily World* and supporting the electoral campaigns of the Party. We did push the paper and had *Daily World* picnics.

We did our work mostly individually, not as a club, but we got together and had good discussions. The electoral work on behalf of Party general secretary Gus Hall was frustrating — collecting signatures meant you were openly in the Party. The bosses red-baited me. We did collect a lot of signatures, but never enough to get on the ballot. I think that was a waste of time. We quietly made fun of Gus's claim of "speaking to millions."

There was a lot of respect for other Party leaders, especially national chairman Henry Winston and Angela Davis. I had always enjoyed study groups, but our own educationals were better than the Party's. The educational work that came from the Party was not impressive. It felt like it came out of the 1950s or earlier. The Party was always predicting the crisis of capitalism, which seemed to us a crisis that affected mostly the working class and not the ruling class. Perhaps the ruling class had a few setbacks here and there, but overall, they just got stronger. It was a social crisis and the way out was not clear. I felt the Party's strategy of the antimonopoly coalition was modeled on the idea of the united front against fascism, but it was not an actual coalition or front.

I was doing a lot of union work — first at Millers Falls Tool, and then I went out on lost time, provided for under the union contract, to help with a first contract at a recently organized shop of women electronic workers at Wesco in Greenfield. It was very exciting to see young women step up as leaders in the first contract fight and then in a twenty-week strike. (UE Local 274 was an amalgamated union of ten different shops.)

The UE local supported the organizing drive, as many members had family with experience working at Wesco. Dave and I were leaders of the strike. The workers struck when it appeared they would never get a decent contract without that action. Striking was their decision. It was so remarkable that the biggest issue for the strikers was a union security clause in the contract. They felt that the boss would otherwise continue to try to undermine the union and the prounion workers. The UE local rallied to their defense. The strike was an incredible experience of union and community support for these workers.

It ended with a massive mobilization of the union and the community, one that affected the employers of other companies. People were going to the picket line and missing work. The other employers were getting nervous. This probably led to the settlement of the strike. Finally, there was an injunction against us, but the terms of the injunction also required the company to bargain to a conclusion under the supervision of the state secretary of labor and industry. We got a contract! This was a huge victory.

UE Conventions

UE conventions were an experience of rank-and-file democratic involvement: reports, committee work, resolutions, and plans of work. Votes were taken on everything. There were great speakers and lots of partying.

In comparison, national Party meetings were ritualized and constrained. People were given five minutes to respond to Gus's long main report and report on what they were doing! There was very little socializing. We were pretty open with friends and UE members about being in the Party. The secretary-treasurer of the UE was Red Block. He was one of the original UE leaders and he had a cantankerous personality. He gave me some warnings about the Party leadership. Party leaders did not like Red, either! I think Gus saw him as a rival.

The Reagan Recession

The election of Ronald Reagan in 1981 and his firing of the air-traffic controllers signaled the beginning of a new antiworker war. It was also the beginning of the Reagan recession. The Party had supported rank-and-file movements for a time, and there was a publication called *Labor Today* that backed these movements. *Labor Today* called for a big meeting in Tonawanda, New York, to begin the organizing for a massive march for jobs in Washington, DC. I was involved in the early organizing for the Jobs March. This was the start of the huge union demonstration that became Solidarity Day. We sent three busloads of people from Greenfield.

In Greenfield, there were mass layoffs at the big manufacturing plants. These were plants owned by multinationals. TRW owned Greenfield Tap and Die; Bendix owned another plant; and Ingersoll Rand owned Millers Falls Tool. This was the beginning of the really significant plant closings in our area. The laid-off workers were facing difficulties getting their benefits and unemployment checks. One of our laid-off members, who was given a hard time at the unemployment office, suffered a heart attack and died. We decided to organize.

UE Local 274 had three hundred people on layoff. We formed an unemployed council. We had a huge effect on the community. We went to Boston to protest the unemployment rules. We got free memberships at the YMCA and free classes at Greenfield Community College. Along with several churches, we established community meals, open to anyone — no questions asked. Community Meals serves to this day. Here was the chance for the Party to take organizing seriously.

In 1982 I traveled to Cuba for the World Federation of Trade Unions Convention, with the North American delegation. We met and talked with union people from all over the world, from Japanese stewardesses to beekeepers from Nepal. We spent time with Polish workers. We toured Cuban factories, schools, and hospitals. We enjoyed the nights in the ice cream park with our young, musical, Cuban translators. Fidel gave a speech about the terrible conditions in the United States — including about murders and violent crimes. Everyone looked at us with sympathy. On a reception line I was kissed by Fidel!

Sectarianism

Back in the United States, Unemployed Councils were springing up across the country, from the Mon Valley in Pittsburgh to Detroit and other industrial areas. It was a real opportunity for the Party. Each council was coming up with imaginative ideas for organizing and creating new working-class forms. But it wasn't led only by the Party. Many left groups were organizing the unemployed as well. Unity was possible. The national leadership in New York didn't like this. According to them, the union and unemployed initiatives were becoming "too democratic."

People were suffering from "the crisis of capitalism." But, unfortunately, the national leadership was more worried about the other left groups than the fight for ultimate goals. There were those who wanted to carry out Party instructions and those who took organizing opportunities seriously.

The national Party leadership decided that they needed to regain control, and so the unemployed councils and trade-union councils were disbanded, the publication of *Labor Today* was suspended, and all went back to the old style of Party officials currying favor with national union leadership.

I think this was the beginning of the end of my Party affiliation. All new ideas were rejected. The Party started criticizing the UE again — the union was "too democratic." I was so excited by the possibilities of working-class democracy, but the contradiction between UE democracy and the Party's distrust of its own membership became more obvious.

I hate sectarianism and I hate labelling. Jim West, then the head of the Party's national control commission (officially, the

Central Review Commission), was the worst, with his lists of who not to associate with and what not to read. If we had read Dorothy Healey's autobiography, *Dorothy Healey Remembers,* we could have been forewarned about the outcome of the fight for change in the Party. Instead, we were told that it was all lies. Healey was an important leader in the Party from Los Angeles who took on the New York leadership, including Gus Hall, in the 1960s and 1970s and was critical of the lack of democracy in the Party nationally and internationally.

Henry Winston's Death

Henry Winston's death in 1986 really affected me. Henry was a beloved leader. He had lost his sight due to inadequate medical treatment while imprisoned during the McCarthy era. He gave honest reports at conventions. It was becoming obvious that Gus called the shots and bribed or threatened people who didn't agree with him. This was not working-class democracy. At the last Central Committee meeting I attended, when we presented a document outlining the need for renewal of the Party, we were met with hostility and personal attacks. That was the end.

The Massachusetts Party was on the side of renewal until the final split that occurred at the 1991 Party convention. A document called "Initiative and Renewal" was signed by 1,200 Party members and presented to the convention. It was met by extreme hostility, and the leadership even called the Cleveland police to come and evict all of us. The firing of the people at the *Daily World*—another end. I had hopes for the Committees of Correspondence. It was a difficult time, with the fall of the Soviet Union. Many of us looked to the South African Party. I was especially impressed with Joe Slovo's paper, "Has Socialism Failed?" It was time to reassess. What should be the Party's relation to the mass organizations and the class? We needed to affirm the centrality of racism and the unity of trade union and mass struggles. I had great admiration for the leaders of this attempt to redirect the Party, especially Kendra Alexander from

Northern California, who tragically died just as we were getting the Committees of Correspondence started.

However, the new leadership and the new structure of the Committees were not different enough from the style of the old leadership and the Party for me to stay connected. I think this problem was not unique to us in the United States. It was happening all over the world. Many Communist parties were undergoing reevaluation and reassessment.

I do think we need a united and active Communist organization that is democratic, based in the working class and open to all the new ways of organizing and looking at the world.

16

A Series of Exposures and Experiences … Some of the Best Years of My Political Life

Chris Townsend[1]

I grew up in central Pennsylvania in the 1960s and 1970s. Things were going downhill for all of that time. You just had to look around. The many manufacturing industries and railroads closed one after the other, and things were failing. The cities and small towns were all beginning to deteriorate to one degree or another, some worse than others. In June 1972, Hurricane Agnes wrecked half of the state, and shortly afterwards the energy crisis of the seventies kicked the whole country in the ass. As a kid you naturally wondered how you would get by when your time came to get pushed out of high school and onto the very crowded job market. My family and school life was fine. Just average working class and boring, but we didn't suffer from — or lack — anything. My folks always put a premium on reading and learning, and I had a great interest in the sciences, in history, and in politics as a result. Both sides of my family were working class and old Republican in orientation. I had an uncle who

1 Originally written and revised May 2021.

was a combat veteran of the Korean War, and he was never the same after his experiences. My family had a relative killed in the Civil War and in World War II, and because of that my father always told us to stay away from the army. I grew up in the era of massive scientific discovery and exploration, so my outlook, I like to think, was based on at least a rudimentary scientific view. I was surrounded by fundamentalist Christians as a youth, and their fanatic anticommunist views always struck me as just plain nuts—even dangerous, since they worshipped the war machine, supported nuclear weapons, you name it.

My early interest in socialism followed a series of exposures and experiences. I came to embrace atheism in revulsion to the religious fanatics all around me. And I was an avid shortwave radio listener as a kid and teenager. Tuning in to all the far-flung stations for news and information was a little like being able to travel. Radio Moscow and Radio Havana Cuba were my favorites. Some of the other English-language services were interesting to me: the British Broadcasting Corporation, Radio France International, and Radio Berlin International, from the German Democratic Republic, among them. The US-sponsored Voice of America was the official government line. To me it didn't differ much from the ordinary corporate media.

For my entire life, the Vietnam War had been raging with no apparent end point or rationale other than being mandated by fanatic anticommunism. Where I lived, you couldn't say anything against the war, even though nobody could explain why we were in another country killing and bombing on a mass scale. It didn't take me more than five minutes to understand why the Vietnamese people resisted our invasion, and why they resisted their own US collaborators. To me, even as a youngster, the entire war was a criminal enterprise propped up for none but illegitimate reasons. In March 1975, the Cambodian military regime collapsed. And then in April the US puppet regime in South Vietnam collapsed and the war thankfully ended. I remember being excited that this deadly fiasco was over. I watched the whole rotten "South" Vietnamese regime collapse on television week after week. In the final weeks of the war, you could also watch live how we were bugging out in a last-ditch helicopter airlift to save our own skins. It was obvious that the people were determined to sweep us out. Hundreds of thousands of the US collaborators were left behind in a panicked state. All these people who had attached themselves to our cause — even if I disagreed with it — were just abandoned. I wondered, "Wow, if we abandon these people, what loyalty do any of these US leaders have to us? And to a small-fry worker like me?" It was apparent to me even in 1975 that our government was going to abandon the working class here in the United States. If anything, I greatly underestimated the extent to which that was going to happen. Take a look around today at the condition of our working class. Appalling. This swirl of events was what helped me make up my mind that I was a Communist, a Marxist, and later a Leninist.

The Vietnam War and its inglorious end for the country spurred my interest in politics, in socialism, and in Communism. I followed very closely the national liberation movements, on the shortwave radio and in what publications I could find. The United States did everything it could to prop up the Portuguese colonial regimes, the Rhodesian outlaw state, and of course the apartheid regime in South Africa. We propped up the Shah in Iran, overthrew the government in Chile, and managed dictators on every continent. Only the Communists opposed all this degenerate and deadly US foreign policy. In high school I stopped reciting the Pledge of Allegiance. This raised eyebrows, but we had enough Mennonite kids in my class who were pacifists and would not say it either, so the teachers just ignored me.

I joined the Democratic Socialist Organizing Committee (DSOC) through the mail in 1977. It seemed pretty level-headed compared to some of the Maoist and Trotskyist sects that were burning out at that time, left over from the 1960s. There was not much you could do to be politically active when you were still a teenager, and there were no local radicals that amounted to much. There were a bare few thousand DSOC members nationwide, and I didn't get to attend my first DSOC meeting until 1979. It was a Youth Section weekend meeting that I really enjoyed, although I truly didn't fit in at all. I was leaving high school and going to work, and almost all of the young socialists at this meeting were either in college or going to college, so that left me on the fringe. I was certainly welcomed, as were the handful of other young workers, and I got to spend a little time with DSOC founder Michael Harrington. He was an impressive figure, and I had already read several of his books. There was not a lot of socialist or Communist literature in circulation back then, and in my case finding it took some effort. I found the *National Guardian,* but at that time it was controlled by wild-eyed ultraleftists. I found *The Militant,* put out by the Socialist Workers Party (SWP), and I enjoyed reading it because of its heavy labor and union coverage. I also found *Soviet Life* and the *Monthly Review,* which I really liked because of their coverage of the third-world struggles then raging. And at the DSOC meeting I was also introduced to a copy of William Z. Foster's *American Trade Unionism,* truly a book that changed my life as a young worker and trade unionist. Even the social-democratic oriented DSOC gave credit to the contributions of Foster, pioneer of industrial union organizing, leader of the Great Steel Strike of 1919, and later the legendary Party trade-union leader. I have always valued this book so much that in 2020 I personally worked successfully to get it back into print, for a new generation of radical trade unionists to benefit from it like I did.

I moved to Florida in 1979, after I got out of high school. I was on my own at seventeen, and the economy was not very interested in me or my labors. I fell in almost immediately to a drive being waged by the Amalgamated Transit Union (ATU) to organize the Tampa workforce. While I was not a radical or even a union activist, several of the leaders of my local in Tampa were bus operators and members of the Communist Party. It became apparent to them that I was an energetic rank-and-file union member with some socialist political underpinnings. We were in the organizing process at that time and these guys were impressive to me. They knew what to do, how to do it, and then you could bet that they got their union work completed. I quickly became a "producer"—I did anything that needed to be done. I signed up too many members to count. I always came to the meetings with fistfuls of signed cards and all of them with the five-dollar initiation fee. I passed out literature at four and five a.m. at the gates. I helped set up and clean up the union hall. I took time before and after work to go around the workplace to talk to other workers and get the word out about our organizing. We won our election, bargained a first contract, and then I was appointed shop steward. Later I was elected to the executive board of Amalgamated Transit Workers (ATU) Local 1464 in Tampa.

I was being noticed as a hard-working organizer, and a couple of the older Communist Party USA (CPUSA) local union leaders started talking to me about joining the Party. I took out a subscription to the *Daily World* and *Political Affairs,* and I purchased some books from them. They were constantly giving me different pamphlets. I enjoyed it all and learned a lot, but I was particularly interested in the Party's labor positions and its labor-organizing history. At that time — 1979 and 1980 — the trade-union presence in the Party was small, scattered, battered in many ways, and still largely underground. As a result of all this process I joined almost immediately, under what was called a "candidate" membership. That meant that I was being evaluated for whether I was up to the standards required for Party membership. I took it seriously and was pretty excited about it, and only later did I figure out that the candidate membership mechanism was from a long-ago period. They were going to let me join no matter what, unless I turned out to be a lunatic, a drunkard or drug user, or had anticommunist views. I held some strong anti-Stalinist views then — as I still have — but none of that got in the way of me being accepted to join.

The Party clubs in Tampa and Saint Petersburg were a fascinating collection of mostly older members and supporters. Being in Florida, we always got a wave of several hundred retirees or friendly ex-Party members who would come down for the winters. The political life of these folks was publicly centered on the peace movement and the need for peace with the USSR. I actually got tired of the immense concentration on the peace movement, since I was eager to talk about the trade-union work then underway locally and nationally. Since I was young, most of the old comrades would have me over for lunch and dinner. They seemed just as interested in me as a young Party recruit as I was in their many decades of activism.

I didn't realize how lucky I was to meet this now-gone generation. A few had been Party members in the 1920s and 1930s. Many were wartime recruits. A few were Spanish Civil War veterans. The majority had been involved in the major labor federations, including the American Federation of Labor, Trade Union Educational League, and the Congress of Industrial Organizations, during their own careers. I met so many that I can't recall all of them now. Some were in the Party, some were not, but all were from the big milieu of Party recruits, supporters, and allies who were of a generation that worked together in the anticapitalist struggles for social change.

Ruth France and Joe Norrick were a couple. Ruth had been hounded out of her job at the United Nations for being a Communist, and her first husband had been the noted civil-liberties attorney Royal France. She had been a prolific writer and played a role in the Party's underground apparatus. Joe was a rank-and-file coal miner from southern Indiana and was thrown out of the United Mine Workers union in an anticommunist purge. He went on to be a founder of and Communist activist in the United Steel Workers union. Willard Uphaus was a Methodist minister and non-Communist socialist who was the executive director of the CIO-led Religion and Labor Foundation, until it was destroyed in the McCarthy repression. Uphaus was also the victim of one of the last McCarthyite jailings, when he was imprisoned for a year in 1960 for refusing to turn over the names of those who subscribed to his World Fellowship of Faiths summer camp in New Hampshire. Bill Sennett was a Spanish Civil War veteran, and after twenty years as a Party functionary he left in response to the 1956 events.[2] He went on to invent the concept of truck-trailer leasing and became wealthy. After his retirement

2 Sennett was swayed primarily by Nikita Krushchev's revelations concerning the Stalin period at the Twentieth Congress of the Communist Party of

Sennett donated large amounts of his fortune to leftist causes, including ambulances for the Sandinista government in Nicaragua. He also endowed *In These Times* magazine in Chicago with the money needed to start publication in 1976. Hugo Gellert had been a lifelong artist and cartoonist, and I think he was from Hungary. Jessica Smith helped found the American-Soviet Friendship Association during World War II and in her later years edited the *New World Review.* In her earlier life she had been a peace activist and Communist, and her second husband was John Abt, a longtime Party attorney. Will Weinstone was one of my favorite old-timers. He had played numerous important trade-union roles in the Party, especially in the founding of the United Auto Workers. Corliss Lamont was a wealthy peace activist and prolific author, and while not connected officially to the Party he was harassed incessantly for his leftist views. All of them were already quite old, but they were all still trying to stay active. Ben Gold, legendary former president of the (CIO) furriers union came over a couple times from his home in Miami. I met Scott Nearing in the winter of 1980 during one of his Florida trips. He was personal friends with the group around Uphaus and other Christian socialists who were active for peace. Nearing had been very active in the nascent Communist Party but drifted away and became a bit of a nut, in my book. An amazing man in his knowledge of food, health, and diet, and certainly a staunch anticapitalist so far as I could figure, he had gone off to live in the wilderness of New England with his second wife, Helen, and they authored numerous books about country living. I recall being disappointed that he wanted to converse more about diet than about his own amazing history.

There was no internet back then, so you got introduced to someone, and if you didn't remember who they were that was it. All had been traumatized to some extent or another by the banning of the Party and the illegal period, so one was careful not to inquire about too many personal details. All of the old-timers

the Soviet Union. See William Sennett, *Reminiscences of William Sennett: Oral History, 1982* (Columbia Center for Oral History, 1982).

seemed to like me well enough, and the fact that I was toughing it out in the shop at that time seemed to give me added standing. With most of the few young people around the Party being students, my crappy job as a city sanitation worker seemed to lend me cachet as a "real" proletarian. I was always excited by the quality of the discussions and deliberations. The old-timers were experts on so many things. And since I was a big reader, all were happy to load me up with new material.

The Party also sent a stream of staff and leaders to Florida to do some organizational work, raise money, and give some a welcome break from the grind. I recall meeting a cast of characters from the Party leadership, but I never met General Secretary Gus Hall, at least not in Florida. Gil Green and Arnold Johnson came a number of times. Both had long careers as Party functionaries, and Green had spent five years underground and five more in jail in the McCarthyite period. I reconnected with Gil Green when I lived in upstate New York. Henry and Fern Winston were a couple, and Henry (Winnie)[3] had been another McCarthy victim, imprisoned after his Smith Act conviction; in prison he lost his eyesight owing to neglect. Henry went on to be the national chairman of the Party before his death in 1986. Fern was his constant companion, and she was active in the women's rights work of the Party. Anne Burlack was a Party stalwart and came out of the textile union struggles. George Meyers was the Baltimore-based trade-union leader of the Party who also came out of the textile industry. Art Shields was a *Daily Worker* and *Daily World* writer for years and years, and he focused on a lot of the big labor fights of the time. Sid Taylor was the Party treasurer, I think, when I met him, since I recall talking to him about money matters. Several others were from the *Daily World* staff. Someone introduced me to the *World Marxist Review* and the *Information Bulletin,* and I became an avid reader until they ceased publication in 1991. There were also speakers from other Left organizations and publications, such as *Freedomways,* a journal of the Black freedom movement, and *New World Review.*

---

3 On the name Winnie, see page 72 of this volume.

Southern civil rights leader Anne Braden was a speaker. The one staff member and several supporters of the National Council of American-Soviet Friendship would also regularly stop in Florida as part of their work. Much of this again centered around Willard Uphaus, the noted Methodist peace activist. I inherited a lot of books and pamphlets from various old comrades at that time. And despite having to move half a dozen times since then, I have held on to all of them. Since I am self-taught, I guess having all of these books and papers has been my substitute for a college degree.

The political discourse in the Party was open and varied, and it was not unusual for someone to take open issue with some Party leader or position. The Soviet Union was not regarded as perfect — far from it. But it was certainly defended on just about every front. All were anti-Trotskyist and anti-Maoist, but only here and there would anyone utter a word aimed at Stalin. The 1956 events in Hungary were painful, and most avoided the whole subject. And given that all of them were persecuted to one extent or another in the McCarthy terror, it didn't surprise me that there were some subjects left unexplored. I got myself into some trouble because I saw the Soviet invasion of Afghanistan in late 1979 as a mistake. It just looked to me even back then that first Carter and then Reagan were going to use it as a trap to bog down the Soviets, although never in a million years could I have imagined what damage was going to be done. Contrary to some conventional wisdom, the Party never kicked me out or did anything to me because of my divergent views. In some ways I think others shared my skepticism and just didn't want to say anything. I was also recruiting new members and helping the Party function within labor circles more than before, so Afghanistan just wasn't the big deal to pick a fight over, I guess.

By chance I met the woman who became my wife, Nancy McFadden, in 1983. I was ready to get out of Florida. The culture is for retirees, not young people. I needed something more substantial as far as both the union work and the political life. So we left together in 1984 and returned to her home in Albany, New York. After Florida, I figured that the Party would be much more developed in Albany. It was a rude awakening. I was exactly the second Party member in the city in 1984. Local civil rights attorney Mark Mishler knocked on my apartment door one day after I had requested contact with the Albany Club, and we are good friends to this day. So, the two of us went to work and just kept grinding away. Back then you had to be discreet about being a member, but despite this Mark went to work on every available opportunity open to him. He gave me a lot of gumption to do the same. After all, I was in a new town with no contacts, and he was a lawyer with a real reputation to protect. I jumped into two different union projects, first with the United Food and Commercial Workers Union (UFCW) and then with the Service Employees International Union (SEIU), so my Party work immediately spread out into the labor work of those unions and the Albany Labor Council. Nancy joined the Party, and then things really took off. She was the key to our distribution of hundreds, and eventually thousands, of *Daily World* and *People's Daily World* copies. Our apartment at the west end of Washington Park in Albany was a place for frequent union and Party club meetings. All three of us were fairly open members of the Party, which really helped. It was still a dicey proposition to be known as a member. Memories of the McCarthy terror in the Albany-Schenectady region were still very much alive. We quickly recruited Martin Manley from Schenectady. He had been active in the then-defunct Irish Republican Clubs, and you could always count on him to pitch in with newspaper distribution and meetings.

All of us went to work, and over the next several years we rebuilt the Party in that part of upstate New York. We slowly grew to ten members, then fifteen, then twenty, and we topped out around twenty-five members. We had members out in Gloversville, New York, the old stronghold of the Fur and Leather Workers Union. We had one member way up in Plattsburgh, near the Canadian border. But we were mostly in Albany, Troy, and Schenectady. Most of our members and supporters were workers in the service industries or in government employment, together with a few students and retirees. Albany is a transient area because of the university, so we had at least another fifteen or twenty members come and go.

Our Party club spent almost all of our time on two areas of concentration: the labor work that I had set in motion and the critical work done by Mishler to make sure that the Party was known among the antiracism and antiapartheid movements. We never did much with the big student population. Our New York Party district staff always tried to order us to go out to the gigantic, old General Electric (GE) works in Schenectady to distribute newspapers; there had once been a huge Party concentration there, in the days when the plant was organized by the United Electrical, Radio, and Machine Workers Union (UE). Most of the time we ignored them. The economy was shifting dramatically, away from manufacturing and into services and public employment. In the end, we kept recruiting union members to join the Party, just not factory workers, so we still looked good.

We did a lot of work in the peace movement. Nancy and I helped revive the Albany Council for American-Soviet Friendship. We enjoyed this and liked getting to meet all the Soviet delegations that would come through town. The FBI was also interested in this project of ours. The FBI would call on our apartment, and we would just tell them to "go away." In 1989 the FBI eventually entrapped a Council staff member in a bizarre prosecution scheme claiming that we were somehow laundering money. The FBI informant was known to us; she was from Buffalo. Her behavior had been suspect for several years, and eventually her perjured testimony was the basis to convict American-Soviet Friendship Council leader Reverend Alan Thomson. She went on to have her own bizarre crash, when in the late 1990s she tried to get a federal pension because of her informing activities and was denied. All of this FBI and grand jury activity just made us even more committed to the cause. Later, when I went to Washington, DC, to work for UE, the FBI visits continued, albeit less and less frequent. I recall one fun episode at our apartment when the FBI called: The agent held up his badge to the peephole in the door to try to prove to me that he was for real. There had been a rash of cop-impersonation cases at that time, so I just called 9-1-1 and reported to our local police that some guy was running around our apartment house telling people he was from the FBI. From our balcony I could see the local police officers spending fifteen or twenty minutes with the agent sorting it out.

I spent a decent amount of time engaged in Party fundraising of various kinds through the years—small stuff, penny-ante stuff, but also quite a few things that were larger and fairly important projects that raised a lot of money for our operations. I also have to chuckle when folks later claimed to be surprised that we were receiving some Soviet subsidies for our work. Of course we were. How else could we do all the things we did with just a few thousand members? And what was wrong with their support anyway? And I am still grateful for whatever they did for us over the many decades that they did it. Am I supposed to be embarrassed somehow that a Communist and workers' government gave our Party some minuscule contributions while all of the big business political parties are gorged on cash from corporations and the rich? Many in the Party were embarrassed by this subject, probably because it was technically illegal in some way. I did not give a damn. Some felt that this money tainted us somehow, but I never felt that way. In hindsight, I think the biggest problem the socialist support caused was that it allowed the Party leadership to operate without worrying about where the members were, how many we really had, and who was really paying the dues to keep things going. No doubt this was a sensitive and difficult issue for many, but I just did not see it as a big problem. Like I said, I was grateful for the support and even proud in some ways that they did what they did.

I was able to take two trips to the Soviet Union paid for by the Soviet government. I had no means to do that on my own, as a worker. We were treated like real comrades and guests, and I learned a lot both times. I am eternally grateful for those opportunities; they were adventures both logistically and politically. Everything I did so far as fundraising I did with great pride, I regret nothing.

The first inkling I had that the Party was heading for trouble was in 1986, when Henry Winston died after a long decline. It is ironic that by 1986 we were growing again, and interest in the Party was growing even more. The glasnost and perestroika periods in the Soviet Union were very helpful in terms of rehabilitating the image of the Communist world. There was new hope and openings for change. We started to hear from long-ago Party members who had dropped out in 1956 or 1958 and still lived in our area. Everyone agreed about this. All of the Party leaders and staff who later claimed that they knew that Gorbachev was the mastermind of some anti-Soviet plan are inventing that today to look so smart and cover their tracks. They are gutless and refuse to own up to the fact that everyone saw what was happening as a welcome development. I remember visiting the Party headquarters on Twenty-Third Street in Manhattan and buying a photo of Gus Hall with Gorbachev. For several years—until things came unglued—everyone wanted to associate themselves with the trend. Those who now claim to have been able to spot all the destruction that was coming were either silent then or are rehabilitating their own roles in what became an historic debacle.

The death of Winston became the seismic event that it was because the national committee immediately abolished his position, rather than allot it to either Angela Davis or Charlene Mitchell. For the first time in decades, we had no public Black–white unity at the highest levels of the Party. In a snap, it was abolished and the change not even explained. The Gus Hall forces had lit the fuse that didn't go off until 1991. From this point on everyone knew that the Hall leadership and the staff he controlled were on the lookout for any Party activists unhappy with this episode or entertaining any other independent positions. I was overlooked on this I think because of my trade-union work and my fundraising. I also did not hold any position in the New York district, so none of the Hall forces would have seen me as a danger.

By the time of the 1991 events our Albany club had held together but had leveled off, owing to all the underlying conflict.

The collapse of the Soviet Union was a blow and hard to fathom. By this time, I was a field organizer for UE and away most of the time. Nancy lived through the whole period and was very demoralized by all of it. She went to the Cleveland Party convention where the split was made official. I was working in West Virginia, and I refused to go. The handwriting was on the wall. The Hall forces were going to "rule or ruin," and that is what happened. Our entire club left to join the Committees of Correspondence, but the long slow decline had set in. It was never the same.

By 1990 I had no hope that the split was to be avoided, and I had little confidence that the opposition could overpower the Hall forces somehow. Partly because Hall controlled the dues rosters and payments, his forces controlled who was a delegate to the convention, and they knew just how to jigger the rules to head off the challenge to their control. Corrupt unions have done what they did in Cleveland for decades. The sloppy finances and membership records were all helpful to the Hall forces when it came to finding reasons to challenge otherwise legitimate delegates. By 1991 my membership came to an end, after eleven years. It just ended sort of like the Soviet Union ended. A strange ending, and it still haunts me today, more than thirty years later. For more than thirty years now, I realize that I belong in a Communist Party, but not *this* Communist Party. Some who left in 1991 went back, but I never have considered it. I saw a presentation by Party leader Sam Webb in 2007 — I came out as a courtesy to a friend who implored me to go — and after his remarks I said hello. He asked me what I thought, and my exact response was to commend him for his efforts, but to point out that "I don't need to rejoin the Communist Party to be a Democrat. I can do that for free." That's how I felt then, and it's how I feel now.

The outcome of the split was what it obviously has been — a total disaster for our movement in the United States. Many people who left the Party did quite well, like we have. We got on with it. You will find former Party members doing creative and critical work all throughout the people's movements. Many are retired by now. Some just faded away. Perhaps it was bound to happen, because of the course of the worldwide Communist movement. I still think, to this day, that any credible study of what the split was — and what it was not — is needed. I found myself on the outside labeled as an "anti–working class" element of some kind, while all the time I have remained a stalwart Marxist-Leninist and trade-union leader. The Party leaders hurling the social democratic charges against those like me who left — namely, Sam Webb and John Bachtell — went on to become the most destructive elements in the Party, with their liquidationist and slavishly pro–Democratic Party orientation.

In a postscript to my Party years, from 1992 until 2013 I was the UE representative stationed in Washington, DC. For almost all of that time I was the unofficial contact for at least twenty-five Communist parties and at least ten or fifteen trade-union groupings. It all grew out of the fact that over time more and more of these groups were growing alarmed with the rightward political drift of the Party, and they did not trust its explanations and analysis of events. After the death of Hall and the ascendency of Sam Webb I had my hands full, as all of these Communist forces wanted some better interpretation of US developments. I did my best to handle the requests for analysis of various developments, and I took at my own expense several trips to Europe and Asia to meet with these groupings. I found it difficult to explain to these forces what the reality was without criticizing the Party, but I did my best. After all, they were asking for a real Marxist analysis of the political moment, they were not asking for an appraisal of the CPUSA and its deterioration. By 2013, when I retired from UE, I had ended this personal consultancy, finding it too exhausting to continue. Maybe I will start it up again when I am retired from my present position.

Overall, my years in the Party were some of the best of my political life. I met too many serious Marxists and Leninists to count, from all over the world. I was lucky to find my way in when I did, despite the 1991 Party split. I saw my work in the years from 1991 to 2008 years in terms of the need to just hang on and preserve some kind of Marxist legacy for the new recruits that were bound to come. I see my work today as trying to reconstitute a new Communist movement, and the young radicals coming out of the woodwork give me lots of hope. Starting with the 2008 crash, then Occupy, then Sanders, and now the Trump years, I have become more convinced than ever that we can rebuild this movement. That's my take. And after all, I am not rich enough to give up.

Fig. 13. The official button for the August 28, 1963, March on Washington, one of the largest protest demonstrations in US history, drawing upwards of 250,000 people, including a sizable number of Communist Party members.

Fig. 14. A women's rights march down Fifth Avenue in New York City on August 26, 1972 marked the anniversary of the signing of the 19th Amendment. A Communist Party contingent, led by members of the National Women's Commission, participated under its own banner.

Select Annotated Bibliography

The works noted below constitute a range of recent and older literature on the dimensions of Communist Party history and experience, particularly in the labor movement, illustrated in the opening volume of *Red Lives: Our Years in the US Communist Party (1950–2000)*. A common thread in several of the listed books, including a few relatively recent ones, is the assumption that the Communist movement in the United States disappeared after 1956 as a result of red-scare persecutions and internal pressures. *Red Lives* challenges this notion. A number of the studies below, however, stand apart, assimilating the diverse histories of participants in the Party and related movements and transcending a focus on leaders. Such works resonate with the great variety of personal accounts constituting *Red Lives,* and in this regard our work amplifies the voices of the Party in a manner characteristic of new approaches to history.

Aptheker, Bettina. *Communists in Closets: Queering the History, 1930s–1990s.* Routledge, 2023.
A foremost leader of the Berkeley Free Speech and Free Angela Davis movements and pioneering feminist scholar, Aptheker critically evaluates the CPUSA's attitudes to LGBTQ+ members. She addresses the experiences of

playwright Lorraine Hansberry and gay rights pioneer Harry Hay, among others.

Deery, Phillip. *Red Apple: Communism and McCarthyism in Cold War New York.* Fordham University Press, 2014.
Deery documents the experience of five Party members in New York City prior to 1960. By detailing the challenges facing Communists in the United States, his portraits demonstrate how Party membership entailed substantial personal risk and how persecution "can test resilience."

Fried, Albert, ed. *Communism in America: A History in Documents.* Columbia University Press, 1997.
In one of the better documentary histories of the Communist Party USA, Fried assumes the Party's end in 1956. Thus he omits the post-1960 span of union, civil rights, anti-repression, and antiwar activities of US Communists documented in *Red Lives.*

Gilpin, Toni. *The Long Deep Grudge: A Story of Big Capital, Radical Labor, and Class War in the American Heartland.* Haymarket Books, 2020.
Gilpin's fascinating account of the Left-led Farm Equipment Workers Union (FE) illustrates the creative contributions of Party members (including her father) to this militant organization, which successfully challenged such firms as International Harvester. She shows how Black–white unity and the building of coalitions were crucial to FE's strength.

Gornick, Vivian. *The Romance of American Communism.* Basic Books, 1977.
Considered a classic of rank-and-file Communist Party reminiscences, Gornick's collection of interviews draws out people's reasons for joining, staying with, or leaving the Party. It treats the period up to circa 1956, and in this respect shares the timeframe of Fried (above).

Haywood, Harry. *Black Bolshevik.* Liberator Press, 1978.
Haywood was a major figure in formulating the Party's thesis that African Americans living in the Black Belt of the South constituted an oppressed nation within the United States. His autobiography includes much experience of

note, including his ultimate denunciation of the CPUSA for dropping the Black Belt thesis.

Heale, M.J. *American Anti-Communism: Combatting the Enemy Within, 1830–1970.* Johns Hopkins University Press, 1990. The author finds the origins of anticommunism in the antilabor outlook of established wealthy groups stretching back two centuries. At the same time, he traces the perpetuation of problematic assumptions that the United States has been a society of universal achievement and equal rights.

Horne, Gerald. *Black Liberation/Red Scare: Ben Davis and the Communist Party.* University of Delaware Press, 1994. Davis, a leading member of the Communist Party, served in the New York City Council representing Harlem in the middle of the 1940s and was convicted under the Smith Act in 1949 for conspiring to teach the forceful overthrow of the government. Horne's well-researched book is a basic text for understanding the McCarthy era.

Howe, Irving, and Lewis Coser. *The American Communist Party: A Critical History, 1919–1957.* Beacon Press, 1957. The authors, editors of the left-liberal magazine *Dissent,* provide a detailed history of the CPUSA until the late 1950s. The material is worth a glance, however skewed by key inaccuracies and the concluding "American Communism as an organized movement had reached the end of the road," representing "the enormous waste of potentially valuable human beings."

Jackson, James E. *Revolutionary Tracings in World Politics and Black Liberation.* International Publishers, 1974. A collection of writings by a prominent Party leader and former tobacco workers organizer, this volume is highlighted by a seminal reevaluation of the Party's original concept that African Americans were an oppressed nation.

Kaplan, Judy, and Linn Shapiro, eds. *Red Diapers: Growing Up in the Communist Left.* University of Illinois Press, 1998. This valuable collection of oral histories illuminates what it was like growing up in the Party environment. Focusing on the contributors' childhoods and youth, the volume includes reminiscences by a few who themselves joined the CPUSA. This distinguishes *Red Diapers* from *Red Lives,* all of whose writers were in the Party, yet for the most part were born and raised outside the Party milieu.

Kovel, Joel. *Red Hunting in the Promised Land: Anti-Communism and the Making of America.* Basic Books, 1994.
Kovel analyzes the careers of such noteworthy anticommunists as Senator Joseph McCarthy of Wisconsin, Senator Hubert Humphrey of Minnesota, and the pro-Nazi priest Father Charles Coughlin of Michigan. He places them in the context of a powerful trend in US history that foments conformity with a status quo of concentrated rule by a few while stigmatizing opponents.

Leonard, Aaron J. *The Folk Singers and the Bureau: The FBI, the Folk Artists and the Suppression of the Communist Party, USA, 1939–1956.* Repeater Books, 2020.
In his documentation of the blacklisting of singers associated with the Communist Party and the Left, Leonard outlines the long reach of the Cold War into the cultural arena. Among the musicians he discusses are Woody Guthrie, Pete Seeger, Josh White, and Oscar Brand.

Monteith, Sharon. *SNCC's Stories: The African American Freedom Movement in the Civil Rights South.* University of Georgia Press, 2020.
Monteith gathers a panorama of accounts by young civil rights activists, among whom may be found several of the contributors to *Red Lives.* Her work sheds light on the experiences of dedicated activists at the grassroots, those whom history books have generally overlooked.

Ottanelli, Fraser M. *The Communist Party of the United States: From the Depression to World War II.* Rutgers University Press, 1991.
Covering a fifteen-year period, Ottanelli goes into depth in favorably reviewing the Party's contributions on numerous fronts. He particularly explores dilemmas facing members as their organization began emerging as a national force.

Pecinovsky, Tony. *Let Them Tremble: Biographical Interventions Marking 100 Years of the Communist Party, USA.* International Publishers, 2019.
Pecinovsky profiles six Communist Party leaders, concentrating on a seventy-five-year interval ending roughly in the 1990s. In the process, he hones in on particular areas of Party work, including youth, racial equality, peace, and civil liberties.

Pettengill, Ryan S. *Communists and Community: Activism in Detroit's Labor Movement, 1941–1956.* Temple University Press, 2020. A local study illustrating historic and extensive involvement of the Party in labor, civil rights, anti-segregation, and housing movements, among others. Pettingill illustrates the meeting halls, bookstores, barber shops, social organizations, churches, autoworkers' locals, and neighborhood clubs where Communists engaged in popular upsurge. McCarthyism virtually decapitated such pivotal undertakings.

Pintzuk, Edward C. *Reds, Racial Justice, and Civil Liberties: Michigan Communists During the Cold War.* MEP Publications, 1997. Though unmentioned by Pettengill, Pintzuk gives greater attention to the use of the Smith Act and the House Un-American Activities Committee against Michigan Party leaders; correspondingly, his treatment of Party civil rights involvements is less extensive, though important.

Schwartz, Harvey. *Solidarity Stories: An Oral History of the ILWU.* University of Washington Press, 2009.
Gathering several dozen contributors covering diverse periods of the Left-led longshore union on the West Coast, Schwartz provides an intimate glimpse into a range of individual experiences, in the manner of Monteith (above) and *Red Lives.*

Storch, Randi. *Red Chicago: American Communism at Its Grassroots, 1928–1935.* University of Illinois Press, 2007.
While covering a relatively brief period, Storch's treatment of Communist Party activism at the grass

roots — neighborhoods, unions, specific industries, and areas of concentration — is exceptional, indicating productive new paths for future historians.

Washington, Mary Helen. *The Other Blacklist: The African American Literary and Cultural Left of the 1950s.* Columbia University Press, 2014.
Analyzing the careers of several prominent Black cultural figures, including painter Charles White and poet Gwendolyn Brooks, the author demonstrates their experiences with the Communist Party, the shape of their political commitments, and how they were impacted by the Cold War.

Books That Influenced Our Authors

In an effort to help readers better understand the intellectual background of the movement and its participants, the editors asked each contributor to share some works that informed their activism and their decision to join the Party. Several responded, and this list collates their contributions. In a few cases, writers shared music or film titles.

Apitz, Bruno. *Naked among Wolves.* Seven Seas Books, 1978.

Aptheker, Bettina. *The Morning Breaks: The Trial of Angela Davis.* Cornell University Press, 1999.

Aptheker, Herbert. *The Nature of Democracy, Freedom, and Revolution.* International Publishers, 1967.

Baldwin, James. *The Fire Next Time.* Vintage, 1993.

Bellamy, Edward. *Looking Backward (2000–1887), or, Life in the Year 2000.* Signet Classics, 2009.

Benedict, Ruth. *Patterns of Culture.* Houghton Mifflin, 2005.

Benedict, Ruth, and Gene Weltfish. *In Henry's Backyard: The Races of Mankind.* Henry Schuman, 1948.

Bill Meyer Music. "Detroit Tribute to Paul Robeson & His Work for Peace." *YouTube,* December 25, 2017. https://youtu.be/CoqAxSDff84.

Boyer, Richard O., and Herbert Morais. *Labor's Untold Story: The Adventure Story of the Battles, Betrayals and Victories of American Working Men and Women.* United Electrical, Radio & Machine Workers of America, 1970.

Brown, Joe David. *The Freeholder.* New American Library, 1976.

Burchett, Wilfred. *Vietnam: Inside Story of the Guerilla War.* International Publishers, 1965.

Carawan, Guy, and Candie Carawan. *Freedom Is a Constant Struggle: Songs of the Freedom Movement.* Oak Publications, 2007.

Childe, V. Gordon. *Man Makes Himself.* Spokesman, 2003.

Colon, Jesus. *A Puerto Rican in New York, and Other Sketches.* International Publishers, 1982.

Dane, Barbara, and Irwin Silber. *The Vietnam Songbook.* The Guardian, 1969.

Davis, Angela Y. *If They Come in the Morning: Voices of Resistance.* Verso Books, 2016.

———. *Lectures on Liberation.* NY Committee to Free Angela Davis, 1971.

———. *Women, Race and Class.* Vintage Books, 1983.

Davis, Benjamin J. *Communist Councilman from Harlem: Autobiographical Notes Written in a Federal Penitentiary.* International Publishers, 1969.

DeCaux, Len. *Labor Radical: From the Wobblies to the CIO.* Beacon Press, 1970.

DeLeon, Daniel. *Two Pages from Roman History.* New York Labor News, 1946.

Divoky, Diane. *How Old Will You Be in 1984? Expressions of Student Outrage from the High School Free Press.* Avon Books, 1969.

Dimitrov, Georgi. *The United Front Against War and Fascism: Speeches Delivered at the Seventh World Congress of the Communist International.* Workers Library Publishers, 1936.

Du Bois, W.E.B. [William Edward Burghardt]. *The Autobiography of W.E.B. Du Bois.* International Publishers, 1968.

———. *Black Reconstruction in America, 1860–1880.* The Library of America, 2021.

———. *The Souls of Black Folk.* W.W. Norton, 2022.

Dutt, Clemens, and Otto Kuusinen, eds. *Fundamentals of Marxism Leninism: Manual.* Foreign Languages Publishing House, 1963.

Engels, Friedrich. *The Origin of the Family, Private Property and the State.* Verso Books, 2021.

Fanon, Frantz. *The Wretched of the Earth.* Translated by Richard Philcox. Grove Press, 2021.

Fast, Howard. *Being Red: A Memoir.* Houghton Mifflin, 1990.

———. *Freedom Road.* Sharpe, 1995.

———. *Spartacus.* North Castle Books, 1996.

Foster, William Z. *American Trade Unionism.* International Publishers, 2020.

Frankl, Viktor E. *Man's Search for Meaning.* Beacon Press, 2017.

Freeman, Jo. "The Tyranny of Structurelessness." *Berkeley Journal of Sociology* 17 (1972–1973): 151–65. https://www.jofreeman.com/joreen/tyranny.htm.

Galeano, Eduardo. *Guatemala: Occupied Country.* Monthly Review Press, 1969.

Gerson, Simon W. *Pete: The Story of Peter V. Cacchione, New York's First Communist Councilman.* International Publishers, 1976.

Giáp, Võ Nguyên. *Unforgettable Days.* Foreign Languages Publishing House, 1975.

Ginsberg, Allen. *Howl, and Other Poems.* City Lights, 1956.

Gold, Michael. *Jews without Money.* Public Affairs, 2009.

Gorky, Maxim. *The Mother.* Translated by Lee Baxandall. Grove Press, 1965.

———. *The Mother.* Translated by Hugh Aplin. Alma Classics, 2020.

Gornick, Vivian. *The Romance of American Communism.* Verso Books, 2020.

Green, Gilbert. *The Enemy Forgotten.* International Publishers, 1956.

———. *The New Radicalism: Anarchist or Marxist?* International Publishers, 1971.

———. *What's Happening to Labor?* International Publishers, 1976.

Hall, Gus. *Racism: The Nation's Most Dangerous Pollutant.* New Outlook Publishers, 1971.

———. *Lame Duck in Turbulent Waters: The Next Four Years of Nixon.* New Outlook Publishers, 1972.

Hobsbawm, Eric J. *Primitive Rebels: Studies in Archaic Forms of Social Movement in the Nineteenth and Twentieth Centuries.* Abacus, 2017.

Jackson, James E. *The View from Here.* Publishers New Press, 1963.

———. *Revolutionary Tracings in World Politics and Black Liberation.* International Publishers, 1974.

Kettle, Arnold. *Karl Marx: Founder of Modern Communism.* Weidenfeld & Nicolson, 1963.

King, Martin Luther, Jr. *Why We Can't Wait.* Beacon Press, 2010.

Lazarus, Emma. *Emma Lazarus: Selections from Her Poetry and Prose.* Emma Lazarus Federation of Jewish Women's Clubs, 1982.

Lenin, Vladimir Il'ich. *Imperialism, the Highest Stage of Capitalism: A Popular Outline.* International Publishers, 1933.

———. *State and Revolution.* International Publishers, 1932.

———. *The Three Sources and Three Component Parts of Marxism.* Progress Publishers, 1969.

Lightfoot, Claude. *Black America and the World Revolution.* New Outlook Publishers, 1970.

———. *Ghetto Rebellion to Black Liberation.* International Publishers, 1968.

London, Jack. *Martin Eden.* Dover Publications, 2017.

Makarenko, Anton Semyonovich. *Learning to Live: Flags on the Battlements.* University Press of the Pacific, 2005.

Mandel, William. *Saying No to Power: Autobiography of a 20th Century Activist and Thinker.* Creative Arts Books, 1999.

Mao Zedong. *On Practice and Contradiction.* Verso Books, 2017.

Marx, Karl. *Capital, Vol. 1.* International Publishers, 1967.

———. *Critique of the Gotha Programme.* International Publishers, 1938.

———. *The Eighteenth Brumaire of Louis Bonaparte.* International Publishers, 1963.

Marx, Karl, and Friedrich Engels. *The Communist Manifesto.* International Publishers, 2014.

Mitchell, Juliet. *Women, the Longest Revolution: Essays on Feminism, Literature, and Psychoanalysis.* Virago, 1984.

Myers, Gustavus. *History of the Great American Fortunes.* Modern Library, 1936.

Neill, Alexander Sutherland. *Summerhill: A Radical Approach to Child Rearing.* Hart Publishing, 1960.

Ochs, Phil. "When I'm Gone." From *Phil Ochs in Concert 1966.* Elektra EKS-7310, 1966, LP.

Ostrovsky, Nikolay. *How the Steel Was Tempered: A Novel in Two Parts.* Translated by R. Prokofieva. Progress Publishers, 1973.

Patterson, William L., ed. *We Charge Genocide: The Historic Petition to the United Nations for Relief from a Crime of the United States Government against the Negro People.* International Publishers, 1970.

Quin, Mike. *On the Drumhead: A Selection from the Writing of Mike Quin.* Pacific Publishing Foundation, 1948.

Reed, John. *Insurgent Mexico.* International Publishers, 1969.

———. *Ten Days That Shook the World.* Penguin, 2007.

Sale, Kirkpatrick. *SDS: The Rise and Development of the Students for a Democratic Society.* Vintage Books, 1973.

Saxton, Alexander. *The Great Midland.* University of Illinois Press, 1997.

Schappes, Morris U. *The Jews in the United States: A Pictorial History, 1654 to the Present.* Citadel Press, 1958.

Seeger, Pete, and the Almanac Singers (Pete Seeger, Tom Glazer, Baldwin "Butch" Hawes, and Bess Lomax); Ernst Busch. *Songs of the Spanish Civil War.* Vols. 1 and 2. Smithsonian Folkways Recordings, SFW40188, 2014 [1961].

Shaw, George Bernard. "Man and Superman." In *Man and Superman and Three Other Plays*. Barnes and Noble Classics, 2003.
Sinclair, Upton. *The Jungle*. Penguin, 1985.
Steinbeck, John. *The Grapes of Wrath*. Penguin, 2006.
Szymanski, Albert. *The Capitalist State and the Politics of Class*. Winthrop Publishers, 1978.
Thoreau, Henry David. *Walden; and, Civil Disobedience*. Penguin, 1983.
Tyner, Jarvis. *Black Liberation*. Young Workers Liberation League, 1970.
———. *New Forms of Racism*. Hall-Tyner Campaign Committee, 1976.
Walker, Alice. *The Color Purple: A Novel*. Penguin Books, 2019.
White, Anne Terry. *Eugene Debs: American Socialist*. L. Hill, 1974.
Williams, Robert F. *Negroes with Guns*. Martino Fine Books, 2013.
Winston, Henry. *Strategy for a Black Agenda: A Critique of New Theories of Liberation in the United States and Africa*. International Publishers, 1973.
Wright, Richard. *Native Son*. Harper Perennial, 2008.
X, Malcolm. *The Autobiography of Malcolm X*. Ballantine, 1992.

Index

Page numbers in italics indicate an illustration.

19th Amendment, 365
"25 Unions Say, 'Cut Workweek'" (Jacques), 77
1199: *1199 News*, 84; AFSCME and, 279; attraction of, 262; Communists and, 319–21; CPUSA and, 262–63; Harvard Hospitals and, 302; North and, 84; Presbyterian Hospital and, 274–77; SEIU and, 28, 263–64, 278, 279. *See also* health-care workers
1960s social unrest, 137–39

Abraham Lincoln Brigade, 18, 35, 110, 197, 267
ABS Speaks, 54
Abt, John, 355
Addington, Wendell, Jr., 64–65, 66
Adelson, Sheldon, 113
Advance Youth Organization, *34*, *212*, 270
Afghanistan, Soviet invasion of, 357
AFL-CIO, 236, 241, 242, 330–31. *See also* CIO (Congress of Industrial Organizations)
Africa: African National Congress, 112, 154; Angola, 58, 59, 63; antiapartheid movement, 59, 60; anti-imperialist movements in, 58–60, Mozambique, 58; NAIMSAL, 19; Republic of New Africa, 51; South African Communist Party, 347; South African Council of Trade Unions, 80
African American leadership: Hall and, 337; Jackson, 71; Mitchell, 300, 321–22, 361; Nicholas, 278; in the peace movement, 100–101; Trade Union Leadership Council and, 80; in the YWLL, 70–71. *See also* Winston, Henry
African Americans: in Arizona, 311, 312; Black student strike, 298, 301; Coalition of Black Trade Unionists, 80, 262; counterculture of, 50; CP and, 297; government workers, 81–82; Hall and, 337; industrial concentration and, 237; League of Revolutionary Black Workers, 46–47, 51, 54, 87, 102, 103; Mississippi Summer Project and, 200; NAACP, 27, *215*, 314; NNLC, 80; in the peace movement, 100–101;

perceptions of, 177; Reuther and, 57; *Rocky Mountain News* and, 316; TULC, 80; UE and, 241; violence against, 121; at Wayne State University, 46; youth, 47, 148. *See also* race and racism
African Liberation Day, 59
air-traffic controllers, 316, 345
Alabama Communists, 19
Albany, New York, 357–59, 361–62
Albert Einstein College of Medicine (AECOM), 275
alcoholism and recovery, 336
Alexander, Kendra, 116, 280, 347–48
Ali, Muhammad, 141
Allan, William "Billy," 41, 52, 74–76, 88, 92
Allen, Ernie, 47
Allende, Salvador, 153
Almond, Gabriel A., 25
Alston, Christopher, 63–64, 99
Amalgamated Transit Union (ATU), 352
American Civil Liberties Union, 316
American Federation of Labor, 354. *See also* AFL-CIO
American Federation of Musicians, 170–71
American Federation of State, County, and Municipal Employees (AFSCME), 85, 206, 279
The American Revolution (Boggs), 62
American-Soviet Friendship Association, 355
American Trade Unionism (Foster), 352
anarchists, 48, 225, 228
Angola, 58, 59, 63
Ann Arbor Sun, 54
Anniversary Tours, 154–55, 159
antiapartheid movement, 59, 60
anticommunism: Christians and, 193, 350; countering, 150; education and, 42; GE and, 306; incongruity of, 74–75; IUE and, 306; loyalty oaths and, 191; Massachusetts State Anti-Communist Commission, 224; nature of, 24–25; Newspaper Guild and, 331; social movement histories and, 114; Student SANE and, 290; unions and, 303, 333; United Mine Workers and, 354; Vietnam War and, 350; at Wayne State University, 47–48; working-class and, 20. *See also* McCarthyism
antidiscrimination laws, 20
antiimperialism, 58–60, 153–54
antimonopoly coalition, 210
Antioch College, 118, 119
antisemitism, 19, 112, 194, 252
anti-Vietnam War movement: Brown and, *35*; CEWVN, 292–93; direct action approach to, 292; FBI and, 341; impact of, 137–38; *Labor Today* and, 333; Morartorium Against the War, 144; NCC, 295; pacifists, 272, 291, 330, 339, 351; Student Mobe and, 139, 272–73; student strike against, 341; teach-in approach to, 291; at UMass, 227–28; at UW, 292–94; W.E.B. Du Bois Club and, *37*; at Wheaton College, 339. *See also* Vietnam War
apartheid, 59, 60, 112
Aptheker, Bettina, *213*, 272–73, 280, 282, 282n2, 289
Aptheker, Herbert, 232, 270, 282n2
Aragon, Louis, 105, 302
Archives, Tamiment Library, 30, 31, 264n4, 333
Area Agency on Aging, 103
Arizona State University Cross Cultural Study Group, 312–13
Armenian genocide, 266
the arts and politics, 99–101, 105, 121, 135–36, 285, 323–26
Askenazi Jews, 265
Association of Black Students, Wayne State University, 54
atomic bomb, 135–36, 293n5. *See also* nuclear disarmament; peace movement

ATU (Amalgamated Transit Union), 352
automation, workers and, 62, 79
automobile industry: Cadillac Assembly plant, 102; Dodge Main plant, 87–89, 97, 102–3; families and the, 27; Ford Hunger March, 63, 64, 98–99; Ford Rouge plant, 42; "Ford Spokesmen Hail Death Car," 83; wage and benefit concessions, 101–2. *See also* General Motors; United Auto Workers (UAW)

Bachtell, John, 363
Baker, General, 87
ballot tampering, 278–79
basic industries, 237
Battle, Buddy, 80
Beatty, Warren, 17
Belafonte, Harry, 268
Bennett, Harry, 98
Berkeley, University of California. *See* University of California Berkeley (UCB)
Bernstein, Bill, 245, 250, 253
Bible scriptures, 328–29
Bicentennial Celebration for Jobs, Freedom, and Peace, 151
Black America and the World Revolution (Lightfoot), 44
Black and Red Collective, 63
Blackburn, Ben, 314–18
Black History Departments, 301
Black Lives Matter, 287
Black Panther Party, 143, 204, 227, 341
Black people. *See* African Americans
Black Power (Boggs), 62
Black Power and the Garvey Movement (Vincent), 47
Black World, 43
Blake, Dave, 58
Blanchard, James, 104
Block, Red, 344
Bloice, Carl, 90, 106, 157, 322
blue-diaper baby, 28, 319
Blue Sheet, 304
Blumberg, Albert E. and Dorothy, 330
Boggs, James and Grace Lee, 61–62
"The Bomb and Tom" (Schaffner), 136
Bonner-Lyons, Pat, 230–31
Booker, Christopher, 47
bookstores, Communist Party, 44–45, 202, 203–4, 335
Boorstein, Edward, 336
Bosch, Juan, *125*
Boston Party organization, 302–9
Boston School Committee, 230–31
Boston School system, 224
bourgeois democracy, 146
Bowman, Arthur, Jr., 47, 61
Bowman, Arthur, Sr., 61
boycotts and sit-ins, 26, 192, 195, 196, 268, 313
Braden, Carl and Anne, 329, 357
Brattleboro Political Action, 341
bricklayers, 327
British Broadcasting Corporation, 350
Bromery, Randolph, 232
Bronx High School of Science, 270
Brooklyn College, 273
Browder, Earl, 29
Brown, Archie, 35
Brown University, 340
Brzezinski, Zbigniew, 46
Burlack, Anne, 356
Butler, Dave, 317
Buxenbaum, Alva, 329

Cadillac Assembly plant, 102
Caetano, Marcelo, 58
Cain, Lee, 87–89
California Communist Party, 21, 61
California Proposition 14, 196
California State College, 119
Camp Nitgedaiget, 219
Camp Unity, 268
Canadian Communist Party, 247
Canadian-US Party School, 202
Capital (Marx), 193
capitalism: colonialism and, 111; crisis of, 343, 346; democratic centralism in relation to, 183; Du Bois on, 33;

in Eastern Europe, 209–10; nature of, 113; transforming thinking about, 256
Capital Times, 295
Carnation Revolution, 58
Carter, Reggie, 47
Carter administration, 68, 80, 84, 85–86, 95, 357
Case, John, 342
Castro, Fidel, *215*, 346
Center for Marxist Education, 270
Central Intelligence Agency (CIA), 236, 331
Central Labor Council, 333
CEWVN (Committee to End the War in Vietnam), 292–93
Chaney, James, 121, 197
charter schools, 172
Chavis, Rev. Ben, 243–44
Che Lumumba Club, 21
Chesman, Naomi, 26
Chicago, Illinois: Chicago Peace Council, 140, 141; ChiTOC, 144; elections and, 148–50; Free Angela movement in, 147–48; independent politics of, 335; Party clubs, 333; Red Squad of, 136–37, 137n2, 142; Skokie suburb of, 134, 143–44; student movement in, 139–44; W.E.B. Du Bois Club in, 201–2
Chile, Popular Unity government in, 336
Chile solidarity movement, 153
China, living in, 176–77
China and the Soviet Union, 147, 177, 298
Chinese Communist Party, 165, 299
Chinese democracy movement, 165
Christians and Christianity, 193, 306n7, 328, 350, 355
Chrysler Corporation, 87–89
Church Committee hearings, 153
CIA (Central Intelligence Agency), 236, 331
CIO (Congress of Industrial Organizations), 76, 303, 306n7. *See also* AFL-CIO
Citizens Against the Tactical Squad, 204
Citizens Party, 149
City College of New York, 188, 274
"The City is the Black Man's Land" (Boggs), 62
city sanitation worker, 356
Civil Rights Movement: Castro and, *215*; Communists and, 19, 115, 115n1, 116, 118, 120–21, 284; effect on the CPUSA, 122–23; Freedom Registering, 198–99; Freedom Summer, 118, 120–21; impact of, 281–82; in Los Angeles, 119; McCarthyism and, 287; poor African Americans in, 121; W.E.B. Du Bois Clubs and, *124*, 196. *See also* Student Nonviolent Coordinating Committee (SNCC)
Clark, Mary, 143
class and ideology, 210–11
class and social movements, 122
class consciousness, 282
Cleaver, Kathleen, 204
climate change, 167
CLP (Communist Labor Party), 87
Coalition of Black Trade Unionists, 80, 262
Coalition of Labor Union Women, 262
coal miners, 319, 354
Cockrel, Kenneth, Sr., 102
Cohen, Abraham, 219, 227
Cohen, David, 342, 344
Cohen, Fannie (Guberman), 219
Cohen, Hyman, 219
Cohen, Madeline (Sivachek), 219
COINTELPRO (Counter Intelligence Program), 20, 298
Cold War, everyday life during, 42–43
Cold War liberals, 20
Coleman, Morris, 284
collective support, 285

College of Physicians and Surgeons (P&S), 274–77
colonialism, Portuguese, 58, 59
colonialism, Soviet Union and, 112
colonizing a worksite, 180, 333
Columbia Presbyterian Hospital Medical Center, 274–77
Columbia University medical library, 274, 275
Comintern debates, 238
Committees of Correspondence for Democracy and Socialism (CCDS): Albany club and, 362; formation of, 22, 264; hope for, 347–48; hospital and drugstore workers and, 263; members of, 115n1, 337, 338; Mitchell and, 321–22; origin and purpose of, 168–69
Committee to End the War in Vietnam (CEWVN), 292–93
Commoner, Barry, 149
Common Sense, 284
Communism: change and, 161; in China, 165; fascism and, 111, 112–13; historical aspects of, 110–12, 114; meaning of, 116; paradox of, 112; in South Africa, 347; split in, 147. *See also* Communist Party, US (CPUSA); socialism
Communist action groups, 205
Communist Control Act, 214
Communist fronts, 205
Communist Labor Party (CLP), 54–55, 87
Communist Manifesto (Marx), 173
Communist Party (CPUSA) Central Committee: change and, 161; on Czechoslovakia intervention, 162–63; democracy and, 347; distrust by, 306–7; Lumumba Club and, 21; meetings of, 334–35; members of, 151, 157, 158, 161, 164, 333; minority report to, 165–66; real existing socialism and, 160–61; West and, 346–47; Winston and, 361
Communist Party (CPUSA) clubs: in Albany, 357–59, 361–62; at Antioch College, 118; for autoworkers, 88, 89; in Boston, 262; in Chicago, 333; in Cleveland, 362; for electrical workers, 333, 334; in Flushing, 191; for hospital and drugstore workers, 263, 264; Irish-Republican Clubs, 358; in Madison and Milwaukee, 298–300; in Massachusetts, 307–9, 342–43; in New York, 262–63; for steelworkers, 333, 334; in Tampa and Saint Petersberg, 353–56; Washington Heights Project and, 274–75
Communist Party (CPUSA) National Committee. *See* Communist Party (CPUSA) Central Committee
Communist Party, US (CPUSA): 1966 convention, *214*; 1969 convention, 299–301; 1991 convention, 22, 165; characterizations of, 24–25; *Daily People's World*, 157; Detroit convention, 89–91; historical aspects of, 28–30, 111; joining the, 25, 69, 142–44, 178, 201, 262, 271, 282, 297–98, 313, 321, 322, 331–32, 342–43, 353; leaving the, 134, 166–68, 185, 209, 237, 259, 264, 280; lessons from, 122; in Massachusetts, 307–9; milieu of, 92; Moscow and, 21; *People's Daily World*, 90, 193–94, 322; *People's World*, 90, 106, 193, 387, 388; policy implementation, 163–64, 182–83; renewal proposal, 347; split within, 22, 164, 361–64; underground, 132, 133–34, 285; upheaval in, 297–98; *The Worker*, 135. *See also Daily Worker*; *Daily World*; Hall, Gus; W.E.B. Du Bois Clubs; Young Workers Liberation League (YWLL)
Communist Political Association, 29
"Communists in the Civil Rights Movement" conference, 115n1
Communist Youth League (KNE), 145

Community Meals, 345
company union, 275
computer operator work, 204
Congress of Industrial Organizations (CIO), 303, 306n7, 339, 354, 355. *See also* AFL-CIO
Congress of Racial Equality (CORE), 121, 195, 289
Congress of Unrepresented People, 293–94
Connolly Youth Union, 145
Cook County courts, 337
Cook County Hospital, 333
cooperation vs. competition, 176
Coors Boycott Coalition, 313
Corbyn, Jeremy, 169–70
cotton-oil processing plant worker, 312
Council for American-Soviet Friendship, 359
Council of Federated Organizations (COFO), 121
counterculture in Detroit, 48–50
counterculture people and joy, 93
Counter-Intelligence Program (COINTELPRO), 20, 298
Cox, Oliver C., 62
CREEM, 43
Crisis, 292–93
Crockett, George W., 45, 51–53, 99
Cuba: Anniversary Tours to, 154, 155; Cuban Missile Crisis, 42, 195, 224; Cuban Revolution, *215*; opening of, 173; Radio Havana Cuba, 350; US blockade of, 153, 195; Venceremos Brigade and, 117; World Festival of Youth and Students in, 76, 81–83, 151, 152, 244
culture, revolutionary, 116
Cunningham, Gene, 46, 61, 76
Cunningham, Merce, 340
CVV (Madison Citizens for a Vote of Vietnam), 296, 297, 298
Czechoslovakia, Soviet intervention in, 161–63, 299, 300, 331

Daily People's World, 157
Daily Worker, 63, 74, 83–84, 221, 267, 356
Daily World: Allan and, 41, 74; distribution of, 358; on Dodge workers, 87; editors for, 106; Eisenscher and, 152; firings at, 347; Fry and, 96; labor coverage of, 80; "For Louis Aragon," 105; A. Max and, 330; on People Before Profits rally, 90; role of, 64; Shields and, 356; writing for the, 76–77, 97, 101, 102, 104, 107, 356
"Dancing in the Streets" (song), 49
Daniel Webster School, 220
Davis, Angela: CPUSA activities and, 178; in Cuba, 280; movement to free, 44, 147–48, 207, 231–32; National Committee and, 361; at People Before Profits rally, 90–91; reputation of, 19–20; respect for, 343; UCLA and, 206; YWLL and, 207
Davis, Leon, 278
Dawson, Kip, 273
Debs, Eugene, 173, 210
De Caux, Len, 76
De Geyter, Chrétien, Pierre, 22
Dellums, Ronald, 86
Deming, W. Edwards, 79
democracy: bourgeois, 146; Chinese democracy movement, 165; CPUSA and, 264, 300, 307, 309, 346, 347–48; democratic centralism, 167–68, 183, 209; expanding, 184; socialism and, 146, 166–67; unions and, 236, 237, 262, 278, 279, 282
Democratic Party: 1964 convention, 199; 1984 convention, 318; in Chicago, 335; CPUSA and, 68–69, 237, 363; of Mississippi, 199; plant closures and, 308; porous aspects of, 67–68; Reagan and, 103–4; SDS and, 330; of West Virginia, 331; working within the, 208; Young Democrats, 271; youth and, 145
Democratic People's Republic of Korea, 157

Democratic Socialist Organizing Committee (DSOC), 351–52
Democratic Socialists of America (DSA), 22, 98, 115, 169, 338
Dennis, Thomas, Jr., 41, 52, 74, 91, 92, 93, 94
Denver, Colorado, 314
Denver Newspaper Guild, 315–16
Denver Post, 316, 317
Depression era, 132–33
Detroit: auto workers, 42; Black politics in, 43–44; Black radicals in, 63–64; cab-driving in, 72–73; capital strike in, 97; Cass Corridor neighborhood in, 45; childhood in, 42–43; CLP in, 54–55; Common Council of, 57, 63–64; counterculture in, 48–50; CPUSA convention in, 77, 89–91, 97; *Detroit Free Press,* 52, 75; Detroit Marxist-Leninist Organization, 60; Detroit Youth Jobs Coalition, 67; Global Books in, 44–45; Grande Ballroom in, 49–50; Hartford Avenue Baptist Church in, 52; labor journalists in, 74–75; legislators, 67; *Metro Times* of, 104; New Bethel Shoot-Out in, 51, 52, 53; People Before Profits rally in, 89–91; during Reagan administration, 97; *Solid Ground* and, 100; Treaty of Detroit, 89; Wayne State University in, 46, 47–48, 54, 62; WDET-FM, 70; Young administration, 48, 53, 80, 95–96, 103; YWLL in, 65–67
The Dialectic of Sex (Firestone), 47
Dickerson, Naomi, 47
disillusionment, 21
Diskin, Lou, 163, 202
Divale, Bill, 206
Dodge Main plant, 87–89, 90, 97, 102–3
Dodge Revolutionary Union Movement (DRUM), 87
Dominican Republic, US military invention in, *125,* 271
Dooley, Tom, 42
Dorothy Healey Remembers (Healey), 347
Dow Chemical, 140
DRUM (Dodge Revolutionary Union Movement), 87
DSOC (Democratic Socialist Organizing Committee), 351–52
Dubeck, Alexander, 162
Du Bois, W.E.B., 33, 232
Dunayevskaya, Raya, 60–61
Durham, Earl, 163

Eastern Europe: Anniversary Tours to, 155; capitalism in, 209–10; Czechoslovakia, 161–63, 299, 300, 331; Hungary, 19, 330, 357; repression in, 112; socialism in, 156–58, 162, 183. *See also* Soviet Union
Economic Notes, 206
economism, 242
Ed H. (Miller Falls Tool worker), 242
education, public, 172
education and social consciousness, 42
education workers, 237
Eisenhower and Castro, *215*
Eisenscher, Judith, 152
Eisenscher, Michael, 288, 289
electoral politics: CPUSA in relation, 19, 69; in Detroit, 48, 53; failed, 334; Hall and, 68–69, 148, 149, 151; J. Jackson and, 318; McGovern and Goldwater and, 291; Michigan CPUSA and, 41, 92; right-wing ascendancy in, 85, 95, 103–4; Trump and, 172; youth and, 145; Youth Rights Candidates, 149
electrical workers, 26–27, 237–38, 333, 334. *See also* International Union of Electrical, Radio and Machine Workers (IUE); United Electrical, Radio, and Machine Workers (UE)
employment discrimination, 195, 196, 201–2
Emspak, Dolores, 302, 302n6

Emspak, Julius, 283, 286–87
The Enemy Forgotten (Green), 330
The Energy Rip-Off (Hall), 72
Engelstein, David, 163–64
environmentalism, 167
Equal Rights Amendment (ERA), 208, 335
Ethical Culture youth discussion group, 269
Evers, Medger, 198
evolution debate, 291
E.W. Scripps Howard Company, 316–17

Fahsen Collective, 299
families, Communist: activities of, 117–18, 132–33; childhood memories of, 224, 267–69; education and, 193; employment and, 262; J. Emspak and, 286–87; Max family, 330; McCarthyism and, 175, 187–89; parental influence and, 178; red-diaper babies, 120, 120n2, 283, 298, 337
Fanon, Frantz, 313
fascism: Communists and, 111, 112–13; fighting, 29, 42, 110, 111, 320, 322; Franco and, 267; in Greece, 154; John Birch Society, 193; Nazi, 164; in Portugal, 58; Soviet Union and, 164; violence and, 202
Federal Bureau of Investigation (FBI): at activities meeting, 163; COINTELPRO program, 20, 298; Council for American-Soviet Friendship and, 357; harassment by, 134–35; informants of, 26, 341; surveillance by, 142; on the W.E.B du Bois Club, 36
Feinsinger, Nathan, 288
feminist nurses, 262
feminists, labor, 208
Ferency, Zoltan, 104
Fifth Estate, 45, 50, 51
the Fight for $15, 287
Fink, Leon, 263
Finnegan's Wake (Joyce), 42
Fisk Rubber Company, 241–42
Fitch, Maurice, 110
Flory, Ishmael, 60, 148
FNLN (National Front for the Liberation of Angola), 59
"For Charlotta Bass" (Jacques), 101
Ford, Gerald, 68
Ford, Henry, 98
Ford administration, 59, 63
Ford Hunger March, 63, 64, 98–99
Ford Motor Company, 83
Ford Rouge plant, 98
"Ford Spokesmen Hail Death Car" (Jacques), 83
"For Louis Aragon" (Jacques), 105
Foster, William Z., 352
Four Essays on Philosophy (Mao), 47
Frabrizio, Ideal, 220, 221, 223, 229–30
Fragments of the Century (Harrington), 98
France, Communist Party of, 105
France, Royal, 354
France, Ruth, 354
Franco, Francisco, 267
Frankie, Peggy Goldman, 41
Franklin, Rev. C.L., 51
Fraser, Douglas, 77, 86
freedom music, 121
Freedom Registering, 198–99
Freedom Riders, 118
Freedom Socialist Party, 313
Freedom Summer, 120–21
Freedomways, 107, 356
Free German Youth, 158
Freeman, Joshua B., 263, 263n3
Free Speech Movement (FSM), 120n2, 200, 213, 282, 282n2, 289, 290
free trade and workers, 78–79
Freiheit, 135
Fried, Clifford, 206
Friedman, Bill, 267
Friedman Joseph (Yusel), 266
Friere, Paulo, 47
front organizations, 133, 333
fruit-export document clerk work, 204

Fry, Pat, 96
FSM (Free Speech Movement), 120n2, 200, *213*, 282, 282n2, 289, 290
functionary work, 269
fundamentalist Christians, 350
Fur and Leather Workers Union, 358

Gaboury, Fred, 77–78, 332, 333
Gaetsewe, John, 80
Ganley, Nat, 74
Garcia, Marcial, 320–21, 322
Garvey, Marcus, 47
gay and lesbian Party members, 31–32
gay rights movement, 122, 172
Gellert, Hugo, 355
General Electric (GE): as aristocracy of labor, 307; colonization of, 180; disciplinary action at, 181; industrial concentration and, 237; in Lynn, MA, 302; on the North Shore, 306; in Schenectady, 286, 359; successes at, 182; WAGE and, 307–9; in Wilmington, MA, 305
General Motors: Cadillac Assembly plant, 102; Dodge Main plant, 87–89, 90, 97, 102–3; Feinsinger and, 288; industrial concentration and, 238; sit-down strike at, 75
German Democratic Republic (GDR), 158, 350
gig work, 73
glasnost, 361
Global Books, 44–45
Gold, Ben, 355
Goldfield, Michael, 19
Goldman, Peggy, 92, 93–94
Goldwater, Barry, 291
Goodman, Andrew, 121, 197
Gorbachev, Mikhail, 161, 280, 361
government workers and activism, 81–82
granite shed work, 220–23
Grayson, Susan, 187
Green, Ben, 148
Green, Gilbert, 163, 280, 330, 356
Greenfield Tap and Die, 345
Green Lantern Eating Co-op, 287
Gregory, Dick, 117, 196
The Guardian, 50
Guild Reporter, 331
Gyroscope, Sperry, 191

Hall, Gus: African Americans and, 337; electoral work for, 343; Healey and, 347; on the labor movement, 254; *Labor Today* and, 333; leadership of, 361, 362; presidential campaigns of, 68–69, 148, 149, 151; real existing socialism and, 156; *Rocky Mountain News* and, 314; Tiananmen Square and, 165; Webb and, 95; writings of, 71–72
Hampton, Fred, 143
Hanible, Janice, 47
Hanna, Cheryl, 107
Harawitz, Jerry, *213*
Harlan County, Kentucky, 290–91
Harlem, *NY*, Castro in, *215*
Harriman, Manny, 267
Harrington, Fred Harvey, 288
Harrington, Michael, 98, 352
Harris, Joseph, 26
Harrison, Wendell, 54
Hartford Avenue Baptist Church, 52
Harvard Hospitals, 302, 304
"Has Socialism Failed" (Slovo), 347
Havens, Richie, 272
Hawkins Jobs Bill, 151
Hayden Robert, 46
Hazard, Kentucky, 290–91
Healey, Dorothy, 21, 61, 300, 347
health-care workers, 27, 237, 261, 262, 263. *See also* 1199
Hegel, G.W.F., 313, 340
Heisler, Bob, 280
Henderson, Erma, 53, 55, 57, 85, 102, 103
"Henry Winston's Laugh" (Pizarro), 323–26
Herald-Statesman, 286
Herndon, Angelo, 110
Hill, Rev. Charles A., 52

Himmelstein, David, 258
Hinton, William, 299
hippies, 226, 247
Hiroshima, Japan, 293n5
Hitler, Adolf, 111, 112, 133
Ho Chi Minh Working Youth Union, 146–47
Holifield, Chet, 208
Holocaust, 112
Holyoke Wire and Cable, 243, 244–46, 248, 255–57
Holyoke Wire and Cable Employee Association, 245, 246, 249–53
Hoover, J. Edgar, 259
Hope Dies Last (Dubeck), 162
Horne, Gerald, 18
hospital workers, 84, 237, 263, 274–77, 387. *See also* 1199
Hotel Theresa, 215
House Un-American Activities Committee (HUAC), 30, 53, 261
housing, public, 225
housing discrimination, 196, 268
housing segregation, 225
Humphrey, Hubert, 287
Humphrey-Hawkins bill, 66
Hungary, Soviet invasion of, 19, 330, 357
Hurricane Agnes, 349

Iggy Pop, 49–50
Illinois District Committee, 151
Illinois Party, 333. *See also* Chicago, Illinois
immigrants, Jewish, 265
immigrants, Turkish, 265
immigrants, Ukrainian, 131–32, 266
imperialism, 113, 114, 238
Imported Publications, 335
industrial concentration, 179–80, 237–39, 302, 304, 307, 334
influenza epidemic, 132
Information Bulletin, 356
Ingersoll Rand, 342, 345
"Initiative and Renewal" document, 264, 347
Insurgent, 140
International Association of Machinists, 207
International Brotherhood of Teamsters, 103, 132, 288–89
International Days of Protest, 295
International Longshore and Warehouse Union (ILWU), 35
International Publishers, 55
International Union of Electrical, Radio and Machine Workers (IUE): anticommunism and, 306; chief union steward for, 239–40; Emspak and, 283; GE and, 309; *IUE L761 News,* 330; Local 201, 305; UE and, 241, 306, 306n7; Williams and, 343. *See also* electrical workers; United Electrical, Radio, and Machine Workers (UE)
In These Times, 355
Intourist, 156–57
Iran, conflicts with, 172
Irish-Republican Clubs, 358
ironworker apprenticeship, 202
Israel, creation of, 122
IUE. *See* International Union of Electrical, Radio and Machine Workers (IUE)

Jackson, James E., 55, 332
Jackson, Jesse, 145, 165, 180, 318
Jackson, Jim, 71
Jacobin, 19
jazz and politics, 70
Jewish cemeteries, repairing, 158
Jewish families, 131–32
Jewish immigrants, 265–66
Jewish People's Institute (JPI), 132
Jim Crow, 26
Jobs March, 345
John Birch Society, 84–85, 193, 244
Johnson, Arnold, 356
Johnson, James, 102
Johnson, Lyndon B., 291
Jones and Laughlin Steel Company, 296

Joseph, Seymour, 84
Journal of Black Poetry, 43
joy and politics, 93
Joyce, Frank, 50–51
Joyce, James, 42
just-in-time production, 79

Kay, Eddie, 276
Kennedy, John F., 136, 192
Kerry, John, 138
keypunch operators, 204
Khrushchev, Nikita, 19, 112, *215*, 330, 354n2
King, Coretta Scott, 277
King, Martin Luter, Jr., 141, 142, 183, 332, 340
Kinoy, Arthur, 61
Kissinger, Henry, 59, 68
Klein, Jim, 17
Kling, Jack, 163, 164
Klu Klux Klan, 330
Knight, Al, 315, 316, 317
Koch Brothers, 113
Komplektova, Alla and Viktor, 157
Korean War, 350
Kramer, Steve, 276–77
Krehbiel, Paul, 313
Kropotkin, Peter, 225, 229

labor aristocracy, 298, 307
Labor Herald, 78
labor movement: anti-Vietnam War movement in, 333; in Canada, 247–48; feminists in, 208, 262; Ford Hunger March and, 98–99; lessons from, 242–43; racism in, 236; Reagan and, 316; reporting on, 75–78; socialists in, 254; upheaval in, 236; young people and, 262. *See also* unions and unionism
Labor Notes, 78
Labor Party, 259
Labor Radical (De Caux), 76
Labor Research Association (LRA), 206
labor theory of value, 284, 285
Labor Today, 78, 236, 331, 332, 333, 334, 345
labor unions. *See* unions and unionism
Labor Unity, 78
Labor Youth League, 55, 330
Ladino language, 265–66
"A Lame Duck in Turbulent Times" (Hall), 68, 71
Lamont, Corliss, 355
Landrum-Griffin Act, *35*
Latino community, 262, 335
League of Revolutionary Black Workers, 46–47, 51, 54, 87, 102
Left ideas, mainstreaming of, 53
Lenin, Vladimir, 145, 168, 183–84, 193, 229–30
Lenin School of the International Department of the CPSU, 336
Lester, Julius, 50
Leviticus 19:33-34, 328
Lewis, John, 270
Lewis, John L., 319
LGBTQ+ rights and equality, 31–32, 122, 172
liberalism and Reagan, 104
liberalism and social movements, 20–21
Liberation, 136
Lightfoot, Claude M., 44, 148, 163, 164, 202
Lima, Mickey, 202
Line, Denise, 64–65
longshoreman work, 204
Looking for the Future (Wofsy), 112
Looney, Ralph, 314
Los Angeles, Civil Rights Movement in, 119
Louisville, Kentucky, 323–26, 329
loyalty oaths, 26, 191–92, 200–201
Lozano, Rudy, 335
Lucky Supermarket shop-in, 195
Luke 4:18, 328–29
Lynd, Staughton, 293, 294

machine shop work, 342

Madison Citizens for a Vote on Vietnam (CVV), 296, 297, 298
Madison Party club, 298–302
Mahaffey, Maryann, 102–3
Malcom X, 215
Mandela, Nelson, 112
Manley, Martin, 358
Mao Zedong, 47
The March of Labor, 78
March on Washington, 270, *365*
Maricopa County, Arizona, 311
marriage equality, 172
Martha and the Vandellas, 49
Marxism: biblical aspects of, 329; *Capital*, 193; Center for Marxist Education, 270; CPUSA and, 55; democratic centralism in, 183–84; Detroit Marxist-Leninist Organization, 60; ideological aspects of, 254; interest in, 340; learning, 283–84; "Marxist Humanism" lectures, 60; science of, 168; studying, 47, 54, 60, 63, 96, 202; W.E.B. Du Bois Clubs and, 196; YWLL and, 145
Marzani, Carl, 296
Massa, Leon, 241, 242, 244
Massachusetts, Quincy, 219–20, 224
Massachusetts Party club, 342–43, 347
Max, Alan, 330
Max, Steve, 284, 330
May Day march, *125*, *126*
McCarren Act, 141, 205, *214*
McCarthyism: anticommunism laws of, 150; awareness of, 55; blacklist of, 30, 175, 188, 189, 331; childhood memories of, 267; Civil Rights Movement and, 287; effect of, 176; gays and lesbians and, 31–32; growing up during, 187–88; HUAC and, 30, 53, 261; impact of, 24–25, 69, 95, 273; informers and informants of, 25–26; Landrum-Griffin Act, 35; Religion and Labor Foundation and, 354; SACB and, 20, *34*, 141, 205; Smith Act defendants, 52, 74, 92, 106, 356; terror legacy of, 73–74; UE and, 241; Winston and, 356. *See also* anticommunism
McFadden, Nancy, 357, 358, 362
McGee, Reg, 99
McGee, Willie, 268
McGovern, George, 145, 149
McPhaul, Art, 63–64
Meany, George, 236, 239
Mein Kampf (Hitler), 111–12
mental health issues, 101, 336
Mesabi Iron Range, 71–72
Metco program, 224–25
Metropolitan Life Insurance, 268
Metro Times, 104
Meyers, George, 91, 331, 332, 356
Michigan Communist Party, 41, 87–89, 92
Michigan Daily, 46
Michigan Governor's race of 1982, 104
Michigan property tax proposition, 84–85
Michigan Six, 52, 61, 74, 92, 106
militancy and union democracy, 236, 237
The Militant, 136, 352
Militant Labor Forum, 273
military budget, 153
military intelligence agencies, 137, 142
Millers Falls Tool Company, 242, 342, 343, 345
Milwaukee Party, 298–300
miners strike, 290–91
Mishler, Mark, 358, 359
Mississippi, Jackson, 120–21
Mississippi Summer Project, 197–98, 199
Mitchell, Charlene, 300, 321–22, 361
Mkalimoto, Ernie, 47
Monk, Thelonious, 100
Monsanto Chemical Company, 241, 343
Monthly Review, 352
Monthly Review Press, 62
Moore, Dave, 99
Moratorium Against the War, 144

Morris, George, 236
Morse, Linda, 273
Moses, Bob, 197–98, 293, 294
Motor City Labor League, 55
Motown, 49
Mozambique, Black Nationalists and, 58
Muravchik, Josh, 270
music and politics, 45, 49–50, 70, 100, 121, 285
Muste, A.J., 339
Myerson, Mike, 280

NAACP (National Association for the Advancement of Colored People), 27, *215*, 314
Nader, Ralph, 256, 257
NAFTA (North American free Trade Agreement), 78–79
NAIMSAL (National Anti-Imperialist Movement in Solidarity with African Liberation), 19
Nasser, Gamal Abdel, *215*
Natambu, Kofi, 100
The Nation, 136
National Alliance Against Racist and Political Repression (NAARPR), 19, 243
National Anti-Imperialist Movement in solidarity with African Liberation (NAIMSAL), 19
National Association of Colored People (NAACP), 27, *215*, 314
National Center of Trade Union Action and Democracy (TUAD), 78
National Committee for a Sane Nuclear Policy (SANE), 269, 290. *See also* Student SANE
National Coordinating Committee to End the War in Vietnam (NCC), 293n5, 294, 295
National Council of American-Soviet Friendship, 357
National Education Association, 331
National front for the Liberation of Angola (FNLA), 59
National Guardian, 352
national health care, 256, 258–59
National Labor Relations Board (NLRB), 253, 277
National Liberation, Socialism, and Imperialism (Lenin), 47
National Liberation Front (NLF), 295, 302
National Mobilization Committee to End the War in Vietnam, 272
National Negro Labor Council (NNLC), 80
National Organization for Black Power, 62
National Public Radio, 70
National Union of Hospital and Healthcare Employees, 278. *See also* 1199
National Urban League, 27
National Women's Commission, *365*
Nazis, 112, 133, 164
NCC (National Coordinating Committee to End the War in Vietnam), 293n5, 294, 295
Nearing, Scott, 355
Nehru, Jawaharlal, *215*
New American Movement, 61
New Bethel Shoot-Out, 51, 52, 53
New Communist Movement, 17, 54, 56–57
Newell, Amy, 250
New Left historians, 17–18
New Left Notes, 136
New Politics convention, 141
News and Letters, 60
Newspaper Guild, 330, 331
New University Thought, 287n4
New World Review, 355, 356–57
New York club, 262–63
New York University Students for a Democratic Society, 271
New York University Tamiment Library, 30, 31, 264n4, 333
NGO-style social service organizations, 66

Nicaragua, Sandinista government in, 355
Nicholas, Henry, 278
Niles Township Student Coalition (NTSC), 142
Nixon, Richard, 42, 192
Nixon, Russ, 296
NLF (National Liberation Front), 295, 302
NLRB (National Labor Relations Board), 253, 277
NNLC (National Negro Labor Council), 80
nonviolence training, 198
Norrick, Joe, 354
North, Dan, 84
North American Free Trade Agreement (NAFTA), 78–79
North Atlantic Treaty Organization (NATO), 210
North Korea, socialism in, 157
Northport, New York, 339
North Shore Party club, 307–9
North Shore region of Massachusetts, 302, 303, 305–6
North Shore School of Jewish Studies, 135
Northwestern University, 144
NTSC (Niles Township Student Coalition), 142
nuclear disarmament, *212*, 269–70
nuclear weapons, 135–36, 153, 167, 293n5
nursing, 262, 263

Oakland High School, 204
Obama, Barack, 113, 172
Obrador, Andrés Manuel López, 172
Occupy movement, 173, 173n4, 184, 364
Oil, Chemical and Atomic Workers, 262
Okemah, Arizona, 311
Overton, Joe, *215*

pacifists, 272, 291, 330, 339, 351
paid administrative leave, 182
Palestinian people, 48
Palmer, Hazel T., 199
Pan African Congress, 59
Paragon Rubber, 232–36, *233*, 239–44
Parchester apartments, integration of, 268
Paris Peace Talks, 302
Parker, DeWitt, 110
Parks, Gene, 296
Patrinos, Sandy, 332–33, 336, 337
pattern bargaining, 89
Paul Robeson Club, 313
Peace and Freedom Party, 207–8
Peace Council, US, 100
peace movement: vs. an anti-imperialist movement, 153–54; antinuclear war demonstrations, 293n5; Black leadership in, 100–101; Brown and, *35*; Council for American-Soviet Friendship, 357, 359; CPUSA and, 160–61; electoral politics and, 150; Promoting Enduring Peace, 154; *Sanity*, 290; Student SANE and, 269–70, 284, 290; at UW, 288; W.E.B. Du Bois Club and, 37
Pecinovsky, Tony, 19
Pedagogy of the Oppressed (Friere), 47
Pennsylvania, Central, 349
Pennsylvania State College system, 331
Pentagon Papers, 147
People Against Racism, 50–51, 301
People Before Profits rally, 89–91, 97
People's Daily World, 358
People's Movement for the Liberation of Angola (MPLA), 59
People's World, 90, 106, 193–94, 322
people-to-people travel, 154
perestroika, 161, 361
Perlo, Victor, 206
philosophy and direct action, 284
piece work, 73
Pinochet military junta, 153
Planned Parenthood, 172

plant closings, 87–89, 90, 102–3, 255–57, 308, 345
plastic factory sealer, 193
Pledge of Allegiance, 351
pluralism, 166
Podemos, 169
poetry and politics, 135–36, 323–26
Poison Cookie Hole, 142
policing: in Detroit, 51; race and racism, 110; Red Squad, 136–37, 137n2, 142, 163; STRESS unit, 48
Polish workers, 252
Political Education Project (PEP), 330
Politics for Peace, 139
Popular Unity Government in Chile, 336
Portside, 171
postal workers' strike, 341
posttraumatic stress syndrome, 227
Potash, Irving, 179
Pottier, Eugène, 22
Prague, socialism in, 158
Presbyterian Hospital, 274–77
Prince, Rob, 314
Professional Air Traffic Controllers Organization, 316
Progressive Party, 133, 306n7
Progressive Youth Organizing Committee (PYOC), 329
Promoting Enduring Peace, 154
Psalm 82:1-5, 328
Psychedelic Stooges, 49–50
public employment and service economy, 359
public housing, 187, 225
public ownership of utilities, 341
public television, 138–39
Purple Gang, 98
Pursel, Kent D., 120n2
PYOC (Progressive Youth Organizing Committee), 329

Queens, New York, 191
Queens College, 273
Quincy, Massachusetts, 219–20
Quincy High School, 224

race and racism: in Boston, 230–31, 302; Castro on, *215*; CPUSA and, 185, 297, 300–301, 317–18, 331–32; Democratic Socialists of America and, 98; development of racial consciousness, 144; in the GDR, 158–59; Hall and, 71; in hiring practices, 195, 196, 201–2; in housing, 268; industrial concentration and, 237; in the labor movement, 236; left-wing organizations and, 61; Lightfoot and, 202; Madison Party on, 300; NAARPR, 243; People Against Racism, 50–51, 301; policing and, 48, 110; racial integration, 116–17, 118; racial violence, 121; *Racism and the Class Struggle*, 62; at the *Rocky Mountain News*, 314–18; students against, 227–28; unions and, 103; war and, 141; while traveling, 119; White and, 103; white workers and, 257–58; Williams and, 242; Zionism and, 122
radio, shortwave, 350
railroad workers, 258
RCA workers, 330
Reagan administration: Detroit during the, 97; Hall and, 314; labor movement and, 316; Reagan Democrats, 104; recession of, 345; Soviet Union and, 357; Stars Wars initiative of, 153, 257
Rebellion in the Unions (Morris), 236
red-baiting, 104, 283, 285, 305, 308, 343
red-diaper babies, 120, 120n2, 267–69, 283, 298, 337. *See also* families, Communist
Red Flash Party club, 333
Redland Daily Facts, 283n3
Reds (film), 17
Red Squad, 136–37, 137n2, 142, 163
Reicher, Julia, 17
Reichstag fire frame-up, 111–12
Reiseburo, 158

Religion and Labor Foundation, 354
religious appreciation week, 192
Republican Party, 113, 327–28
Republic of New Africa, 51
Republic Steel, 133
Retail, Wholesale, and Department Store Union, 278
Reuther, Victor, 333
Reuther, Walter, 42, 57–58, 80, 89, 89n2, 333. *See also* United Auto Workers (UAW)
Revolutionary Communist Party, 313
Richmond, Al, 193–94
right-to-work state, 312
Rivera, Dennis, 279
Robert F. Wagner Archives, New York University, 30
Roberts, Leslie, 47
Robeson, Paul, 23, 52, 133, 151
robots and workers, 62, 79
rock 'n' roll, 49, 285
Rocky Mountain News, 27, 313, 314–18
Rodney, Walter, 313
Rohr Industries, 207
Roman Catholic Church, 306n7
Roosevelt High School, 285
Roosevelt Hospital, 277
Roosevelt University, 337
Rosenberg, Julius and Ethel, 192
Rosie the Riveter, 42
Ross, Mollie, 266
Runnels, Frank, 102
Russia, czarist, 110, 111, 112
Russian Jews, 219

Salazar, António de Oliveira, 58
salted worksites, 180
Salvucci, Tony, 220, 221, 222
sandblasters, 222
Sanders, Bernie, 169, 172, 364
Sandinista government, 355
San Francisco Ballet, 109–10
San Francisco State College, 206
Sanity, 290
Savannah State University, 338
Save Our Union movement, 263, 263n3, 278–79
Savio, Mario, 200
SCEF (Southern Conference Education Fund), 329
Schatz, Phil, 74
Schenectady, New York, 283, 286, 358–59
schools, Communist Party (CPUSA), 71, 202–3, 247–48, 332
Schwerner, Michael, 121, 197–98
scientific and technological revolution, 167
Scottsboro Boys, 235
SDS. *See* Students for a Democratic Society (SDS)
Seabrook nuclear power plant, 341
Seale, Bobby, 204
sectarianism, 295–96, 346–47
Seeing Red (film), 17
segregation: battles against, 26; fight against, 138, 281; housing, 225; in Kentucky, 327; school, 117–18, 312; school in Boston, 224; Woolworth's and, 192, 284. *See also* boycotts and sit-ins; Civil Rights Movement
self-employment, 210, 211
Selma, Alabama, *124*
Sennett, Bill, 354
Sephardic Jews, 265–66
service economy and public employment, 359
Service Employees Union (SEIU), 28, 263–64, 278, 279, 358
Sevy, Lisa, 267
sexism at the *Rocky Mountain News*, 314–18
Shapiro, Andrea, 332, 337
Sheraton Palace Hotel, 196
Sherman, Howard, 206–7
Shields, Art, 356
shop-ins, 195
shorter workweek, 79, 80
shortwave radio listener, 350
Shostakovich Trilogy, 109–10
Siegel, Leni, 213

silicosis, 222, 235
Simms, Harry Hersh, 110
Sinclair, John, 49, 54
single-payer health insurance, 258–59
sit-ins, 26, 192, 195, 196, 268, 313
sit-ins and boycotts, 192
Sixties, social unrest of, 137–39
Sklar, Martin J., 271
Skokie, Illinois, 134, 143–44
Slovo, Joe, 347
small businesses, 210
Smith, Jessica, 355
Smith Act defendants, 52, 74, 92, 106, 356
SNCC. *See* Student Nonviolent Coordinating Committee (SNCC)
socialism: anarchy and, 228; Christians and, 355; democracy and, 146, 166–67; early interest in, 350; in Eastern Europe, 162, 183; "Has Socialism Failed," 347; hierarchical approach to, 238–39, 255; influence of, 179; as irreversible, 209–10; a new openness to, 169–70; a new socialist movement, 171–73; real existing, 156–61; Socialist Club at University of Wisconsin, 287–88; Socialist Party, 221, 290; Socialist Study Group, 271; Socialist Unity Party, 158; Socialist Workers Party, 58, 228, 272, 273, 295, 313, 352
social tourism, 155–56
Soglin, Paul, 296
Solidarity Day, 345
Solid Ground, 100
South Africa, 122
South African Communist Party, 347
South African Council of Trade Unions, 80
South End, 46–47, 48, 76
Southern Conference Education Fund (SCEF), 329
Southern Patriot, 329
Southern Student Organizing Committee (SSOC), 329, 330
South Shore Coalition for Human Rights, 225
South Works plant of US Steel, *127*
The Soviet Bloc (Brzezinski), 46
Soviet Peace Committee, 154
Soviet Union: Anniversary Tours to, 154–57; attitudes toward, 298; capitalists in, 210; China and, 147, 177; collapse of, 22, 264, 362; colonialism and, 112; Communist Party, 336, 354n2; CPUSA and, 30; defending the, 357; establishment of, 111; fascism and, 164; Gorbachev and, 161, 280, 361; Hitler and, 112; invasion of Hungary, 19, 330, 357; Lenin School in, 336; prestige of, 164–65; Radio Moscow, 350; real existing socialism in, 156–58; subsidies from, 360; travel to, 154–56, 157, 360; World Federation of Democratic Youth, 81. *See also* Stalin, Joseph
Spanish Civil War veterans, 354–55
Spanish Jews, 265–66
Spanish-speaking workers, 276
Spock, Benjamin, 117
SSOC (Southern Student Organizing Committee), 329, 330
Stalin, Joseph: attitudes toward, 357; historical aspects of, 110; paradox of, 112; revelations about, 19, 330, 354, 354n2; US Communists and, 30, 353
Starobin, Bob, *213*
State and Revolution (Lenin), 193
State University of New York (SUNY), 271, 331
Steele, James, 70–71, 81
steelworkers: in Chicago, 335; Great Steel Strike, 352; industrial concentration and, 334; Jones and Laughlin Steel Company, 296; Party club, 333; prestige of, 27; at Republic Steel, 133; United Steelworkers, 254, 262, 354; at U.S. Steel, *127,* 334, 335

Steinberg, Jerry, 304
Stitt, Sonny, 100
Strategic Defense Initiative, 257
STRESS (Stop the Robberies, Enjoy Safe Streets), 48
strikes: Black student strike, 298, 301; capital strike in Detroit, 97; Great Steel Strike, 352; national student strike, 272–73, 341; postal workers' strike, 341; Student strike at UMass, 227–29
Student Committee for the National Committee for a Sane Nuclear Policy (Student Sane), 269–70, 284, 290. *See also* National Committee for a Sane Nuclear Policy (SANE)
Student Mobilization Committee against the War in Vietnam (Student Mobe), 139, 272–73
student movement: Black student strike, 298, 301; in Chicago, 139–44; Free Speech Movement, 120n2, 200, *213*, 282, 282n2, 289, 290; Liberal Youth of Niles Township, 136–37; national student strike, 272–73, 341; NTSC, 142; for school integration, 270; Student Mobe, 139, 272–73; Student SANE and, 269–70, 284, 290; Students for fair Housing, 196–97; at UCB, 289–90; at UMass, 227–29; at UW, 292–93, 298, 301; workers compared to, 137
Student Nonviolent Coordinating Committee (SNCC): Berkeley Friends of, 197; Congress of Unrepresented People event of, 293–94; Friends of, 329; Lester and, 50; in Mississippi, 121; Mississippi Summer Project of, 197–98; Moses and, 197–98; parents of, 197; training school of, 197; at UCB, 282. *See also* Civil Rights Movement
Student SANE, 269–70, 284, 290
Students for a Democratic Society (SDS): in Chicago, 142; Common Sense and, 284; founding of, 329; High School, 139; *New Left Notes*, 136; at NYU, 271; Political Education Project of, 330; at UW, 290
Students for Fair Housing, 196–97
Studies on the Left, 271, 287, 287n4
substance-abuse counseling, 335–36
Subversive Activities Control Board (SACB), 20, *34*, 141, 205
Supporting Staff Association (SSA), 275
Sykes, Frank, 98

Taft-Hartley Act, 92
Tamiment Library, New York University, 30, 31, 264n4, 333
Tampa, Florida, 352–57
Taylor, Sid, 356
Teaching Assistants Association, 301–2
teach-in movement, 291–92
Teamsters, 103, 132, 288–89
Teixeira, Ed, 247, 248
television news and the sixties, 138–39
textile union, 356
Thiemy, Al, 241–42
Thomas, Norman, 270, 290, 327
Thomson, Rev. Alan, 359
Tiananmen Square, 165
Tisch Amendment, 85
Tormey, Don, 242–43
"To Save the Soul of America" (Jacques), 100
trade agreements and workers, 78–79
Trade Union Educational League, 354
Trade Union Leadership Council (TULC), 80
Trade Union League, 242
trade unions. *See* unions and unionism
Treaty of Detroit, 89, 97
Tribe, 54
Trotsky, Leon, 60, 178
Trump, Donald J., 171, 364
Trumpism, 171
TRW Corporation, 244–45, 249, 250, 253, 255, 345. *See also* Holyoke Wire and Cable
Turkish immigrants, 265, 266

Turner, Doris, 278–79
Tyner, Jarvis, 148, 149, 151

UCB. *See* University of California Berkeley (UCB)
UCFW (United Food and Commercial Workers Union), 358
UCLA (University of California), 25, 206
UE. *See* United Electrical, Radio, and Machine Workers (UE)
Ukrainian immigrants, 131–32, 266
Unemployed Councils, 99, 346
Union Democracy in Action, 78
unions and unionism: *American Trade Unionism,* 352; anticommunism and, 303; class consciousness in, 305; coal-miners union, 319; colonized worksites, 180; corruption and, 362; democracy and, 262, 278, 279, 282; discipline cases, 181–82; elected officers of, 239–40, 243–45; electrical workers, 26–27; faculty members and, 331; family and, 286; forcing change in, 236; granite-cutters, 221; industrial concentration and, 179–80, 237–39, 302, 304, 307, 334; legislators and, 67; mergers, 278, 279; race and, 103; RCA workers, 330; salted worksites, 180; Solidarity Day, 345; steel workers, 133; steelworkers, 27; strike funds, 241; textile, 356; trade union councils, 346; transit-union organizing, 27; wage and benefit concessions, 101–2. *See also specific unions and organizations*
United Auto Workers (UAW): Administration Caucus of, 80; Alston and, 63; childhood memories of, 42; democracy and, 262; Feinsinger and, 288; Fraser and, 77, 86; GM sit-down strike of, 75; Local 600 Credit Union, 61; Reuther and, 42, 57–58, 80, 89, 89n2, 333; Robeson and, 52; Runnels and, 102; Weinstone and, 355. *See also* automobile industry
United Electrical, Radio, and Machine Workers (UE): conventions of, 344; democracy and, 346; economism and, 242–43; Emspak and, 283; family and, 27, 286; GE and, 309, 359; at Holyoke Wire and Cable, 248, 249–53, 256; IUE and, 306, 306n7; layoffs, 345; Local 424, 191; at Monsanto, 241; national health care and, 258–59; steelworkers and, 334; at USM, 303–5; in Vermont, 342; in Washington D.C., 363; at Wesco, 344. *See also* electrical workers; International Union of Electrical, Radio and Machine Workers (IUE)
United Farm Workers, 307
United Food and Commercial Workers Union (UFCW), 358
United May Day Committee, *126*
United Mine Workers, 354
United Mineworkers of America, 262
United Nations General Assembly, *215*
United Rubber workers, 241
United Shoe Machine Company (USM), 303–5, 307
United States Steel, 27
United Steelworkers, 262, 354
University of California Berkeley (UCB): Berkeley Students for Fair Housing, 196–97; FSM at, 120n2, 200, *213*, 282, 282n2, 289; graduation from, 201; minority journalists program, 313; Richmond at, 193; student movement at, 289–90; Vietnam Day, 293; W.E.B. Du Bois Club at, 36
University of California Los Angeles (UCLA), 25, 206
University of California Riverside, 206–7
University of Colorado Boulder, 313
University of Illinois, 149, 337

University of Massachusetts (UMass), 47, 225–29, 232, 343
University of Michigan Ann Arbor, 46
University of Washington Tacoma, 338
University of Wisconsin (UW): Black student strike at, 298, 301; entering, 286; History Department, 296; Madison Committee to End the War in Vietnam, 292–93; Socialist Club at, 287–88, 290; Teaching Assistants Association, 301–2; teach-in movement at, 291, 293; W.E.B. Du Bois Clubs at, 290; WISEM at, 288–89
Uphaus, Williard, 354, 357
Upheaval in the Quiet Zone (Fink), 263
Urban League, 313, 314
US-GDR Friendship League, 158
USM (United Shoe Machine), 303–5
U.S. Steel Company, 27, *127*, 334, 335, 336
utilities, public ownership of, 341

Venceremos Brigade, 19, 96
Vermont, 341
veterans, Spanish Civil War, 354
victory gardens, 305
Vietnam Day, 293
Vietnam Summer, 141
Vietnam War: draft of the, 200–201, 201n3, 285, 286–87; impact of, 351; veterans of the, 225, 226; working-class Struggle linked to, 350–51. *See also* anti-Vietnam War movement
Voice of America, 350–51
Voices of the Future, 154, 159
voter registration, 121, 198–99
Voting Rights Act, 172, 199

WAGE (Win Against GE), 307–9
wage and benefit concessions, 101–2
wages, rise in, 20
wages of the US Communist Party, 101, 160
Walker, Thomas, 47
Walker, Tom, 60
Wallace, Henry, 306n7
Warren, Elizabeth, 172
Warsaw Pact countries, 162–63, 164
Washington, Harold, 335, 336
Washington Heights Project, 274–77
Washington Labor for Peace, 331, 333
Watson, John, 47
Wayne State University, 46, 47–48, 54, 62
Weather Underground, 341
Webb, Sam, 94–95, 362, 363
W.E.B. Du Bois Clubs: in Chicago, 140–41; Civil Rights Movement and, *124*, 196; community organizing for, 201–2; FSM and, 200; *Insurgent*, 140; in NYC, 272; Pecinovsky and, 19; SACB and, 141; school of, 142; Student Mobe and, 272–73; at SUNY New Paltz, 270–71; at UCB, 195–96; at UW, 290; YWLL compared to, 146
Weinberg, Jack, 289
Weingarten rules, 182
Weinstone, Will, 300, 355
welfare state, expansion of, 20
Wellman, Saul, 52, 61, 74
Wesco, 344
West, Don, 331
West, Jim, 164, 346–47
Westchester Discussion Group, 284–86, 292
West Virginia AFL-CIO, 331
Wheaton College, 339
Wheeler, Tim, 80
White, Dave, 278–79
White, Jack, 72, 103
White Panther Party, 49
Williams, Harold, 241, 242, 342–43
Williams, James, *127*
Win Against GE (WAGE), 307–9
Winston, Henry: at CPUSA convention, *214*; death of, 347, 361; in Florida, 356; "Henry Winston's Laugh," 323–26; at May Day march, *126*; nickname of, 72; at People Before

Profits rally, 91; People Before Profits rally and, 89; respect for, 343
Winter, Carl, 106
Winter, Helen, 74
Wisconsin Historical Society, 291, 303
Wisconsin State Journal, 301
Wisconsin Student Employees Association (WISEA), 288–89
women: Coalition of Labor Union Women, 262; electronics workers, 344; ERA, 208, 335; feminist nurses, 262; at Holyoke Wire and Cable, 248–49; labor feminists, 208; National Women's Commission, 365; sexism at the *Rocky Mountain News*, 314–18; SNCC and, 197; Women for Peace, 135; Women for Racial and Economic Equality, 333; Women's Conference of Concerns, 85; *Women's Estate*, 47; women's movement, 122, 261, 340, 365; Women Strike for Peace, 208
Woods, Sylvia, 148
Woolhandler, Steffi, 258
Woolworth sit-ins, 192
The Worker, 134, 136
workers compensation insurance, 235
working-class: anarchists, 229; anticommunist reforms and, 20; blue-diaper baby, 319; broadening the thinking of, 254–59; changing nature of, 167; communists, 232–33; CPUSA in relation, 26–27, 92; democracy, 346; free trade and, 78–79; ideology and, 210–11; legislators as, 67; in Madison, 298; old Republicans, 349–50; socialism and, 111; solidarity, 180; students compared to, 137; Vietnam War in relation to, 350–51; workers' funeral dirge, 346; *Working-Class New York*, 263; Workmen's Circle, 266. *See also* unions and unionism
World Federation of Democratic Youth, 81
World Federation of Trade Unions Convention, 345–46
World Fellowship of Faiths summer camp, 142, 354
World Festival of Youth and Students, 76, 81–83, 151, 152, 244
World Marxist Review, 356
World War I, 28
World War II, 29, 42, 112, 133, 355
Worthington Compressor Company, 242
WREE (Women for Racial and Economic Equality), 333

Yank (quarry worker), 220–21
Yosemite National Park, 194
Young, Coleman A., 48, 53, 80, 95–96, 103
Young Communist League, 63, 98, 132
Young Democrats, 271
Young Lords, 143
Young People's Socialists League (YPSL), 266
Young Socialist Alliance (YSA), 272, 273, 295
Young Turks movement, 266
young voters movement, 149
Young Workers Liberation League (YWLL): 1972 presidential election and, 148–49; Boston School Committee and, 230–31; in Chicago, 146; delegation to Vietnam, 146–47; in Detroit, 64; Divale and, 206; founding of, 144–45; Free Angela movement and, 147–48, 207, 231–32; International Association of Machinists and, 207; leadership in, 151; members of, 65–67; organizing committee, 203; Peace and Freedom Party and, 207–8; relations with CPUSA, 144–45; Steele and, 70; Voices of the Future program, 154
Youth March for Jobs, 151
youth organizations: CPUSA and, 32–33, 144–45, 274, 330; Ethical

Culture youth discussion group, 269; international, 145; Labor Youth League, 55, 330; Liberal Youth of Niles Township, 136–37, 145; PYOC, 316; World Federation of Democratic Youth, 81; Young Communist League, 63, 98, 132. *See also* W.E.B. Du Bois Clubs; Young Workers Liberation League (YWLL)
Youth Rights Candidates, 149
YWLL. *See* Young Workers Liberation League (YWLL)

Zagarell, Mike, 106, 280
Zeitlin, Maurice, 296
Zionism, 122

About the Editors

Jay Schaffner, the son of Ukrainian Jewish immigrants, was born in 1952 and grew up in Skokie, a Chicago suburb. As a teenager he participated in civil rights marches and anti–Vietnam War actions, becoming a leader of the area's high school antiwar and young voters' movements and later the Chicago Peace Council. He was in Students for a Democratic Society and the socialist, multiracial W.E.B. Du Bois Clubs and then, at sixteen, joined the Communist Party, running as a Communist for University of Illinois trustee when he was twenty-two. In 1970, Schaffner helped found the Young Workers Liberation League, and in 1974 he became a national officer. After moving to New York in 1975, he was elected to the CPUSA national committee, first in 1979 and then at every convention until 1991, when he left the Party. In 1990 he became a secretary for Local 802 of the American Federation of Musicians, later supervising its recording department. He negotiated electronic media agreements and was twice voted to the executive board. A founding moderator of *Portside,* he continues collaborating with the progressive news website. In retirement, he cochairs a tenant committee in his housing cooperative. He belongs to the New York State Committee of the Working Families Party. Married, he has two children and four grandchildren.

Paul Friedman was born on February 20, 1947, in New York City. His family moved from the Bronx to Flushing, Queens, in 1955. Paul attended Bronx High School of Science and New York University, where he received his bachelor of science degree. He served as a national coordinator of the Student Mobilization Committee to End the War in Vietnam and youth director of the New York State district of the Communist Party while on hiatus from college. From 1970 to 1973, Paul worked as a research technician in the pediatric cardiology department at the Columbia College of Physicians and Surgeons at the Presbyterian Medical Center. He joined the staff of Local 1199 in 1973 as an organizer and eventually worked as assistant director of organizing for 1199's National Union of Hospitals and Health Care Employees. Prior to his retirement in 2019 Paul served in various leadership positions at 1199 Service Employees International Union; Local 100 Hotel Employees and Restaurant Employees Union; Committee of Interns and Residents; and New York State Nurses Association. Paul participated in or led campaigns throughout the United States that brought over twenty thousand new members into these unions.

Cindy Hawes was born in Pasadena, California. She grew up in the Altadena-Pasadena area before going off to study at the University of California, Santa Barbara. Cindy spent her junior year abroad in Madrid, Spain, and it was during that year that she traveled with other US students to the Soviet Union. That trip, as well as other travels, sparked an interest in socialism. After graduating, she continued her studies in Mexico, and when she returned to the United States she started a career in journalism and joined the Young Workers Liberation League and eventually the Communist Party USA. Cindy moved to New York in 1977 to be a staff member at the *Daily World;* in 1981 she became the *Daily World's* correspondent in Mexico City and, in 1988, in Los Angeles. She left the paper in 1989, and subsequently the Party, and for the next three years taught first grade in East Los Angeles. In 1992, she returned to Mexico City, where she worked with both the national and international press there until her retirement. She currently devotes her time to translation and her own writing.

Geoffrey Jacques is a poet, writer, and editor who has been an activist and worker in the peace, labor, and left-wing political movements since the 1970s. Born in Detroit in 1953, he was the *Daily World* correspondent in that city from 1978 to 1983, and a New York City–based *Daily World* staffer from 1983 to 1985. He has worked as a business representative and organizer for Local 802 of the American Federation of Musicians, and from 1990 to 1996, he was assistant editor, then associate editor, of *1199 News,* the monthly magazine of 1199 SEIU, the New York City–based health and hospital workers union. He was the founding managing editor of the journal *New Labor Forum* and has published articles in many other journals and periodicals. Jacques earned his PhD in English from the City University of New York (CUNY), and has taught classes in English and US literature, African American studies, American studies, writing, and humanities at York College, CUNY; John Jay College of Criminal Justice, CUNY; New York University; the University of California, Santa Barbara; Pacifica Graduate Institute; California Institute of the Arts; and elsewhere. His books include the poetry collections *The Orchestra of Wind Chimes* (2023) and *Just for a Thrill* (2005), both from Wayne State University Press, and the literary-critical study *A Change in the Weather: Modernist Imagination, African American Imaginary* (University of Massachusetts Press, 2009). His poem, "Trump," appeared in 2019 in the journal *Black Renaissance/Renaissance Noire.* His essay "A New Civil Rights Movement, a New Journal," an introduction to the online archive of the complete run of *Freedomways* magazine, appears on the open-access Reveal Digital–Independent Voices portal at JSTOR. Since 2014, he has been a moderator for Portside. He and his wife, Sherri L. Barnes, live in Ventura, California, and Detroit, Michigan.

Timothy Johnson worked as a reporter for *People's World* (1985), and *People's Daily World* (1985–1990). He joined the Communist

Party in Chicago in 1983 and lived in Chicago, Los Angeles, and New York City. He also served on the Party's African American Equality Commission from 1987 to 1991.

Carol Pittman was born to Communist parents—her father an African American who left Georgia during the great migration, her mother a German Jew who left Germany in 1938. Both were lifelong journalists and wrote for and edited *People's World, Daily World,* and *People's Daily World.* As a teen in San Francisco Carol joined the high school activist group Students Organized Education and Action League and was active in both the civil rights and anti–Vietnam War movements. She joined the Bay Area youth club of the Communist Party USA at seventeen. She was briefly a member of the Black Panther Party. She studied ethnography at Karl Marx University in Leipzig, Germany. She is multilingual, speaking English, German, Spanish, and Russian. Upon returning to the United States and New York City, Carol joined the Young Workers Liberation League and was active in the Chile Solidarity Movement. While Youth Council coordinator of the National Coalition for Economic Justice, she helped organize the National Youth March for Jobs in the mid-1970s, then the largest national youth mobilization for jobs. Carol became education director for the New York Party and a state committee member, and was a leader of the fight for change. She left the Party in 1991. Her work as community-outreach coordinator for a local hospital's pediatric resource center led to becoming an organizer for Local 1199, Registered Nurse Division. After leaving 1199 she became director of NY Jobs with Justice and the Workers' Rights Board. She was a moderator of Portside from 2003 to 2014. As community affairs coordinator and then associate director for political and community organizing of the New York State Nurses Association, she coordinated NYSNA's labor-community work, building solidarity and organizing the response to hospital closings. Carol is now retired, a grandmother, and volunteers at a local food pantry, a community writing workshop, and the Brooklyn Botanic Garden.

Donna Ristorucci (née Hackman) was born in 1947 in Jamaica, New York. She knew she was a socialist at the age of eleven. The oldest of three children, she asked her father on a ride home from her grandparents, "Why can't everyone just have everything they need?" He replied, "That's socialism." Her parents were leftists, but McCarthyism put the kibosh on any activism. In high school, Ristorucci worked in peace and civil rights activities, especially the 1964 boycott for school integration. She joined the W.E.B. Du Bois Club in 1965 and the Communist Party in 1966, following its first open convention since McCarthyism. At City College she became immersed in anti–Vietnam War and open-admissions struggles on campus. She left school to work full-time for the Du Bois Clubs. She helped organize the US delegation to the 1968 World Youth Festival in Bulgaria. A founder of the Young Workers Liberation League, Ristorucci was its New York education director. She participated in the Party's national council and New York State leadership until moving to Jersey City in 1979. In 1971, Ristorucci became the *Daily World's* youth editor, serving on the editorial board. She eventually edited *World Magazine,* the paper's weekly supplement. During her years at the paper, she gave birth to three sons. She left the paper and the CPUSA in 1987. After working at a labor-law office, Ristorucci was hired by Teamsters Local 237, a public-employee union, as associate editor of its newspaper. Returning to school at night, she earned a BA in labor studies in 1991. In 1995 she became founding editor of 237's retiree newspaper and assistant director of the Retiree Division. She retired in 2012—still a Communist, still anti-imperialist, still going to demonstrations (although not quite as many).

Born in Brooklyn, New York, in 1953, **Daniel Rosenberg** came to the Communist movement in 1970. His parents were Communist Party members and community leaders in civil rights, peace, labor, and other movements. Fearing that the McCarthyite red scare of the 1950s would impose a Nazi-type regime in the United States, the Party urged his parents to go "underground"—with him in tow—to escape persecution. They moved through various cities until returning to Brooklyn. Rosenberg soon stumbled into public school. Each day lasted a century. He read Lenin and Marx in the summer of 1969, entering eleventh grade with both conviction and verbiage. From the last row in class, he held forth, in contrast with his general silence during the previous decade. He soon joined the Young Workers Liberation League, the Party's new youth organization. He would hold League leadership positions and later local posts in the Communist Party. He served on the Party's history and international commissions (the latter owing to his representing the League in the anti-imperialist World Federation of Democratic Youth). He has a doctorate in history from the City University of New York. He taught at Adelphi University for thirty-five years. He has written several pieces about Party history.

Jackie Saindon worked for most of her life as an adult educator, teaching adults to read, as well as teaching English to second-language learners. She has also been a community activist, serving on the school board, the library board, and various other community organizations. For many years, until her retirement in 2018, she was a part-time assistant professor in the Language and Literacy Department of the University of Georgia. She was born into a Communist Party family and grew up as a "red-diaper baby." Her father was sent to New York in 1952 to join other Party members sent to work in industrial settings. During that period, she read Marxist literature that had been hidden in her family's basement. She was an active member of the W.E.B. Du Bois Club and later of the industrial section of the Party, working with grassroots members of the International Garment Workers Union and District 65 United Auto Workers, organizing office workers to join the union already established by warehouse workers. She currently lives in Athens, Georgia, where she is co-coordinator of an adult literacy program and works with community groups and the school district to revitalize their adult and family literacy programs.

www.ingramcontent.com/pod-product-compliance
Lightning Source LLC
LaVergne TN
LVHW010556100826
845148LV00014B/2738

* 9 7 8 1 6 8 5 7 1 2 9 0 7 *